Computational Modeling of Behavior in Organizations

The Third Scientific Discipline

Computational Modeling of Behavior in Organizations

The Third Scientific Discipline

Edited by
Daniel R. Ilgen and Charles L. Hulin

AMERICAN PSYCHOLOGICAL ASSOCIATION
WASHINGTON, DC

Published by
American Psychological Association
750 First Street, NE
Washington, DC 20002

Copies may be ordered from
APA Order Department
P.O. Box 92984
Washington, DC 20090-2984

In the UK and Europe, copies may be ordered from
American Psychological Association
3 Henrietta Street
Covent Garden, London
WC2E 8LU England

Typeset in Berkeley Book by UpperCase Publication Services, Ltd., Reston, VA

Printer: Automated Graphic Systems, Inc., White Plains, MD
Cover Designer: Naylor Design, Washington, DC
Project Manager: UpperCase Publication Services, Ltd., Reston, VA

Library of Congress Cataloging-in-Publication Data
Computational modeling of behavior in organizations : the third scientific discipline / edited by Daniel R. Ilgen and Charles L. Hulin.
p. cm.
Includes bibliographical references and index.
ISBN 1-55798-639-8 (alk. paper)
1. Organizational behavior—Mathematical models. 2. Organizational behavior—Computer simulation. I. Ilgen, Daniel R., II. Hulin, Charles L., 1936-
HD58.7 .C66 2000
658.3—dc21

99-089792

British Library Cataloguing-in-Publication Data
A CIP record is available from the British Library.

Printed in the United States of America
First Edition

Dedicated to

Willard S. Vaughan and Steven T. Seitz

who introduced us to the benefits of
computational modeling, the third scientific discipline

APA Science Volumes

Attribution and Social Interaction: The Legacy of Edward E. Jones

Best Methods for the Analysis of Change: Recent Advances, Unanswered Questions, Future Directions

Cardiovascular Reactivity to Psychological Stress and Disease

The Challenge in Mathematics and Science Education: Psychology's Response

Changing Employment Relations: Behavioral and Social Perspectives

Children Exposed to Marital Violence: Theory, Research, and Applied Issues

Cognition: Conceptual and Methodological Issues

Cognitive Bases of Musical Communication

Cognitive Dissonance: Progress on a Pivotal Theory in Social Psychology

Computational Modeling of Behavior in Organizations: The Third Scientific Discipline

Conceptualization and Measurement of Organism–Environment Interaction

Converging Operations in the Study of Visual Selective Attention

Creative Thought: An Investigation of Conceptual Structures and Processes

Developmental Psychoacoustics

Diversity in Work Teams: Research Paradigms for a Changing Workplace

Emotion and Culture: Empirical Studies of Mutual Influence

Emotion, Disclosure, and Health

Evolving Explanations of Development: Ecological Approaches to Organism–Environment Systems

Examining Lives in Context: Perspectives on the Ecology of Human Development

Global Prospects for Education: Development, Culture, and Schooling

Hostility, Coping, and Health

Measuring Patient Changes in Mood, Anxiety, and Personality Disorders: Toward a Core Battery

Occasion Setting: Associative Learning and Cognition in Animals

Organ Donation and Transplantation: Psychological and Behavioral Factors

Origins and Development of Schizophrenia: Advances in Experimental Psychopathology

The Perception of Structure

Perspectives on Socially Shared Cognition

Psychological Testing of Hispanics

Psychology of Women's Health: Progress and Challenges in Research and Application

Researching Community Psychology: Issues of Theory and Methods

The Rising Curve: Long-Term Gains in IQ and Related Measures

Sexism and Stereotypes in Modern Society: The Gender Science of Janet Taylor Spence

Sleep and Cognition

Sleep Onset: Normal and Abnormal Processes

Stereotype Accuracy: Toward Appreciating Group Differences

Stereotyped Movements: Brain and Behavior Relationships

Studying Lives Through Time: Personality and Development

The Suggestibility of Children's Recollections: Implications for Eyewitness Testimony

Taste, Experience, and Feeding: Development and Learning

Temperament: Individual Differences at the Interface of Biology and Behavior

Through the Looking Glass: Issues of Psychological Well-Being in Captive Nonhuman Primates

Uniting Psychology and Biology: Integrative Perspectives on Human Development

Viewing Psychology as a Whole: The Integrative Science of William N. Dember

Contents

Contributors

Kathleen M. Carley, Carnegie-Mellon University

Michael D. Coovert, University of South Florida

James H. Davis, University of Illinois

Richard P. DeShon, Michigan State University

David W. Dorsey, Personnel Decision Research, Inc.

Jeffrey R. Edwards, University of North Carolina

Mark Fichman, Carnegie-Mellon University

Kathy A. Hanisch, Iowa State University

John R. Hollenbeck, Michigan State University

Charles L. Hulin, University of Illinois

Daniel R. Ilgen, Michigan State University

Norbert L. Kerr, Michigan State University

David M. Krackhardt, Carnegie-Mellon University

Bibb Latané, Florida Atlantic University

J. Miller McPherson, University of Arizona

Liberty J. Munson, University of Illinois

Nigel Nicholson, The London Business School

Craig A. Olson, University of Wisconsin

M. Anjali Sastry, University of Michigan

Donald P. Schwab, University of Wisconsin

Steven T. Seitz, University of Illinois

Garold Stasser, Miami University

Michael J. Zickar, Bowling Green State University

Foreword

In early 1988, the APA Science Directorate began its sponsorship of what has become an exceptionally successful activity in support of psychological science—the APA Scientific Conferences program. This program has showcased some of the most important topics in psychological science, and the conference participants have included many leading figures in the field.

As we enter a new century, it seems fitting that we begin with a new face on this book series—that of the Decade of Behavior (DoB). The DoB is a major interdisciplinary initiative designed to promote the contributions of the behavioral and social sciences to address some of our most important societal challenges, and will occur from 2000 to 2010. Although a major effort of the DoB initiative will be related to informing the public about the contributions of these fields, other activities will be put into place to reach fellow scientists. Hence, the series that was the "APA Science Series" will be continued as the "Decade of Behavior Series." This represents one element in APA's efforts to promote the Decade of Behavior initiative as one of the partner organizations.

Please note the Decade of Behavior logo on the inside jacket flap, as well as on the title page. We expect this logo will become a familiar sight over the next few years. For additional information about the DoB, please visit http://www.decadeofbehavior.org.

As part of the sponsorship agreement with APA, conference organizers commit themselves not only to the conference itself, but also to editing a scholarly volume that results from the meeting. This book, the first in the Decade of Behavior series, is such a volume. Over the course of the last 12 years, we have partnered with 44 universities to sponsor 57 conferences on a wide variety of topics of interest to psychological scientists. The APA Science Directorate looks forward to continuing this program, and to sponsoring other conferences in the years ahead.

We are very pleased that this important contribution to the literature was supported in part by the Scientific Conferences program. Congratulations to the editors and contributors on their sterling effort.

Richard McCarty, PhD
Executive Director for Science

Virginia E. Holt
Assistant Executive Director for Science

Preface

We live in a stochastic, dynamic, nonlinear world. Myriad loosely connected economic, financial, political, cultural, and technological conditions are responsible for the dynamics of environments within which organizations function today. Because of environmental dynamics and uncertainty, as organizations grow, they differentiate internally and add functions and subsystems to cope with different elements in their environments. As they differentiate, they add integrative functions to manage and coordinate the work of earlier differentiation. Environmental changes and the mechanisms that organizations have developed to cope with their environmental uncertainty and dynamics represent a quantum leap in complexity and nonlinearity of organizations as sociotechnical systems from what they were a generation ago.

Employees' behaviors match the complexity of their organizational contexts. Patterns of behavior generate locally chaotic regions in otherwise deterministic systems (see Chapter 4, by Munson & Hulin). As students of human behavior in organizations, our task is to expand our understanding of such behaviors. Theories and research methods have advanced dramatically over the past few decades; they now offer a number of sophisticated and creative ways for dealing with the domains of our discipline. However, our methods and our theories remain far better suited for the deterministic and linear corners of that domain than for the well-populated chaotic regions of it—an area where dynamic, nonlinear, stochastic processes hold sway. We handicap ourselves and our research efforts if we continue to use deterministic models and limited research methods to explore equally limited regions of our total domains of behavior in organizations.

In this book we turn to computational modeling as a means for building theory and asking questions about the nature of organizational behavior in complex, dynamic, and stochastic conditions. Computational models do not provide all the answers. They do provide answers that lie beyond the scope of most of our current research methods, both in the field and in theoretical deduction and induction.

Unfortunately, most researchers with interests in organizational behavior have ignored computational modeling as a method for studying phenomena that exist somewhere between the organizational and individual levels. The purpose of this edited volume is to begin to rectify this problem. We have invited a number of people who are using computational models to share that work with you. In doing so, we asked them to describe their work in ways that make clear the unique contributions of computational modeling to the problem at hand. In many cases, the mathematical and computer models incorporated in the simulations of the theoretical models are extremely complex; in others, they are models of simplicity and accessibility (see

Chapter 9, by Latané). We have asked the authors to provide sufficient detail of the method and the results obtained from computational modeling for you, the reader, to see the ways in which the method can offer insights into understanding the behaviors of interest. We have provided examples of uses of computational modeling ranging from faking on personality tests to group interactions to interactions among subpopulations of people to the adaptive restructuring of organizations. It is our hope that those examples will clarify the wide variety of issues in organizations that can benefit from computational model research and stimulate readers to consider these approaches in their own work.

Computational Modeling of Behavior in Organizations

The Third Scientific Discipline

CHAPTER 1

Introduction to Computational Modeling in Organizations

The Good That Modeling Does

Charles L. Hulin
Daniel R. Ilgen

Thousands of Chicago commuters eagerly anticipated the October 5, 1994, completion date for the final phase of a 3-year reconstruction project that had disrupted traffic throughout the northwest quadrant of the city. The expressway opened on time, but within 2 weeks commuters were reported to be "surprised" when faced with more back-ups, more congestion, and more delays. Rush hour commuting time increased 20%, and traffic volume rose 15% from the weeks preceding the opening of the new road in spite of the improved capacity for automobile traffic ("Rebuilt Kennedy," 1994).

Urban highways, streets, and roads are structural elements of any city's transportation system—a complex, dynamic, open system. Many of us often are unwilling participants in such systems, and we can sympathize with the Chicago commuters. We are as surprised as they are by the result of expanding the capacity of the expressway.

Not everyone, however, was surprised at the outcome of the improved system in Chicago. People who develop and test computer models of traffic flows would have been surprised by any other outcome. Well-developed computer and formal models of urban commuter traffic behavior conclude exactly what was observed. Those models predict outcomes well, and their predictions are often counterintuitive (Arnott & Small, 1994). For example, the Pigou–Knight–Downs paradox identifies conditions under which adding more lanes of traffic in a restricted access area, such as an expressway or a bridge, will lead to no change in capacity (reported in Arnott & Small, 1994). Unfortunately, policy decisions about building highways are made by elected officials with agendas other than moving traffic, not by computer modelers.

Policymakers are not alone in overlooking the value of computer models for understanding human behavior in complex, dynamic, open systems. Until recently, computer models—hereafter referred to as "computational models"—have been largely ignored by those studying or managing the behaviors of people in organizations. This myopia occurs despite computational modeling's value for understanding cognition (Lewandowski, 1993; Posner, 1989), management science (Williams et al., 1994), and organizational theory (Carley & Prietula, 1994). This book addresses this oversight.

Computational modeling refers to a loosely interrelated set of research tools that have been developed to address questions about the functioning of complex systems, including the behaviors of individuals in those systems, that cannot be addressed using other, more traditional, research methods. Models are used to ask "What if. . . ?" questions about such systems:

- What would happen to turnover rates in a specified organization if unemployment rose from 6% to 7% and if sanctions on absences were reduced by a given amount?
- What would happen to the spread of AIDS and population demographics in a country if the pool of women of marriageable age became seriously depleted from the spread of AIDS itself?
- What would happen to the usefulness of a personality test used as a selection device if 75% of the items in it could be faked by takers, rather than 25%, and the predictive validity of the test was .30?

Those questions and others like them are poorly addressed using traditional experimental or regression-based approaches to the study of human behavior. Different forms of computational modeling, however, yield answers that often are counterintuitive but are nevertheless important to policymakers.

The variety of approaches based on computational modeling precludes a satisfying definition of the process. In general, the approaches begin with a series of statements written in propositional calculus, or "if . . . then" form. The statements may represent theories or a set of competing theories of human behavior or other elements of a system. They are then used to generate computer algorithms that can simulate behaviors of the elements in the system and the output of the system as a whole. The behavior of the elements of the computational model, or virtual, system can then be compared with the empirical traces of behaviors of similar elements in the real-world, or mundane, system. Computer simulations can be viewed as experiments done "in silica" rather than in "in vitro," where the output of one iteration or simulated time period of a dynamic, stochastic, complex system represents the results of one experiment and becomes the input for the subsequent, linked experiment for the next time period.

This general statement about computational modeling is too simple, because some modeling is done by asking what kinds of simulated conditions are needed before the elements in a system will behave as they would under the assumptions of a specified model or theory. Here the emphasis is on finding the conditions under which simulated systems conform to the propositions of abstract models or theories.

Some computational models ask questions about conditions that may not exist today on earth. These counterfactual conditions can often be used to illuminate situations that do exist and may even occur frequently.

Background

Enduring epistemological questions address the interfaces between theory and research methods and between research methods and data. Theory is the source of all hypotheses, but not all hypotheses are amenable to evaluation by all methods, and not all methods will yield data that can answer questions drawn from all theories. Cronbach (1957, 1975) articulated these limits when he contrasted the two major research disciplines of scientific psychology: the experimental and the correlational disciplines. The two scientific disciplines make fundamentally different assumptions about the interface between data and theory. Each has strengths and weaknesses for studying behavioral and cognitive processes in psychology. The two approaches occasionally complement each other; the strengths of one can overcome the weaknesses of the other. They produce fundamentally different data, and each discipline proceeds from a view of the world unique to its approach.

Experimental designs rely on control over one set of variables to draw inferences about the effects of the controlled variables on other variables, which are allowed to vary freely. Among the controlled variables, homogeneity among cases (e.g., people or groups) that the variables describe is created by experimental manipulations and random assignment of subjects to conditions. By contrast, correlational designs maximize the heterogeneity of the systems or of individuals within the systems being compared. This strategy assumes that by maximizing heterogeneity on one or two causal variables thought to be operating, the effects of variables irrelevant to those under examination will be minimized by random shocks and stochastics inherent in the systems. The signal in correlational designs is normally treated as noise in experimental designs. The two research disciplines, even when applied to the same research question, frequently yield results that cannot be reconciled.

Few informed scholars question the contributions to knowledge of data generated through either of these disciplines. Ilgen (1985) noted that even in the field of industrial-organizational (I/O) psychology, long a bastion of the individual differences/correlational research tradition, the question is one of *when*, not *if*, experimental research methods should be used to address certain research questions.

Misfits Between Research Methods and Models in Organizational Research

Experimental methods and cross-sectional correlational analyses of individual differences often represent "epistemological misfits" for studying phenomena of interest in organizational behavior. They are used because researchers assume they are all we have. Organizational employees are dynamic, open systems nested within dynamic and open organizational systems. Causal theories developed to explain their behaviors often incorporate constructs—and relationships among constructs—that take into account the complex interdependent and dynamic nature of behavior in organizational settings. Both correlational and experimental methods are used to evaluate the fit of data to such theories. The data for these static analyses are observations at a single point in time or, at best, a few observations across a limited and arbitrary time interval; they are snapshots of a stream of behavior whose headwaters and destination are unknown. The settings for the pictures are determined by ease of access to the banks of the stream. These snapshots do not allow dynamic causality to unfold across time at its own cadence. Static data often cannot directly answer questions about the models they are supposed to help evaluate. Experimental and correlational methods depend on data that are confounded with time in ways that are not well understood.

Observations of a stream of behavior taken at arbitrary times are as likely to miss important manifestations of the unfolding of a dynamic process as they are to trap it. Even if some of the manifestations are captured, these images are but uncertain and intermittent illuminations projected on the viewing screens of static designs. This problem is troublesome; the cadences of social and behavioral processes may not unfold linearly with respect to the clock–time continuum. Different forces at work in these processes unfold and have different cadences with regard to one another. Panel or longitudinal studies cut into the stream of time almost blindly, beginning and ending with little theoretical basis. Arbitrary intervals of 6 months or 24 months may capture rather different pictures of a time–behavior trajectory, depending on the equally arbitrary entry point into the time stream and the array of forces at work during the interval spanned by the study. See, for example, longitudinal research efforts by Munson, Hulin, and Drasgow (in press) and Glomb, Munson, Hulin, Bergman, and Drasgow (1998). Their results contribute to our understanding of the effects of a potent job stressor, sexual harassment, on women's job and psychological outcomes. We must be concerned, however, about the unintended constraints of the 2-year intervals on the outcomes of the processes being studied.

Our attempts to understand dynamic processes of organizational behaviors using one of the standard research disciplines do not resemble a well-edited movie. The results are more like a slide show constructed from a drawer full of unnumbered pictures; each picture represents a pure moment in an organization, crystallized in time. We select pictures at random, examining them to discover details we may have missed. Some we number and retain; others we throw back into the drawer. We try to assemble the pictures into a sequence that can be riffled to generate apparent motion, believing that this process approximates the underlying dynamics of behavioral processes. But if the pictures we number and reassemble are temporally too close to each other, they will be nearly identical. From such a sequence, we might conclude that the organization and the processes frozen in the pictures were in stasis, that nothing important changes across time. If the pictures are temporally too remote, they will resemble each other only slightly. Myriad changes from one picture to the next may mask any changes in the processes we want to understand. True change is lost in the noise of the Brownian movement of elements of the images. We will conclude that the organization and the behavioral processes in it are random or, at best, chaotic systems.

In this way, sequences of static snapshots of the same organization can lead to divergent conclusions. The accuracy of each moment in the life of an organization is not the issue. The pictures of frozen moments are accurate, but they are not true; they lead to the wrong conclusion. Sometimes we get the pictures assembled correctly and choose the appropriate time intervals, but we may not know it when we have done so. The time intervals we impose on organizational processes are chosen without regard to a sound database or well-developed theory of organizational time. This arbitrariness frustrates our attempts to understand truly dynamic organizational processes.

Computational Modeling: The Third Scientific Research Discipline

In spite of nearly universal reliance in social and behavioral sciences on one of the two traditional research disciplines, they neither define nor exhaust the domain of research strategies. Computational modeling and its subset, computer simulations, are examples of a general research method that falls outside the domains of experimentation and correlational approaches. Computational modeling has strengths orthogonal to the strengths of either traditional research discipline. Simulations and modeling offer advantages over the severely bounded rationality of human reasoning. Computational modeling is a third research discipline not captured by either of the two described by Cronbach (1957, 1975). Modeling is the "redheaded stepchild" of organizational research methods; it is useful for a number of issues important to behavior in organizations, but it has been little used and is little appreciated.

Research in the two familiar disciplines begins with theory—theory that is informed by our construing of organizational realities as we understand them and by our knowledge of human behavior in general. The theory becomes a network of elements and constructs linked by propositions about the nature of their interrelationships. Such theories incorporate constructs whose indicators and manifestations can be observed, measured, and/or manipulated so inferences can be made about the reasonableness of the proposed theory. We advance understanding by evaluating the fit, one study at a time, of observations to the theoretical network of linked elements and constructs. Confidence in a theory increases if there is a good fit. If there is not a good fit, modifications in the theory are proposed that produce a better fit to observations. These modifications are evaluated as new observations are matched to them in the next step. We conduct and evaluate our current studies within the broader framework of earlier studies on the same or related constructs. No study done today is the first one done on an important question. Any modifications we make to our theories need also be congruent with previous findings.

Research with computational models also begins with theory and ends with evaluating the fit of observations. The theory, also informed by construals of organizational reality and of human behavior, is expressed in the form of formal algorithms of the nomological network, a propositional calculus of "if . . . then" statements. Then, the nodes of the net and the connections between them are modeled with computer simulations whose inputs are data sampled from variables with distributions based on known characteristics of the constructs the variables represent. Outputs of model at time n, the nth iteration or simulated behavioral episode, serve as inputs to time $n+1$ iterations so the model in a very real sense changes as a function of its own past behavior across time or episodes. Logical criteria for stopping the modeling process are selected a priori, and output of the computer simulation is obtained for all time periods or iterations. That output may then be evaluated with respect to observational data similar to those used to evaluate the degree of fit for correlational or experimental research. The difference is that simulation data represent a standard of comparison that has incorporated complex interactions among constructs in the theory that are consistent with known conditions and with theory but often could not have been predicted because of the single cycle (or very limited time horizon) of our theories constructed from real-time data.

An epistemological mismatch occurs when "causal" explanations, which imply known temporal ordering of events or variables, are evaluated with static designs. These evaluations rest on assumptions that generally are not defensible in behavioral research. Even with the most sophisticated analytic programs available, at best we can conclude that hypotheses derived from a specific model, selected on theoretical grounds from among many possible models, are not inconsistent with the patterns of the data that were obtained. Covariance structure analyses are a major advance over a naïve falsification approach that tests implications of a model or theory one at a time. The larger the number of hypotheses or causal links that are tested simultaneously, the lower the a priori probability that empirical support will be found for the model that generated them. The larger the number of low a priori links among constructs that are tested and supported, however, the greater the reduction of entropy in the relevant space. Although consistent with modern epistemology, claims for causality made on the basis of such results must be cautious.

The modeling research tradition provides a correction to the limitations of our two standard research paradigms; it creates a triangulated view of cross-sectional inquiries and controlled-setting experiments for devising and testing causal, dynamic theories. The passage of time, real or simulated, is necessary before we can assign directions with some degree of certainty to the links among the constructs in our models. Paradoxically, modeling research allows a degree of realism not possible in experimentation and a serial perspective not possible even in panel-based analyses.

The output of one iteration in a simulation, perhaps modified by stochastic shocks and dynamic feedback, becomes the input for the next iteration. Iterated output of simulations of dynamic systems allows us to tease apart dynamic forces whose effects become clear only as we examine the traces of those forces interacting over periods of time (computational or real) and in complex settings (virtual or mundane). Temporal cadences and intrinsic periodicities inherent in antecedent-behavior processes are fragmented into noise by controlled experiments and cross-sectional snapshots of relations among individual differences. These cadences and the trajectories they follow become the signals rather than background noise in computational modeling as they unfold across iterations or behavioral episodes. Dynamic processes are rarely captured, even in panel designs, which usually span time intervals based on rules of thumb or convenience rather than on sound empirical data or theoretical propositions. Munson et al. (in press) and Glomb et al. (1999) provide examples of the complexities of interpreting results from longitudinal empirical studies of dynamic behavioral processes.

Cross-sectional studies can establish the existence of a relation between a cognitive or affective state and a contemporaneous behavioral response. These internally valid relations may cast more shadows than light when used to illuminate the fundamental dynamics of feedback effects of behavioral responses onto antecedent cognitions. They are a necessary and important part of our database. We rely on those results when we design our longitudinal empirical studies or computational modeling efforts. But we need to go beyond these studies and their limitations to provide us with the information that will reduce our uncertainty about important organizational processes. We face significant problems extending our research efforts in organizational behavior to account for a broader range of dynamic issues. These problems cannot be solved by the same thinking that generated them.

Applications of Modeling

The following discussion of useful applications of computational modeling techniques draws from a number of content areas. The underlying problems that the examples illustrate exist in different forms in many organizational research areas and in policy decisions concerned with controlling behaviors in organizations.

Operations on Large and Unreliable Data Sets

Many problems require policy decisions based on very large data sets. Computer models can integrate all available data and project "if . . . then" outcomes based on the courses of action selected by the human operators and the dynamics and stochastics of the process. For example, programmers can select from a number of possible interventions into the comorbidity of AIDS, sexually transmitted diseases, and tuberculosis. Another example is that of integrating indicators of system functioning and troubleshooting problems in complex social–technical systems. Nuclear power plants, for instance, are extreme examples of complex social–technical systems replete with stochastic dynamic feedback and feedacross loops and high levels of interdependencies. Troubleshooting such systems and using computer modeling to trace the cascading effects of mechanical malfunctions, transient electronic signals, misread and misinterpreted signals, and misset control inputs easily illustrate the need and optimal locations of firewalls between subsystems to trap and prevent the cascading of compounded errors (Perrow, 1984). Computational modeling programs can operate on fallible, unreliable, and incomplete data and integrate across observations to remove the effects of random errors. "Fallible," "unreliable," and "incomplete" describe most of our empirical databases.

Behaviors in Interdependent Social–Technical Systems

Social–technical systems almost always involve nonlinear, stochastic, dynamic interdependencies among many components. The number of interdependent components and their degree of interdependence in such systems precludes closed-form analytic solutions. Initial conditions and nonlinearities in the systems may introduce elements of local chaos in the midst of highly deterministic systems. These systems require numerous solutions and are exquisitely sensitive to initial conditions and the dynamic processes that are stochastically triggered. The dynamic elements in these systems require simulations over many time periods to evaluate the equilibria points or to determine whether the system will reach static or dynamic equilibrium under all starting conditions. An example of computational modeling applied to such a system is the evaluation of the expected results of different theoretical models of organizational withdrawal (Hanisch, Hulin, & Seitz, 1996, in press; see also Hanisch, Chapter 3, this volume, and Munson & Hulin, Chapter 4, this volume).

Interdisciplinary Problems

Policy decisions often must be based on extensive interdisciplinary databases and perspectives from a variety of approaches. The ability of any discipline-bound model or single investigator to integrate relevant information from multiple sources is likely to be severely compromised. Useful models or theories often span disciplines in ways that exceed our cognitive capacities. Complex models projecting the spread of AIDS and HIV are examples of such policy issues that require input from several disciplines—including epidemiology, population demographics, sociology, and psychology (Seitz & Mueller, 1994). Evaluation of the implications of competing conflict and peace strategies involves a similar type of policy analysis (Seitz, 1994).

High Risk of Harm

The financial costs of operational errors resulting from incorrect decisions may be unacceptably high, and errors may place an unacceptable number of humans at risk.

One problem in this category is the evaluation of different air traffic control systems using artificial intelligence concepts that project future positions of aircraft in free-flight conditions. Different configurations of information displays in cockpits in a proposed new method of controlling aircraft under instrument flight rules is another example of a system that would require extensive modeling followed by empirical research before adoption (Wickens, 1999).

General Advantages of Modeling

Modeling serves theory development and operational uses with equal facility. It is nearly impossible, for example, to derive analytically all the implications of a complex, deterministic model or theory. It is impossible to derive analytically the implications of stochastic, nonlinear, dynamic models. Computational modeling can contribute significantly during early phases of research on complex theories by illuminating the interface between theory and data. It allows investigators to explicate the implications of theoretical assumptions and propositions. These efforts require that the theories or models, often framed as literary metaphors, be translated into precisely stated "if . . . then" propositional inventories. These inventories, in turn, are translated into the language of mathematics or (fuzzy) set theory for use in simulations or modeling.

Emergent properties of complex models that are unanticipated by the model developers, as well as unrecognized aspects of interrelated theoretical propositions, can be studied during subsequent phases of research on a model or theory. Emergent properties might include the asymptotes, if such exist, for different behaviors being modeled; the trajectories by which outputs approach their asymptotes; the equilibrium (or lack thereof) of the model's output after *N* iterations; or the covariance structure among all the outputs of a model or theory. Interactions among manifestations of different processes and constructs can generate local regions in the space being modeled that cannot be understood within linear frameworks.

Information is available from the output of computational modeling that cannot be known and, depending on the complexity of the models, is not derivable analytically before simulations are run (Simon, 1992). Emergent system properties have been discovered that were neither evident nor expected based on the behavior patterns of all elements composing the system, including people. Emergent properties have been discovered in astrophysics that defined black holes (Smarr, 1985), in the behavior of people (Luce, 1995), in the spread of AIDS (Seitz, 1994), in memory processes (Lewandowski, 1993), and in the withdrawal behaviors of people (Hanisch, Hulin, & Seitz, in press). Unanticipated emergent properties of systems and models (e.g., black holes) are as scientifically informative as empirically verified relations and links among indicators of constructs.

Computational modeling is efficient; simulations can be concentrated in regions of theoretical space that maximize information. For example, if it is important that we learn about the expected results of using specific kinds of compensation packages, we can use modeling to explore the effects of specific plans on, say, variance of pay among employees or expected correlations between pay levels across years. If the links between compensation packages and the accuracy of performance evaluations represent the areas in which we know least, these can be modeled without the necessity of evaluating all elements of the domain.

It is effective; we can usefully model what cannot be studied empirically. We cannot study empirically all relevant characteristics of environments, organizations, and important organizational behaviors. Empirical research has extensively explored the regions of organizational and theoretical space likely to be encountered in "normal" research or practice. These explorations have typically examined processes in these regions one or two variables at a time. Standard empirical research on organizations located at the margins of the organizational space is nearly impossible for three reasons: (a) the infrequency of events in this region; (b) the density of sampling required to obtain stable estimates of relations among low base-rate behaviors and other variables; and (c) the likelihood of higher-order interactions among contextual or environmental characteristics, organizational parameters, and individual differences. Modeling can extend our knowledge from the explored areas to the extremes of the domain where little is known.

Information is densest at the margins of a young research field, but research tends to be densest in the center of the research field, where cases are easiest to obtain and pressures to solve practical problems may be the greatest. Organizational research is a young field. Applications and extensions of theoretical models to the boundaries of our field will provide much information and reduce uncertainty about how people behave in organizations located throughout organizational space.

To study the margins of a research field often requires resources beyond our reach. Pilot research to identify salient properties of the margins of our knowledge, as well as the identifying logistics necessary to obtain data and observations from organizations and people within those margins, are serious impediments to progress. Computational modeling often can be used to simulate individual behavior in organizations and environments that define the margins. The discovery of black holes in space, identified by simulating the behavior of gases in zero gravity of deep space, represents an example of the ability of the modeling process to provide information from the boundaries of a research field. In this latter case, we knew the laws of gas dynamics and we knew about zero gravity in deep space. Applications of the laws of gas dynamics in zero gravity provided the information needed to identify black holes.

Computational modeling and simulation are consistent with modern views of epistemology and the needs to use an encompassing view of the total theoretical and organizational space to link limited, ad hoc theories. The usefulness of theories should be judged by the extent to which they address questions in all regions of the theoretical space under consideration (see Seitz, Chapter 2, this volume), not by whether a few specific hypotheses cannot be rejected. Hypotheses derived from local ad hoc theories are unlikely to be refuted because of their limited scope. But if the theories are evaluated using a metric of uncertainty reduction, those theories will likely be found deficient when contrasted with theories that address the expected relationships throughout the space under study. Computational modeling can provide information about broad theories and models that comprise many improbable links among constructs. These constructs, in turn, comprise many manifest indicators.

Few managers or engineers would implement a complex technical or social–technical system without first conducting extensive modeling—scenario evaluations—to determine the probable results of the system's behavior under a variety of environmental and human inputs. They identify cascading or compounding errors caused by small technical problems or human errors and erect firewalls to trap the effects of those errors and limit the damage to the total system. Managers charged with responsibility for human resource systems can exercise the same caution by modeling organizational interventions into human resource systems.

Models normally contain random shocks and stochastic links from individual variables or events to other variables and constructs. As we specify the content of the major source of the random shocks, we begin the process of replacing stochastics with events with known distributions and expected effects. For example, young, single parents in the work force may have child care problems, a source of shocks that influence tardiness, attendance, or job attitudes. Health problems for older workers may be a source of shocks for this segment of the work force. Alcohol abuse problems related to Monday absences may be random shocks for still another group of employees. Computational modeling can build in provisions for different distributions of stochastic shocks, based on known empirical relations, for different segments of the work force and begin to account for a greater variety of influences on behaviors and other outcomes. To the extent that these stochastics are based on known content relations and differences, we can begin to move from models with many sources of random variation to models reflecting a greater degree of determinism.

Computational modeling can be used to construct comprehensive theories and useful models from local ad hoc theories. We can identify the regions of organizational and environmental space in which subsets of available models generate results consistent with empirical data. Those models can be linked computationally to each other and generalized to other regions of the space by extending environmental and organizational parameters and constraints that identify and define new regions of space. Such hybrid models may never be evaluated for their usefulness in all regions of the space to which they are generalized. However, if they account for important variance in the regions in which they can be tested, we have more confidence in their usefulness when applied to regions of the space to which they have been extended by general theory and known parameters.

Each of the following chapters and commentaries by recognized social and behavioral scientists contributes to our knowledge and understanding of a specific domain related to organizational behavior. The breadth and variety of the topics addressed and the models that have been simulated—from stochastic unfolding models to nonlinear, dynamic, stochastic models and from user-accessible Excel programs to million-line–long C++ software—attest to the potential of computational modeling to complement and extend our knowledge of behavioral processes in organizations. Exploitation of this third research discipline to other domains in organizational research will yield information about topics that may be but poorly studied using one of our traditional research disciplines. The field of organizational research will be richer and our understanding of organizational behaviors at the boundaries of our domains will be greater if researchers increase their efforts to exploit computational modeling and simulations of behavior processes in organizations.

Blurring the Distinctions Between the Traditional Research Disciplines

Research is advanced by theory but is constrained by technology. Research technology and relevant theory must be in synchrony before modeling can become a well-used research tool. Computer technology has provided us with machines that allow complex models to be evaluated. Computer programming languages make this aspect of computational modeling accessible to researchers without requiring a PhD in computer science.

The linkage between technology and modeling can be seen in physics. Janus, a newly developed computer, is based on 9,072 Pentium Pro processors operating in parallel (Johnson, 1997). Janus has the electronic muscle to perform a trillion floating-point operations each second: a *teraflop* capacity. Until recently, physicists were described as either experimentalists or theorists. The availability of a teraflop computer blurs distinctions among researchers by contributing to the development of a third research discipline, labeled *numerical analysis* in physics. Some physicists argue that numerical analysis based on computational modeling is the branch most likely to lead to the next major breakthrough in physics.

Scientists who recreate biological reactions in test tubes are said to be working "in vitro." Researchers who conduct experiments inside computers' silicon chips are working "in silica." Information produced in silica is treated as equivalent to the information produced by experimentation or theoretical analysis. Experiments that are unthinkable in physical terms will be conducted in teraflop machines, and the knowledge produced will further our understanding of the systems and processes studied in silica. Janus was recently used, for example, to analyze what would happen if a meteor 0.6 miles in diameter were to hit the earth, vaporize portions of the oceans, and set off tidal waves. Such an experiment can be done only in silica.

Developments in numerical analysis in physics, astrophysics, astronomy, and related soft science fields have not been paralleled by analogous developments in computational modeling in behavioral sciences. Developments in computer capacity and flexible programming languages are no longer roadblocks to the developments of computational modeling in these areas. We have the hardware needed for our modeling efforts. The software can be developed.

Theory, the second part of the modeling enterprise, is the element that may be a significant impediment to the adoption of modeling in organizational science. As Latané (Chapter 9, this volume) notes, our theories seldom lend themselves to precise expression. Deriving consequences from verbally stated theories is difficult, and propositional calculus becomes nearly impossible. Translating literary theories into quantifiable point estimates is similarly difficult. In addition many theories stand too close to the data they were formulated to explain. Ad hoc theories explain the data that generated them—that the theories were generated to account for. Generalizability to other manifestations in the same domain or to conceptually more remote domains is questionable, and interest in modeling such theories is understandably limited. Organizational researchers are indeed often constrained in modeling studies by the state of our theoretical developments; this problem is more real than apparent. Several of the authors in this volume, however, demonstrate that verbal theories are translatable into computer algorithms with promising results. Similar efforts in other research domains in organizational studies may yield similar benefits.

Plan for the Book

This book presents 10 chapters by behavioral scientists from a variety of backgrounds. The work of each writer illustrates different approaches to computational modeling in content areas related to organizational behavior. It is our hope that the chapters will serve as an introduction to computational modeling for researchers in organizational behavior and in I/O psychology and stimulate them to use the tools of computational modeling to ask important research questions of their own.

This chapter and the following chapter by Seitz prepare the groundwork for this book by discussing computational modeling nontechnically and generally, as it might be applied to questions in the area of organizational behavior and I/O psychology. The chapters develop the case that computational modeling could profitably be used more extensively in organizational research than it currently is being used. Specifically, the authors argue that many of the models of behavioral processes we are attempting to evaluate empirically in our collective areas of interest are dynamic models containing nonlinearities and other elements of chaotic systems. Evaluating such models using one of the two traditional research disciplines, experimentation and correlational analyses, often creates epistemological misfits between the models and the hypotheses and between the hypotheses and the data. Deriving closed-form analytic solutions to formal statements of the consequences of these models is often impossible. In many cases, computational modeling represents an attractive alternative to experimentation or correlational analyses of individual differences as a way of evaluating the usefulness of these models.

The chapters of the book follow a "micro to macro" scheme. The book begins with chapters focusing on individuals and ends with chapters on how organizations operate within their environments. Specifically, the chapters first cover topics such as personality assessment and individual withdrawal behaviors; then focus on groups, individuals, and organizational systems (e.g., pay, group formation, effects of information distribution in groups); and, finally, address macro aspects of organizations functioning in volatile competitive and social environments.

This ordering may be a holdover from the past. The flexibility and power of computational modeling make it easy for researchers to assess simultaneously the effects of variables sampled from societal and organizational levels as well as from individual and group levels. The capacity and power of our computer systems and the flexibility of our programming languages may contribute to the quietus of the distinctions between macro and micro research that have ill-served us for the past 30 years. Investigators now can routinely simulate the additive and interactive effects of variables drawn from multiple levels. The knowledge gained through the simulations of theoretical models will offer important guidance to this field, possibly blurring macro and micro distinctions.

Discussants—one for each modeling chapter—comment on how the chapters illustrate the advantages of modeling and further the understanding and appreciation of modeling for the readers. The discussants were asked to serve neither as critics of what was written in the chapters nor as acolytes of the modeling process or the findings. Their goal was to provide an alternative perspective on modeling and on the usefulness of the modeling process as applied to research on organizational behaviors. They were given a difficult task, and they executed it well.

We hope these chapters will stimulate readers to apply modeling in their own research specialties. The potential applications are limited only by our "wetware," not by our hardware or software.

References

Arnott, R., & Small, K. (1994). The economics of traffic congestion. *American Scientist, 82,* 446–455.

Carley, K. M., & Prietula, M. J. (1994). ACTS theory: Extending the model of bounded rationality. In K. M. Carley & M. J. Prietula (Eds.), *Computational organization theory* (pp. 65–88). Hillsdale, NJ: Erlbaum.

Cronbach, L. J. (1957). The two disciplines of scientific psychology. *American Psychologist, 12,* 671–684.

Cronbach, L. J. (1975). Beyond the two disciplines of scientific psychology. *American Psychologist, 30,* 116–127.

Glomb, T. M., Munson, L. J., Hulin, C. L., Bergman, M., & Drasgow, F. D. (1999). Structural equation models of sexual harassment: Longitudinal explorations and cross-sectional generalizations. *Journal of Applied Psychology, 84,* 14–28.

Hanisch, K. A., Hulin, C. L., & Seitz, S. T. (1996). Mathematical/computational modeling of organizational withdrawal processes: Benefits, methods, and results. In G. Ferris (Ed.), *Research in personnel and human resources management* (Vol. 14, pp. 91–142). Greenwich, CT: JAI Press.

Hanisch, K. A., Hulin, C. L., & Seitz, S. T. (in press). Computational modeling of temporal dynamics and emergent properties of organizational withdrawal behaviors and models. In M. Erez & U. Kleinbeck (Ed.), *Work motivation in a cross-national perspective.* Hillsdale, NJ: Erlbaum.

Ilgen, D. R. (1985). Laboratory research: A question of when, not if. In E. A. Locke (Ed.), *The generalizability of laboratory experiments: An inductive survey* (pp. 257–268). Lexington, MA: D.C. Heath.

Johnson, G. (1997, September 5). Giant computer virtually conquers space and time. *The New York Times.*

Lewandowski, S. (1993). The rewards and hazards of computer simulations. *Psychological Science, 4,* 236–242.

Luce, R. D. (1995). Four tensions concerning mathematical modeling in psychology. *Annual Review of Psychology, 46,* 1–26.

Munson, L. J., Hulin, C. L., & Drasgow, F. D. (in press). Temporal dynamics and sexual harassment: Assessing the effects of sexual harassment over time. *Personnel Psychology.*

Perrow, C. (1984). *Normal accidents: Living with high risk technologies.* New York: Basic Books.

Posner, M. I. (Ed.). (1989). *Foundations of cognitive science.* Cambridge, MA: MIT Press.

Rebuilt Kennedy hasn't been a moving experience. (1994, October, 16). *The Chicago Tribune,* Section 2, pp. 1–2.

Seitz, S. T. (1994). Apollo's oracle: Strategizing for peace. *Synthese, 100,* 461–495.

Seitz, S. T., & Mueller, G. E. (1994). Viral load and sexual risk: Epidemiologic and policy implications for HIV/AIDS. In E. H. Kaplan & M. L. Brandeau (Eds.), *Modeling the AIDS epidemic: Planning, policy, and prediction* (pp. 461–480). New York: Raven Press.

Simon, H. A. (1992). What is an explanation of behavior? *Psychological Science, 3,* 150–161.

Smarr, L. L. (1985). An approach to complexity: Numerical computations. *Science, 228, 403–408.*

Wickens, C. (1999). Automation in air traffic control: The human performance issues. In M. Scerbo and M. Mouloua (Eds.), *Automation technology and human performance: Current issues and trends* (pp. 2–10). Mahwah, NJ: Erlbaum.

Williams, T. J., Bernus, P., Brosvic, J., Chen, D., Doumeingts, G., Nemes, L., Nevins, J. L., Vallespire, B., Vliestra, I., & Zoetekouw, D. (1994). Architectures for integrating manufacturing activities and enterprises. *Computers in Industries, 24,* 111–139.

CHAPTER 2

Virtual Organizations

Steven T. Seitz

Virtual reality was, until recently, largely the realm of science fiction writers and their aficionados. *Frankenstein* was Mary Shelley's (1818/1984) virtual representation for the evils of industrialization. The monster metaphorically illustrated how the machine age would come back to haunt and destroy its human creators. Shelley's model was man himself, assembled with stitched limbs and transplanted brains, then energized by the not-so-heavenly powers of a lightning storm. Other metaphoric models are common in Western thought. Plato's allegory of the cave, in which he depicts the world itself as a virtual representation of abstract Truth and Knowledge accessible only to well-trained philosophers, is a well-known example.

Social reality as we know it, or as we think we know it, is a daunting landscape to paint. We shall only paint a corner of that landscape here—namely, that of human organizations. The enterprise is not new. There once was a time when organization charts were the virtual representation of organizations. Somewhat later, communication links, nodes, and boundary spanners became their virtual representation. Then came a time when decision heuristics or "rules of thumb" were used to represent organizational processes. The latter were particularly popular among those committed to case studies. Simon's *Administrative Behavior* (1997) recast the metaphor in terms of information theory, but the simpler tools of observation and reflection were then no longer adequate to testing the conceptualizations he proposed. Many scholars continued their quest for more and denser case studies, perhaps to illustrate Simon's insights, but also because many believed that the growing volume of case studies would somehow reveal everything we really wanted to know. The quest for intersubjectively verifiable evidence in the study of human organizations led researchers down two additional paths: (a) an extensive overview of many different organizations in varied settings and (b) an intensive examination of single processes with all other relevant processes held constant. The first of these used statistical techniques that essentially controlled for different processes or properties by maximizing variance in a multivariate pool. The second used experimental designs that sought to isolate and study single processes by deliberately holding constant all other causal variables except those introduced as treatments. Along the way, both approaches subtly lost sight of organizations in real-world action.

The dilemma was both methodological and epistemological. The older virtual representations of organizations appeared either near intellectual bankruptcy (organization charts) or too soft and idiosyncratic (case studies) to reach beyond description into scientific explanation. The more scientific research designs objectified or deconstructed organizations to a point where parts became surrogates for the whole and the organization itself got lost in a reductionist frenzy. Like the King's horses and men working on Humpty Dumpty, it became increasingly difficult to put the "organization" back together again.

Virtual Organizations

A virtual organization is a functional representation of a real organization. Already this representation creates a Janus-faced problem. Just as an organization is more than its organization chart, so too a virtual organization cannot and should not be a caricature of the real organization it seeks to represent. A problem with so-called toy universes is that in the effort to simplify, we may reduce a real organization to a figment of the modeler's imagination. Hindsight warns against oversimplification; foresight unveils an equally serious problem. Critics of computational modeling charge that computational modelers are caught in a chicken-and-egg conundrum. They argue that creating a functional representation of a real organization requires the type of detailed understanding that flows from extensive preliminary research and discovery.

Those critics' prevailing epistemology solves the latter problem by begging the question. The myth of science-as-cumulation rests on the comforting notion that our scientific task is limited to breaking a problem into small and tractable components. The reintegration of these components is simply dismissed as nonproblematic. The tower of science and knowledge will be built when individual researchers have created enough bricks of knowledge. We seem to have assumed that the benefits of division of labor seen in organizations also will apply to the study of organizations. Some researchers work on problems of decision making, some work on negotiation and resolution of conflict, and still others work on problems of supervision. Because each researcher is an expert in his or her specific area, it is assumed that gains from specialization will be realized. The work of reintegrating the local bits of knowledge produced by individual researchers into a coherent statement of the parallel and interacting processes in organizations is left to a few macrotheorists and unspecified others whose specialty is the integration of multiple, conflicting chunks of evidence.

In the real world, this rarely happens. The intellectual division of labor has produced jargons that isolate specialists and render both inter- and intradisciplinary communication difficult. The devil is in the details, and the shards of eggshell seldom again make the image of poor Humpty Dumpty. Despite the persistent myth that a gallant genius would one day succeed where the King's men failed, a general theory of human organizations has yet to unscramble organizational research.

Computational modeling leads down a difficult but alternative path to the quixotic quest for the gallant genius; it is not a captive of the chicken-and-egg conundrum. No general theory of human organizations may exist, but there are many partial theories and many theories of local (as opposed to global) space behaviors. These are the building blocks of computational modeling. The pages that follow describe a method that emphasizes the importance of comparing competing models and of gluing together the bits and pieces of previous work. The logic is stunningly simple. Each partial theory purports to model one segment or another of the organizational landscape. Like the many artistic renditions of the Crucifixion, there are elements common to all of them despite differences in style. Renditions also may have idiosyncrasies, elements thought important by one artist, yet ignored by another. When compared side-by-side, some renditions end up telling different stories, and sometimes the stories told are seemingly contradictory. When the renditions are flatly contradictory, we can test competing accounts against their empirical referents. When the renditions are plausibly complementary, we can explore hybrid accounts that synthesize the partial perspectives into more comprehensive ones.

Again, virtual organizations are functional representations of real organizations. The study of virtual organizations requires the marriage of theory and observation. The proper metaphor here is marriage, not parentage. The positivist tradition holds that theory will naturally emerge from concatenated observation. The rationalist tradition holds that observation itself is fully structured by intuitively identifiable principles of human reason. Both of these epistemologies are parentage metaphors, where thought or knowledge is either the cause or the effect of observation. A marriage metaphor suggests that each tradition brings its own resources to the union and that the symbiosis of the whole is irreducible to its individual parts.

We shall finally argue that the study of virtual organizations is eminently scientific. The core of this argument has two well-known principles. First, any and all claims must be, at least in principle, falsifiable (Popper, 1959/1992). This means that claims, in some sense or other, must be empirically testable. Our approach, however, is decidedly at odds with naïve falsificationism. Second, all findings must be intersubjectively verifiable (Kaplan, 1964). Findings must be replicable.

Comparing competing models is simultaneously a logical and an empirical exercise. Let us begin with two degenerate cases. First, there may be many different ways to explain a single observation or a few observations. In this sense the single observation is theoretically overidentified. For convenience we label this *overidentification error I* (OE I). We often find this situation when researchers offer competing ad hoc hypotheses to explain an empirical observation. It often takes the form of "Well, I think that's because. . . ." Here science bears a striking similarity to political pundits offering opinions on "events of the day." A seemingly opposite case occurs when many different observations conform to a single theoretical assertion or a few assertions. In this sense the single theoretical assertion is observationally overidentified. For convenience we label this *overidentification error II* (OE II). Here the theoretical claims are so vacuous that virtually any finding can be read in support of the theoretical claim. It often takes the form of "Well, everything I see confirms my original judgment." We again find parallels with political pundits who, with conclusion in hand, label each and every event as proof positive of their original claim. In the case of OE I errors, the observations contain too little information to help differentiate good theoretical claims from bad ones. In the case of OE II errors, the theory contains too little information to permit contradiction or falsification by real-world events.

To avoid OE I or OE II errors, the study of virtual organizations ideally should combine (a) many observations and (b) many theoretical assertions. Both the observations and the theories must contain sufficient information to make it possible to test and to falsify competing theoretical claims. The illuminating power of theory is thus judged by the range of things it anticipates and their potential falsifiability. The chances that diverse domains of observation fit the dictates of a heterogeneous set of theoretical claims decrease with the information content of the observations and the information content of theoretical claims. In terms of significance testing, the a priori probability of "information-rich" observational patterns conforming to dictates of several information-rich competing theories is vanishingly small.

Computational Modeling

Computational modeling is not simply an extension of mathematical modeling. It represents a significant departure, both methodologically and epistemologically. The older mathematical modeling traditions required that formulated problems be mathematically tractable. This requirement had two consequences: (a) A calculus of several variables quickly was reduced to a calculus of few variables, and (b) the resulting toy universes were justified in terms strikingly similar to the science-as-cumulation epistemology. The implied belief was that little models would naturally concatenate with others and that their synthesis would be a nonproblematic outcome of normal science. That did not happen. What may be worse, the practice generated bodies of research in such areas as rational choice, which had limited empirical fit, although it was, for the most part, logically coherent.

When the elders of a remote island tribe were asked whether the Americans had really walked on the moon, the elders replied no, because "no man could live long enough to climb that far." The same problem appears when mathematical modelers are asked to pass judgment on computational modeling. They see it from the vantage of reduced equation sets worked out with pencil and paper. Computational modeling simultaneously allows the researcher to model a large set of heterogeneous theoretical claims, map them into an equally expansive range of observations, and model the observations that would be generated by the various information-rich theories. From the perspective of a mathematical modeler, however, this complexity becomes so daunting that the computational model is dismissed as a black box, and the evidentiary exercise is reduced to manipulating parameters to fit a target observation. The science of computational modeling thrives on the complexity that mathematical modelers ignore because the analytic solutions so prized by mathematical modelers are beyond pencil-and-paper technologies.

The key to the science of computational modeling lies in the information–theoretic approach to explanation introduced at the end of the last section. A good defense attorney limits the information a guilty client provides, because the more the client says, the greater the chance of self-incrimination. This occurs in part because the more information that is provided, the greater the chance is to find an inconsistency or contradiction with the facts. The more complex my story, the lower its a priori empirical probability. Changing one parameter value in a coupled, nonlinear model does not have isolated consequences for just a single observation. If you do not have the correct story, changing one or another claim (or parameter) increases the chance that other factual mismatches will appear. Similarly, the more complex the story, the greater the chance for an internal inconsistency. A computational modeling strategy quickly reveals logical inconsistencies that lie hidden beneath verbal turf. The same strategy allows the researcher to simulate the dynamics of complex, information-rich theories and to compare patterns of virtual instantiations to their real-world counterparts.

Computational modeling is the appropriate vehicle for studying virtual organizations. Computational models allow the functional instantiation of real organizations. Modern software architecture allows a single program to contain several competing models and to test those models against large or expansive databases. Developmental work is now underway in the area of computational theorizing, where the logical components of competing models are hybridized through interplay with one database and then tested against a different, independent database. Many of the algorithms guiding computational theorizing are already in place, some of which are illustrated later in this chapter.

Principle of Explanation

Overidentified systems, those generating either OE I or OE II errors, are characterized by high degrees of theoretical or observational entropy. With OE I, entropy is high because we have too many pundits and too little evidence to ponder. OE II entropy is high because anything seems consistent with our vague or broad-stroke expectations. Some cacophony or noise exists in either case. A flock of vultures (theories) shrieking and striking for a simple morsel (datum) is about as unstructured as the perceptual world of a person with paranoid schizophrenia (theory), who sees danger lurking in any shadow and beyond every turn (data).

The concept of entropy is used here in its information–theoretic sense: randomness or disorder or irregularity in a situation (Shannon & Weaver, 1949). When more information is transmitted than an encoding system can structure, it appears as "noise." In physical systems, such as telephone communications, the task is to control the signal-to-noise ratio. In explanatory systems, the task is similar. If the answer to "What do you make of this?" is "It could mean a dozen things," then noise dominates signal. If the answer to "What should we look for?" is "The evidence is everywhere," then noise also dominates signal. By way of contrast, if the answer to "What do you make of this?" is "There is only one or, at best, a few processes that could produce that pattern," then the signal is strong. Similarly, if the answer to "What should you look for?" is "There is a definite set of things that must appear, and a second set of things that must not appear," then the signal is also strong.

Attributing seemingly unrelated "bad" events to "angry gods" is an attempt to reduce the entropy in a domain of observation. It does so at the cost of an OE II: Everything evinces the mood of the gods, and tautologically, the mood of the gods is seen everywhere we choose to look. Circularity or tautology is a sign of OE II reasoning. Ad hoc theorizing, the spinning of explanations as each finding emerges, is also an attempt to reduce the entropy in a domain of observation. It does so at the cost of an OE I: Meaning is in the eye of the beholder, knowledge is a personal construction of reality, and intersubjective verifiability gives way to the blooming of a thousand intuitions. A proliferation of opinion and assertion is a sign of OE I reasoning.

Entropy remains high if a theory lacks discriminating power among potential observables. In this respect, "angry gods" are entropic explanations. Entropy also remains high if there are nearly as many accounts for an observable as there are observers. In this respect, a multitude of buzzing theorists still produces entropic explanation. In contrast, a good theory should do the following:

- impose considerable structure on the situation and, by so doing, essentially convert what may be initially regarded as noise into signal
- have an a priori probability of fitting observables that is quite low; the chance of finding the signal amid all the noise should initially appear quite remote.

A good theory is improbably accurate (Good, 1975; Rosenkrantz, 1980). It has discriminatory power, and it speaks on matters when other theories remain silent.

A slightly more formal way of looking at this information–theoretic view of explanation is captured in the following discrete case formulation of relative entropy (see Shannon & Weaver, 1949). Suppose we represent a theory's set of claims as $\{C_1, \ldots, C_k\}$. We represent the a priori probability of each claim as $p(C_1) = c_1$, etc. Given theory *T*, the conditional probability becomes $c_1|T$. The theory's entropy is represented as T_E. Now:

$$T_E = \frac{\{\sum_{1}^{k} [c_k|T \times \log(c_k|\sim T) + (c_k|\sim T) \times \log(c_k|\sim T)]\}}{\{k \times \log(.5)\}} \qquad (2.1)$$

For a single consequence C_k, the value of T_E is largest when the a priori probability of a consequence c_k is 50/50, or .5. The value of T_E is smallest (i.e., entropy is lowest) when the a priori probability of consequence c_k is very small (see Table 2.1).

Theories with limited amount of informational claims (i.e., theories with a small number of consequences) are characterized by greater entropy than are theories with more informational claims. A low-entropy theory seeks to convert large amounts of what we might take to be noise into meaningful signal. A consequence that we already expect and for which a theory simply adds its voice contributes little to reducing entropy. Similarly, a consequence that we continue to expect, even when the theory cannot be supported, contributes little to reducing entropy. Theoretical claims that are unexpected and which would not be expected outside the framework of a particular theoretical matrix are the building blocks for a low-entropy theory. A low-entropy theory is one that claims to convert large amounts of what we otherwise might take to be noise into a meaningful signal.

We can illustrate this simple algorithm with the following three cases. Each case guides use of the algorithm even when we have limited data for instantiating the algorithm. In case one, suppose we have a single observation that is predicted by a half-dozen different theories. Because the observation is widely expected, we set its a priori probability to $[1- (1/n) + \alpha] = .84$, where *n* is the number of theories anticipating the same observation and α is a small constant between .00 and .01. Because several theories anticipate the observation, we set the a priori probability of $(c_k|\sim T)$ to .5. Knowing the theory thus adds nothing to expectation regarding the anticipated

TABLE 2.1

Entropy features of an information–theoretic view of explanation

VERBAL	FORMAL	HIGH ENTROPY	LOW ENTROPY
Number of consequences	For $\{C_1 \ldots C_k\}$	k is small	k is large
A priori probability, given *T*	For c_k|T	c_i is large	c_i is small
A priori probability, given ~*T*	For $(c_k\|\sim T)$	$(c_k\|\sim T)$ large	$(c_k\|\sim T)$ small

observation; it remains just as likely to happen as not happen. Its T_E score is .711 (with a maximum value of 1.0, namely, much entropy or noise).

In case two, suppose we have a theory for which any of a half-dozen observations meet its test. In this case, for each observation C_k, we set $c_k|T$ to $1/n$ = .167, where n is the number of different observations that meet the theoretical test. Because we do not know whether the various observations would occur if the theory were false, we set $(c_k|{\sim}T)$ to .5. The T_E score here is .932, or again, lots of entropy or noise.

In case three, suppose that the theory requires six observations to occur simultaneously. For comparison, we estimate the a priori probability of each element in the set at $.167^6 = .0000214$. In the absence of additional information, we will assume that the occurrence of all six consequences if the theory were false is $.5^6$ = and hence set $(c_k|{\sim}\mathrm{T})$ to .015625. The T_E here is .094, a situation where the entropy or "noise" is substantially controlled vis-à-vis signal or "explanation."

This simple goodness-of-fit measure illustrates our information–theoretic approach to explanation. Our goal is the functional rather than total representation of a real organization. Parsimony is not the guide to explanation under these circumstances; the reduction of observational entropy through the wise use of theory is the core principle. We want a general theory of human organizations that will produce a theoretical entropy score (T_E) near zero when tested against real-world analogs. We have suggested two derivations from this logic: (a) comparing competing models and (b) synthesizing partial theories into more comprehensive ones. Like any modern field of scientific inquiry, the study of human organizations has its characteristic division of intellectual labor. Within the larger domain comprising human organization, scholarly subcommunities focus on selected functional components. When scholars within these subfields disagree, they generate the raw materials for comparing competing models. Across subfields, the raw materials exist for coupling or synthesizing partial models into more comprehensive ones. In both cases, the ultimate goal is to find a functional representation of human organizations that minimizes explanatory entropy and avoids OE I or OE II reasoning.

Illustration: Saving Intellectual Capital

Suppose we have a large organization preparing for layoffs with two fundamental goals: (a) to maintain its core intellectual capital and (b) to reduce its peripheral human capital. Let us set an equally daunting research task: to gain sufficient understanding of the transition dynamics to provide pragmatic assistance as decision makers formulate and implement the layoff plan. We are not studying an organization in its maintenance phase, nor are we studying an organization undergoing normal change. This illustration focuses on an organization undergoing drastic transformation.

If we were to use a case study approach, we would essentially reason by analogy. Thus, organization A is like organization B and, based on the asserted similarity, we would use the good and bad lessons learned in organization A to inform and guide the policies in organization B. Reasoning by analogy is not proof in the scientific sense, but it attempts to draw lessons from history. The problem, of course, is that analogies are inherently entropic. Organization B could be said to be like many, many other organizations in one way or another, and it is precisely in determining which of these ways are relevant that we overidentify possible explanations and things being explained. Reasoning by analogy is an example of OE I: There are nearly as many potential comparisons as there are case experts recommending the appropriate comparison.

If we were to use an experimental design, we would face similar problems, but for drastically different reasons. We would first have to begin with the concluding knowledge being sought, namely, the few factors that are causally related to keeping critical intellectual capital but that allow peripheral human capital to disperse. A conclusion in search of supporting evidence is an example of OE II: the truth is known, let the facts conform (or else revise the obviously misguided measurement indicators). If we try to avoid starting with a conclusion in search of supporting evidence, then we may find ourselves in a situation remarkably similar to overidentified explanation in case studies (OE I): Each varying factor is a potential explanation, and hence an entropic abundance of explanations exists. A further complication comes into play if more than one possible outcome is associated with varying any particular factor. We either are back to assuming the knowledge being sought (i.e., which outcome is relevant to the research question), or we have an overabundance of possible explanations.

Suppose we look at extensive comparative analyses. Because the problem at hand is dynamic in the sense that it is a process that unfolds over time, it would be inappropriate to use a cross-sectional analysis of variance or regression. Even if we were to assume that there was a statistically adequate set of organizations in the process of downsizing and that at any instant we had organizations in the sample representing all phases of the downsizing process, we still would be substituting analyses of variance across stages or levels for dynamic analysis. The more nonlinear the process, the greater the sampling density required. We gain only modest ground by introducing panel or time-series designs, in part because the data demands expand geometrically and in part because the indicator problem persists. If modest changes in the sample result in significant changes in parameter estimations or, worse still, in shifts in the relative importance of contributing variables, then the data model has an overabundance of potential explanations and falls prey to OE I.

Computational modeling begins where each of these approaches runs into difficulties. Logical models are developed to instantiate plausible explanations, whether they are complementary or contradictory. Data models are developed to instantiate measurement or observation patterns that are expected to flow from each of the potential explanations at any given point in the unfolding dynamic process. The logical models incorporate temporal dynamics, and thus, by derivation, so do the data models. The logical models thus represent processes. User-controlled iterations, or *time-steps,* allow complex dynamics to unfold with feedback, even if there is no "reduced form" equilibrium derived from an analytic solution. At any point in the unfolding process, the implied structure of the observed universe can be induced and compared with the results of a data model instantiated at that juncture of the logical process. Explanations with low entropy map into highly structured data models that, in turn, provide large amounts of information about the expected structure of the observational or empirical universe. The a priori chance of such a fit is small. A good theory imposes an a priori extensive structure on expected observational patterns and for which, if the test is successful, and despite its low a priori probability, the data model provides empirical confirmation of the predicted pattern.

In a sense, computational modeling seeks to turn overidentification problems (OE I or OE II) on their heads. If several theories purport to explain an observable phenomenon, then we try to make them competing explanations; namely, What other expectations follow from each vantage point, and what observations should not be found if a given explanation is correct? Here we are converting an OE I problem (too many explanations of too few observations) into a test of competing theories. An OE II problem, that everything is evidence of the initial claim, must first be subjected to a falsification test: Is there anything that would disprove this explanation? If this test is passed, then we proceed to comparatively evaluate the information load of the OE II explanation against the information load of any other competing theory attempting to explain the same set of observables.

Now let us cast the problem as a concrete example of organizational layoffs. We will assume that the layoffs generate unusual stress on the survivors and that the stress vis-à-vis layoffs increases negative attitudes toward the organization. The task is to minimize the impact of negative attitudes among the workers most central to the continued viability of the organization's mission. To minimize this impact, in turn, requires that the core intellectual capital be provided with incentives (or disincentives) designed to minimize departure of target personnel. For simplicity of discussion, we will assume that we already know the following information. First, the external employment opportunities for the targeted group are modestly greater than the opportunities available to those leaving the organization involuntarily. Second, the targeted group has the same age and tenure distribution as the peripheral workers, and any correlation between attitude valence and age or tenure is equivalent in the two groups.

The remaining research difficulties are daunting. First, there are several empirical traces of worker withdrawal. They include the obvious issues, such as turnover and early retirement, but they also include less obvious forms, such as wasting time on the job, tardiness, absence, and so forth. Second, there are many different accounts of

(a) the relation between attitudes and resulting behaviors, (b) the expected structural relation between the empirical traces of withdrawal behaviors and their attitudinal antecedents, and (c) the feedback dynamics as attitudinal change and withdrawal trace behaviors occur. Some explanations see each attitude or behavior as independent packets operating in isolation from one another. Other explanations suggest progression or spillover (see Hanisch, Chapter 3, or Munson and Hulin, Chapter 4, this volume). Third, the relation between organizational sanctions or incentives (or environmental variations, such as differential reemployment opportunities) and the attitude–behavior nexus remain largely unexplored.

It would be simple to conclude that the state of knowledge is inadequate to provide policy guidance to organizational decision makers. The larger issue, however, is whether the classical research methodologies can ever adequately prepare us to understand these dynamics sufficiently to provide forecasting capabilities. The possibility space implied by multiple empirical traces of withdrawal, the many alternative accounts of the relation between attitude–behavior packets, the many alternative feedback scenarios, and the ill-defined impact of boundary constraints (organizational carrot-and-stick policies and the larger unemployment environment) is too large to exhaust by case studies or experimental designs in a lifetime of research. The data demands for extensive cross-sectional and longitudinal analyses are similarly beyond reasonable reach.

Computational modeling thrives in this research environment. Regarding the logical side of the coin, alternative accounts of the relation between attitude–behavior packets become competing models. The feedback scenarios are computational productions of the models as the time-steps unfold. The various boundary constraints can also be simulated by aggregating the attitude–behavior model components with contextual and environmental components. (Conversely, these processes can be disaggregated to allow closer scrutiny of each layer of this compositional causality.) These scenarios generate vast quantities of simulation information, and hence the pragmatic task shifts from gathering information to comparing and analyzing simulation results.

Looking at the empirical side of the coin, these dynamic computational models tell us what constellation of multiple observables we should expect at one or another phase of an unfolding withdrawal process. The correlative data models link these logical predictions to their empirical expectations. Let us begin by positing two competing explanations: (a) an "independent forms" model and (b) a progression model. For simplicity we shall say that in the independent forms model, withdrawal attitudes are really separate attitudes and that changes in one have no bearing whatsoever on changes in another. Also for simplicity, we shall say that in the progression model, the withdrawal attitudes are, in fact, hierarchically rankable in terms of degree of withdrawal and that an individual moves from one level to another if there is no satisfaction forthcoming. Based on an independent forms model, we might expect that (a) downsizing has an isolated impact on one or two separate attitudes,

(b) any withdrawal behavior that occurs feeds back onto its isolated attitude correlate, and (c) over time the negative shock of downsizing would dissipate even without feedback. Based on a progression model, we might expect that (a) downsizing affects lower level forms of withdrawal first, (b) unsatisfactory feedback cascades to more severe forms of withdrawal, and (c) across the time trajectory, the withdrawal behaviors become more serious as the employees quickly progress through the less serious to the more serious overt behaviors. In each of these instances, the expected empirical trace is different between models and at different points along the unfolding trajectory. We now have the basis to test competing models. This particular test focuses on aggregate patterns, but we can also explore individual trajectories within these aggregate patterns using standard Monte Carlo designs.

Data previously generated by case studies, experimental designs, and extensive comparative analyses can provide empirical benchmarks for the simulation results. In this respect, computational modeling works hand-in-hand with the older technologies. Because the computer can quickly do rote repetitive tasks, it can rapidly produce alternative scenario analyses that would not be possible in a lifetime of observation.

Illustration: Extensions to Emergent Technologies

Now suppose we wish to study organizations charged with the development and dissemination of new technologies. To make things interesting, we will assume that the potential uses for the new technologies are not well known. The potential markets are ill defined, and the proper mix of research, development, and production personnel are only vaguely understood. The consulting task is to help management position the organization to maximize the ability to deliver tailored products to emergent market niches and to minimize cost inefficiencies. We have deliberately chosen an example that is not at or near steady-state equilibrium and that does not have obvious analogs in previous case histories.

Computational modeling is a fast and relatively inexpensive technique for exploring alternative scenarios or "state instantiations." This is the situation confronting us here, where neither the potential markets nor the technical uses nor the appropriate personnel mix is well understood. Second, computational modeling can draw from the basic discoveries of experimental design, help explore their synthesis, and then help weave logical stories that produce virtual consequences. Testing in this case would follow a two-stage strategy. First, the synthetic web of explanatory principles would be used to regenerate empirical traces documented in other case studies or extensive statistical analyses. This stage ensures that we have a good handle on the various causal forces that may be at work in this case. Successful concatenations would then be used to generate alternative virtual scenarios in the case at hand. The process, in a sense, generates plausible futures. This crafty weaving of theory and evidence, experiment and description, logic and statistical pattern, is the sine qua non of computational modeling.

This approach uses previous discoveries from experimental or statistical work to provide baselines for behavioral dynamics. The proposed procedure assumes that there is some continuity in human attitudinal and behavioral dynamics but that these dynamics come into play differently in different contexts and that they may even interact with contexts. For example, suppose we posit that some significant proportion of a Western work force is moderately or highly motivated by a desire for achievement. How this motivation for achievement affects behaviors under conditions of high risk and high uncertainty may differ from contexts of low risk and low uncertainty. We then "play out" the logical implications of alternative scenarios. For example, one baseline scenario might be that circumstances of high risk and high uncertainty have no effect on achievement motivation and therefore no impact on observable behaviors. Another scenario might hold that achievement-motivated behaviors decrease linearly with risk and uncertainty, and a third might hold that achievement-motivated behaviors exponentially decrease as risk and uncertainty increase. Each of these "what if" scenarios generates patterned "logical" findings that can be compared with known results from controlled studies.

The logical decomposition of nonlinear processes into isolated components is a typical intervening step on the way to full-fledged scenario analyses of complex problems for which few or no empirical analogues exist. We essentially vet the processes taken singly and then explore the complex patterns when the processes are concatenated in a computational model.

Conclusion

Virtual reality is a functional representation of a real-world target of inquiry, such as a large-scale organization undergoing rapid personnel change or one facing a new product or environment challenge. Computational modeling is the methodology we recommend for building virtual realities. Part of that methodology, in turn, is the use of information–theoretic principles to marry substantive theory and observation. This approach helps us avoid the problems of ad hoc theorizing (OE I) and the problems of circular, vague, and nonfalsifiable explanations (OE II). Another part of that methodology emphasizes the need to compare competing models. The proper test, therefore, is not whether a claim is statistically unlikely given a null hypothesis (betting against "nothing") but whether one concatenated set of claims and empirical confirmations has greater information content than another concatenated set of claims and empirical confirmations. In short, the test of a good model or theory is how much work it can do for us. Computational modeling allows us to extend research agendas beyond those possible through case studies, experimental design, or statistical analysis. It seeks to supplement, not replace these older methodologies. It also provides us with tools for modeling possible future states (i.e., prediction) while drawing heavily on "postdiction" for testing and validation. NASA scientists modeled the behavior of the small rover and made the appropriate adjustments before sending it on its journey. Computational modeling allows us to bring the same level of insight to understanding and guiding organizations in a fast-paced and ever changing social universe.

References

Good, I. J. (1975). Explicativity, corroboration, and the relative odds hypotheses. *Synthese, 30,* 39–73.

Kaplan, A. (1964). *The conduct of inquiry: methodology for the behavioral sciences.* New York: Thomas Y. Crowell.

Popper, K. R. (1959/1992). *Logic of scientific discovery.* New York: Routledge.

Rosenkrantz, R. D. (1980). Measuring truthlikeliness. *Synthese, 45,* 463–487.

Shannon, C. E., & Weaver, W. (1949). *The mathematical theory of communication.* Urbana: University of Illinois Press.

Shelley, M. W. (1984). *Frankenstein.* New York: Bantam Classics. Original work published 1818.

Simon, H. A. (1997). *Administrative behavior* (4th ed.). New York: Free Press.

CHAPTER 3

The Impact of Organizational Interventions on Behaviors

An Examination of Different Models of Withdrawal

Kathy A. Hanisch

Hanisch (1995b) defined *organizational withdrawal* as a construct denoting "various behaviors employees engage in to remove themselves from their job or avoid their work" (p. 604). Employees' withdrawal behaviors have interested organizational researchers both theoretically and practically for well over a half-century. An understanding of the causes of these behaviors can help employers who have struggled to deal with high turnover and absenteeism rates. In addition to turnover and absenteeism (two frequently studied forms of withdrawal), being late, leaving work early, playing computer games or surfing the web on work time, taking long lunch or coffee breaks, making excuses to go somewhere to get out of work, making frequent trips to the restroom, moonlighting, excessive chatting with coworkers, missing meetings, and drinking alcohol at work are examples of other organizational withdrawal behaviors (Fisher & Locke, 1992; Hanisch, 1995a; Hanisch & Hulin, 1991). The antecedents of these behaviors have received considerable attention, particularly with regard to the behaviors of absenteeism and quitting. Dissatisfaction with one's work, supervisor, and coworkers is among the reasons given for these behaviors (see Hanisch, Hulin, & Roznowski, 1998, for an overview of the relations among job attitudes and withdrawal behaviors). Although the antecedents of some withdrawal behaviors have been extensively evaluated, an examination of the relations among different forms of withdrawal and how organizational interventions or environmental events might affect relations among employees' withdrawal behaviors is needed.

Researchers, often at the request of employers, have attempted to predict, understand, and even control withdrawal behaviors because of their costs to organizations. Unfortunately, each withdrawal behavior usually has been studied in isolation; we have little empirical information about the relations among withdrawal behaviors. This lack can be attributed to researchers' myopic focus on one withdrawal behavior at a time as well as difficulties inherent in studying these relations. Possible reasons for the lack of systematic inquiry into the relations among withdrawal behaviors include the following:

- It is difficult to measure multiple forms of withdrawal in a single study.
- Practitioners need to control one behavior (e.g., lateness problem, high turnover rate) for practical purposes.
- The behaviors are low base-rate behaviors and have skewed distributions that create difficulties for analysis.
- Time is important in the relations among withdrawal behaviors, and most social scientists' approach to research focuses on cross-sectional data collections.
- Researchers have a tendency to not recognize explicitly that antecedents are complex and that people may respond to them by engaging in multiple behaviors (see Hanisch, 1995a, for a detailed discussion of these points).

This chapter uses computational modeling to provide information about relations among employee withdrawal behaviors when an organizational intervention is imposed during a simulation. Specifically, it describes an evaluation of the effects of organizational interventions on targeted and other withdrawal behaviors, comparing different theoretical models of the relations among withdrawal behaviors.

Models of Withdrawal Behaviors

Several theories or models describe what the relations among withdrawal behaviors should be like. Each model hypothesizes different functions of enacted withdrawal behaviors and implies different structures among the withdrawal behaviors. The models include the independent forms of withdrawal model, the compensatory behaviors withdrawal model, the progression of withdrawal model, the spillover model of withdrawal, and the alternate forms of withdrawal model. The original descriptions of all the models focused on two or three behaviors: absenteeism, quitting and, occasionally, lateness. Since these models were developed, possible additional withdrawal behaviors have been identified, such as leaving work early, retiring early, and playing computer games at work (Hanisch, 1995a; Hanisch & Hulin, 1990, 1991). The following sections briefly describe each model. (For details, see Hanisch, Hulin, and Seitz, 1996, and the references by the original authors of the models at the end of this chapter.)

Independent Forms of Withdrawal Model

In March and Simon's (1958) original statement of the independent forms of withdrawal model, absenteeism and quitting were assumed to be unrelated because they have different functions and consequences for employees who quit or are absent. March and Simon hypothesized that being absent from work and quitting one's job should be psychologically and statistically independent. The independent forms model describes the process of organizational withdrawal as follows: Employees choose to withdraw from an organization by being absent *or* by quitting. The behaviors may have common antecedents, but they have different functions and consequences for the employees. March and Simon argued that dissatisfaction, or motivation to withdraw, is "general and holds for both absences and voluntary turnover" (p. 93). Absences are hypothesized to reduce negative job attitudes by removing the employee temporarily from the stresses of their day-to-day tasks. Quitting reduces stress from a specific job by removing the person permanently from the organization and required work tasks. The limited empirical results that are available, however, do not support this model.

Compensatory Behaviors Withdrawal Model

The compensatory behaviors withdrawal model, first described by Hill and Trist (1955), assumes that enacting a single withdrawal behavior in varying amounts (e.g., once, several times) in response to negative organizational attitudes or work-related stress is sufficient to reduce job stress and dissatisfaction. That is, enacting any one withdrawal behavior reduces negative attitudes and the necessity for enacting other withdrawal behaviors. Hill and Trist observed that absences were a characteristic of "stayers" rather than "leavers." Those who were not absent were more likely to quit than those who had been absent in the past. From this observation they concluded that absenteeism compensated for any job dissatisfaction that may have been experienced by the "absence-prone" employees, making it unnecessary for them to quit.

In this model, all withdrawal behaviors appear to have the same psychological function: relieving job dissatisfaction and job stress. Any withdrawal behavior, once enacted, compensates for other withdrawal behaviors, making them unnecessary.

Progression of Withdrawal Model

Several articles contain elements of the progression of withdrawal model. Baruch (1944) described absences from work as "short-term quits." Herzberg, Mausner, Peterson, and Capwell (1957) argued that the problems of absenteeism and turnover should be considered jointly because "the small decision which is taken when the worker absents himself is a miniature version of the important decision he makes when he quits his job" (p. 103). Melbin (1961) argued that leaving a job is the outcome of a chain of experiences leading to a final break with an organization: "High absenteeism (lateness and absence) appears to be an earlier sign, and turnover (quitting and being fired) the dying stage of a long and lively process of leaving" (p. 15).

Rosse and Miller (1984) described and Rosse (1988) provided a partial empirical test of this model.

The progression of withdrawal model specifies that in response to negative job attitudes, people enact a stochastically ordered sequence of withdrawal responses. These responses range from minor acts, such as daydreaming or frequent trips to water fountains and restrooms, to lateness or leaving work early to absences from meetings, and abuse of sick and personal leave. Finally, the responses become more major withdrawal behaviors, such as unexcused absences, quitting, or early retirement. A generic ordering of these withdrawal behaviors in terms of degree of withdrawal is implied in this list. The order would most likely vary, depending on organizational differences that summarize technological and work force differences; job classifications within organizations and, perhaps, such individual differences as gender, age, or years of organizational service. As with the other withdrawal models, it is assumed that each of an employee's withdrawal behaviors has a feedback effect onto his or her job attitudes and withdrawal tendencies. However, the progression of withdrawal model also assumes that the effects of the feedback—that is, the amounts by which job dissatisfaction and withdrawal tendencies decrease—will vary as a function of the degree of withdrawal the behavior represents. Taking frequent trips to the water fountain or long coffee breaks, for example, are a less severe degree of withdrawal than being absent from work; enacting those behaviors should have minor effects on job dissatisfaction or withdrawal tendencies, compared with behaviors that represent a higher degree of withdrawal.

The progression of withdrawal model hypothesizes that employees enact withdrawal behaviors in a stochastically ordered sequence. The withdrawal behavior most likely to be enacted initially would be one of the milder forms of withdrawal. If this form of withdrawal reduced job dissatisfaction and job stress to a tolerable level, the employee would either repeat the same or a similarly severe withdrawal behavior to maintain the status quo and a tolerable level of job dissatisfaction and stress. If the chosen withdrawal behavior does not reduce job dissatisfaction or job stress to tolerable levels, the employee would be expected to increase the severity of the enacted withdrawal behaviors in the next behavioral time cycle (e.g., the next day, week, or month).

Spillover Model of Withdrawal

Beehr and Gupta (1978) argued that withdrawal behaviors should be positively intercorrelated—that there should be a nucleus of withdrawal behaviors that occur in concert. Aversive work situations should generate nonspecific negative attitudes and nonspecific withdrawal tendencies that allow employees to avoid the aversive parts of their work. The nonspecific avoidance tendencies, according to the spillover model, then "spill over" from one withdrawal behavior to another. Thus, an aversive work situation may generate several different withdrawal behaviors at the same time or several occurrences of the same behavior. The behaviors enacted depend on the behavior—one can quit a job only once, for example—and the situational constraints imposed on one or some subset of the withdrawal behaviors.

To account for any spread of withdrawal behaviors from the one initially enacted, this withdrawal model points to mechanisms that function independently of the attitudinal antecedents that triggered the initial behavior. This process may reflect habituation. Another descriptive metaphor for the spillover model is "behavioral diffusion" from one withdrawal behavior, once enacted, to other behaviors, which occurs without any necessary feedback effects on job attitudes.

Alternate Forms of Withdrawal Model

The positive intercorrelations among all withdrawal behaviors that should be generated by spillover effects from one behavior to another are a possible weakness of the spillover model. Eagley (1965) has shown that environmental constraints, instantiated by unemployment, can decrease the probability that an employee will quit his or her job. If environmental conditions or organizational constraints suppress or effectively eliminate one or more of the possible withdrawal behaviors, is it reasonable to assume, as the spillover model does, that all withdrawal behaviors will be suppressed similarly?

The alternate forms of withdrawal model (Mobley, 1977; Rice & Trist, 1952) addresses possible model–data fit problems for the spillover model that are caused by environmental constraints on one or a subset of withdrawal behaviors. It hypothesizes that different withdrawal behaviors are substitutable. This model assumes that aversive work conditions, through their effects on job dissatisfaction, will lead to organizational withdrawal. However, external economic conditions, organizational sanctions for different behaviors, and reinforcement histories of people who have enacted different withdrawal behaviors will largely determine the specific withdrawal behavior that is enacted (Hanisch, 1995a). According to this model, when constraints are placed on one withdrawal behavior, the probability of an alternate form of withdrawal increases. The assumption of the substitutability of behaviors in the alternate forms model is likely to be important only when a set of events constrains an employee from enacting one or more withdrawal behaviors that might otherwise have been selected.

Some jobs have severe sanctions on tardiness because the output of one employee is the input for the next employee. These long-linked technologies (e.g., assembly lines) require all employees to be present during the times they are scheduled to work or face harsh consequences (e.g., termination). Under such conditions, tardiness might be enacted as a withdrawal response infrequently, even among those with extremely negative job attitudes. The negative sanctions for tardiness may outweigh the relief the behavior provides from job stress. In this scenario, according to the alternate forms model, alternatives to tardiness such as drinking before work, absenteeism, or quitting should increase. Other organizations may place severe sanctions on absenteeism, thereby suppressing it as an alternative, or may have benefit packages that encourage "early" retirement, increasing the likelihood of this form of organizational withdrawal. Some jobs, because of their structure and constraints, make it virtually impossible to wander around and look busy or miss meetings. In these jobs, some subsets of withdrawal behaviors are unlikely, but other forms of withdrawal are likely to be substituted for the constrained withdrawal behaviors.

Summary of Withdrawal Models

Structural relations among different withdrawal behaviors are a crucial part of the evidence that should be evaluated to reach conclusions about the validity of the five withdrawal models under different conditions. All the models have static and dynamic structural relations among different withdrawal behaviors; frequencies of behaviors under different environmental conditions are their core outcomes. In addition to theoretical and structural differences, the models have different implications for organizational practice. Empirical research on the models is limited; little research exists on multiple forms of withdrawal within single studies, and there is even less on multiple forms of withdrawal over multiple time periods. Research has evaluated relations among a few withdrawal behaviors in ad hoc organizational samples located in different environmental settings (although these settings are usually not described in publications). All the models cannot be correct; some of them have implications that are contradictory to the implications of other models. This fact highlights the need to evaluate the implications of the models across different situations defined by macroenvironmental factors (e.g., unemployment) or organizational conditions (e.g., sanctions on absenteeism) over several or many time periods. Our traditional research methods are unable to do this type of evaluation.

This chapter evaluates three of the five models, including the spillover model, the compensatory model, and the progression of withdrawal model. The independent forms model was not included because most of the empirical literature in this area indicates that withdrawal behaviors are related in some manner (see Hanisch et al., 1998). The alternate forms model was not included because its focus is on constraints placed on one withdrawal behavior, leading to the probability that another form of withdrawal will increase. Relations among the behaviors without an external force impinging on at least one of them are not addressed, thereby making this model incomplete. In many respects, the alternate forms model resembles the compensatory model, except that in the alternate forms model, the employee is "encouraged" to engage in a different withdrawal behavior because another behavior is blocked by either an organizational intervention or an environmental event.

Incentive and Sanction Programs and Withdrawal Behaviors

One function of human resource managers is to monitor, measure, evaluate, and suggest possible solutions to problems in organizations. Jewell (1998) indicates that the total costs of absenteeism to American organizations exceed $25 billion a year including direct pay, benefits, and indirect costs of employees' absences (e.g., temporary replacement employees, administration to reorganize work around an absent employee). Dalton and Enz (1988) reported that 1 million employees each day will not attend their regularly scheduled work in the United States. Tyler (1997) estimated the cost of absenteeism at $572 per employee each year; others have estimated the total annual cost at $40 billion ("Expensive Absenteeism," 1986). Taylor (cited in Wagner & Bankshares, 1990) estimated total paid sick leave costs at approximately $7 billion, or $116 per employee per day. Because of the costs associated with employee withdrawal, human resource managers and organizational researchers are involved in generating solutions to decrease turnover and absenteeism as well as other negative behaviors (Dalton & Mesch, 1991). Actions taken by management in organizations involve the implementation of sanctions or incentives to foster desired behaviors. In some situations, management is interested in encouraging certain withdrawal behaviors—such as early retirement—based on cost considerations, productivity of employees, or both. In other situations, managers want to encourage attendance and do so through the use of incentives or sanctions.

Absenteeism Interventions

Several different types of incentive and sanction programs have been implemented to deal with problematic withdrawal behaviors, and absenteeism has received some attention in the scientific literature. Different approaches to combating absenteeism have different underlying theories of human behavior. For example, punishment will combat absenteeism only if people make conscious decisions about attending. Similarly, wellness programs will increase attendance if absenteeism is mostly the result of illness. Aamodt (1996) described the decision-making theory of absenteeism as follows: Employees make a decision each day as to whether they will or will not attend work. The process most likely includes weighing (consciously or unconsciously) the consequences of going to work against the consequences of not going. If this description is accurate, absenteeism can be reduced by increasing the advantages of going to work and increasing the disadvantages of not going. Based on this theory, attendance can be increased in several ways that have been studied in some detail.

Wagner and Bankshares (1990) completed a meta-analysis of the effectiveness of absenteeism control methods used by organizations. The increase or decrease in absenteeism in each study was converted into an effect size statistic (*d*) using Hunter, Schmidt, and Jackson's (1982) methods. Based on 4 studies, the absenteeism method found to have the highest effect size was well pay (d = .86), which is paying employees for unused sick leave. This was followed by flextime (d = .59, 10 studies), compressed work schedules (d = .44, 5 studies), discipline (d = .36, 12 studies), and recognition (d = .36, 6 studies). Types of discipline might include providing a warning system with levels for frequency of occurrence (e.g., three verbal warnings, three written warnings, 1-day suspension, termination), less popular work assignments, and firing employees. Recognition programs might include employers providing feedback or praise for good performance as well as an outward display of recognition, such as perfect attendance certificates, coffee mugs, plaques, pins, and watches.

The remaining four methods evaluated by Wagner and Bankshares (1990) included (a) wellness programs, (b) financial incentives (e.g., paying employees a financial bonus for certain levels of attendance), (c) games (e.g., playing poker at work—each employee gets a playing card every day he or she attends during the week, and the person with the winning hand at the end of the week receives a prize or cash award), and (d) record keeping, which had effect sizes of .18, .17, –.08, and –.34, respectively. All of these effect sizes were based on 6 or 7 studies.

Interventions on Early Retirement or Turnover

The decision to take early retirement may be affected by either an incentive or a sanction provided by the organization. If the organization is interested in decreasing its older work force, it might sweeten an early retirement incentive program by offering a retirement cash buyout or agreeing to increase the monthly pension payment by a certain percentage. If an organization wanted to maintain its current work force for some time, however, it might raise the age at which it contributes to the health benefits of retirees, making early retirement less desirable.

Decisions to quit may be affected by an incentive to stay, but they also are likely to be affected by the economic climate, specifically the unemployment rate. The effect of a relevant high unemployment rate for an employee probably would be a devaluation of his or her contributions and difficulty finding alternative employment. This situation results in competition from others as well as a reduced market of employers hiring in organizations. Relevant low unemployment would have the opposite effect; an employee's contributions would be of more value, and one's current employer may offer inducements to encourage the employee to remain with the organization.

The simulation results presented below provide for interventions on absenteeism, early retirement, and turnover; all the interventions, as evaluated here, sanction and are meant to discourage the three behaviors. Of interest is the effect on other behaviors included in the simulation if such interventions are imposed during the simulation runs. The simulation runs evaluate absenteeism individually across three models, whereas turnover and retirement are evaluated jointly across the three models. Comparisons with the base models (simulations with no interventions), as well as similarities and differences across the three models, also are presented.

WORKER: A Computational Modeling Program

Researchers can take many approaches to modeling, including what is modeled and the contents of those models. The type of modeling presented here is best described as a "dynamic feedback systems perspective" to modeling (Roberts, Andersen, Deal, Garet, & Shaffer, 1983). The systems approach emphasizes the connections among the various components that constitute a system and, in this case, a dynamic system. WORKER is a computational modeling software program (Seitz, Hanisch, & Hulin, 1997) that was developed to evaluate the expected relations among withdrawal behaviors. This program can simulate the withdrawal behaviors of individuals in organizational environments.

The user sets the initial conditions in WORKER to create a simulated organization of employees with specified age, years of organizational service, gender, and job classification distributions. The user sets the structure of the initial employee attitudes in the organization. In addition to the work force characteristics, the user can set constant or varying unemployment levels.

The user also controls organizational characteristics that simulate different levels of sanctions, or "carrots and sticks," wielded by an organization to influence the frequencies of specific organizational withdrawal behaviors. These sanctions can be altered at any point in the simulation by means of the intervention module in the WORKER program. This function permits the user to simulate an organizational intervention, perhaps in response to one or more behaviors becoming too frequent (e.g., absenteeism).

WORKER is based on fuzzy set theory and fuzzy calculus. These basic mathematical operations are combined with thresholds and feedback dynamics. Negative attitudes that fail to reach the necessary threshold may still be translated into manifest behaviors at user-defined probability rates. Similarly, attitudes that exceed the necessary threshold may not get translated into manifest behaviors, again based on user-defined functions. This stochastic component of the program allows the probability of translating an attitude into a behavior to vary with the strength of the attitude. See Hanisch et al. (1996) for more details on the operation of the WORKER program.

This chapter focuses on the effects of organizational interventions imposed 10 years into a 20-year simulation of different models of withdrawal. Specifically, interventions were imposed on absenteeism in one evaluation of the models and on turnover and early retirement in a second evaluation of the models. The results from the base runs, in which no interventions were imposed during the simulation, were used to compare the results from the intervention simulations. The potential effect of the interventions on attitudes, behavioral propensities, and frequencies of all modeled withdrawal behaviors is of interest. If different patterning is evident as the withdrawal process unfolds across time and across different models, this would imply that studying isolated withdrawal behaviors may result in misleading conclusions. By modeling the patterning among withdrawal behaviors, we can observe how the withdrawal process will be enacted; through these observations, we can gain a better understanding of how the different behaviors may be affected over time.

Method

The organization created for the simulations consisted of an employee population of 300 with equal proportions of male and female employees. Ages of the employees were sampled from a normal distribution that had a mean of 38 years and a standard deviation of 4.2; the range was from 18 to 65. Years of organizational service were sampled from a uniform distribution that ranged from 0 to 20 years. Unemployment was set at a constant 6% for the simulation runs. The computer-generated simulees with the characteristics described above will, for ease of reference, be referred to throughout this chapter as employees.

The four withdrawal behaviors simulated were turnover, early retirement, absenteeism, and tardiness. The user-controlled parameter that determines the initial relation between the attitude toward the behavior and the behavior is the *loading* of the attitude on the common attitude vector. These loadings control the intercorrelations and structure among the attitudes in the initial simulation period and are shown in Table 3.1. A second parameter associated with the behaviors is referred to as the *threshold.* The threshold, stochastically imposed for each behavior, determines the point at which the attitude is translated into a behavior with a given probability. For the simulations completed here, attitudes above the threshold were translated into behaviors with a probability of .80; the further the attitude is above the threshold, the more likely the behavior is to be enacted. Attitudes below the threshold were translated into behaviors with a probability of .20; the further the attitude is below the threshold, the less likely the behavior is to be enacted. A range of threshold values was set for the behaviors, consistent with their descriptive labels; they are presented in Table 3.1. A final parameter, relevant for only one of the models simulated in this study, is called the *degree of withdrawal* and refers to the "belongingness" of the behavior to the fuzzy set of organizational withdrawal. The greater the degree of belongingness, the more severe or extreme the behavior. This parameter influences stochastically the order of behavioral choice in the progression of withdrawal model only. The values assigned in this simulation run were .25 (tardiness), .50 (absenteeism), .70 (early retirement), and .80 (turnover).

TABLE 3.1

Initial parameter settings for simulation runs

BEHAVIOR	LOADING ON COMMON VECTOR	THRESHOLD VALUES
Tardiness	.50	.15
Absenteeism	.50	.50
Turnover	.75	.75
Early retirement	.85	.70

Base and Intervention Runs

The three models—spillover, compensatory behaviors, and progression of withdrawal—were each initially evaluated for the 20 years in the simulation (1990 to 2010) to obtain the baseline results for the simulated organization. In each time period, each behavior was either enacted or not for each employee, depending on the rules of the specific model used (i.e., spillover, compensatory behaviors, progression of withdrawal) and the attitude of the employee. Attitudes were updated for the next period on the basis of feedback from the behaviors enacted in the previous time period, stochastics that influence attitudes that do not lead to behaviors, and other conditions imposed by the specific model being evaluated. Hanisch et al. (1996) described these dynamic workings of WORKER's algorithms for specific simulations.

In all simulation runs included in this study, the effects of stochastics influence all results and introduce a degree of randomness into the results that adds verisimilitude; they also make the results less clean than they would be if the stochastics were not included. At the system or organizational level for this study, large sample sizes somewhat ameliorate these effects. At the individual level, a behavior enacted or not enacted because of the stochastically imposed threshold may cause two employees with identical attitudes to diverge dramatically toward their final states. Hanisch et al. (1996) showed both individual and organizational effects.

The output from each iteration of the simulation consists of those behaviors enacted during the time period and the attitudes and behavioral propensities at the end of the time period. The attitudinal results, behavioral propensity results, and proportion of employees who enacted the different behaviors during the simulation of the four withdrawal behaviors for each model are shown in separate graphs for each simulation run.

Absenteeism Intervention

For each simulation using one of the three withdrawal models, an intervention on absenteeism of .90 (scale from 0 to 1.00) was imposed in the year 2000. This was an increase from its baseline value of .40 (considered a neutral value). The attitudinal results, behavioral propensity results, and proportion of employees who enacted the different behaviors are presented and compared with the outcomes of the base runs (i.e., the simulations without the intervention) for each model.

Turnover/Early Retirement Intervention

Interventions equivalent to making turnover and retirement undesirable for employees (.90 sanction) were imposed in year 2000 of the simulation run. The information of interest was the effect of the intervention on the turnover/early retirement attitudes, behavioral propensities, and behaviors as well as on the other withdrawal behaviors included in the simulation for each of the three models of withdrawal.

Results

Spillover Model Results

Figures 3.1, 3.2, and 3.3 present the attitudes, behavioral propensities, and proportion of employees enacting behaviors that the spillover model generated across the 20-year time-period simulations, which were completed under the baseline, absenteeism intervention, and turnover/early retirement intervention conditions, respectively.

Absenteeism Intervention

The effects of the intervention on absenteeism can be seen by comparing Figures 3.1 and 3.2. The effect of the intervention relative to the baseline condition results (Figure 3.1) is to double the attitude toward absenteeism while decreasing the absenteeism behavioral propensity by approximately half its baseline value (compare Figures 3.1A to 3.2A and 3.1B to 3.2B). No changes occurred in the other attitudes or in the behavioral propensities for turnover or retirement as a result of the absenteeism intervention. The behavioral propensity for tardiness, a behavior similar to absenteeism (both are work withdrawal behaviors and have the same common vector loading), increases slightly under the absenteeism intervention condition relative to the baseline condition. With regard to the proportion of employees who enacted the four behaviors, there is a decrease in absenteeism and a slight increase in tardiness, whereas turnover and early retirement follow the movement of absenteeism (compare Figures 3.1C and 3.2C) from the baseline to intervention conditions.

Turnover/Early Retirement Intervention

The early retirement/turnover intervention results shown in Figure 3.3 provide another evaluation of an intervention under the spillover model. As can be seen by

FIGURE 3.1

Results for the spillover model under the baseline condition

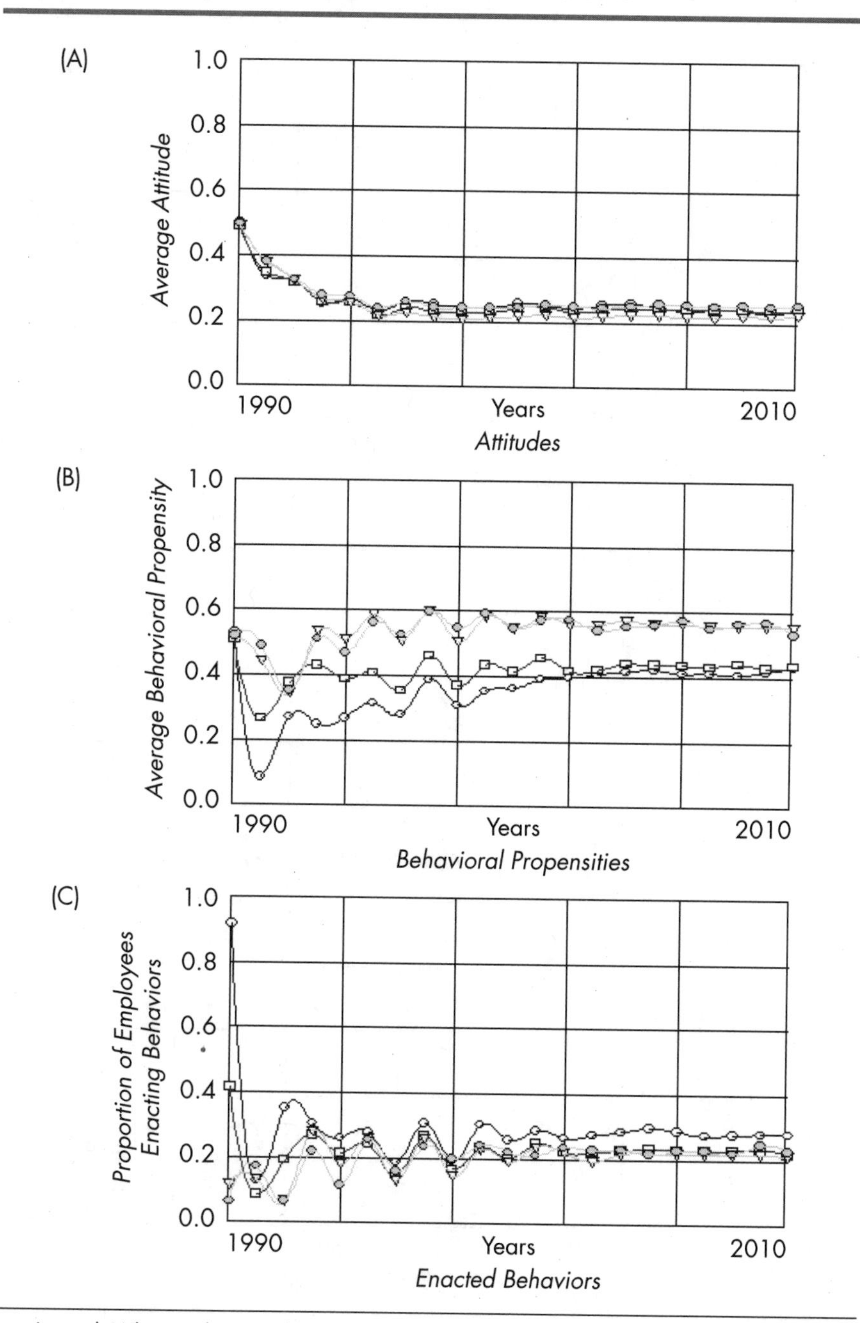

Legend: White circles = tardy; grey circles = turnover; rectangles = absent; triangles = unexpected retire.

FIGURE 3.2

Results for the spillover model under the absenteeism intervention condition

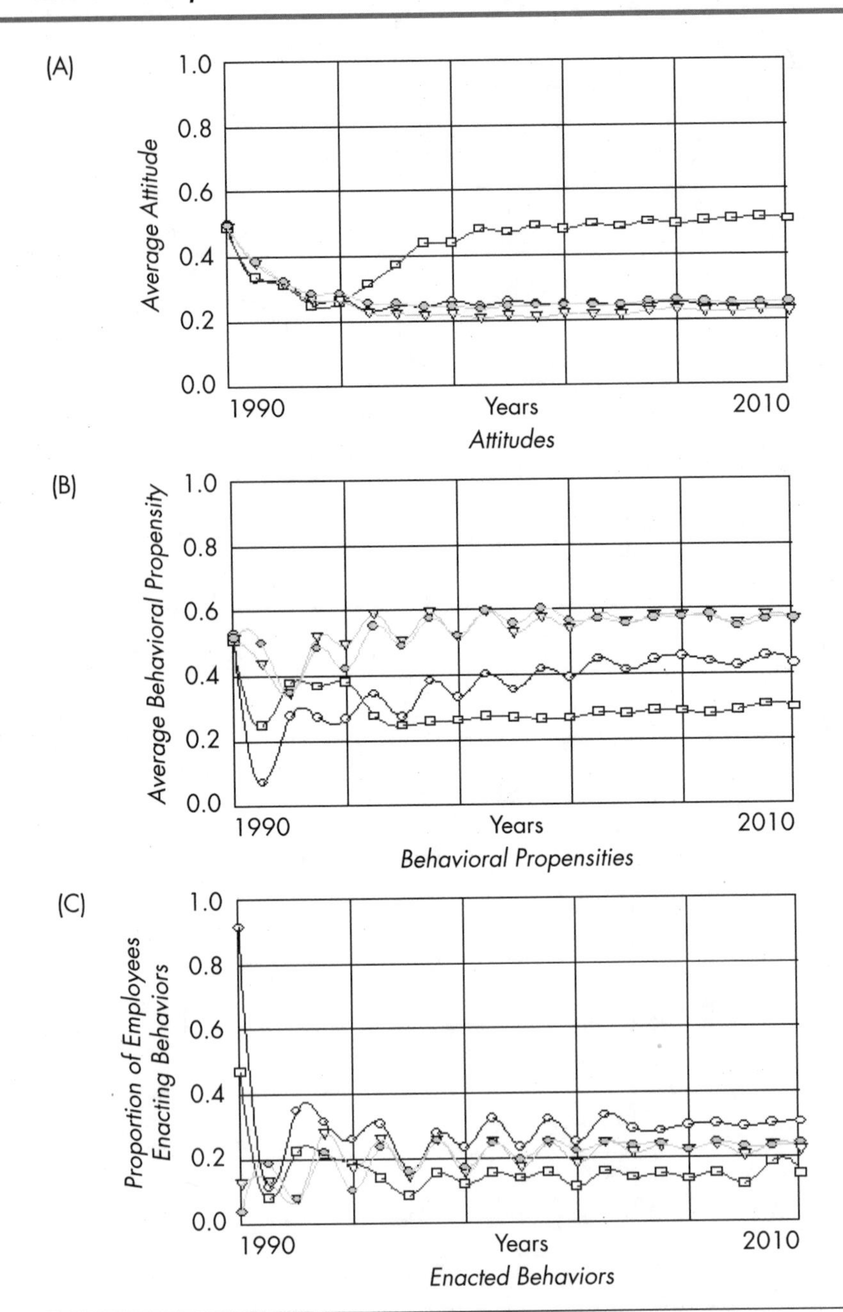

Legend: White circles = tardy; grey circles = turnover; rectangles = absent; triangles = unexpected retire.

FIGURE 3.3

Results for the spillover model under the turnover/early retirement intervention condition

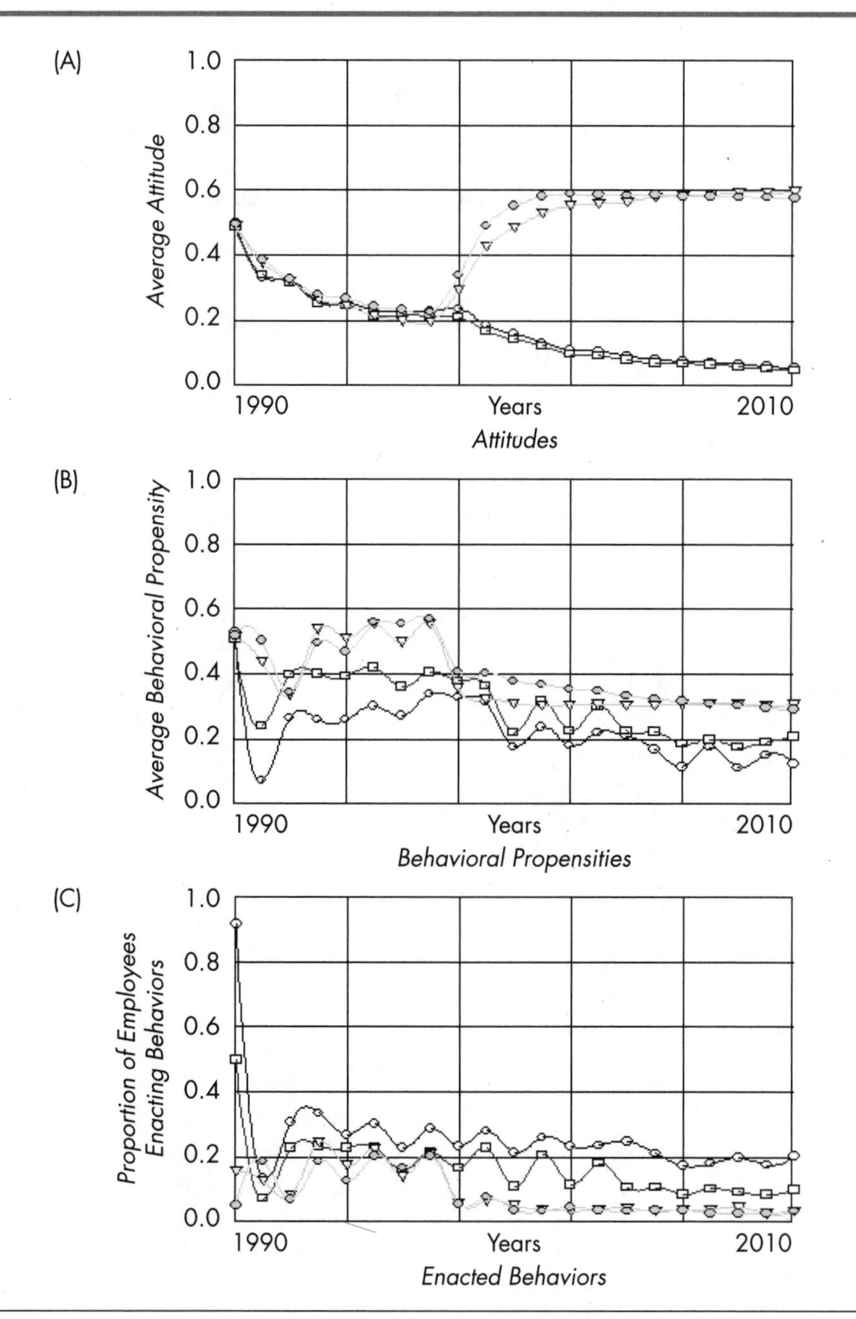

Legend: White circles = tardy; grey circles = turnover; rectangles = absent; triangles = unexpected retire.

comparing Figures 3.1A and 3.3A, there is a large increase in the attitude toward turnover and early retirement, whereas the attitudes toward absenteeism and tardiness decrease. All the behavioral propensities decrease from the baseline results, with the largest decline occurring in tardiness (see Figure 3.3B). With regard to the proportion of employees enacting behaviors, a large decrease in turnover and early retirement exists, as does a decrease in both absenteeism and tardiness from the baseline to intervention conditions (compare Figures 3.1C to 3.3C).

Compensatory Withdrawal Model Results

The parallel results generated by the simulations of the compensatory model are shown in Figures 3.4, 3.5, and 3.6. Figure 3.4 presents the baseline results for the simulation, and Figures 3.5 and 3.6 present the findings for the absenteeism and turnover/early retirement interventions, respectively.

Absenteeism Intervention

In the case of absenteeism, the attitude toward the behavior increases (compare Figures 3.4A and 3.5A), whereas the behavioral propensity decreases from baseline levels (compare Figures 3.4B and 3.5B). Only small changes occur in the attitudes for the other behaviors after the intervention is imposed. The behavioral propensities, however, change significantly as a result of the intervention, with a flattening of the values within the behaviors relative to their baseline values (see Figure 3.5B). Early retirement and turnover are at similar levels for the behavioral propensities and are slightly higher during the intervention simulation. The value for tardiness flattens out, and there is a steady increase in that behavioral propensity over time.

The proportion of employees who enacted the different behaviors in the intervention run are shown in Figure 3.5C. The values in that figure indicate less fluctuation over time in the enactment of the behaviors; the peaks and valleys are less prominent then they are under the baseline condition (see Figure 3.4C). The proportion of employees engaging in absenteeism decreases after the intervention and, in general, there is a fairly even suppression of the other behaviors over time.

Turnover/Early Retirement Intervention

A somewhat different picture of the effects of the intervention on turnover and early retirement for the compensatory model is shown in Figure 3.6. As expected relative to baseline values (Figure 3.4), the attitudes toward the two behaviors increase (see Figure 3.6A), their behavioral propensities decrease (see Figure 3.6B), and the proportion of employees enacting the behaviors decrease (see Figure 3.6C). The attitudes toward tardiness and absenteeism decrease, and the behavioral propensities decrease relative to baseline values. Note that after the intervention, turnover has the highest attitude values and also the highest behavioral propensity values compared with the other behaviors. Turnover and retirement switch their rank order in the

FIGURE 3.4

Results for the compensatory behaviors withdrawal model under the baseline condition

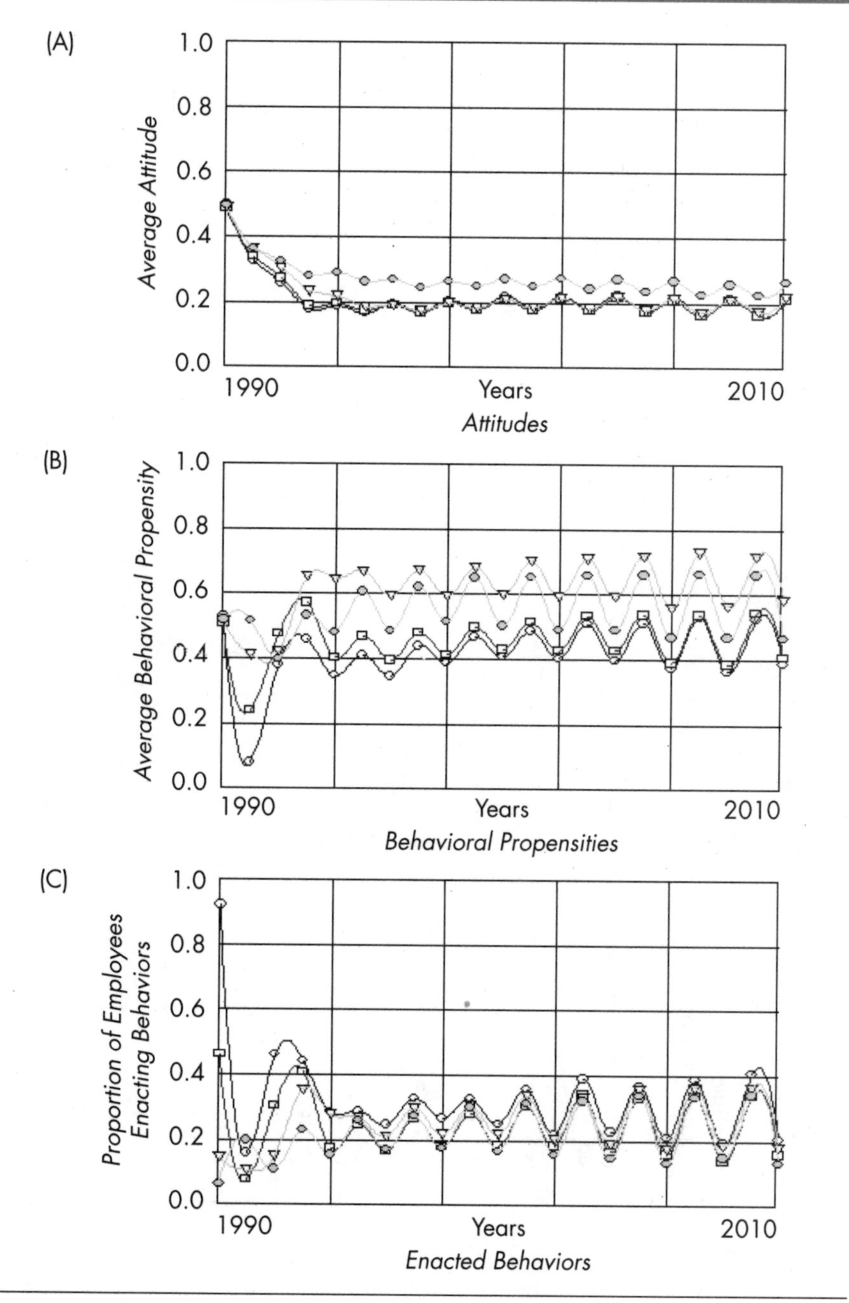

Legend: White circles = tardy; grey circles = turnover; rectangles = absent; triangles = unexpected retire.

FIGURE 3.5

Results for the compensatory behaviors withdrawal model under the absenteeism intervention condition

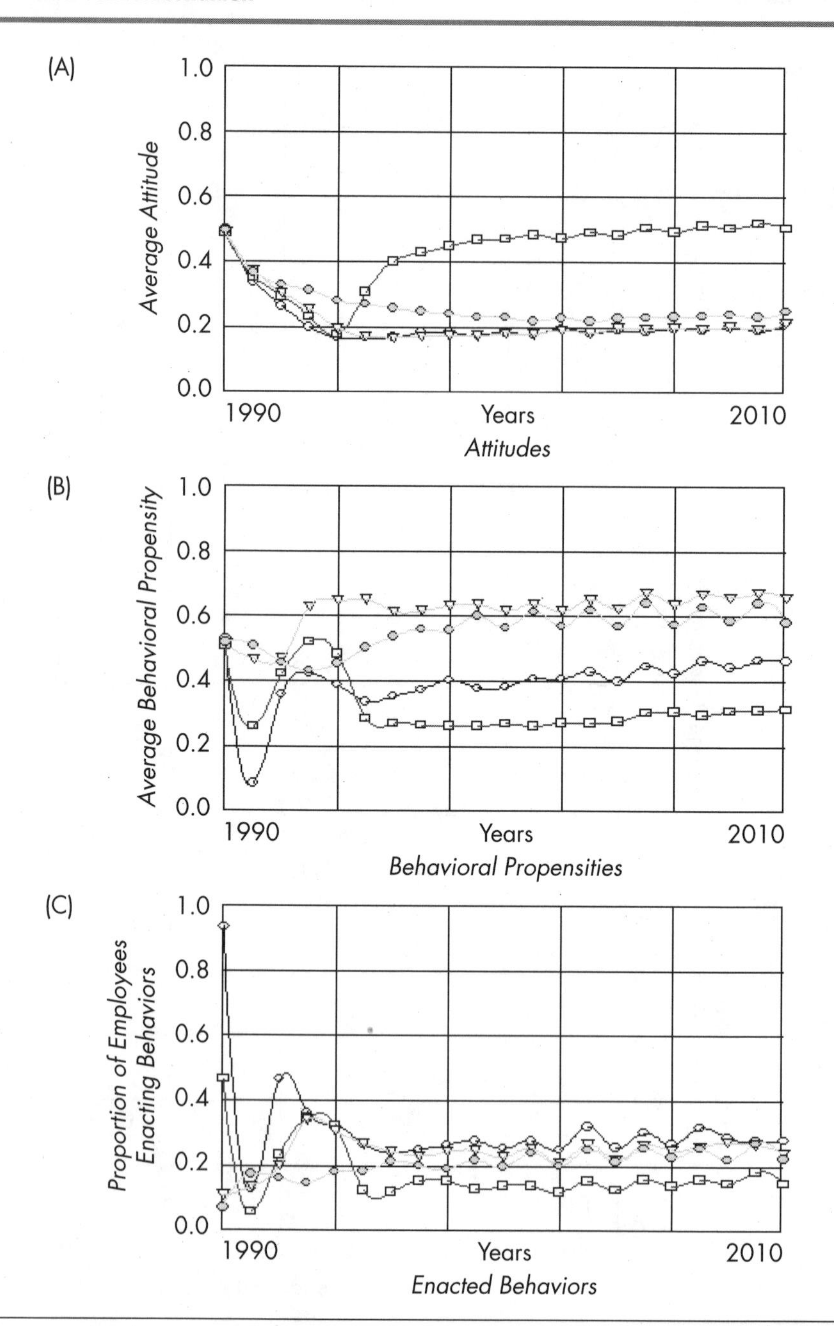

Legend: White circles = tardy; grey circles = turnover; rectangles = absent; triangles = unexpected retire.

FIGURE 3.6

Results for the compensatory behaviors withdrawal model under the turnover/early retirement intervention condition

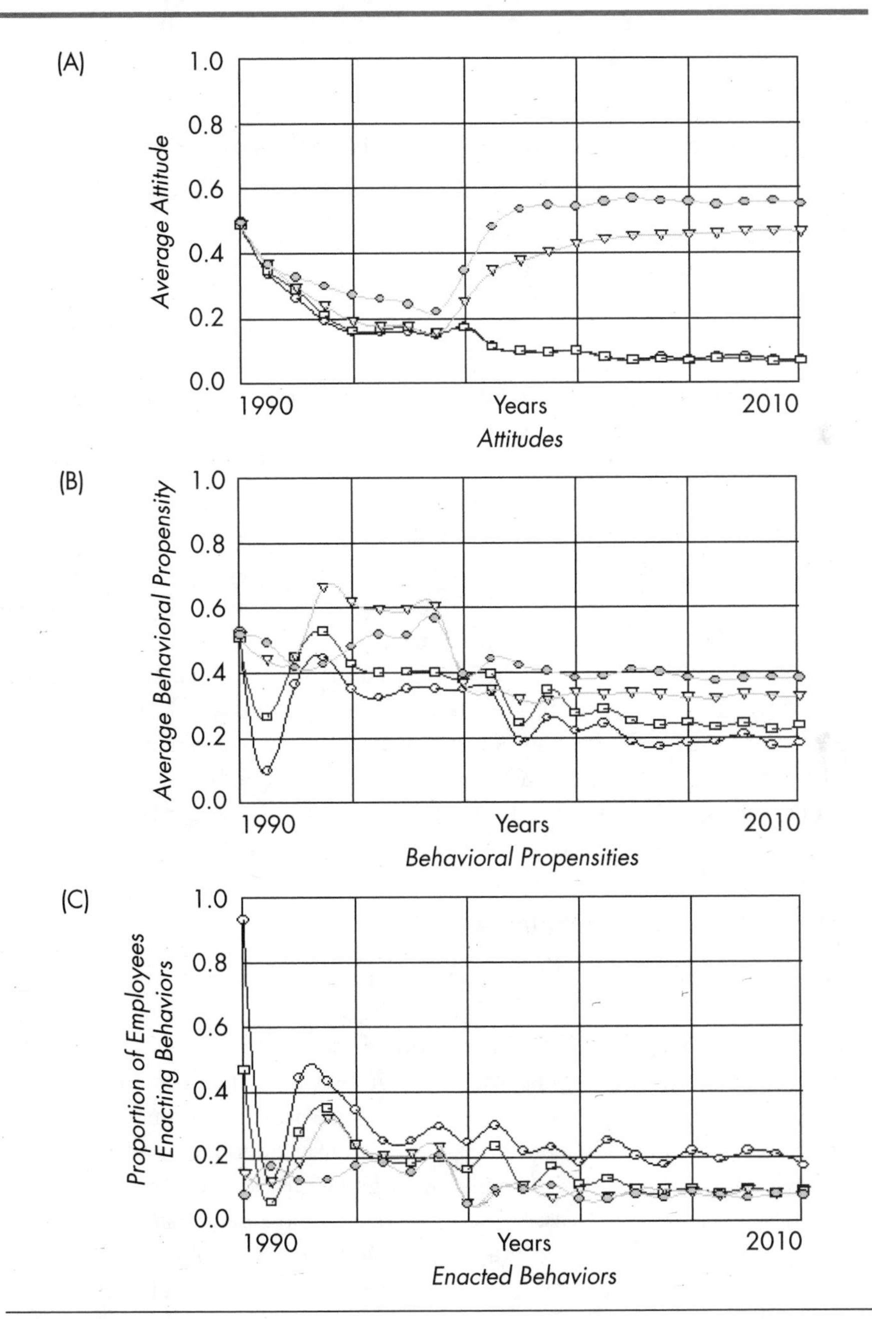

Legend: White circles = tardy; grey circles = turnover; rectangles = absent; triangles = unexpected retire.

behavioral propensity figure after the intervention is imposed, a change that is consistent with the difference in the attitudes between the two behaviors. Finally, the proportion of employees who enacted absenteeism declines after the intervention, whereas the proportion enacting tardiness also decreases, in general, to the lowest values in the baseline simulation.

Progression of Withdrawal Model Results

The baseline simulation results for the progression of withdrawal model are shown in Figure 3.7; Figures 3.8 and 3.9 show the results for the absenteeism and turnover/early retirement interventions, respectively.

Absenteeism Intervention

A comparison of Figures 3.7 and 3.8 reveals an increase in the attitude toward absenteeism, a decrease in its behavioral propensity, and a decrease in the proportion of employees who enacted absenteeism; the intervention on absenteeism had the anticipated effect on that behavior. Evaluating the other behaviors in the simulation indicates that there was little fluctuation in the employees' attitudes but increases in their behavioral propensities. Specifically, all the behavioral propensities increase from between approximately .30 and .50 (see Figure 3.7B) to between .65 and .90 (see Figure 3.8B). The ordering of the behavioral propensities stays the same as in the baseline simulation, although there is more distance, or spread, between the behaviors. The proportion of employees who enacted the behaviors stayed about the same for tardiness in the intervention run, although there is less fluctuation across time relative to the baseline simulation (see Figures 3.7C and 3.8C). Early retirement decreases after the intervention, whereas turnover has fewer low values and does not fluctuate as much as during the baseline simulation.

Turnover/Early Retirement Intervention

Evaluating the results of the intervention on turnover and early retirement indicates that the attitudes toward both behaviors increase from the baseline simulation, whereas the absenteeism and tardiness attitudes decrease to very low values (see Figure 3.9A). The behavioral propensities for turnover and retirement are essentially equivalent after the intervention is imposed; absenteeism and tardiness follow the same trajectory and have higher values after the intervention than under the baseline condition. The proportion of employees enacting turnover and retirement in the intervention simulation decreases to very low values, and absenteeism and tardiness increase relative to the baseline condition. The proportion of employees enacting the latter two behaviors becomes level over time after the intervention is imposed.

FIGURE 3.7

Results for the progression of withdrawal model under the baseline condition

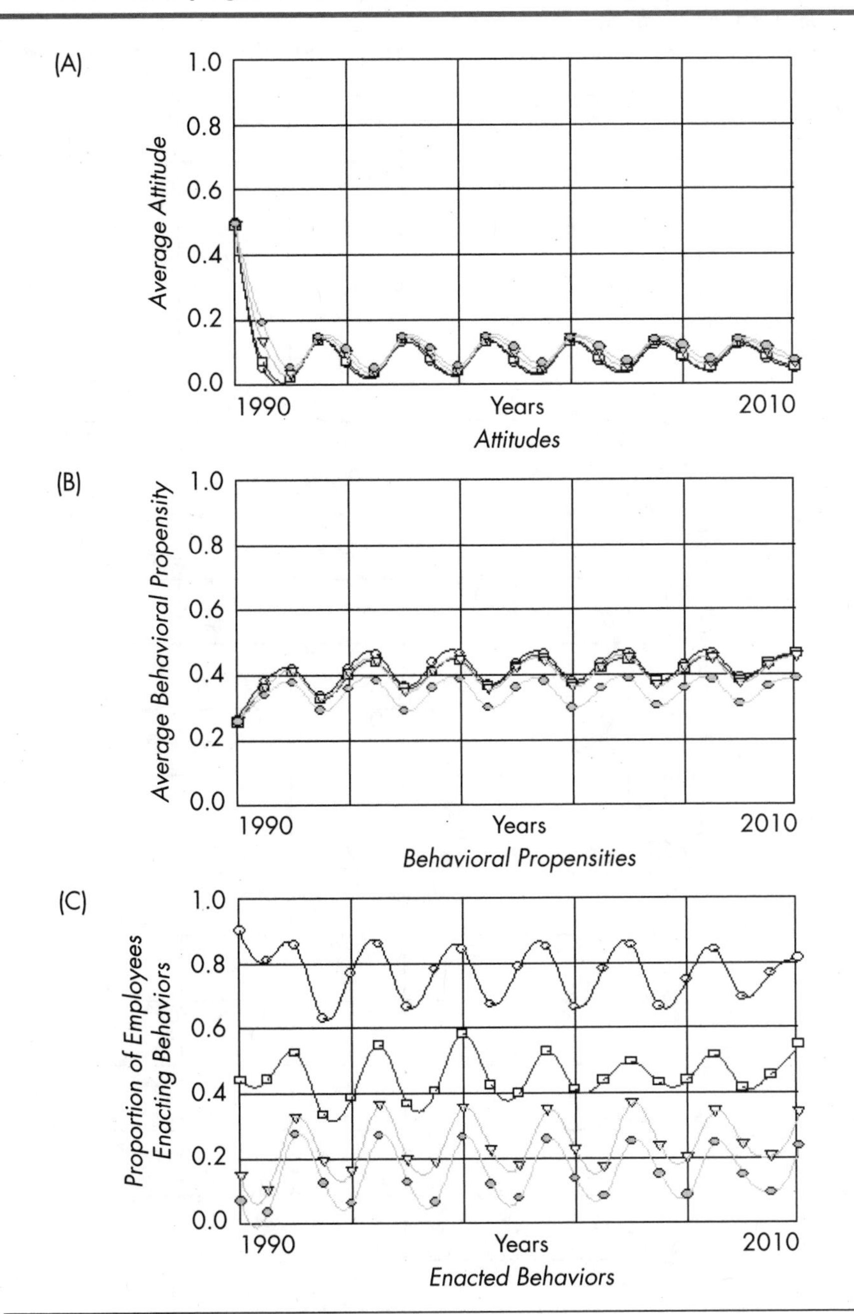

Legend: White circles = tardy; grey circles = turnover; rectangles = absent; triangles = unexpected retire.

FIGURE 3.8

Results for the progression of withdrawal model underthe absenteeism intervention condition

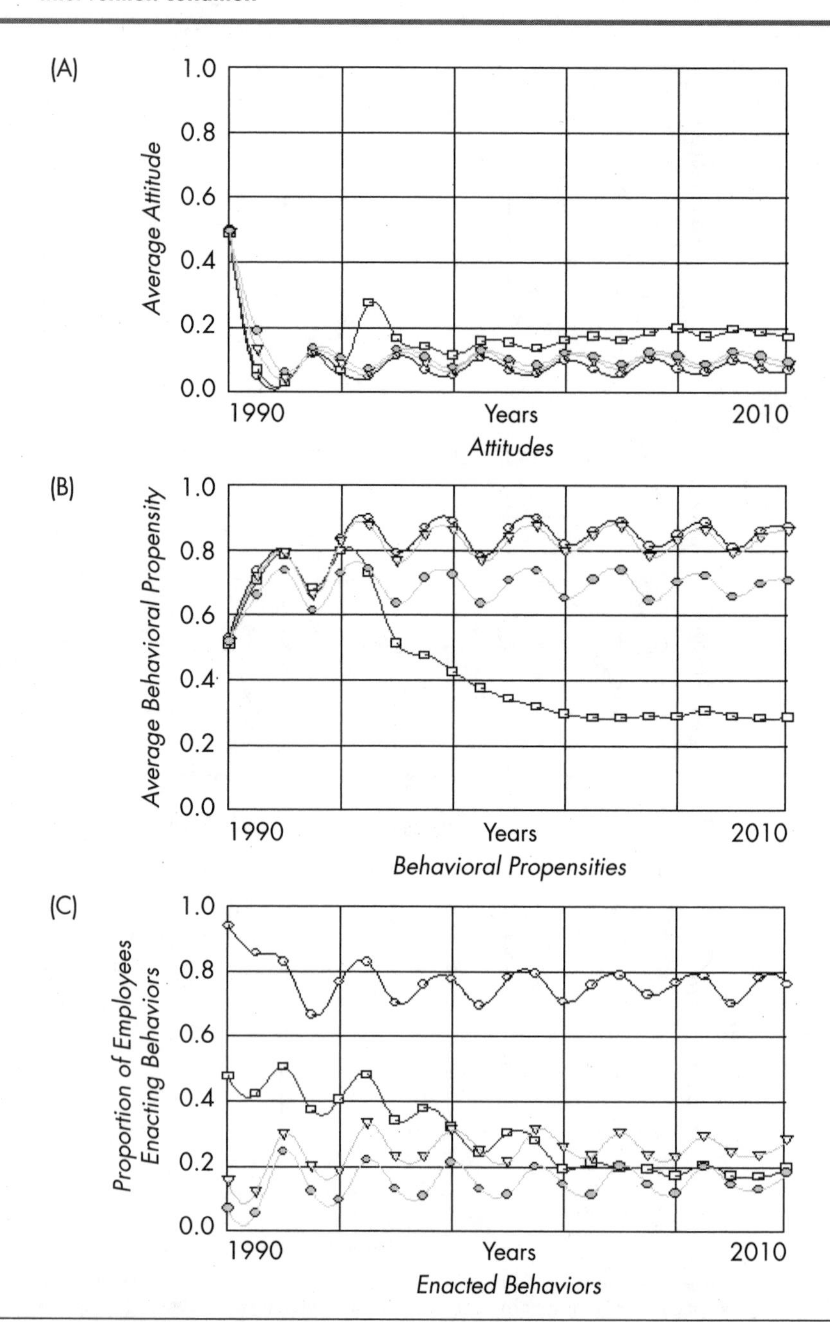

Legend: White circles = tardy; grey circles = turnover; rectangles = absent; triangles = unexpected retire.

FIGURE 3.9

Results for the progression of withdrawal model under the turnover/early retirement intervention condition

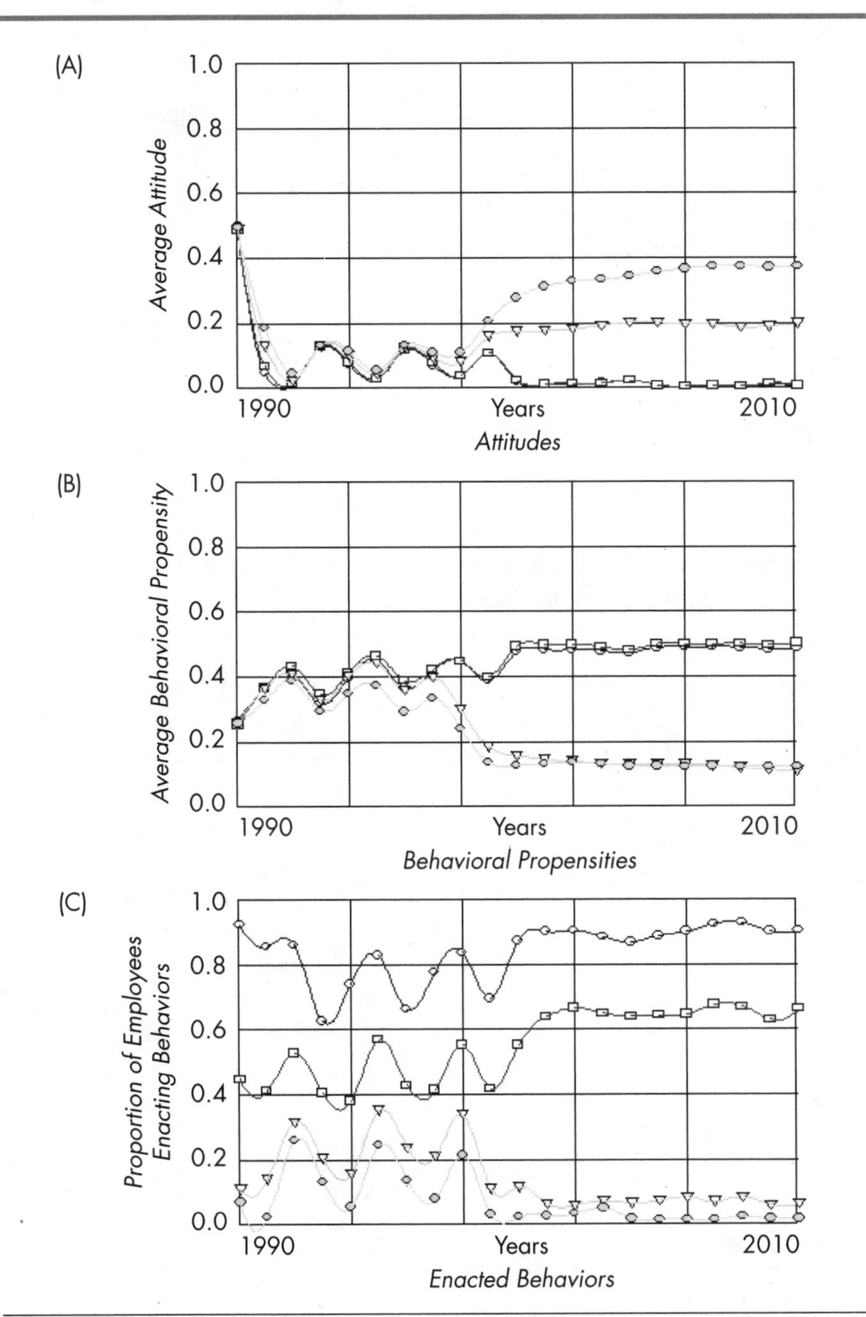

Legend: White circles = tardy; grey circles = turnover; rectangles = absent; triangles = unexpected retire.

Comparison of Withdrawal Model Results for the Absenteeism Intervention

Examining the results of the absenteeism intervention across models provides another way to evaluate this study of multiple behaviors. The graphs for the attitude values for the spillover (Figure 3.2A) and compensatory (Figure 3.5A) models are very similar; absenteeism increases and steadies around .50, and the other attitudes across the two models have similar patterns. The attitude results for the progression of withdrawal model (Figure 3.8A) are more suppressed for all behaviors, and the attitude toward absenteeism hovers around .20. Similar patterns are found for the behavioral propensities and proportion of employees enacting the behaviors: The spillover and compensatory model results are very similar, whereas the results for the progression of withdrawal model are unique. The behavioral propensity for absenteeism decreases to approximately the same level as in the spillover and compensatory models but does so from a much higher starting point in the progression of withdrawal model. In addition, tardiness, absenteeism, and early retirement have behavioral propensity values between .65 and .90 in the progression of withdrawal model, compared with values between .40 and .60 in the spillover and compensatory models.

Comparison of Withdrawal Model Results for the Turnover/Early Retirement Intervention

The results across the three models for the turnover/early retirement intervention simulation follow a somewhat similar pattern as was found with the absenteeism intervention simulation. The results for the spillover (Figure 3.3) and compensatory (Figure 3.6) models are similar to each other, whereas the progression of withdrawal model (Figure 3.9) results have a different structure. For example, attitudes toward turnover and early retirement are again not as high in the progression of withdrawal model as they are in either the spillover or compensatory models. More separation exists between the behavioral propensities in the progression of withdrawal model than in either of the other two models. Turnover and early retirement are suppressed to behavioral propensity values of about .10 after the intervention, but they are between .30 and .40 in both the spillover and compensatory models. The proportion of employees enacting behaviors also varies quite dramatically with the progression of withdrawal model, showing a great deal of fluctuation in values: The leveling-off proportions for tardiness and absenteeism after the intervention are approximately .90 and .65, respectively, whereas the proportions for these behaviors in the spillover and compensatory models are approximately .20 and .10, respectively.

Discussion

The results presented here for the two simulated interventions are not intuitive and imply that manifestations of withdrawal, when studied only using cross-sectional designs, may lead to misleading conclusions. The different manifestations of withdrawal should be studied over time and as a covarying set of behaviors, rather than individually.

Important emergent properties of these three models across the two interventions are seen in the withdrawal behavior results. As a check on the programming of the intervention results, the attitudes toward the behaviors increased, the behavioral propensities decreased, and the proportion of employees enacting the behaviors decreased for the targeted behaviors. This was true across all evaluated models and over time. The interesting findings of this simulation study are the effects of the interventions on the other available withdrawal behaviors. For ease of presentation and discussion in this chapter, employees had four withdrawal behaviors from which to choose, including tardiness, absenteeism, early retirement, and turnover; the assumption within the WORKER program is that employees can enact one or more of these behaviors within a time period in accordance with the specifications of the particular model of withdrawal.

The spillover, compensatory, and progression of withdrawal models provided an interesting and informative comparison across the two interventions evaluated in this study. Perhaps most surprising and counterintuitive is the similarity of the final intervention results across the spillover and compensatory models. The baseline simulation results are different, particularly when examining the behavioral propensity and proportion of employees who enacted the behaviors; there is more fluctuation in the graphs for the compensatory model and spillover model than would be expected given the verbal descriptions of the models. The general pattern to the baseline results for the two models is similar with regard to ranking the behaviors in terms of behavioral propensities or the proportion of employees who enacted behaviors. The progression of withdrawal model also has fluctuations that resemble the compensatory model in behavioral propensities and proportion of employees who enacted behaviors at baseline; the baseline results more generally are quite different from either the compensatory or spillover model results.

In the absenteeism intervention simulation evaluated under the spillover and compensatory models, the change in the proportion of employees enacting behaviors was slightly reduced for all the withdrawal behaviors. In the progression of withdrawal model results, when the intervention was imposed on absenteeism, the proportion of employees enacting behaviors decreased for all behaviors except tardiness, the behavior most similar to absenteeism in the simulation. Relative to the baseline simulation results, less fluctuation occurred in the proportion of employees enacting tardiness, and the values over time either increased or decreased slightly. Given these intervention results, a human resource manager deciding whether to impose a sanction on absenteeism would not need to be concerned, in general, with its effect on the frequency of the other withdrawal behaviors.

Examination of the turnover/early retirement intervention results in the spillover and compensatory models reveals a pattern similar to that of the absenteeism intervention. In the spillover model, the proportion of employees enacting all the behaviors decreases. The compensatory model results are more stable under the intervention than the baseline condition, with a general decrease in the proportion of employees enacting behaviors.

A different finding is evident in the progression of withdrawal model results. The proportion of employees enacting turnover and early retirement in the intervention condition decreases, but both absenteeism and tardiness increase. When the two most extreme behaviors were unavailable to employees, they progressed to the other behaviors, resulting in a larger increase in their enactment of absenteeism than tardiness. This is likely the result of absenteeism's greater similarity, in terms of degree of withdrawal, to turnover and early retirement than tardiness.

Except for the progression of withdrawal model results, the intervention decreased the targeted behavior as well as the other withdrawal behaviors. In the results for the progression of withdrawal model, a human resource manager would need to determine the value of the decrease in the behaviors of turnover and early retirement relative to the increase in absenteeism and tardiness to decide whether the benefits of the intervention outweighed the costs.

Future Research and Conclusions

This study evaluated the relations among four withdrawal behaviors under several conditions, with the focus on sanctions imposed on withdrawal behaviors. The results of this study are interesting and provide a useful starting point for testing and eventually understanding the relations and patterning among employee withdrawal behaviors. Any one of the theoretical models may be correct under different circumstances, or we may find that the "best" model in terms of prediction and understanding of employee behaviors is a hybrid of two or more of the models hypothesized many years ago. A future study should evaluate additional behaviors as well as the effects of incentives, or "carrots," on employees' behavioral patterns.

An important component of simulation or modeling work is to validate some subset of the results by conducting an empirical study. The results presented here provide a useful starting point for designing a study to collect data on several withdrawal behaviors to evaluate a subset of these findings. The time has come to expand the scientific inquiry regarding employee withdrawal behaviors beyond studying turnover *or* absenteeism in a single study. More complicated research designs that include multiple time periods and multiple behaviors would significantly further our understanding of this important area for researchers, employers, and employees. The results of the simulations suggest that the patterning among employees' withdrawal behaviors is important for understanding the process of employee withdrawal; verification of those results with empirical tests is needed.

Computational modeling can address substantive issues in many content areas and serve as an initial testing and research design avenue. New information is frequently available from computational modeling results; depending on the complexity of the models, that information may not have been derivable before the simulations were done. System properties can emerge that were neither evident nor expected on the basis of individual behavior patterns. Such discoveries in the area of organizational withdrawal are fully expected if computational modeling is systematically used. Computational modeling, as one of several available research tools, should be a useful guide to researchers as they strategically plan how to more accurately and completely answer questions about the employee withdrawal process. In addition, the research results should provide helpful advice and guidance for employers who must manage employees' withdrawal behaviors.

References

Aamodt, M. G. (1996). *Applied industrial/organizational psychology.* Pacific Grove, CA: Brooks/Cole.

Baruch, D. W. (1944). Why they terminate. *Journal of Consulting Psychology, 8,* 35–46.

Beehr, T. A., & Gupta, N. (1978). A note on the structure of employee withdrawal. *Organizational Behavior and Human Performance, 21,* 73–79.

Dalton, D. R., & Enz, C. A. (1988). New directions in the management of employee absenteeism: Attention to policy and culture. In R. S. Schuler & S. A. Youngblood (Eds.), *Readings in personnel and human resource management* (pp. 357–366). St. Paul: West.

Dalton, D. R., & Mesch, D. J. (1991). On the extent and reduction of avoidable absenteeism: An assessment of absence policy provisions. *Journal of Applied Psychology, 76,* 810–817.

Eagley, R. V. (1965). Market power as an intervening mechanism in Phillips Curve analysis. *Economics, 32,* 48–64.

Expensive absenteeism. (1986, July 7). *Wall Street Journal,* p. 1.

Fisher, C. D., & Locke, E. A. (1992). The new look in job satisfaction research and theory. In C. J. Cranny, P. C. Smith, & E. F. Stone (Eds.), *Job satisfaction* (pp. 165–194). New York: Lexington.

Hanisch, K. A. (1995a). Behavioral families and multiple causes: Matching the complexity of responses to the complexity of antecedents. *Current Directions in Psychological Science, 4,* 156–162.

Hanisch, K. A. (1995b). Organizational withdrawal. In N. N. Nicholson (Ed.), *The Blackwell encyclopedic dictionary of organizational behavior* (p. 604). Cambridge, MA: Blackwell.

Hanisch, K. A., & Hulin, C. L. (1990). Job attitudes and organizational withdrawal: An examination of retirement and other voluntary withdrawal behaviors. *Journal of Vocational Behavior, 37,* 60–78.

Hanisch, K. A., & Hulin, C. L. (1991). General attitudes and organizational withdrawal: An evaluation of a causal model. *Journal of Vocational Behavior, 39,* 110–128.

Hanisch, K. A., Hulin, C. L., & Roznowski, M. (1998). The importance of individuals' repertoires of behaviors: The scientific appropriateness of studying multiple behaviors and general attitudes. *Journal of Organizational Behavior, 19,* 463–480.

Hanisch, K. A., Hulin, C. L., & Seitz, S. T. (1996). Mathematical/computational modeling of organizational withdrawal processes: Benefits, methods, and results. In G. Ferris (Ed.), *Research in personnel and human resources management* (Vol. 14, pp. 91–142). Greenwich, CT: JAI Press.

Herzberg, F., Mausner, B., Peterson, B., & Capwell, D. (1957). *Job attitudes: Review of research and opinion.* Pittsburgh: Psychological Services of Pittsburgh.

Hill, J. M., & Trist, E. L. (1955). Changes in accidents and other absences with length of service: A further study of their incidence and relation to each other in an iron and steel works. *Human Relations, 8,* 121–152.

Hunter, J. E., Schmidt, F. L., & Jackson, G. B. (1982). *Meta-analysis: Cumulating research across methods.* Beverly Hills, CA: Sage.

Jewell, L. N. (1998). *Contemporary industrial/organizational psychology.* Pacific Grove, CA: Brooks/Cole.

March, J. G., & Simon, H. A. (1958). *Organizations.* New York: Wiley.

Melbin, M. (1961). Organizational practice and individual behavior: Absenteeism among psychiatric aides. *American Sociological Review, 26,* 14–23.

Mobley, W. H. (1977). Intermediate linkages in the relationship between job satisfaction and employee turnover. *Journal of Applied Psychology, 62,* 237–240.

Rice, A. K., & Trist, E. L. (1952). Institutional and subinstitutional determinants of change in labor turnover. *Human Relations, 5,* 347–372.

Roberts, N., Andersen, D., Deal, R., Garet, M., & Shaffer, W. (1983). *Introduction to computer simulation: The system dynamics approach.* Reading, MA: Addison-Wesley.

Rosse, J. G. (1988). Relations among lateness, absence, and turnover: Is there a progression of withdrawal? *Human Relations, 41,* 517–531.

Rosse, J. G., & Miller, H. E. (1984). Relationship between absenteeism and other employee behaviors. In P. S. Goodman & R. S. Atkin (Eds.), *Absenteeism: New approaches to understanding, measuring, and managing employee absence* (pp. 194–228). San Francisco: Jossey-Bass.

Seitz, S. T., Hanisch, K. A., & Hulin, C. L. (1997). *WORKER: A computer program to simulate employee organizational withdrawal behaviors.* University of Illinois at Urbana–Champaign and Iowa State University.

Tyler, K. (1997). Dependability can be a rewarding experience. *HR Magazine, 41*(9), 57–60.

Wagner, T. J., & Bankshares, D. (1990). A meta-analytic review of absenteeism control methods. *Applied HRM Research, 1,* 19–22.

COMMENT:

Comparing Models of Withdrawal Using a Computational Model

Mark Fichman

Computational modeling is a powerful new method for theoretical analysis. Such models are now essential in many areas in the physical, biological, and behavioral sciences. For example, computational models are the best instantiations of theories in climate modeling. Computational models describe a system's behavior by instantiating a set of theoretical premises; the computational implementation allows one to draw inferences from theoretical premises. Theoretical implications are derived by executing the computational model. Put simply, in computational models, "assumptions are stated as computer programs that simulate the structures of the real world, and inferences are drawn by operating a computing machine" (Dutton & Starbuck, 1971, p. 3). Hanisch and her colleagues (Hanisch, Hulin, & Seitz, 1996) have developed a computational model (WORKER) of organizational withdrawal, which Hanisch describes in Chapter 3. I want to use Hanisch's work to identify this approach's strengths and to recommend steps for improving such modeling of organizational behavior.

Why Use Computational Models?

Computational models are relatively new tools for theoretical analysis. Any new model, computational or otherwise, should suggest observations, inferences, and plausible explanations that other theories do not offer. Computational models offer several distinctive features for theory building.

First, computational models make explicit the assumptions about mechanisms or processes (Simon, 1977) that generate behavior. WORKER requires the theorist to articulate a full specification of the theory. When researchers undertake theoretical tests and examine conflicting claims, ambiguous or incomplete statements about assumptions and mechanisms often cause difficulty. Depending on how one understands a set of theoretical assumptions, a new result can suggest confirmation of a theory to one person, disconfirmation of a theory to a second, and a need for modification to a third. Tetlock and Manstead (1985) found this pattern in critical competitive tests between cognitive and self-presentational explanations of cognitive dissonance effects: Ambiguous theoretical statements resulted in contentious debates. Much work was done in order to define the conditions under which a particular theory holds. One can argue that such debate leads to new knowledge. However, if the theoretical statements offered had been more explicit, the path toward a more refined statement of such attitude change phenomena as insufficient justification might have been smoother and traveled more quickly. Computational models demand more clarity in theoretical statements. This requirement may help us understand and resolve theoretical disputes more quickly and effectively.

Second, computational models facilitate exploration of a theory's implications. The theorist can vary model parameters and assumptions to evaluate their role in the generation of particular predicted effects. One can do *Gedanken* experiments in a disciplined way, exploring the theoretical space in a way that might be less tractable using other analysis tools. For example, Schultz and Lepper (1996) implemented a connectionist network soft constraint satisfaction model of cognitive dissonance reduction in the free choice and insufficient justification experimental paradigms, which are two classic dissonance theory problems. They identified several new predictions. In particular, they computationally derived the implications of free choice between undesirable alternatives, a condition never considered by dissonance theorists. These implications were tested empirically and confirmed. Not only is their computational model consistent with past results, it also suggests new results, which is precisely what we want from a theoretical statement. What is particularly striking is that their results were found for cognitive dissonance, an area in which literally hundreds of studies have been done and the level of researcher interest and motivation has been extremely high for several decades.

It is the capacity to execute and evaluate such thought experiments that makes computational modeling attractive. An important corollary of this attribute is the ability to study complex processes that do not readily lend themselves to analysis and closed-form solutions. A complex behavioral process often requires the specification of many variables and processes in such complex interrelationships that it is difficult to do the theoretical analysis in any other way than by simulation. Cognitive theorists have recognized this difficulty, and cognitive models such as SOAR (Laird, Newell, & Rosenbloom, 1987) and ACT–R (Anderson, 1993) attest to the value of computational models for analysis of complex behavior.[1]

[1]It is not a coincidence that the author's affiliation and the affiliation of the models cited are the same. Computational modeling is a passion at Carnegie-Mellon University with many partisans.

WORKER, a computational model of withdrawal, is designed to achieve the goal of a more completely articulated, explicitly stated process model of attitudes and behaviors, focusing particularly on the attitudes and behaviors linked to withdrawal. Hanisch explores its implications for different models of withdrawal in a way that could not be readily done using other theoretical tools for analysis. WORKER uses the strengths of computational modeling, integrating many processes and variables and making explicit assumptions and mechanisms.

Is Computational Modeling a Good Choice for Theoretical Analysis of Motivated Behavior Such as Withdrawal?

The value of a computational approach to analyzing streams of motivated behavior was first recognized by Atkinson and Birch[2] (1974), who studied achievement motivation and the dynamics of action computationally. Given a set of psychological processes and empirically grounded assumptions about their interaction, Atkinson and Birch showed that dynamic motivational analysis was feasible using a computational model.

In WORKER, the need to *explicitly* specify processes and mechanisms highlights both the extent and limits of our knowledge. Hanisch et al. (1996, particularly Tables 1 and 2) provided the precise specification of attitude–behavior relations in WORKER. Attitude–behavior feedback is specified such that if a behavior is taken, the attitude toward that behavior declines in the next unit of time (i.e., the propensity to undertake a behavior declines after it has been taken). If a behavior is not enacted, the propensity increases until that propensity passes a threshold. This reasonable set of assumptions is consistent with the several theoretical models being developed and tested here. Motives that are unfulfilled increase over periods, whereas motive fulfillment reduces attraction for a behavior. Precise functional forms for these relationships are specified. What is unclear is the theoretical status of and empirical basis for these particular functional forms.

Constructing WORKER is a good research strategy for this problem. What are some of the benefits for withdrawal research? Hanisch can study the interrelation among many behaviors, allowing consideration for substitution effects between behaviors (Miners, Moore, Champoux, & Martocchio, 1995; Youngblood, 1984). Hanisch studies different withdrawal models that suggest interrelations among withdrawal behaviors (e.g., progression of withdrawal), simultaneously analyzing a larger set of interrelated behaviors than others have done. Most analysis of withdrawal

---

[2]A former colleague of Hanisch and her colleagues in the Department of Psychology, University of Illinois at Champaign-Urbana.

has focused on one, two or, at most, three behaviors. WORKER allows analysis of a larger family of behaviors, behaviors for which there is evidence of interrelationships (Hulin, 1991). Theoretically, it is clear that one must look at all withdrawal behaviors simultaneously, given the theoretical perspective underlying WORKER (Hulin, 1991).

One way to increase the benefit of WORKER is to make the best use of results from other work. For example, absence and turnover are correlated .33 in a recent meta-analysis (Mitra, Jenkins, & Gupta, 1992). How can Hanisch take greatest advantage of this result? First, ask whether and under what conditions WORKER reproduces relationships between behaviors, such as turnover and absence, that approximate those found empirically. Second, constrain the appropriate parameters in the model to reflect empirical estimates that are currently available. A difficulty in many computational models is finding plausible parameter estimates and starting values. Meta-analyses may be useful in helping modelers set such constraints. Alternatively, one can use such estimates to test model validity. Interestingly, although the work reported here and other work casts doubt on the independent forms model, in results reported elsewhere (Hanisch et al., 1996, Tables 4, 5, and 6), the correlation of turnover and absenteeism behavioral propensities is .33 in the independent forms condition, .44 in the compensatory condition, and .60 in the progression of withdrawal condition. Surprisingly, using independent forms generates the closest estimate for propensities to the Mitra et al. (1992) result for actual behaviors. In Tables 7, 8, and 9 of Hanisch et al. (1996), the correlations between behaviors in WORKER are much lower than Mitra et al.'s (1992) estimate, with correlations near zero where estimates are reported. One would like to see these estimates closer to the values reported in the field or, at least, understand why they differ.

Modelers must assess model sensitivity. In WORKER, what is the sensitivity of the analyses to variation in the initial values for the transition map parameters? To construct these maps, one needs to specify a functional form, parameter values, and the structure of the relations between behaviors. Theoretical positions, such as progression of withdrawal, give insufficient information to make these specifications—often no more guidance than the sign of the relationships. WORKER forces the modeler to make these decisions. Having made the specifications (maybe with the help of empirical estimates), the modeler must ask how sensitive the model is to variation in these specifications. It is difficult to evaluate, except by explicit computational experimentation, what assumptions and specifications drive the observed results and how sensitive the model is to variations in these specifications. We earlier noted the advantages of explicitly stated assumptions in a computational model. Now that we have them, we can and must ask what their impact is on the observed results. Are the results highly sensitive to particular parameter values, or are they robust?

Does WORKER Facilitate the Exploration of the Theory's Implications?

Because WORKER was designed to draw out the implications of models such as the progression of withdrawal model, we can ask whether the demonstration offered here provides insight into how these models work. Hanisch offers two ways to study this question. First, examine the baseline models that suggest the operation of these models. Second, consider the intervention results, which essentially are experimental manipulations. The baseline models (Figures 3.1, 3.4, and 3.7) exhibit the spillover, compensatory behaviors, and progression of withdrawal models. The first 10 years of each intervention simulation also are essentially baseline models, because interventions only occur in the second 10 years of these estimates. Both the compensatory and progression of withdrawal baseline models show regular oscillation. This pattern suggests a problem with WORKER; there is insufficient consideration for the organizational context. Why should everyone's behavior covary so tightly? An organization cannot tolerate this in its working population. The high degree of regularity at the organization level occurs because the models are aggregations of *simulated individuals,* not *simulations of interacting groups of people* in an organization. No interdependencies between people exist that would tighten constraints on such behavior. When simulating organizations, one has to simulate the interdependent nature of the system. This is not modeled here, but it is an essential extension. Withdrawal behavior occurs in an organizational context, and that context has to be captured by more than interventions as constraints on independent individuals.

Without interdependence, much that is organizational is lost in WORKER. Even if one is aggregating individuals and not modeling interdependence directly, demographic changes and manpower flows should be considered. Is turnover completely modeled? Are people who leave replaced? If so, what kinds of people are the new entrants? People age and are promoted. How does that change their behavior propensities and attitudes? Aggregating with a simple set of assumptions about demographics and manpower flows may generate more plausible and interesting results than these baseline models suggest.

A surprising and puzzling result is that all the interventions have substantial effects between 2 and 6 years before their implementation at the 10-year point in the simulations. In Figures 3.2a and 3.5a, for example, attitudes seem to change after only 5 years (1995), but the intervention is scheduled for 2000. The early baseline years 1 through 10 in Figures 3.2 and 3.5 seem surprisingly different graphically from the baseline models in Figures 3.1 and 3.4. This variation suggests some instability (given stochastic components and, consequently, different initial conditions in what may be a dynamic system), which may require looking at more than just one simulation or replication. It may be necessary to run sufficient replications to assess solution stability.[3] Interestingly, the intervention results, other than seeming to start too early given their implementation, do suggest that the compensatory behaviors and spillover models are not as dissimilar as one might assume and are distinctly different from the progression of withdrawal model. All three models behave roughly as one would expect. However, if one thought that absence cultures and norms (Drago & Wooden, 1992; Johns & Nicholson, 1982; Martocchio, 1994) evolve in organizations and in groups in organizations, one might expect that those norms and culture would not respond quite as quickly or completely as they seem to in these simulations. This social dimension of absence could be studied in WORKER, possibly as part of the interdependence structure in the organization.

For WORKER to help us better understand withdrawal, steps should be taken to improve communication between researchers and ease adoption of WORKER. Success for a computational model, as with any theory, would be widespread adoption and use (Peters & Olson, 1983). WORKER is a theoretical statement about withdrawal. Successful theories must be communicated clearly and completely, so that others can use them. To use any theory, I must be able to readily apply it. To use Naylor, Pritchard, and Ilgen's (1980) theory of behavior in organizations, for example, I get the book off my shelf, read the appropriate sections, and try to apply the theory. Cohen, March, and Olsen (1972) developed the "garbage can" computational model of organizational decision making. The theory is formally stated as a computer program that is an appendix to the paper, so that anyone can examine, compile, and execute the garbage can model. When Bendor, Moe, and Shotts (1996) analyzed the theory, they simply took the article, compiled the code, and ran the model to derive the garbage can model's implications for conditions of interest to them. Consider ECHO, Thagard's (1989) computational model of explanatory coherence. He initially made the code available on diskette, then made it available on the Internet, and now provides the model as Java code that can be accessed via the World Wide Web.[4] This is how a computational model should be shared. For others to use WORKER, the theory, they need to be able to grab it and use it, as one would ECHO from the web or a book from the shelf. Open, available code is essential. We want to rapidly disseminate new theories so that our science can move forward.

Creating WORKER or any computational model requires a different set of skills from those we now teach. Computational modeling is an important new method,

[3]One of the perverse outcomes of simulations is that precisely because you can explore more conditions and run many replications, decisions about when to start and stop running a simulation model are somewhat harder to make than in the field, where many other constraints take hold. Nevertheless, one can and should estimate how many replications to run as one sees the variation across replications.

[4]See http://cogsci.uwaterloo.ca/ for the Computational Epistemology lab. By using Java, Thagard bypasses many of the difficulties of compiling code on multiple platforms, allowing users easier access to the program or theory.

possibly a third scientific discipline. For this discipline to thrive, we must rethink our profession's norms and practices. Creating and implementing WORKER requires skills and training more akin to the training now received in computer science or computational physics. Computational modelers are theorists. They must invest significant time and effort acquiring modeling skills to complement their disciplinary knowledge. The traditional professional researcher role in psychology and organizational behavior is the researcher as both theorist and empiricist. Most papers have both theoretical and empirical components, and most of us do a mixture of empirical and theoretical work. We tell our students to develop *and* test theories. This professional model *will not work for computational modelers* and probably will not continue to work for other theorists as our field embraces increasingly sophisticated and complex types of theoretical tools. We must recognize and value efforts such as WORKER on their own terms, where the theorist's role is to generate theory, and the modeler should not be "required" to test the theory as well. Asking others to emulate the efforts of Hanisch and her colleagues in developing WORKER and then also asking those same people to do empirical research based on their theoretical efforts will not do. It demands too much of the researcher and does not allow them sufficient resources to develop their skills and the models themselves. In advocating this view of the theoretical enterprise, I am suggesting that the division of labor between theory and empirical testing often found in other disciplines may be right for us if we are to take maximum advantage of this new set of exciting computational tools. If efforts such as WORKER are to thrive (and they should), we have to think differently about how we disseminate theories and the division of labor in psychological and organizational science.

References

Anderson, J. (1993). *Rules of the mind.* Hillsdale, NJ: Erlbaum.

Atkinson, J. W., & Birch, D. (1974). The dynamics of achievement-oriented activity. In J. W. Atkinson & J. O. Raynor (Eds.), *Motivation and achievement* (pp. 271–325). New York: Winston.

Bendor, J., Moe, T. M., & Shotts, K. (1996). *Recycling the garbage can: An assessment of the research program.* Unpublished manuscript.

Cohen, M., March, J. G., & Olsen, J. P. (1972). A garbage can model of organizational choice. *Administrative Sciences Quarterly, 17,* 1–25.

Drago, R., & Wooden, M. (1992). The determinants of labor absence: Economic factors and workgroup norms across countries. *Industrial & Labor Relations Review, 45*(4), 764–778.

Dutton, J. M., & Starbuck, W. (1971). *Computer simulation of human behavior.* New York: Wiley.

Hanisch, K. A., Hulin, C. L., & Seitz, S. T. (1996). Mathematical/computational modeling of organizational withdrawal processes: Benefits, methods, and results. In G. Ferris (Ed.),

Research in personnel and human resources management (Vol. 14, pp. 91–142). Greenwich, CT: JAI Press.

Hulin, C. (1991). Adaptation, persistence and commitment in organizations. In M. D. Dunnette & L. M. Hough (Eds.), *Handbook of industrial and organizational psychology* (Vol. 2, 2nd ed., pp. 445–505). Palo Alto, CA: Consulting Psychologists Press.

Johns, G., & Nicholson, N. (1982). The meanings of absence: New strategies for theory and research. In B. M. Staw & L. L. Cummings (Eds.), *Research in organizational behavior* (Vol. 4, pp. 127–172). Greenwich, CT: JAI Press.

Laird, J. E., Newell, A., & Rosenbloom, P. S. (1987). SOAR: An architecture for general intelligence. *Artificial Intelligence, 33,* 1–64.

Martocchio, J. (1994). The effects of absence culture on individual absence. *Human Relations, 47*(3), 243–262.

Miners, I. A., Moore, M. L., Champoux, J. E., & Martocchio, J. J. (1995). Time-serial substitution effects of absence control on employee time-use. *Human Relations, 48*(3), 307–326.

Mitra, A., Jenkins, G. D., & Gupta, N. (1992). A meta-analytic review of the relationship between absence and turnover. *Journal of Applied Psychology, 77*(6), 879–889.

Naylor, J. C., Pritchard, R. D., & Ilgen, D. R. (1980). *A theory of behavior in organizations.* New York: Academic Press.

Peters, J. P., & Olson, J. (1983). Is science marketing? *Journal of Marketing, 47,* 111–125.

Schultz, T. R., & Lepper, M. R. (1996). Cognitive dissonance reduction as constraint satisfaction. *Psychological Review, 103*(2), 219–240.

Simon, H. (1977). *On judging the plausibility of theories.* Boston: Reidel.

Tetlock, P. E., & Manstead, A. (1985). Impression management versus intrapsychic explanation in social psychology: A useful dichotomy? *Psychological Review, 92*(1), 59–77.

Thagard, P. (1989). Explanatory coherence. *Behavioral and Brain Sciences, 12,* 435–502.

Youngblood, S. (1984). Work, nonwork, and withdrawal. *Journal of Applied Psychology, 69*(3), 106–117.

CHAPTER 4

Examining the Fit Between Empirical Data and Theoretical Simulations

Liberty J. Munson
Charles L. Hulin

True experiments in organizations are difficult to conduct. They have limited temporal spans that may destroy the underlying behavioral cadences—natural unfolding of behaviors—that are of interest to organizational researchers. Further, survey studies in organizations are typically cross-sectional; those few that are longitudinal have short time spans that are chosen for practical rather than theoretical reasons. Computational modeling is an alternative research strategy that can be used to address issues in which the passage of time is necessary to allow behavioral processes to occur and for feedback from those behaviors to influence subsequent behaviors. Modeling can improve our understanding of how some patterns of human behavior in organizations unfold over time. Used in this way, computational modeling is a bridge between dynamic theories and empirical data; modeling can inform us about the structure of data that should be obtained if a specific model or theory is an accurate account of some process of interest.

A vital part of modeling is the examination of the fit or congruence of empirical data to the predictions and results that theoretical models produce through simulations. Comparisons of theoretical and empirical relations between behaviors, attitudes, or other phenomena of interest can provide information about the usefulness of applying a particular model of behavior to an organizational setting. This chapter focuses on model–data fit by comparing data obtained from an organizational survey with output generated by several dynamic models of behavioral processes within organizations.

The authors thank Michael Zickar and Joseph Rosse for their comments and suggestions on an earlier draft of this chapter. Their efforts improved the final product. We also thank Steven Seitz for his invaluable contributions to the development of the WORKER program and his patience in explaining, many times, that the output of dynamic models may be nearly as complex as observations on the system the dynamic models simulate . . . but easier to understand because we can toggle modules on and off to study experimentally the operations of the modules one at a time. We thank him for his patience as well as his more material contributions.

The specific behavioral focus of this chapter, *organizational withdrawal* (defined as employees' attempts to remove themselves from aversive job environments through a variety of behaviors, including tardiness, absenteeism, leaving work early, quitting, or unexpected retirement; see Hanisch, 1996, and Hulin, 1991), is amenable to computational modeling. WORKER (Hanisch, Hulin, & Seitz, 1996; Hanisch, Chapter 3, this volume) is computational modeling software developed to simulate organizational withdrawal behaviors; it uses a library of theoretical models as well as organizational, environmental, and individual-differences parameters to simulate organizational withdrawal processes.

Models of Withdrawal

We use enacted behaviors as manifestations of an underlying construct of withdrawal; they are the basis for estimating and understanding this construct. Five models that hypothesize patterns among organizational withdrawal behaviors and, implicitly, the meanings of those behaviors and the general construct they define, have been offered in the literature. They include the independent forms model (March & Simon, 1958), compensatory behaviors model (Hill & Trist, 1955), spillover model (Beehr & Gupta, 1978), alternative forms of behavior model (Mobley, 1977; Rice & Trist, 1952), and progression of withdrawal model (Baruch, 1944). This simulation will evaluate the structure of withdrawal behaviors simulated by the independent forms, compensatory, spillover, and progression of withdrawal models as described by Hulin (1991) and Hanisch (this volume), using the WORKER software described by Hanisch.

Although the statements of these models are substantially different, they all appear to share one important characteristic: They all assume that withdrawal behaviors are functional. That is, they assume that behaviors are enacted to reduce the job dissatisfaction or job stress that precipitated the behaviors. Behavioral functionality implies that there should be dynamic feedback links from enacted withdrawal behaviors to their antecedent cognitive states and attitudes. Except for the independent forms of withdrawal model, the models share another characteristic: They hypothesize that different withdrawal behaviors are dynamically linked. The occurrence of one withdrawal behavior is linked, in different ways in those four models, to the occurrence of other withdrawal behaviors as well as to its antecedent cognitions and attitudes. In these characteristics, the models are consistent with the classical, and still relevant, theories of attitude–behavior relations discussed by Doob (1947) and Thurstone (1931).

Although they share important characteristics, the models are contradictory in some ways. They cannot all be accurate accounts of withdrawal, but they all have some supporting data, suggesting that they may be *locally* accurate and useful accounts of the withdrawal process. The strengths of computational modeling allow us to study the implications of components of these organizational withdrawal models that cannot be efficiently studied using traditional research methods.

Some Problems With Empirical Studies

Empirical studies of organizational withdrawal have been impeded by problems that prevent adequate evaluations of the usefulness of the different models. These problems include:

- low base rates of the behaviors
- the complexity of the interacting environmental and individual characteristics that influence withdrawal decisions and behaviors
- implicit temporal requirements dictated by dynamic feedback functions
- the need to assess and study several behavioral manifestations of the general withdrawal construct.

Some of these problems are statistical (e.g., low base rates of most withdrawal behaviors). Others reflect habits of our research rather than endogenous problems. For example, repeated studies of one withdrawal behavior at a time are done as though such studies could be combined later into a general statement of the withdrawal process. The optimistic view of research and promised development of large-scale theories offered by logical positivism have not been realized in research and theory in this, or perhaps any, area of psychology.

This chapter uses computational modeling to address some model–data fit issues in patterns of reported organizational withdrawal behaviors. By using computational modeling of withdrawal behaviors in a virtual representation of the organization from which the empirical data were obtained, we can address a number of epistemological issues with the impedimenta listed earlier in this section having minimal impact.

Computational modeling allows us to deal effectively with an unacknowledged problem in the study of functional behaviors. These behaviors, which are assumed to be precipitated by an antecedent cognitive and emotional state, have feedback effects that reduce the stress that led to the enacted withdrawal behaviors. Time and temporal factors play a role in all studies that address these and related issues in organizations. However, a useful theory of organizational, or perhaps even psychological, time remains elusive and unformulated.

How long is long enough for a cause (job dissatisfaction) to have an effect (withdrawal behavior)? How much time is too much, when a third variable (economic conditions) may change and threaten the inferential validity of a study? Time is necessary for behaviors and their feedback to unfold in research on organizational withdrawal. The amount of time required, however, is unknown. Modeling studies can finesse the ambiguity in clock-time intervals required for behaviors.

Identifying the particular dynamic model of withdrawal that is operating within an organization has implications for management. Knowing the appropriate model may prescribe the types of interventions that will reduce targeted behaviors and proscribe others, because of the modeled effects on the frequencies of other withdrawal behaviors (Hanisch, this volume). Computational modeling allows researchers to identify the models that account for patterns of behaviors within a particular organization and reduce uncertainty about many factors that influence the withdrawal process. Good theories are practical.

WORKER Software

WORKER, developed by Hanisch et al. (1996), is a computational modeling software program designed to simulate withdrawal behaviors. (Details of WORKER can be found in Hanisch, this volume, and in Hanisch et al., 1996.) Extensive testing and validation on the fuzzy inference engines in WORKER document the realism captured by this modeling software. WORKER is based on fuzzy set theory and fuzzy calculus. These basic mathematical operations are combined with stochastically imposed thresholds and feedback dynamics to simulate employees' process of behavior selection. Stochastic thresholds allow negative attitudes that are more extreme than a user-defined value to be translated into manifest behaviors at rates less than 1.00 and attitudes less extreme than the thresholds to be translated stochastically into manifest behaviors at user-defined rates greater than .00. Feedback from an enacted behavior back to the attitude associated with it also is stochastically augmented. Feedback is normally set to $X_i + \delta$, where X_i is the feedback from the ith behavior and δ is a draw from a distribution $N(0, \sigma^2)$.

No claim is made that the virtual organizations recreate all the mundane realism of functioning organizations. A virtual organization does not have to be as complex as the organization it simulates, nor does it have to mimic the organization in every detail to produce output that is useful for model testing; aircraft simulators do not have to fly to teach pilots to fly. We must, however, guard against creating toy universes. We have attempted to set those characteristics that have direct influences on the behavioral process being modeled.

Purpose

This chapter describes the power of computational modeling as a research tool for illuminating the theory–data interfaces and for assessing model–data fit. Practical benefits of computational modeling for management are also an integral goal of our research efforts.

Data from structured interviews of employees in an organization were used to create a virtual copy of the organization in WORKER. Simulations then generated expected withdrawal behaviors based on each of the theoretical models of organizational withdrawal. Correlations among the simulated withdrawal behaviors generated by each model were compared with correlations generated from the interview data to determine which theoretical model provided the best fit to the empirical data for this organization.

Method

Participants

A total of 127 women provided the data for this study. All the women were faculty or staff members at a large midwestern university, and the mean age category was 40 to 44 years. Of the women, 117 women (94%) were white; 5% were African American; and 1% were Asian, Hispanic, or another ethnicity. Most (70%) were married or living with someone. The proportion of women who reported having attended or graduated from college was 53%. All participants had at least a high school diploma.

Procedure for Interview

Letters were sent to each department or unit head explaining the research and interview process. Each woman selected in the sample then received a letter explaining the purpose of the study, followed by a telephone call to set up a time for the interview and to answer any questions the participant had. To increase participation, we offered each woman $20. Research participants were informed that their participation was voluntary and that their responses were not anonymous but were confidential.

Participants read the questions on the computer screen and keyed their responses directly into a laptop computer. The interviewer remained in the room to answer any questions that might arise during the completion of the survey but was positioned so that he or she could not see the computer screen. For further details, procedures, see Munson, Hulin, and Drasgow (in press).

Instrument

Two scales provided the information needed to input the withdrawal behaviors and sanctions to be modeled by WORKER.

Work Withdrawal Scale

This scale, developed by Hanisch (1990) and Hanisch and Hulin (1990, 1991), represents one of two hypothesized dimensions of organizational withdrawal. Work withdrawal focuses on the behavioral attempts of the employee to escape from work and work tasks. The work withdrawal scale consists of 12 items with a 7-point response scale, ranging from *never* to *all of the time.* This scale assesses the self-reported frequency of engaging in the following behaviors: tardiness, absenteeism, taking long breaks, missing meetings, taking drugs or drinking alcohol after work, doing poor work, checking the time frequently, ignoring tasks unrelated to performance review, letting others do your work, making excuses to get out of work, using equipment for personal use, and tampering with equipment so that work cannot be accomplished. Coefficient α for this scale was .69. However, only 8 behaviors were modeled in WORKER, partly because the software can simulate only 10 behaviors at a time, and partly because several of the behaviors were nearly redundant and had equal reported frequencies, suggesting that only one of a pair of behaviors would be needed to assess model–data fit. Coefficient α of the 8 items was .60. The relatively low α coefficients for the scales are similar to those reported elsewhere (Fitzgerald, Drasgow, Hulin, Gelfand, & Magley, 1997) and reflect the heterogeneity of the behaviors that is required to assess adequately the behavioral construct of work withdrawal.

Sanctions

Perceived sanctions were assessed by asking how severe the punishment would be for engaging in each of the withdrawal behaviors included in the work withdrawal scale. The work withdrawal item was immediately followed by the appropriate sanction item. The 4-point response scale ranged from *very severe* to *no one would care or notice.*

Procedure for Computer Simulation

Demographic information from the survey was used to create a virtual organization in WORKER. Age in the virtual organization was normally distributed; the mean was 42 years, and the standard deviation was 7. These values were estimated from the distribution of responses across age categories. Tenure ranged from 3 to 35 years and was normally distributed, with a mean of 23.5 and a standard deviation of 2.4. The values were estimated from the categorical tenure variable.

The behaviors selected for modeling met important properties that distinguished them from the other behaviors. Behaviors were chosen based on their perceived sanctions and reported frequencies. To ensure that behaviors with a range of sanctions were included, the behaviors with the highest perceived sanction (personal use of equipment) and the lowest (postwork impairment) were included in the simulation. The most frequent behavior (tardiness) and the least frequent behavior (tampering with equipment) also were included.

Tampering with equipment had no variability in the reported frequency of the behavior (i.e., no one reported engaging in this work withdrawal behavior). Although setting the behavioral threshold high will potentially prevent any simulated employees from engaging in this behavior, tampering with equipment may still occur in simulations because of the stochastic nature of the behavioral thresholds. Employees may engage in the behavior even when their intentions are below the threshold. In the case of the progression of withdrawal model, for instance, everyone may progress through the milder behaviors without reducing their dissatisfaction or stress and eventually enact the most extreme behavior, tampering with equipment. Given the theoretical tenets underlying progression of withdrawal (progression through withdrawal behaviors occurs in a stochastically ordered sequence from least severe to most severe), this behavior may occur in the simulation of this model.

Some behaviors were eliminated because they were highly similar in terms of frequency and sanctions to other behaviors already included. The 8 behaviors remaining were as follows:

- missing meetings
- postwork impairment (drinking or doing drugs after work)
- tampering with equipment
- absenteeism
- tardiness
- doing poor work
- personal use of equipment
- daydreaming

We set the loadings for the attitudes on the common vector in the attitude space, which controls the correlations among the attitudes, to .4, .7, and .9 in three separate runs for each model. The settings span the range of loadings that can define a general job-attitude construct (Roznowski & Hulin, 1990). Loadings of the attitude variables of .4 on a common vector define a weak general attitude, loadings of .7 define a strong general attitude, and loadings of .9 are rarely encountered but were included to span the possible range of values. Done this way, the loadings allow us to estimate effects that the intercorrelations of the attitudes defining a general job attitude construct may have on the simulated behaviors or attitudes.

The settings allowed the manipulation of the attitude space among the employees in the virtual organization. A strong general attitude space is one in which few differentiations exist, both among different attitudes and among the different behaviors to which the attitudes are linked. A weaker general attitude vector defines an attitude space with clear differentiations among the attitudes and, consequently, among the behaviors. We used the common vector loadings to achieve different attitude spaces.

The common vector loadings had small effects on the correlations among the enacted behaviors across time. The simulations using higher loadings generated higher intercorrelations among the behaviors for more iterations than did the lower loadings. Differences attributable to manipulated attitude space characteristics nearly disappeared by the end of the simulation. The results presented in the sections that follow are based on runs using loadings on the common vector set at .7.

Behavioral thresholds were estimated using the frequencies of the behaviors reported by the sample of organizational employees. The behaviors reported to be most frequently enacted at the organization were set to have the lowest thresholds in the virtual organization; those with lower frequencies were set to have higher thresholds. These frequencies were then rescaled to have a mean of .5 and a variance of .25 to conform to the requirements of WORKER.

Unemployment was set at 6% throughout the simulation. Organizational sanctions were set using the perceived sanctions reported by the participants. The 4-point response scale was transformed to have a mean of .5 and a standard deviation of .25, so the sanctions could be input into WORKER's sanction scale, which ranges from 0 to 1.

Once the organization was created, each model of withdrawal was used to simulate withdrawal behaviors. Correlations among the behaviors and attitudes were obtained across 20 iterations, with each iteration representing a behavior cycle or time period. Correlations among simulated behaviors were compared with the correlations among frequencies of reported withdrawal behaviors. The model that generates a structure among the simulated withdrawal behaviors that fit the empirical data structure, evaluated by calculating root mean squared discrepancies, gains support as the most likely locally useful model of withdrawal; it is the model that provides the "best" fit to this specific organization.

Results

Based on the empirical data, the simulated correlation matrix among the withdrawal behaviors should have the following properties (among others): (a) Most of the entries are positive and of moderate strength, (b) the correlation between tampering with equipment and other behaviors should be near zero (no variability in organizational sample because no one reported engaging in this behavior), and (c) most of the correlations between postwork impairment and other withdrawal behaviors should be small (see Table 4.1 above the main diagonal for the empirical correlations).

Comparisons between the intercorrelations based on the empirical and simulated behaviors suggested that the progression of withdrawal model was not a useful representation of the withdrawal process as represented by the empirical data; it was therefore eliminated from further analysis. An inspection of the cross-sectional intercorrelation matrices among the simulated behaviors obtained after 5, 10, and 20 iterations suggested little variability in the behaviors; nearly all the entries in the correlation matrix were near zero. A graph of the simulated behaviors based on this model showed that the employees progressed through the behaviors quickly and that by the 5th iteration, nearly all the employees were engaging in 5 of the 8 withdrawal behaviors simulated. The root mean square residual (RMSR), calculated by comparing the empirical matrix with the one obtained after the 10th iteration, was

TABLE 4.1

Correlations obtained from the empirical data and from the simulation based on independent forms model (10th iteration)

	MISS MEETINGS	POSTWORK DRINKING	TAMPER WITH EQUIPMENT	ABSENT	MAKE EXCUSES TO GET OUT OF WORK	TARDY	PERSONAL USE OF EQUIPMENT	DAYDREAMING
Miss meetings		.07	.00	.18	.19	.21	.00	.15
Postwork drinking	.02		.00	.04	.09	.04	.24	.20
Tamper with equipment	.07	.02		.00	.00	.00	.00	.00
Absent	.26	.03	−.01		.37	.29	.15	.16
Make excuses	.24	.06	.07	.27		.16	.29	.27
Tardy	.15	.00	−.12	.32	.26		.11	.11
Personal use of equipment	.03	.11	.08	.19	−.17	.14		.42
Daydreaming	.27	.00	.08	.29	.24	.10	.27	

Note: The correlations obtained from the empirical data are presented above the diagonal. The correlations among the withdrawal behaviors simulated by the independent forms of withdrawal are shown below the main diagonal.

.15, also suggesting that the behaviors simulated by the model did not fit well with the empirical data. (Note that the output generated after the 10th iteration was used to calculate each RMSR reported below.) This does not mean that the progression of withdrawal model is not a useful representation of the withdrawal process in general; rather, these findings suggest that this model as simulated is inappropriate for this organization. A modification of the progression of withdrawal model programmed into WORKER, which is designed to slow the process of progressing through behaviors, improves the model–data fit without violating the basic assumptions of the model. However, even with a slower progression through the stochastically ordered behaviors, the progression of withdrawal model is unlikely to yield correlations or behavior structure that would resemble this organization, because tampering with equipment should become progressively more frequent in the progression of withdrawal model. This simulation does not comport with what is occurring within this organization. A further modification increasing the feedback from enacted behaviors to precipitating attitudes and behavioral intentions also would be required.

The spillover model was examined as a second possible model of the empirical data. It generated many negative correlations among the simulated behaviors. The RMSR between the empirical and simulated behavior matrices was .14, a negligible improvement over the progression of withdrawal model but still unsatisfactory for these analyses.

Empirical data also were compared with the behaviors simulated by the alternative forms and compensatory models; the output data generated from the simulations of the two models were nearly indistinguishable from each other. The correlations among the behaviors and among the attitudes at each time interval were nearly identical across the two models, regardless of the value of the common vector. Indeed, the underlying assumptions of the two models are difficult to distinguish. WORKER's output reinforced the theoretical similarities between the models during the simulations of this virtual organization. If the organizational data fit one of the two models, it would fit the other equally as well. We note, however, that the description of the compensatory model appears to focus on situations in which one withdrawal behavior is blocked by an external or internal force. This model might provide a better fit to the empirical data in other local situations with one popular behavior blocked by environmental exigencies.

The correlation matrix for the behaviors for both models was positive; nearly all the values were high, ranging from .40 to .70. All the correlations between tampering with equipment and the other variables were zero, as were the correlations between postwork impairment and the other behaviors. However, the empirical data suggest that the correlations should not be that high; indeed, the highest correlation in the empirical data was .42, between personal use of equipment and daydreaming. The RMSR for both models exceeded .26; the models simulated behaviors that did not fit the empirical data well. The two models were rejected as possible explanations of the withdrawal process at this organization. We are not suggesting that the models should be rejected in general; they only appear to be inappropriate for the empirical data from this organization in the neutral economy we simulated.

The independent forms model generated simulated data with the best fit to the empirical data. The correlations among the simulated behaviors were of the appropriate direction and magnitude. Some correlations had small negative values that should have been positive and small, but this was the only problem with the output generated from this model. Comparing the empirical correlations with the theoretical correlations derived from the independent forms models, the similarities far outweigh the differences. The RMSR was .08, suggesting that this model provided a reasonable representation of the empirical data. The correlations among behavior frequencies simulated by the independent forms model are shown in Table 4.1 below the main diagonal.

Additional Evidence

At the end of each behavioral interval iteration, WORKER produces updated values for each attitude–behavior frequency. Correlations among the attitudes within one time period, correlations among the frequencies of one behavior across time periods, and correlations among the values of one attitude across time periods also provide information about the models of withdrawal. These correlations and frequencies cannot be compared with any empirical counterparts in this study; the latter empirical data were not available from the interviews. Correlations, however, can be compared with data from other studies in the literature. Correlations of the frequencies of one behavior or one attitude across time provide information about the stability and dynamics of attitudes and behaviors simulated by the independent forms model. Stability across time, moderated by the temporal interval between assessments of the attitudes or behaviors, is found in most studies of individual behaviors (Henry & Hulin, 1987, 1989; Hulin, Henry, & Noon, 1990) and work attitudes (Smith, Kendall, & Hulin, 1969). Table 4.2 shows the correlations among the values of one attitude—toward missing meetings—across eight time periods below the diagonal. The parallel correlations of the simulated behaviors of missing meetings across the same iterations are shown above the diagonal.

The correlations above and below the diagonal all are positive. The correlations among the attitudes should be larger than the intercorrelations among the behaviors because the latter correlations are attenuated by nonnormal distributions of behaviors frequencies. The correlations are the largest for adjacent time intervals and become progressively smaller as the time periods become more remote from each other. These patterns of correlations conform to general findings in the literature. The consistency between the superdiagonal structure of the matrices shown in Table 4.2 and previous empirical studies lends further support to our conclusions about the usefulness of the independent forms model of withdrawal in this organization. The

TABLE 4.2

Correlations among simulated attitudes toward missing meetings and simulated behaviors of missing meetings across 8 iterations (independent forms)

TIME PERIOD	6	7	8	9	10	11	12	13
6	.13	.23	.26	.30	.20	.12	.08	.03
7	.76	.08	.31	.45	.41	.23	.14	.03
8	.67	.92	.10	.33	.49	.38	.19	.19
9	.64	.88	.97	.17	.37	.41	.40	.28
10	.62	.88	.95	.98	.08	.46	.40	.32
11	.62	.87	.95	.97	.99	.06	.71	.63
12	.61	.87	.94	.95	.98	.99	.09	.67
13	.60	.86	.94	.94	.96	.97	.98	.07

Note: Intercorrelations of simulated attitudes toward missing meetings are below the diagonal. Intercorrelations among simulated behaviors are above the diagonal. Correlations between simulated attitudes and simulated behaviors are shown in the main diagonal.

level of correlations between attitudes from adjacent time periods is much higher than expected, but the pattern is consistent with other empirical data. This higher-than-expected level of correlations can be reduced by increasing the impact of the feedback from enacted behaviors onto the attitudes that precipitated the withdrawal behaviors.

Discussion

Correlations among behaviors simulated from the independent forms model fit most closely with the empirical correlations among the reported behaviors. This outcome does not mean that the other models are not useful descriptions of how the withdrawal process may unfold over time. This result means that the independent forms model is the most useful local model; it provides the best description for this organization operating in an environment of fixed unemployment that we simulated. Much additional research on the usefulness of all of these withdrawal models in different organizations operating under different sets of environmental restrictions is needed.

Interface Between Data and Theory

Computational modeling can illuminate interfaces between theory and data, as we did in this chapter. It can tell us what empirical data to expect based on theoretical models operating within configurations of organizational parameters and environmental constraints, and it will aid in interpreting and understanding the construct of withdrawal as well as models that claim to describe the withdrawal process.

Computational modeling can be used to do what those who developed the verbally stated, metaphorical theories did not do: provide statements about the empirical evidence that would be generated by the operation of the theory in specific organizations and environments.

Explorations across all regions of the environmental and organizational parameters must be done before general statements about the organizational withdrawal process can be made. However, even when discrepancies are found regarding the usefulness of different models in some local regions of the total space, computational modeling can be used to generate overarching theoretical models that identify the organizational and environmental characteristics and parameters that allow the discrepant as well as the consistent findings to be integrated into a general statement of the withdrawal process.

Model–Data Fit

The empirical data in this study were obtained by slicing into an unfolding, dynamic system at arbitrary times. We have no idea how long this process has been unfolding for this sample of employees in this organization, making it difficult to determine which iteration of the simulation should be used as a comparison. Yet, the problem of time is not unique to withdrawal. It is an influence on all studies—whether modeling or empirical—of dynamic processes in organizations. Computational modeling requires that we acknowledge the role of time in the functional processes we have studied.

Empirical correlations reflect common method variance as well as construct variance. However, given the levels of the empirical correlations among reported frequencies of behaviors and their fit to simulated behaviors, the effects of common method variance appear to be trivial and do not generate artifactually high correlations. An unconventional use of computational modeling in this area would be to simulate data assuming no common error variance and compare the results to empirical data in which there may be common error variance. If we have identified the appropriate model, such comparisons should allow us to evaluate the influence of common error variance across a wide variety of distributions and assumptions.

The independent forms, spillover, and progression of withdrawal models produced low intercorrelations among behaviors in spite of the high loadings of attitudes on a common vector. These low intercorrelations appear to be a function of the dynamics of the models rather than probative evidence about a general construct of work withdrawal. Hulin (1991) derived the expected values of correlations among behaviors assuming a strictly unidimensional general behavioral construct and found similar low behavioral intercorrelations. Empirical correlations among enacted behaviors often are a poor guide to the underlying constructs unless the results that would be generated by the operation of the general construct are known rather than assumed. Empirical correlations among behaviors, for example, are influenced by the degree to which the behavior loads on a common vector, the distributional properties of the behavior, the unreliability of the behaviors, and any dynamic dependencies that may exist among pairs of behaviors in addition to their loadings on a common vector. All of these factors may reduce correlations substantially below unity. Correlations among behaviors in the .20 range can be generated by a strongly unidimensional model (Hulin, 1991).

Computational modeling is not a stand-alone research procedure. Well-articulated theoretical models are needed to provide the propositional calculus, the "if . . . then" statements, that generate the inference algorithms of the program. Appropriate empirical data are needed against which the structures of the simulated data can be compared. Relevant, empirically derived parameters and characteristics of environments and organizations are needed to provide a setting in which people behave and to enable the operation of these influences on behavioral processes.

Although the five models in the theoretical library of WORKER were described a number of years ago (see Hulin, 1991, for a description), the specific structures among the enacted behaviors that would be produced by each of the models were not explicated until they were simulated by computational modeling research (Hanisch et al., 1996). These withdrawal models, which have substantially different implications for organizational practice, were not evaluated by even the most routine test: What data structure would be expected if a given model provided an accurate description of the withdrawal process? This chapter provides a beginning to that process.

References

Baruch, D. W. (1944). Why they terminate. *Journal of Consulting Psychology, 8,* 35–46.

Beehr, T. A., & Gupta, N. (1978). A note on the structure of employee withdrawal. *Organizational Behavior and Human Performance, 21,* 73–79.

Doob, L. W. (1947). The behavior of attitudes. *Psychological Review, 45,* 135–156.

Fitzgerald, L. F., Drasgow, F., Hulin, C. L., Gelfand, M. J., & Magley, V. J. (1997). The antecedents and consequences of sexual harassment in organizations: A test of an integrated model. *Journal of Applied Psychology, 82,* 578–589.

Hanisch, K. A. (1990). *A casual model of general attitudes, work withdrawal, and job withdrawal, including retirement.* Unpublished doctoral dissertation, University of Illinois at Urbana–Champaign.

Hanisch, K. A. (1996). Organizational withdrawal. In N. N. Nicholson, R. Schuler, & A. Van de Ven (Eds.), *The Blackwell encyclopedic dictionary of organizational behavior* (p. 604). Cambridge, MA: Blackwell.

Hanisch, K. A., & Hulin, C. L. (1990). Job attitudes and organizational withdrawal: An examination of retirement and other voluntary withdrawal behaviors. *Journal of Vocational Behavior, 37,* 60–78.

Hanisch, K. A., & Hulin, C. L. (1991). General attitudes and organizational withdrawal: An evaluation of a causal model. *Journal of Vocational Behavior, 39,* 110–128.

Hanisch, K. A., Hulin, C. L., & Seitz, S. T. (1996). Mathematical/computational modeling of organizational withdrawal processes: Benefits, methods, and results. In G. Ferris (Ed.), *Research in personnel and human resources management* (Vol. 14, pp. 91–142). Greenwich, CT: JAI Press.

Henry, R. A., & Hulin, C. L. (1987). Stability of skilled performance across time: Some generalizations and limitations on utilities. *Journal of Applied Psychology, 72,* 457–462.

Henry, R. A., & Hulin, C. L. (1989). Changing validities: Ability–performance relations and utilities. *Journal of Applied Psychology, 74,* 365–367.

Hill, J. M., & Trist, E. L. (1955). Changes in accidents and other absences with length of service: A further study of their incidence and relation to each other in an iron and steel works. *Human Relations, 8,* 121–152.

Hulin, C. L. (1991). Adaptation, persistence, and commitment in organization. In M. D. Dunnette & L. M. Hough (Eds.), *Handbook of industrial and organizational psychology* (2nd ed., pp. 445–505). Palo Alto, CA: Consulting Psychologists Press.

Hulin, C. L., Henry, R. A., & Noon, S. L. (1990). Adding a dimension: Time as a factor in the generalizability of predictive relationships. *Psychological Bulletin, 107,* 328–340.

March, J. G., & Simon, H. A. (1958). *Organizations.* New York: Wiley.

Mobley, W. H. (1977). Intermediate linkages in the relationship between job satisfaction and employee turnover. *Journal of Applied Psychology, 62,* 237–240.

Munson, L. J., Hulin, C. L., & Drasgow, F. (in press). Longitudinal analyses of dispositional influences and sexual harassment: Effects on job and psychological outcomes. *Personnel Psychology.*

Rice, A. K., & Trist, E. L. (1952). Institutional and subinstitutional determinants of change in labor turnover. *Human Relations, 5,* 347–372.

Roznowski, M., & Hulin, C. L. (1990). The scientific merit of valid measures of general constructs with special reference to job satisfaction and job withdrawal. In C. J. Cranny & P. C. Smith (Eds.), *Job satisfaction: How people feel about their jobs and how it affects their performance* (pp. 123–164). New York: Lexington Books.

Smith, P. C., Kendall, L., & Hulin, C. L. (1969). *The measurement of satisfaction in work and retirement.* Chicago: Rand McNally.

Thurstone, L. L. (1931). The measurement of social attitudes. *Journal of Abnormal and Social Psychology, 26,* 249–269.

COMMENT:

Modeling Withdrawal

Theoretical, Empirical, and Methodological Implications

Nigel Nicholson

The vision of science is binocular: One eye, empiricism, searches for a better understanding of the phenomena (i.e., data) our senses present to us, thereby seeking to improve our ability to predict and control them. The other eye, theory, looks beyond to what we cannot yet see (but might), telling us where and how we should look for understanding. It is essential that they work together for true depth perception. The worst science has been monocular—dust bowl empiricism versus armchair speculation.

Historically, both eyes of science have benefited from mechanical invention. Some of our most important discoveries have come from technologies that, like new lenses, sharpen and enlarge vision, from Tycho Brahe's telescope to the Hubble. Mathematics and logic are technologies in this sense: They both reveal and order. Technologies are rejected when they fail to work—when they lack internal consistency. The same applies to models in general (Chapanis, 1961) and computational modeling in particular, which, as undertaken by Munson and Hulin, does exactly as they describe: mediates between theory and empiricism.

To be successful, this modeling has three requirements. First is internal consistency. The model has to work, to which end computer technology is a major new resource, allowing the consistency of ever more complex models to be rigorously tested. Second, the elements of the model need to relate with some fidelity to known phenomena—plausible correspondences must hold between constructs and reality. Third, the model must generate interpretable outcomes; valid criteria should exist against which to judge the meaningfulness of the outputs of modeling.

Against these standards Munson and Hulin's method is impressive, demonstrating the value of the approach for the rigorous testing of theory and for the guidance of future empiricism. Therefore, this commentary does not attempt a critique of the technique, but rather considers what it suggests for theory and empiricism in its chosen domain, namely, the relationship between organizational attitudes and behavior.

Attitudes and Behavior: The Case of Withdrawal

The study takes as its theoretical point of origin the notion that there is a family of behaviors that share a common attitudinal cause. This attitudinal cause, negative sentiments toward the workplace, is also a family of valences, although the authors do not discuss this possibility. For example, many different aspects of work may be the object of negative affect (conditions, supervision, and so on). The withdrawal behaviors remove the individual from the source of the affect.

The authors are not the first to take the reasonable position that there is a simple causal linkage between job dissatisfaction and these behaviors (e.g., March & Simon, 1958), especially absence. Absence is the quintessential withdrawal behavior, because it removes the person from the source of dissatisfaction for longer than most alternative avoidance routines in work and for less long than the more drastic termination of the employment relationship (turnover).

The early literature on absence and turnover treated the link with dissatisfaction as a specific form of the more important broad relationship in social psychology between attitudes and behavior. With absence, as in other areas, research repeatedly encountered the recalcitrant empirical reality that the relationship is often weak and unreliable. Over the past three decades, confident claims about dissatisfaction as the main predictor of absence have been found to be unsupportable (Farrell & Stamm, 1988; Hackett, 1989).

Two responses to this failure are possible. The first is a theoretical rejection of the construction of the relationship. One extreme account holds that attitudes are ephemeral and artifactual creations of social science methodology rather than causal entities in human psychology. Another account treats them as epiphenomena—they have no causal power as passive or reactive sentiments. Rather, as in expectancy valence theory, they are the outcomes of behavior more than the cause of them.

The second explanation is methodological, although in reality it is a methodological recasting of some aspects of the theoretical critique. It is that either the independent or dependent variables, or the measurement of the relationship between them, is misspecified. Misspecification of variables usually means that they are incommensurate in specificity (e.g., a general attitude measure, such as dissatisfaction with work, is tested in relation to a highly specific behavior, such as absence). Misspecification of the relationship, in this context, means that the attitudes and the behaviors have independent causes (and effects), which may sometimes be mediated by unmeasured other variables. This undoubtedly is the case, especially in relation to the focal behaviors. Absence may be caused by factors beyond a person's control, such as illness and accidents, which have a minimal or only indirect bearing on attitudes.

Conversely, a person may feel negative about work as a result of factors that absence (as "withdrawal") might not remove (e.g., dissatisfaction with pay might be exacerbated by absence that leads to loss of pay).

All of these observations have merit in some measure. It can be argued that the attitudes that researchers seek to relate to absence and other behaviors are the wrong variables and that more dynamic motivational constructs should be in the frame. Research periodically has confirmed that alternative constructs are better predictors of these behaviors, such as intent to leave for turnover (Mobley, 1982) and attendance motivation for absence (Fichman, 1988). Research also suggests that behaviors may be misspecified. One of the most notable demonstrations in relation to absence was Smith's (1977) finding that absence was predicted much better for a single day under adverse weather conditions. In effect, the behavior was "purified" of extraneous determinants by the barrier to attendance created by the conditions. Finally, on the misspecification of the relationship, two ingenious longitudinal studies have illustrated the possibility of bidirectional relationships. Clegg (1983) and Tharenou (1993) both found evidence for a reverse causal relationship to the conventional modeling of attitudes as independent and behavior as dependent variables. In both cases, the sign of the relationship is negative as predicted, although we also may entertain the possibility that under some circumstances it may not be (i.e., that absentees have more positive work attitudes than regular attenders). Such relationships are well within the capacity of computational modeling to test.

Now let us look at the Munson and Hulin simulation and how it addresses these issues.

Modeling Withdrawal: The Evidence of the Present Study

Theorists and researchers seek to overcome the difficulties described in the previous section through their use of the withdrawal concept. It represents, in the work of Munson and Hulin and earlier research, the attempt to specify the attitude–behavior relationship in the work domain correctly (or optimally) by developing a generalized underlying attitudinal construct that specifically relates a family of behaviors that "withdraw" a person from work. Let us look at how Munson and Hulin's work attempts this feat.

First, the attitude, like attendance motivation and intention to leave, seems to be a behavioral orientation. Munson and Hulin do not elaborate on the psychological essence of the construct, but this interpretation is clearly implied by the use of Hanisch's scale and the setting of common vectors in the model. How reasonable is this as a proposition, namely, that people will vary over time and circumstances in their disposition to withdraw from work by various means? One may give a generally affirmative answer from plentiful evidence that humans are hardwired to withdraw from or avoid noxious stimuli (Goleman, 1995). Moreover, we may assume without difficulty that individuals differ in their sensitivity to environmental noxiousness and hence in their dispositions to withdraw. To this we may add a consideration absent in the model, but which could be readily incorporated: Individual thresholds for the appraisal of positive and negative experiences differ as stable properties of the person (i.e., a personality construct amounting to susceptibility to negative appraisal). Both personality and stress research (Cooper & Payne, 1991) support this possibility. Within the model, however, individuals are treated alike within a simple feedback model. Changes in attitudes trigger behaviors, which then feed back to reduce the attitude.

But what if the attitude were less open to this feedback? That is, what if people with personalities encompassing a high disposition to withdraw require frequent recourse to the behaviors to effect a change in feeling, and those with low dispositions to withdraw never make recourse to the behaviors? The result would be much as Hulin himself and others have observed, a J-curved (negative binomial) distribution of these infrequent behaviors—most people exhibiting none of them, and a minority experiencing many of them. Future work with the system could readily incorporate a dispositional moderator to enlarge on the effects of such population difference. Thresholds could be set for the attitudes that differentiate among subpopulations as well as for each behavior. Results from research on demographic correlates could help here (e.g., the greater propensity of women and low-status workers to negative affect and of older workers to more positive affect).

Turning to the behaviors, we must ask the question "Is it equally reasonable to propose that the work behaviors under consideration are appropriate; that is, are they capable of satisfying the disposition?" Here we are on more speculative ground. Yes, it can be imagined that any of the eight behaviors identified could do so, although in every case, other motives seem to be equally or more plausible candidates: poor time management (missing meetings), social motives (postwork impairment), aggression (tampering with equipment), sickness (absence), inadequate skills (doing poor work), nonwork goals (personal use of equipment), and creative impulses (daydreaming). None of these possibilities presents a fundamental objection to the research. They only suggest limitations to the likelihood of a clear, generalizable positive relationship being found between the attitude and the behavior. In absence research, it is well recognized that the problem is that absence is a multiply determined behavior (Nicholson & Martocchio, 1995). The behavior may (a) serve different ends at different times or places, (b) serve one goal covertly while overtly serving another, and (c) serve one goal for one person and a different one for another. This was demonstrated in an unusual and painstaking piece of absence research by Hackett, Bycio, and Guion (1989). They found among a sample of nurses that idiographic, intraindividual longitudinal analysis could explain additional variance.

Point (a) suggests that unseen forces may channel attitudes down particular behavioral paths. Munson and Hulin cleverly recognize this in their incorporation of sanctioning regimes and unemployment levels into the modeling environment.

However, there is room to go much further, as the authors imply. It is well known that the causes of absence depend on context (Nicholson & Johns, 1985). The more general theoretical point is that any attitude to be expressed as a behavior requires a facilitating context. Research suggests that factors may operate at a group level of analysis (work group, factory site, company), a level that sets conditions for quite different sets of relations to operate. Far from being what Munson and Hulin call "mundane characteristics" whose "influence on organizational withdrawal process is likely to be minor," many group level factors may completely mediate the process. For example, company rules and worker-shared norms may mean that in a given setting, one withdrawal behavior may be an accepted and accessible expression of sentiment. In another, quite different behaviors may be the only currency in which employees express their feelings.

Point (b) is closer to the authors' implicit position—that different behaviors are equally potent paths to motivational goals, but this fact may not be apparent from mere observation. Indeed, a main purpose of this kind of modeling is to tease out the latent commonalities in motivations underlying superficially disparate behaviors. Certainly, it is known that "sickness" as a cause of absence is not a simple matter of physical risk through exposure to viral or other hazards. It is also a function of susceptibilities that have attitudinal correlates (Harvey & Nicholson, in press). It is quite tenable that people who are motivated to withdraw will get sick without being aware of the connection. The same reasoning can apply to the other behaviors. The question for the authors is, rightly, an empirical one. Will the data support this account? Note that the positive correlations among the items in Hanisch's scale are not a sufficient test of the idea, since the measure is attitudinal.

Point (c) (idiographic individual differences) complicates the picture further. This point is a recasting of the earlier observations about the likely relevance of both stable individual differences and contextual factors, namely, that we can expect both of them to relate not only to attitudes but also to behaviors. *Context* will affect behaviors through the constraints and opportunities of structural factors (e.g., by virtue of his or her role or position in an organization, a person will have greater or lesser access to a behavior than another person). Missing meetings, postwork impairment, tampering with equipment, and personal use of equipment seem especially likely to be open to this possibility. Relevant *individual-difference factors* may often be constitutional. Postwork impairment, absenteeism, doing poor work, and daydreaming all seem likely to be associated with individuals' physical condition, mental powers, addictions, and so forth. Again, we may say that Munson and Hulin's method is designed to answer the question empirically about what relationships are consistent with which explanatory accounts, and it has the virtue of offering possibilities for the incorporation of modeling individual and group contextual constraints that might give rise to different patterns.

Thus, we can envisage computational modeling creating environments in which (a) individuals are differently distributed according to various characteristics that are related to the behaviors and in which (b) thresholds differ in the access they afford to the behaviors at the group level. This refinement could go a long way to further explicating the functioning of "absence cultures" (Nicholson & Johns, 1985), perhaps extending the notion to provide a coherent account of "withdrawal cultures."

Turning to the specification of the relationship, as we have seen, Munson and Hulin envisage a one-way causal flow with feedback loops. This approach is founded, as we have seen, on the strong theoretical presumption of withdrawal theory that the family of withdrawal behaviors are reactive "pain avoidance" (Nicholson, 1977), rather than proactive, goal-directed behaviors. I have suggested above how the 8 behaviors might serve goals other than reducing work-related negative affect. Some of the goals might even eliminate or reverse the feedback loops of the model. For example, a worker under conditions of weak supervision who is free to take time off without sanction may have higher absence *and* higher satisfaction than a worker who is under a strict supervisory regime. The former worker is using his absence to consume additional satisfactions outside the workplace. Again, it seems as though the model is flexible enough to incorporate the possibility of these and other kinds of causal relationships (i.e., to look, in effect, beyond the withdrawal model in the attempt to predict unwanted or dysfunctional work behaviors). Clearly, adding these other relationships is to ask the modeling method to enter a new realm of complexity, whereby people with multiple motives engage in similar behaviors for different reasons. However, research suggests that this is the reality with which such empirical modeling must come to terms.

What Do the Results Imply?

Munson and Hulin's modeling, measured against the three criteria discussed at the start of this essay, passes the first test—internal consistency—by virtue of its ability to produce results of any kind. Much of the above discussion has been devoted to the second criterion, how elements correspond to external reality. More can be said about this, but by and large, it has fidelity to what is known about human psychology and behavior, although, as I have argued, room exists for refinement and enlargement. Turning to the third criterion, how interpretable are the findings? Two approaches exist to interpretation: (a) considering the criterion against which model fit is judged and (b) examining the interpretations that the obtained patterns of results will bear.

The first approach has obvious weaknesses. Although data were gathered with great care, the sample looks unusual—women in university employment. As I have suggested above, boundary conditions for empirical relationships between attitudes and work behaviors include individual difference and work context variables. We need to consider the possibility that the model with the best fit will not generalize to a good fit with equivalent data gathered from quite different populations and contexts, such as male factory workers. Further advances in the method, according to this observation, would seem to require not only incorporation of new variables to represent group and individual differences but also a wider range of empirical data sets against which to assess fit. The likely conclusion would be that different models would be revealed to be associated with particular organizational environments and with different subpopulations within them, as defined by their psychological or demographic characteristics.

The results themselves are extremely encouraging for the method at a general level, because they show how different sets of assumptions concatenate to produce visible outcomes that can be matched with observable patterns in organizational behavior. The method yields an especially valuable benefit in helping to resolve the persistent and tricky issue of shared method variance. The findings are reassuring to generations of researchers for whom shared method variance is held up as a major flaw in their survey methodologies.

The results here, interestingly, favor the independent forms model of relationships among the variables. The results, therefore, are pointing in directions suggested in the above discussion—that these behaviors are incommensurate in how they serve psychological needs. The independent forms theory holds that the behaviors have, according to Johns (1997), "different antecedents, functions, and consequences, and should thus be studied independently" (p. 124). For theoretical reasons similar to the arguments advanced above, this is the position that predominated in my own work. In addition, if we were to accept the results of Munson and Hulin's exploration as conclusive, then the withdrawal theory, in effect, has little to offer and can be abandoned. Doing so would be premature, however. Far from closing this door, it opens it, along with several others in a hall of possibilities. There is great value in using this method to explore the implications of our theoretical assumptions in the structure of data. This method also is useful for examining the structure of data produced by models to consider what kinds of theories the data might currently support or suggest for the future. For example, in Munson and Hulin's modeling, after several iterations "nearly all the employees were engaging in 5 of the 8 withdrawal behaviors simulated" (p. 76). This result is inconsistent with what one would expect to find on the basis of the individual differences argument above, and like this commentary, it suggests that differential susceptibilities need to be incorporated.

Indeed, recent research on personality has begun to conclude, much as Hanisch and Hulin (1990) argued, that we may be underestimating its predictive validity because of misspecification of the behaviors to be predicted. When one looks at families of related behaviors or at behaviors over a long enough time span, the predictive validity of personality measurement increases dramatically (Ones, Viswesvaran, & Schmidt, 1993). Similarly, although the results in the present test are not sympathetic to a similar line of argument for withdrawal, they do offer the possibility of defining the contexts and populations where the construct might be visibly important to understanding organizational behaviors. In short, Munson and Hulin's work demonstrates the capacity of computational modeling in this and related areas to function as a powerful technology that can maintain a flexibly searching, keenly focused, and far-sighted scientific vision of organizational behavior.

References

Chapanis, A. (1961). Men, machines, and models. *American Psychologist, 16*, 113–131.

Clegg, C. W. (1983). Psychology of employee lateness, absence, and turnover: A methodological critique and empirical study. *Journal of Applied Psychology, 68*, 88–101.

Cooper, C. L., & Payne, R. L. (1991). *Personality and stress: Individual differences in the stress process*. Chichester, UK: Wiley.

Farrell, D., & Stamm, C. L. (1988). Meta-analysis of the correlates of employee absence. *Human Relations, 41*, 211–227.

Fichman, M. (1988). Motivational consequences of absence and attendance: Proportional hazard estimation of a dynamic motivation model. *Journal of Applied Psychology, 73*, 119–134.

Goleman, D. (1995). *Emotional intelligence*. London: Bloomsbury.

Hackett, R. D. (1989). Work attitudes and employee absenteeism: A synthesis of the literature. *Journal of Occupational Psychology, 62*, 235–248.

Hackett, R. D., Bycio, P., & Guion, R. M. (1989). An idiographic–longitudinal analysis of absenteeism among hospital nurses. *Academy of Management Journal, 32*, 424–453.

Hanisch, K. A., & Hulin, C. L. (1990). Job attitudes and organizational withdrawal: An examination of retirement and other voluntary withdrawal behaviors. *Journal of Vocational Behavior, 37*, 60–78.

Harvey, J., & Nicholson, N. (in press). Minor illness as a legitimate reason for absence. *Journal of Organizational Behavior.*

Johns, G. (1997). Contemporary research on absence from work: Correlates, causes and consequences. In C. A. Cooper & I. T. Robertson (Eds.), *International review of applied psychology, 1997* (Vol. 12, pp. 126–138). Chichester, UK: Wiley.

March, J. G., & Simon, H. A. (1958). *Organizations*. New York: Wiley.

Mobley, W. H. (1982). *Employee turnover: Causes, consequences and control*. Reading, MA: Addison-Wesley.

Nicholson, N. (1977). Absence behavior and attendance motivation: A conceptual synthesis. *Journal of Management Studies, 14*, 231–252.

Nicholson, N., & Johns, G. (1985). The absence culture and the psychological contract: Who's in control of absence? *Academy of Management Review, 10*, 397–407.

Nicholson, N., & Martocchio, J. J. (1995). The management of absence: What do we know? What can we do? In G. R. Ferris, S. D. Rosen, & D. T. Barnum (Eds.), *Handbook of human resources management* (pp. 597–614). Oxford: Blackwell.

Ones, D. S., Viswesvaran, C., & Schmidt, F. L. (1993). Comprehensive meta-analysis of integrity test validities: Findings and implications for personnel selection and theories of job performance. *Journal of Applied Psychology, 78,* 679–703.

Smith, F. J. (1977). Work attitudes as predictors of attendance on a specific day. *Journal of Applied Psychology, 62,* 16–19.

Tharenou, P. (1993). A test of reciprocal causality for absenteeism. *Journal of Organizational Behavior, 14,* 269–287.

CHAPTER 5

Modeling Faking on Personality Tests

Michael J. Zickar

Personality traits are integral individual-differences variables for the science and practice of industrial–organizational (I/O) psychology and have been endorsed as valid predictors of job performance in personnel selection (Barrick & Mount, 1991; Tett, Jackson, & Rothstein, 1991). In spite of a resurgence of interest in personality theory in applied psychology, concern about the transparency and fakeability of personality items has led some researchers to question the usefulness of personality tests for employee selection.

Concern for the susceptibility of personality tests to dissimulation began shortly after the advent of structured personality tests. Meehl and Hathaway (1946) developed indices to identify invalid responses in the Minnesota Multiphasic Personality Inventory (MMPI), one of the first structured personality inventories. The effects of nuisance variables (e.g., social desirability) and motivational states (e.g., faking "good" or feigning a mental illness) on personality test scores also have been explored. Recent debate has focused on whether faking distorts the measurement properties of personality tests. Some research has concluded that faking does not decrease the predictive validity of personality tests (Hough, Eaton, Dunnette, Kamp, & McCloy, 1990), whereas other research suggests that faking can affect hiring decisions (Douglas, McDaniel, & Snell, 1996).

Previous research on faking has used experimental designs in which some participants are instructed to fake. Other research has used nonexperimental designs in which applicant responses are compared with those of a sample of incumbents, whose motivation to fake should be less. Both strategies have severe limitations. With experimentally induced faking research, it is unclear whether the process that participants use to fake in those experiments is similar to the process used by applicants who fake (Kroger & Turnbull, 1975). In the applicant sample paradigm, it is nearly

I would like to thank the students in my graduate measurement seminar for commenting on an earlier draft of this chapter. Additional thanks are given to Scott Highhouse, Daniel Ilgen, and Charles Hulin for their comments and suggestions.

impossible to distinguish applicants who faked from honest applicants—who, after all, would admit to faking? Because of the limitations of the two methodologies, modeling and computer simulation can be used to address some initial questions about the effects of faking.

Modeling of individuals responding to personality items allows researchers to determine the effects of the responding strategy (e.g., faking, malingering, carelessness), the role of measurement context (e.g., job application, academic research, concurrent validation), and how the response style and contextual variables can influence decisions made on the basis of personality instruments. In the modeling context, factors that are difficult to manipulate experimentally, such as test validity, can be examined through the use of Monte Carlo simulations. Data from the simulations provide useful information to organizational consumers of personality tests. Before discussing such research, it is necessary to review some basic psychometric concepts that are used in this simulation research.

Item Response Theory

Traditional test theory, commonly designated Classical Test Theory (CTT), is the basis for most commonly used scale development techniques, such as examining item–total correlations and internal consistencies (Gullicksen, 1950; Lord & Novick, 1968). CTT has served the basic needs of applied psychologists by providing tools for data analysis that require few assumptions. A limitation of CTT, however, is that it is not effective for modeling how people respond to items (Hambleton & Swaminathan, 1985). Sophisticated analyses and applications, such as adaptive testing, interpreting mean differences between different groups, and identifying atypical item response patterns, require an understanding of individual item responses.

Item response theory (IRT) relates characteristics of items and characteristics of individuals to the probability that a person will respond affirmatively to an item. The cornerstone of IRT is the *item response function* (IRF). This function is a nonlinear regression of the probability of affirming item i on a latent trait, θ. Several possible forms to this regression line exist. For dichotomously scored items, the two-parameter logistic (2PL) model and the three-parameter logistic (3PL) model are commonly used. A class of *polytomous* models can be used for items with more than two options.

The formula for the 2PL model is

$$P(u_i = 1|\theta) = \frac{1}{1 + e^{-1.7a_i(\theta - b_i)}}, \tag{5.1}$$

where the probability that an individual with a latent trait, θ, affirms an item i (i.e., $u_i = 1$) is a function of two parameters: a discrimination parameter, a_i, and a location or threshold parameter, b_i. The probability of affirming items with high a parameters varies sharply as a function of θ, whereas the probability of affirming items with low a

parameters varies weakly as a function of θ. Low a parameters are usually associated with items that measure other unintended traits instead of (or in addition to) the intended θ. Items with high b parameters will be endorsed only by respondents with large, positive θs, whereas items with low b parameters will be endorsed by everyone except people with the most extreme negative θs. This model assumes that individuals with the lowest θ values will have a zero probability of affirming the item.

The 3PL formula, an extension of the 2PL, includes an additional item parameter, c_i, which is often called a *pseudoguessing* parameter. The c parameter introduces a nonzero lower asymptote to the IRF so that even respondents with large negative θs will have a nonzero probability of affirming the item. The c parameter may be warranted when faking is expected (i.e., individuals with the lowest trait scores will still be expected to endorse the items with nonzero probability). This model also may be appropriate even for situations in which there is no motivation to fake, if certain items are saturated with social desirability and often are not affirmed because doing so might make the respondent feel bad about his or her self-image.

IRT models assume that the latent trait, θ, is the dominant individual determinant of item responses. Therefore, only unidimensional scales are to be analyzed by these models. Because no test or scale is ever strictly unidimensional, it is necessary to establish the amount of multidimensionality that can be tolerated with unidimensional IRT models. Drasgow and Parsons (1983) demonstrated that deviations from strict unidimensionality will not destroy the fidelity of these models as long as an appropriate factor analysis demonstrates that the first factor has a much larger eigenvalue than secondary factors. Unfortunately, many personality constructs may have higher levels of multidimensionality than the levels Drasgow and Parsons (1983) found acceptable. For multidimensional data sets, nonparametric IRT models (Levine, 1984) or multidimensional models (Reckase, 1997) should be used.

Figure 5.1 presents IRFs (using 2PL and 3PL models) estimated for an item from the Sociability scale of the Hogan Personality Inventory (Hogan & Hogan, 1992). Based on the IRF, one can trace the probability of affirming an item as a function of θ. For example, individuals with θ equal to 0.0 would be expected to have an 80% probability of affirming that item. The 2PL and 3PL IRFs do not differ much throughout the θ continuum, except at extremely low ($\theta < -2.0$) sociability levels. Therefore, individuals with θs equal to −3.0 would be predicted to affirm the item around 5% of the time if the 2PL model is used; however, the 3PL model predicts that that item should be affirmed 15% of the time by the same group. Decisions about which model is most appropriate should be based on an evaluation of goodness-of-fit. .

Modeling Faking Using IRT

IRT is a powerful measurement technique that, when creatively applied, can answer problems that previous measurement theories were ill-equipped to answer. IRT-based tools, if extended appropriately, have the potential to provide further advances

FIGURE 5.1

Item response functions for a personality item

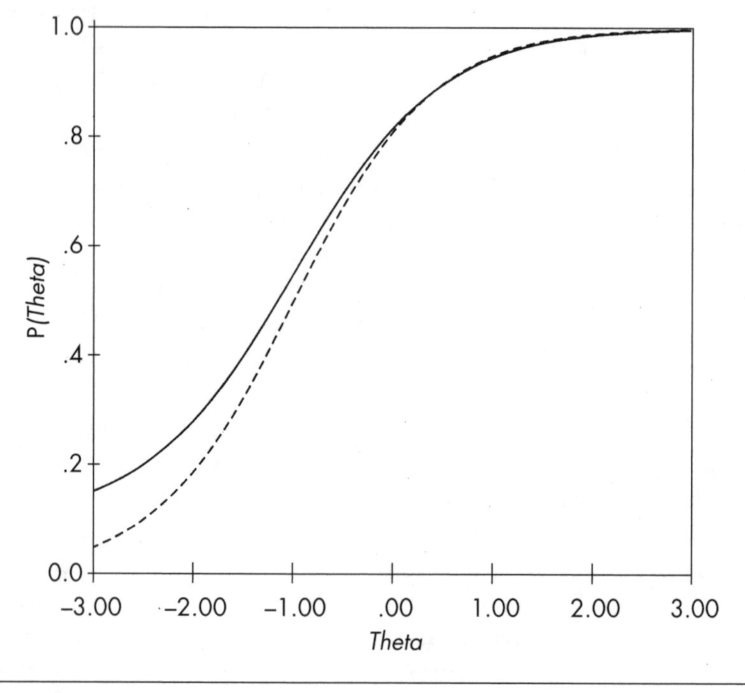

in personality measurement. The following research uses IRT as the foundation for simulation research to determine the effects that faking may have on the measurement properties of tests.

Does Faking Matter?

Many studies have shown that subjects can manipulate personality scale scores when instructed. Subjects instructed to fake good receive higher scores than subjects instructed to answer honestly (White, Nord, Mael, & Young, 1993). Subjects also can feign illnesses or portray themselves in a poor light (Gilles, Rogers, & Dickes, 1990). In addition, research has demonstrated that in applicant settings, applicants often provide false information to self-report questionnaires (Anderson, Warner, & Spector, 1984). Despite this evidence, some psychologists have concluded that faking is *not* a problem in selection contexts (Barrick & Mount, 1996; Hough & Schneider, 1996; Ones, Viswesvaran, & Reiss, 1996). This conclusion is based on the finding that when validity correlations are corrected for social desirability (a common index of faking good), validity correlations do not increase substantially

(Christiansen, Goffin, Johnston, & Rothstein, 1994; Hough et al., 1990). This result suggests that the overall bivariate distribution between predictor and criterion is not distorted by faking.

Simulation research by Zickar, Rosse, Levin, and Hulin (1997), however, suggested that faking may cause local distortions in the bivariate distribution even while not significantly distorting the overall correlation. They hypothesized that though the validity correlation might not be distorted by faking, there might be specific changes in the rank ordering of applicants that would make decisions based on personality tests less useful than the validity coefficient suggests. This hypothesis would be difficult to test with empirical data because it is never clear, in an applicant sample, which respondents are answering honestly.

Zickar et al. (1997) used a simulation methodology that allowed the form and magnitude of faking to be specified. Simulation methodology also allowed true parameters to be "known" so that the effects of faking could be better understood. The simulation demonstrated that when some portion of a sample is faking and some is responding honestly, the validity correlation is typically not affected to a large degree. A disproportionate number of fakers, however, received the top score. The true trait scores of those fakers tended to be lower than those of the simulated honest people who also received the highest score. These results bring into question the conclusion that faking does not distort decisions based on test scores.

Zickar et al.'s (1997) simulation was built directly around an IRT framework. IRFs were estimated for the 2PL model using data from the Army's Work Orientation scale from the Assessment of Background and Life Events (ABLE; White et al., 1993). The estimated IRFs then were used to generate item responses for a simulation data set. Responses for honest respondents were generated with the following five-step process using custom-written Turbo Pascal software.

1. For each simulated respondent, a θ was sampled from a normal distribution.
2. Steps 2–4 generated the item response data for each simulee. The probability of affirming the item given the θ chosen at step 1 [i.e., $P(u = 1|\theta)$] was computed using the 2PL formula and the estimated item parameters from the ABLE data set.
3. Next, a random variable, τ, was sampled from a uniform distribution ranging from zero to one.
4. If τ was less than or equal to $P(u = 1|\theta)$, then the item was recorded as affirmed; otherwise, the item was recorded as not affirmed.
5. A criterion score was simulated by randomly choosing a value from a correlated bivariate distribution. This guaranteed that the criterion score would be correlated with the q distribution. The correlation between the q and criterion distributions was varied across simulation conditions.

The process for simulating the faking respondents' data was identical, except for step 2. A model needed to be formulated to describe how fakers respond to personality items. As long as the faking model allowed $P(u = 1|\theta)$ to be computed, faking data could be simulated with a similar process as the normal data. In the Zickar et al. (1997) research, a θ-shift model was hypothesized to model the process that respondents use to fake good on personality tests. In this model, individuals who were faking responded to items that were verifiable and objective (e.g., "Did you participate in high school athletics?") with their honest θ (see Becker & Colquitt, 1992). On items that were not easily verifiable (e.g., "Are you generally happy?"), however, respondents responded to the items with $\theta + \delta$, where δ was a specified amount of bonus points. δ may vary according to a person's motivation to fake, faking ability, or the perceived verifiability of the item. In Zickar et al. (1997), δ was systematically manipulated across simulation conditions so that its effects could be directly examined. Adding δ to θ ensured that fakers would have a higher probability of affirming the item than would be expected given their latent trait level. For this simulation, items were deemed fakeable or nonfakeable based on previous research (Zickar & Drasgow, 1996).

The three factors manipulated in this simulation were (a) the percentage of fakers in a sample, (b) the amount of faking those fakers did (i.e., δ_{Mean}), and (c) the correlation between the θ distribution and the criterion score distribution (i.e., the true validity correlation of the test). Crossing all levels of the three factors led to 210 simulation runs.

Results showed that the decrease in validity resulting from faking was generally minimal, even with large percentages of fakers in the validation sample. The drop in validity was largest when the faking magnitude, δ, was large and the percentage of fakers in a sample was near 50% (see Figure 5.2). However, even in the most extreme faking conditions, the validity under faking conditions decreased only 25% from conditions with no faking. In operational settings with less extreme faking conditions, decrements in validity may be attributed to sampling error and, hence, raise little concern.

Despite the small decreases in validity, significant distortions occurred in the rank ordering of simulees; those with observed scale scores at or near the maximum possible score were more likely to have faked. Even when only 5% of the sample was slightly faking, 15% of the simulees that obtained the top score on the scale were faking. When 25% of the sample was moderately faking, 63% of the simulees that obtained the top score were faking. These results are important because fakers with high observed scores tended to have lower θs than honest simulees with the same observed scores.

The results suggest that in conditions of faking combined with top-down selection, (a) fakers will be disproportionately hired, (b) the fakers hired will be of lower quality than expected (i.e., they will have lower θs than honest people with the same score), and (c) the validity coefficient will not provide an indication of these problems.

FIGURE 5.2

Validity decrement as a function of % fakers in a sample and faking magnitude: true validity, $\rho = .30$

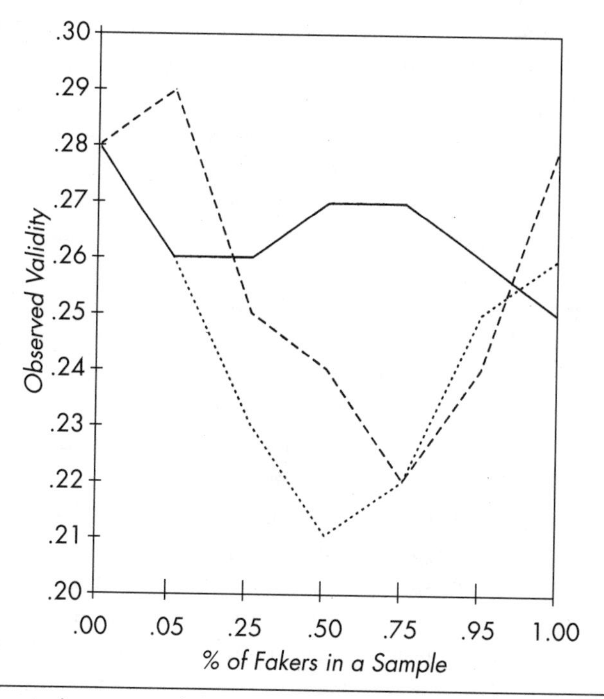

This simulation paradigm also can be used to answer a series of "what if" questions that are not possible with experimental data sets. For example, what would be the effects on validity if . . .

- fakers faked on all items
- a large variation existed in the motivation to fake among fakers
- more-discriminating items were used.

By answering these questions in a simulation context, practitioners who use personality tests in selection programs can better understand potential problems that may remain hidden if only traditional research strategies are used.

Extension of Simulation

After the earlier simulation was completed, an additional Monte Carlo study was conducted to test the effects of three additional variables on the validity coefficient: the percentage of fakeable items, the correlation of faking magnitude with θ, and the standard deviation of the faking magnitude within a sample (Zickar, 1997). The number of fakeable items was fixed at nearly 50% in the previous study, whereas it was given a range of four values in this research: 25%, 50%, 75%, and 100%. The validity decrement should be related to the percentage of items faked in a sample, with higher percentages of faked items leading to larger validity decrements. The correlation of δ (faking magnitude) with θ also was allowed to vary. The range of the correlation was –.40, –.20, .00, .20, and .40. The validity decrement should be relatively small with a positive correlation and relatively large with a negative correlation. Some researchers have hypothesized that social desirability (a surrogate for faking magnitude) should be positively related to certain personality traits, whereas others claim that there should be a negative relation. By modeling this correlation, the ramifications of the different positions can be tested. Finally, the standard deviation of δ was varied from 1.0 (the previous study's value) to 5.0 and 9.0. Large values of this standard deviation would indicate that the sample had applicants who greatly varied in motivation to fake. People with small δs may already be employed or especially honest, whereas those with large δs may be unemployed and, perhaps, dishonest. Depending on the hiring circumstances, respondents may be relatively homogeneous in faking motivation or they may differ greatly.

The same data generation process as in Zickar et al. (1997) was used, except that the faking model was modified to accommodate the three manipulated factors. Results from the simulations suggested that different factors worked in combination to produce validity decrements. The effects both of faking variability and of the correlation of faking with the criterion depended on the percentage of items faked. The impact of these factors was greatest when 75% of the items were deemed fakeable. The effects of these factors diminished as the number of fakeable items approached either 0% or 100%. This result is similar to the finding in the previous simulations, which suggests that the validity decrement will be greatest when around 50% to 75% of the sample is faking.

The sample variability of faking led to decreases in validity; however, there were no substantial differences between the $\sigma = 5$ or $\sigma = 9$ conditions. Perhaps these values were larger than some threshold at which the validity decrement reaches a floor effect. With 50% of the items faked, the validity decrement for the $\sigma = 1.0$ condition was –.09 (.21 with true validity of .30). With both $\sigma = 5.0$ and $\sigma = 9.0$, the decrement was –.13. These values were averaged across the correlation of δ with θ conditions, because there was no interaction between that factor and faking variability. The effects diminish when 100% of the items are fakeable, with the decrements equal to –.07, –.08, and –.08 in the respective conditions.

The relation between validity decrement and correlation between δ with θ (i.e., $\rho_{\delta\theta}$) followed the same pattern. With 50% of the items faked, the decrement for the $\rho_{\delta\theta} = .40$ condition was –.07. With a correlation equal to 0, the decrement was –.12, whereas the decrement for $\rho_{\delta\theta} = -.40$ was –.14. The differences between the decrements became minimal as the percentage of items faked became close to 0% or

100%. The results suggest that when faking is related to the construct of interest, faking will result in less of a decrement than when faking is unrelated to or negatively correlated with the construct.

These results further the understanding of the role of contextual variables in research conducted to test the effects of faking on validity decrement. It may be that previous applicant studies on faking did not have a large enough range of faking motivations (i.e., low variability in faking) to show a significant decrease in validity stemming from faking. These results also generalize previous findings to include the number of items faked. The higher the number of items that people fake, the greater the drop in validity should be. It is unclear, though, why validity decreased less when 100% of the items were faked, compared with when only 75% of the items were faked.

A Better Model of Faking

Both of the previous simulation studies were based on a model of faking that was not tested to see if it fit the data of actual fakers. To increase confidence in the simulation research, it was necessary to gain an empirical understanding of the response process of fakers and to generate reasonable estimates for the different simulation parameters. Therefore, analysis of empirical data was conducted (Zickar & Robie, 1999).

Because it is usually impossible to gather a pure sample of fakers from applicant data, experimentally induced faking was used in an attempt to understand applicant faking. Researchers analyzed an archival data set in which participants were instructed to either answer honestly or to fake by choosing what they felt to be the best answer (Young, White, & Oppler, 1991). Data were analyzed from three experimental conditions: Respondents were told (a) to answer honestly, (b) to ad lib fake good, or (c) to fake good based on coaching they received. In the coached fake-good condition, respondents were given practice items and the correct answer was identified by a coach. In the ad-lib faking condition, respondents were given no coaching. Three personality scales were analyzed: Nondelinquency, Work Orientation, and Emotional Stability, all of which had been used in validation research to predict military performance criteria (White et al., 1993).

Because the items each had three ordered options, a polytomous IRT model was chosen to model these data. Samejima's (1969) graded model was designed to analyze polytomous data with ordered options (e.g., disagree, neutral, and agree) and has been shown to model Likert-type data well (Maydeu-Olivares, Drasgow, & Mead, 1994). In this model, each item is characterized by *option response functions* (ORFs) instead of IRFs. The ORF is similar to the IRF, except that the y-axis is the probability of endorsing a particular option instead of the probability of affirming the item. In the graded response model, a discrimination parameter (a) and $m - 1$ threshold parameters (where m is the number of options) are estimated for each item. The ORFs are constructed based on the item and threshold parameters.

Polytomous IRT can model faking behavior in two ways: (a) Faking can be considered to be a function of the items changing when faked, or (b) it can be a function of a person's trait scores changing when faking. The *changing items paradigm* models faking as a change in item and option parameters from the honest to faking condition. This paradigm assumes that the latent traits of respondents (i.e., θs) are *not* changed by faking. Although the physical structure and wording of items does not change when faked, the perceptions of the same item may differ between honest respondents and fakers. The changes in perceptions may relate to changing expectations of the consequences of choosing particular options, to different frames of reference, or both. The primary research goal under this paradigm is to determine the nature of the ORF changes across different faking and honest conditions.

The *changing persons paradigm* models the process of faking as a change in the person's latent trait. Whereas most IRT theorists believe that θ is a relatively stable individual characteristic that is unrelated to the testing instrument, the changing persons paradigm assumes that the faking individual's θ is temporarily and consciously changed to improve personality test scores. The primary research goal of this paradigm is to determine the amount of the θ shift. With this paradigm, item parameters may be allowed to vary across conditions. By allowing item parameters to vary, differences in item parameters across conditions signify that the amount of θ shift is not constant but differs across items. If item parameters were not allowed to vary, then the changing persons paradigm would assume that the change in θ is constant across all items.

Neither paradigm can be considered more correct than the other, because both models should provide identical statistical fit to data. They differ in that the overall mean difference in θ across conditions is directly modeled in the changing persons paradigm, whereas in the changing items paradigm, the overall mean shift is absorbed into the ORF shift.

Changing Items Modeling

One recurrent finding was that the threshold parameters were more negative in the faking conditions, with the coached condition having more negative thresholds than the ad-lib condition. Both faking conditions had more negative thresholds than the ORFs that were estimated from the honest conditions. This negative shift in thresholds suggests that, compared with honest respondents with identical θs, fakers are more likely to choose the most positive option. Comparing the thresholds across each option, the response probabilities for the most positive option tended to be most affected by faking, whereas the least positive option was relatively unaffected by faking. This outcome suggests that respondents who were likely to choose the least positive option when responding honestly would still be predicted to choose the same option when faking.

The discrimination parameters tended to be highest for the coached condition and the lowest for the honest condition. The increase seemed paradoxical; it was hypothesized that faking would reduce discrimination parameters because the process of faking was thought to reduce the role of θ in process of answering items. One explanation for the increase in item discriminations was that the meaning of θ had changed across faking conditions and that in faking conditions, shared variance increased. To explore this hypothesis, a series of nested confirmatory factor analyses were conducted. Factor loadings and error variances remained constant across experimental conditions, but the factors were more highly correlated in the faking conditions. The higher factor intercorrelations could be explained with the introduction of an additional common factor, on which all items load, irrespective of scale. Common variance therefore increases, although this common variance is independent of the common variance attributed to the scale constructs. The IRT model is unable to distinguish different sources of variance shared by all items, so an increase in common variance is unrelated to the content variance. This additional source of shared variance may be similar to the common factor that Schmit and Ryan (1993) identified as an "ideal employee" factor and that Christiansen (1998), using a classical test theory approach, labeled an "increase in true score variance."

Changing Persons Modeling

For the changing persons paradigm, the mean difference between fakers and honest respondents was calculated and then modeled through an equating process (Baker, 1992). Equating eliminates mean differences between two groups, allowing ORFs to be compared across dissimilar groups. After equating, only 13 of the 112 ORF comparisons had significant differences between ORFs across faking and honest conditions. This relatively few number of differences suggests that the θ shift used by fakers was relatively constant across items. For security reasons, item content was not available; it thus was not possible to determine reasons for the 13 differences.

Along with examining differences after equating, it was possible to compare the differences in θ distributions across conditions. The mean θ of the honest group was always lower than that of the coached condition, and it was lower than the ad-lib condition was in comparison with the honest condition This result suggests that coached faking was more extreme than ad-lib faking. The means of the ad-lib faking respondents were higher than the means for the honest groups, except for the nondelinquency scale, in which the honest respondents had a mean of 0.03 compared with the mean of ad-lib fakers, which was fixed at 0.00. The mean θs for the honest group taking the nondelinquency scale were closer to zero (i.e., –0.21 in the coached comparison and 0.03 in the ad-lib comparison) than for the other scales (e.g., for the emotional stability scale, –0.70 for the coached comparison, and –0.13 for the ad-lib comparison). This finding suggests either that the nondelinquency scale was more difficult to fake than the other two scales or that respondents chose to fake less for this scale. Standard deviations for the honest group were all in the range of 0.38 to 0.56 (the faking standard deviation was always fixed at 1.0), suggesting that there was less variation in the honest sample than in the faking samples. Also, the standard deviations were always less for the coached faking comparisons, suggesting that there was more variance in θ scores when respondents were not given instructions on how to fake good.

Future Research and Conclusions

These investigations of faking using IRT-based simulations and analyses illustrate the potential of IRT to answer difficult questions that traditional measurement frameworks and empirical research designs are poorly equipped to answer. One of the benefits of the initial simulation work was the development of a formal model of faking (i.e., the θ shift). This initial model was used with a range of values that analysis of empirical data later demonstrated to be largely unrealistic. The development of the θ-shift model, however, helped frame the problem in a way that suggested the empirical data collection and analyses that would further develop the model. This process of using empirical data to fine-tune a computational model also has been used by Pete, Pattipati, and Kleinman (1993) to develop a model of team decision making.

The next logical step in this research would be to replicate the Zickar et al. (1997) simulation using the information learned from the empirical modeling of the experimental faking data (Zickar & Robie, 1999). This new simulation would include the addition of shared content variance between all items that was unrelated to the criterion variable. Also, the empirical results could be used to develop an appropriate range of faking variances so that the variability of the faking sample could be sufficiently large. The range of faking magnitudes also would be further restricted based on the same analysis.

Modeling personality response data with IRT models resembles computational modeling in that a mathematical formula, along with estimated item and person parameters, is used to represent the response process. As shown in this chapter, this modeling of personality at the item response level can provide a foundation for conducting computer simulation research that can help answer questions that cannot be satisfactorily answered with empirical data.

References

Anderson, C. D., Warner, J. L., & Spector, C. E. (1984). Inflation bias in self-assessment examination: Implications for valid employee selection. *Journal of Applied Psychology, 69,* 574–580.

Baker, F. B. (1992). Equating tests under the graded response model. *Applied Psychological Measurement, 16,* 87–96.

Barrick, M. R., & Mount, M. K. (1991). The big-five personality dimensions and job performance. *Personnel Psychology, 44,* 1–26.

Barrick, M. R., & Mount, M. K. (1996). Effects of impression management and self-deception on the predictive validity of personality constructs. *Journal of Applied Psychology, 81,* 261–272.

Becker, T. E., & Colquitt, A. L. (1992). Potential versus actual faking of a biodata form: An analysis along several dimensions of item type. *Personnel Psychology, 45,* 389–406.

Christiansen, N. D. (1998, April). *Sensitive or senseless? Using social desirability measures to identify distortion.* Paper presented at the meeting of the Society for Industrial and Organizational Psychology, Dallas.

Christiansen, N. D., Goffin, R. D., Johnston, N. G., & Rothstein, M. G. (1994). Correcting the 16PF for faking: Effects on criterion-related validity and individual hiring decisions. *Personnel Psychology, 47,* 847–860.

Douglas, E. F., McDaniel, M. A., & Snell, A. F. (1996, August). *The validity of non-cognitive measures decays when applicants fake.* Paper presented at the meeting of the Academy of Management, Nashville, TN.

Drasgow, F., & Parsons, C. K. (1983). Application of unidimensional item response theory models to multidimensional data. *Applied Psychological Measurement, 7,* 189–199.

Gilles, J., Rogers, R., & Dickes, S. (1990). The detection of faking bad response styles on the MMPI. *Canadian Journal of Behavioural Science, 22,* 408–416.

Gullicksen, H. (1950). *Theory of mental tests.* New York: Wiley.

Hambleton, R. K., & Swaminathan, H. (1985). *Item response theory: Principles and applications.* Boston: Kluwer-Nijhoff.

Hogan, R., & Hogan, J. (1992). *Hogan personality inventory manual.* Tulsa, OK: Hogan Assessment Systems.

Hough, L. M., Eaton, N. K., Dunnette, M. D., Kamp, J. D., & McCloy, R. A. (1990). Criterion-related validities of personality constructs and the effects of response distortion on those validities. *Journal of Applied Psychology, 75,* 581–595.

Hough, L. M., & Schneider, R. J. (1996). Personality traits, taxonomies, and applications in organizations. In K. R. Murphy (Ed.), *Individual differences and behavior in organizations* (pp. 33–88). San Francisco: Jossey-Bass.

Kroger, R. O., & Turnbull, W. (1975). Invalidity of validity scales: The case of the MMPI. *Journal of Consulting and Clinical Psychology, 43,* 48–55.

Levine, M. V. (1984). *An introduction to multilinear formula score theory* (Measurement Series 84–4). Champaign: University of Illinois, Department of Educational Psychology.

Lord, F. M., & Novick, M. (1968). *Statistical theories of mental test scores.* Reading, MA: Addison-Wesley.

Maydeu-Olivares, A., Drasgow, F., & Mead, A. D. (1994). Distinguishing among parametric item response models for polychotomous ordered data. *Applied Psychological Measurement, 18,* 245–256.

Meehl, P. E., & Hathaway, S. R. (1946). The K factor as a suppressor variable in the MMPI. *Journal of Applied Psychology, 30,* 525–561.

Ones, D. S., Viswesvaran, C., & Reiss, A. D. (1996). Role of social desirability in personality testing for personnel selection: The red herring. *Journal of Applied Psychology, 81,* 660–679.

Pete, A., Pattipati, K. R., & Kleinman, D. L. (1993). Distributed detection in teams with partial information: A normative-descriptive model. *EEE Transactions on Systems, Man & Cybernetics, 23,* 1626–1648.

Reckase, M. D. (1997). The past and future of multidimensional item response theory. *Applied Psychological Measurement, 21,* 25–36.

Samejima, F. (1969). Estimation of latent ability using a response pattern of graded scores. *Psychometric* Monograph No. 17.

Schmit, M. J., & Ryan, A. M. (1993). The Big Five in personnel selection: Factor structure in applicant and nonapplicant populations. *Journal of Applied Psychology, 78,* 966–974.

Tett, R., Jackson, D., & Rothstein, M. (1991). Personality measures as predictors of job performance: A meta-analytic review. *Personnel Psychology, 44,* 703–742.

White, L. A., Nord, R. D., Mael, F. A., & Young, M. C. (1993). The assessment of background and life experiences (ABLE). In T. Trent & J. H. Laurence (Eds.), *Adaptability screening for the armed forces* (pp. 101–162). Washington, DC: Office of the Assistant Secretary of Defense.

Young, M. C., White, L. A., & Oppler, S. H. (1991 October). *Coaching effects on the assessment of background and life experiences (ABLE).* Paper presented at the meeting of the Military Testing Association, San Antonio, TX.

Zickar, M. J. (1997). Computer simulation of faking on a personality test. In G. Alliger (Chair), *Faking matters.* Symposium at the annual meeting of the Society of Industrial-Organizational Psychology, St. Louis.

Zickar, M. J., & Drasgow, F. (1996). Detecting faking on a personality instrument using appropriateness measurement. *Applied Psychological Measurement, 20,* 71–87.

Zickar, M. J., & Robie, C. (1999). Modeling faking good on personality items: An item-level analysis. *Journal of Applied Psychology, 84,* 551–563.

Zickar, M. J., Rosse, J., Levin, R., & Hulin, C. L. (1997). *Modeling the effects of faking on a personality test.* Unpublished manuscript.

COMMENT:

Computational Models of Personality and Faking

Richard P. DeShon

The effects of social desirability and faking on personality measurement are, at best, ambiguous. It appears that people can fake responses on personality measures when instructed to do so, but the extent of actual faking in real settings is unclear. Presumably, faking and socially desirable response patterns undermine the psychometric properties of personality measures, but the magnitude of the effects is not well understood. Zickar's research on modeling the effects of faking using item response theory (IRT) provides answers to many of these problems.

To evaluate the contribution of Zickar's modeling of the faking process to the area of personality assessment, it is useful to clearly specify criteria that are relevant to the evaluation of computational models. Computational modeling has at least three advantages over traditional methods of scientific inquiry.

First, computational models can provide answers to research questions that are not easily addressed through traditional research methods. For example, once a computational model of a system is developed, it is possible to examine the behavior of the system under a huge variety of parameters. Many of the critical questions relating to the effects of social desirability and faking on personality measurement are not easily answered through empirical research. As Zickar's chapter highlighted, it is not easy to precisely manipulate validity in empirical research. Furthermore, in an actual setting it is difficult to identify which people are responding honestly and which are responding inaccurately. However, Zickar's results speak to what can happen under various parameters of the model and only indirectly address what actually happens in real-world selection contexts. The importance of this process should not be underestimated, but the generalizability of the results must be explored through more traditional research techniques. When developing computational models of behavioral phenomena, it is critical that the models be grounded in actual behavior. A thorough development of a computational model of any system requires the recognition that the relationship between computational modeling and empirical research is dynamic and cyclical.

Second, computational modeling often makes mathematically intractable problems accessible and, as a result, may lead to interesting insights into the behavior of the system. Zickar's IRT analysis of simulated data clearly demonstrated some interesting results. Specifically, the validity of personality measures does not appear to be greatly influenced by the presence of faking, even under fairly extreme parameterizations. However, the relative rank ordering of the top-scoring individuals greatly favored the fakers. As such, meta-analyses of validity coefficients would likely result in the conclusion that faking has no effect, even though fakers would be disproportionally selected in a top-down selection model. In retrospect, this result *could* have been deduced logically, but the fact is that the question did not arise until a computational model of faking behavior was implemented.

Third, and perhaps most important, modeling a system requires that the system be carefully analyzed and that assumptions concerning system behavior be stated explicitly. Unfortunately, this important aspect of computational modeling is not highlighted in Zickar's approach to assessing faking on personality measures. One of the major advantages of computational models is that they encourage the modeler to make explicit a number of otherwise implicit assumptions. IRT, however, involves a number of frequently unstated assumptions, and the statistical model does not encourage the explication of assumptions. In fact, the term *item response theory* is a bit of a misnomer. It is not a theory of how people generate responses to items, but rather a general model for analyzing the results of the item generation process (Goldstein & Wood, 1989). Perhaps the limited attention given to the assumptions of this particular computation model reflects the typical approach to measurement in IRT.

What are some of Zickar's implicit assumptions that guide the modeling of faking on personality measures? The language he uses suggests that he is modeling personality as a stable, individual-difference *trait,* which appears to be most consistent with the "Big Five" view of personality. He never explicitly defines the core construct of personality, however. This omission is unfortunate because numerous models of personality exist and the process of faking may differ substantially across the various theories. In fact, many personality psychologists strongly disagree with the Big Five characterization of personality (e.g., Block, 1995; Mischel & Shoda, 1995). The fact that this treatment requires no conceptual model of personality is analogous to modeling responses on a knowledge test without having a model of cognition that specifies how knowledge is encoded, stored, and retrieved.

Similarly, when constructing computational models, it is critical that variables in the model be defined as explicitly as possible. Unfortunately, many variables and processes used in Zickar's presentation are undefined. For instance, Zickar repeatedly refers to the concepts of "motivation to fake" and "faking ability." These are key constructs in any model of response generation on self-report measures of personality, but they receive virtually no conceptual development or explication. The concepts are operationalized in the simulations, but without conceptual definitions it is quite difficult to evaluate the appropriateness of the operationalizations. So, for instance, in the Zickar, Rosse, Levin, and Hulin (1997) simulations, motivation to fake was manipulated by adding points to the latent trait on items that were "fakeable." This operationalization assumes that the motivation to fake is equivalent across respondents and the entire range of personality. Perhaps more important, without clear construct definitions it is difficult to see why this manipulation would not be consistent also with individual differences in the *ability* to fake responses. The Zickar (1997) simulations extended the operationalizations of motivation to fake by incorporating individual differences in that motivation (i.e., the standard deviation of the faking bonus points) and by allowing the amount of faking to be correlated with the latent trait. These are certainly important extensions of the simulations, but the distinction between the motivation and the ability to fake remains unclear.

In contrast to these sources of ambiguity, an important aspect of Zickar's treatment of faking is the development and clear specification of the faking process. Zickar distinguishes between the changing persons model and the changing items model of faking. Faking in the changing items model occurs through a difference in item parameters between simulated fakers and nonfakers. Faking in the changing persons model occurs by adding points to the person's latent "true score" and assumes that "the faking individual's θ is temporarily and consciously changed to improve personality test scores" (p. 104)

The clarity of presentation on the various models of the faking process allows one to evaluate the conceptual underpinnings of the model and to either agree or disagree with the model's assumptions. For instance, there is some ambiguity with respect to the appropriateness of modeling the faking process as a change in item parameters or as a temporary change (or state) in the person's latent trait. Although these models of faking may be statistically equivalent, it seems somewhat contradictory to view personality as a stable individual-difference trait and to then have a latent trait that changes as a function of motivation to fake. Only the item-faking process is justifiable from a conceptual perspective.

Conclusions

Zickar's modeling of faking on self-report measures of personality addresses an important question and provides convincing results on the effects of faking. Much of the research presented in his chapter could not have been carried out using traditional methods, and the attempt to model the process led to interesting insights into the effects of faking. My only serious criticism concerning this modeling work is one of omission. Zickar is no more guilty of failing to clearly state the assumptions underlying his research on personality than virtually all current research on personality assessment. However, he approached this topic through computational modeling and missed an opportunity to clearly highlight many unstated assumptions common in this research area. Similarly, Zickar could have better integrated the existing literature on computational models of personality (e.g., Mischel & Shoda, 1995) and explored the overlap of these distinct approaches.

Although Zickar's IRT modeling of faking on personality measures is quite useful and has led to important insights, much theoretical, empirical, and computation work is still required to understand the process. From a practical perspective, the Big Five trait approach to personality is useful and important. The approach taken in the development of the Big Five traits was primarily empirical, however, and it is surprisingly devoid of theory that could be used to guide empirical and computational research. The Big Five model does not specify how personality develops, why it differs from person to person, and how it might change over time. It simply assumes that there are stable individual differences in personality that relate to important outcomes. Perhaps more important, this approach to personality assessment does not encourage a careful analysis of situations and situational moderators of behavior. Fortunately, other theories of personality better specify the theoretical aspects of the construct and are more conducive to modeling and empirical research. I am particularly fond of Mischel and Shoda's (1995) approach, and a rudimentary computational model of their theory of personality already exists.

From a computational modeling perspective, more work is needed on the precise implementation of the constructs most relevant to faking on self-report measures of personality. Specifically, personality needs to be implemented in a manner consistent with a comprehensive theory of personality. It may turn out that the latent trait approach used in IRT is entirely appropriate, or a more complex model of personality may be required. Presumably, responses to the questions on self-report measures of personality are generated through the processing of information in the cognitive system. If so, the large knowledge base that has been developed in the area of computational modeling of cognitive processing (e.g., connectionist architectures and production systems) could be used to model the response generation process in personality. In addition, the constructs of ability to fake and motivation to fake need to be clearly articulated and operationalized in ways that demonstrate their unique contribution to observed scores on these measures. Finally, more empirical work is needed to provide reasonable parameters for any computational model of the faking process that might be developed.

References

Block, J. (1995). A contrarian view of the five-factor approach to personality description. *Psychological Bulletin, 117,* 187–215.

Goldstein, H., & Wood, R. (1989). Five decades of item response modeling. *British Journal of Mathematical and Statistical Psychology, 42,* 139–167.

Mischel, W., & Shoda, Y. (1995). A cognitive–affective systems theory of personality: Reconceptualizing situations, dispositions, dynamics, and invariance in personality structure. *Psychological Review, 102,* 246–268.

Zickar, M. J. (1997). Computer simulation of faking on a personality test. In G. Alliger (Chair), *Faking matters.* Symposium at the annual meeting of the Society of Industrial–Organizational Psychology, St. Louis.

Zickar, M. J., Rosse, J., Levin, R., & Hulin, C. L. (1997). *Modeling the effects of faking on a personality test.* Unpublished manuscript.

CHAPTER 6

Simulating Effects of Pay-for-Performance Systems on Pay–Performance Relationships

Donald P. Schwab
Craig A. Olson

The simulation described here was motivated by our interest in employee work outcomes as a function of human resources (HR) system variables. HR variables form a part of the "context" for employees. Increasingly, those who study HR systems are calling for theory and, especially, research that brings context to the study of organizational behavior (OB) and HR (Cappelli & Sherer, 1991; Jackson & Schuler, 1995; Mowday & Sutton, 1993). Management and organizational systems, labor and product markets, and legal requirements are examples of interesting and potentially important contexts for such research.

Research elaborating on contextual variables is particularly important to advancing organizational practice. For example, how should managers develop and implement HR systems (e.g., compensation systems) to obtain desired employee responses? More broadly, how should various HR systems, such as compensation, promotion, and staffing, be combined to achieve organizationally desirable outcomes? An informative body of empirical research is developing that addresses this sort of question using macro (firm-level) outcome measures (see, e.g., MacDuffie, 1995).

Although widely recognized as important, research that combines individual and organizational levels of analysis has been problematic (Rousseau, 1985). Problems include the identification of sampling frames and difficulties in obtaining responses from both organizations and employees. Much research has obtained responses only from employees. Those studies have used employee perceptions to measure key organizational variables, a practice that has been criticized for obvious reasons (Cappelli & Sherer, 1991; Mowday & Sutton, 1993).

This chapter describes one effort to address the challenges of research designed to cross individual and organizational levels. The substantive problem focused on relationships between the financial rewards obtained by employees and their performance. We examined those relationships as a function of variation in organizational compensation systems and as a function of other HR management characteristics hypothesized to affect the relationships (e.g., the quality of performance measurement).

The study was conducted using a computer simulation. "Employees" were created and grouped into labor forces that were "employed" by organizations with different HR system characteristics. The labor forces were followed over time to observe how relationships between pay and performance varied across the organizational settings.

This chapter begins with a summary of the study, which is brief and omits detail important for a thorough understanding; the complete study is reported in Schwab and Olson (1990). We include a brief rationale for the theoretical framework, describe the simulation, and identify challenges we confronted in performing it.

The second portion of the chapter describes some of our experiences with this simulation. One reason simulations may be an infrequent form of research is that researchers experience difficulty in conducting them. Here we emphasize the challenges of identifying and rationalizing the variables and parameter values that constitute the simulation framework, not the difficulty in setting up the computer programs to run simulations. We also discuss problems encountered in communicating simulation results.

The last section of the chapter describes research that might be performed using a simulation like ours. We offer suggestions for extending our work and for addressing other substantive issues.

The Study

Overview

The simulation was designed to study how well performance-based pay programs and related HR management systems link individual employee pay to their performance. This focus was stimulated by our interest in compensation, especially how compensation systems influence employees. We picked performance-based pay systems among managerial and professional employees ranging from entry level to upper middle management.

To carry out the simulation, we created hypothetical managerial and professional labor forces within sets of organizations. Each set of organizations differed in pay programs and other characteristics, which are described in the sections that follow. Labor forces within organizations were then followed for 10 time periods to observe how pay systems and other differences built into the organizational sets influenced pay–performance relationships among the employees.

Dependent Variables

Two dependent variables were developed to capture pay–performance relationships among labor forces in each organizational set. Both involved relationships (expressed as correlation coefficients) between true (reliably measured) performance and pay obtained within a labor force. The unit of analysis was thus the labor force of an organization within each set.

One cross-sectional dependent variable was the correlation of employee performance in a particular period and the pay increment associated with performance in that period. This is analogous to reports from field case studies (Auster & Drazin, 1987; Medoff & Abraham, 1980, 1981) of pay increase–performance relationships, except that our relationship was based on true rather than observed (unreliable) performance measurement, for reasons to be explained shortly.

The second dependent variable (longitudinal) was the correlation of true accumulated performance with accumulated pay increases in any given time period. For example, values for this variable in the third time period represented the correlation of employees' performance summed over three periods, with their pay increments summed over the same three time periods. This longitudinal measure is a better indication of how well pay is linked to performance over an employee's tenure with an organization. We know of no field research that has investigated longitudinal relationships between pay and performance histories, probably because such data generally are not readily available.

Independent Variables

Variation in the two dependent variables was studied as a function of differences in several characteristics hypothesized to influence pay–performance relationships. Of course, differences in pay systems were of primary interest. Although four specific levels of this variable were created, only the two contrasting classes of merit and bonus systems are summarized here. Merit systems were operationalized by building periodic pay increases into base pay for subsequent periods. For example, a merit pay increase of 7% in one time period is added to base pay in all future periods in which the employee is with the organization. In each subsequent period, merit increases are thus typically built on top of a higher base pay. Although currently out of favor, merit systems remain the dominant form of pay system for middle-level managers and professionals (Milkovich & Newman, 1996).

Merit systems were contrasted with bonus systems; the latter provide pay increments that do not become a part of base pay in the subsequent time period. Advocates argue that bonus systems are more motivational because they link pay more closely to performance (Lawler, 1971, 1981).

The likely presence of error in performance measures is a major criticism of all individually based pay-for-performance systems (Milkovich & Newman, 1996). A voluminous literature documents such errors (see Murphy & Cleveland, 1991). To capture the implications of errors in performance measures, we created two levels, representing high and low performance measurement error.

Although not of central interest, two rules representing promotion also were created. Promotions are typically associated with pay increases and thus were included because of the possibility for interaction with pay-for-performance rules. To maximize differences, one treatment promoted employees randomly from lower to higher job levels as job vacancies were created by turnover. The other treatment promoted individuals based solely on their observed performance.

An additional variable became an issue because the study followed employees through 10 time periods. Specifically, we had to make assumptions about the stability of true performance over time; little empirical evidence was available to guide us. We thought it reasonable to suppose that people systematically differ in characteristic levels of performance but that they nevertheless experience some random variation around this characteristic level from period to period. Consequently, we created two levels that varied the size of the random variation around baseline performance levels.

Method

Simulations of the type constructed here are analogous to experiments (Whicker & Sigelman, 1991). The independent variables—pay system (two merit and two bonus), measurement error (high and low), promotion rules (random and performance based), and performance stability (high and low)—were crossed and balanced in a between-subjects factorial design to create organizational sets. Time periods represent a within-subject factor.

The sample consisted of 640 identical (subject to several uncorrelated errors) managerial and professional labor forces that were created using Monte Carlo simulation procedures. These labor forces were then randomly assigned to the experimental conditions in the first time period. Relationships among pay, observed performance, job level, and job and organizational tenure in the first time period were established consistent with relationships obtained in three field studies of managerial and professional labor forces (Auster & Drazin, 1987; Gerhart & Milkovich, 1989; Kahn & Sherer, 1988). In the simulation, a measure of true performance for each employee was created from observed performance, subject to the two measurement-error levels

In subsequent time periods, changes in job level, both performance levels, and pay were made according to rules associated with each level of the manipulated independent variables within each experimental treatment level. First, true performance was established as a function of a constant value and one of the two levels of a random component representing performance stability. Second, promotions and corresponding promotion pay increases were carried out as a function of vacancies created by turnover and one of the two promotion rules. Turnover was held constant at 10% per period. The size of each organization's managerial and professional labor force also was held constant; reductions in labor force brought about by turnover in one time period were replaced with external hires in the next. Observed performance was established from true performance using one of the two measurement error levels. Finally, observed performance was used to generate appropriate merit or bonus pay increases.

Results

Among the many findings, only two that were unanticipated are summarized here. These two also were robust across different methods of measuring them and across different time periods. They also serve to illustrate both the promise and the problems of simulation as a methodology for acquiring knowledge about organizations.

Measurement Error Consequences

One interesting finding involved the consequences of measurement error. Effects of unreliability on zero-order relationships are well known (e.g., Schwab, 1999). Unreliability in either an independent or dependent variable attenuates the correlation between the variables relative to the true-score relationship. We thus expected that the more reliable measurement of performance condition would result in a substantially higher relationship between pay and true performance, other things being equal.

This turned out not to be the case. Measurement reliability had a small relative effect on relationships between true performance and pay increases, even at the outset. In the first time period, high and low levels of measurement error were .401 and .451, respectively. By the end of 10 periods, the effect of measurement error was almost completely vitiated among the organizations' labor forces (a high level of .268 and a low level of .270).

This unexpected result occurred for two reasons. First, as noted above, relationships between pay and performance were specified initially based on previous field research, which reported only modest relationships between observed (and hence true) performance and pay. Thus, variation in measurement error had a small effect in part because of the modest relationship between pay and performance already present. Second, the relationship between pay and true performance over time was further attenuated by the modest relationship between pay and performance of new entrants to each organization. The assimilation of the new entrants further reduced the effect of measurement error on pay–performance relationships in subsequent time periods.

This finding illustrates that an outcome which is clear in the abstract (e.g., the consequence of measurement error for true-score relationships) is not necessarily unambiguous when embedded in a dynamic system. Organizational prescriptions based on isolated relationships may be of limited value in predicting outcomes in complex ongoing systems.

A caveat also is appropriate. Pay–performance relationships were not varied at the outset of the simulation, nor were they varied among new entrants brought in during the course of the simulation. As a consequence, we cannot speak to the relative role of measurement error in situations where initial pay–performance relationships differ from those studied.

Merit Versus Bonus Systems

The literature suggests that bonus systems should link pay with performance better than merit systems for two reasons (see Lawler, 1981; Schuster & Zingheim, 1992). First, managerial and professional pay systems typically provide pay increases as a percentage of base pay. Employees with equal performance levels obtain pay raises of an equal percentage. All employees in a job category receive the same base pay in bonus systems; thus, employees observed to have equal performance obtain equal pay increases. Alternatively, because merit systems result in unequal base pay levels as a function of earlier merit increases, equal performance in any pay period can lead to unequal dollar pay increases. In the cross-section then, it is argued that bonus systems will more closely tie current pay increments to current performance levels.

Second, merit systems typically have pay ranges established around pay rates for jobs. This administrative procedure keeps pay rates for jobs within an acceptable pay hierarchy for rates across jobs. However, the pay ceilings on those ranges should eventually constrain pay increases for employees who provide meritorious performance in time period after time period.

To our surprise, we found that merit systems performed as well as the bonus systems in the cross-section, and they did better longitudinally. Illustrative findings are summarized in Table 6.1, which shows that both systems performed about the

TABLE 6.1

Median pay–performance correlation coefficients among current employees in the 1st, 6th, and 10th time periods

DEPENDENT VARIABLE AND TIME PERIOD	MERIT	BONUS
1st	.426	.426
6th		
Cross-sectional	.428	.410
Longitudinal (time periods 1–6)	.518	.382
10th		
Cross-sectional	.436	.432
Longitudinal (time periods 1–10)	.558	.394

Note: These are median correlation coefficients formed from the averages obtained by the two merit pay systems and the averages obtained by the two bonus pay increase systems.

same when compared within a time period; compared longitudinally, however, merit pay was superior.

The explanation for these seemingly anomalous findings resides largely in the contrasting consequences of measurement error in observed performance versus the stability of true performance over time. Measurement error implies that performance will be imperfectly rewarded with pay in each time period. Over time, however, the average observed performance tends to converge on the true underlying performance level. Merit systems that build pay increments into base pay capitalize on any performance stability, whereas bonus systems, because they have no longitudinal "memory," do not.

Consequences of pay range ceilings in merit systems, if any, depend on a number of other characteristics of the system and labor force. Those characteristics include (a) the width of pay ranges and the size of merit increases, (b) error in performance measurement and the longitudinal stability of true performance, (c) how frequently the organization's pay level is increased and by how much, (d) promotion rates and the rules for assigning pay rates given a promotion, and (e) turnover. The merit systems designed in our study resulted in relatively little range restriction, although, of course, alternative systems could be created that would provide more consequential constraints.

On Simulating Organizational Environments

Ideally, the description above provides a sense of how the simulation was conducted and something about the more interesting results obtained. This section explains why we used a simulation to investigate this topic and describes challenges we confronted in its conduct and presentation.

Why Simulation?

The method of the study did not spring full-blown from our knowledge of, interest in, or experience with simulation. Rather, the issues investigated and the theoretical framework employed in the study were generally motivated by our substantive interests and knowledge. Our belief that organizational reward systems need investigation using organizations as the unit of analysis was stimulated by the reasons articulated at the outset of this chapter. Interest in relationships between performance and monetary rewards among employees reflect long-time academic interests.

Familiar empirical methods seemed unattractive for the topic as defined at this general level. Experimentation would have required more organizational cooperation than we could even imagine. A survey of organizational practices was unappealing because of measurement problems and lack of control.

Simulation was an attractive option because it liberated us from many of the problems associated with conducting empirical research in organizations. In particular, we did not have to worry about obtaining participation from organizations or their employees. We did not have to worry about data availability, measurement or manipulation development, or response rates and missing data. The choice also was fortuitous because it allowed us to investigate consequences of measurement error on pay–performance relationships, an issue that could not be investigated with field or experimental methods.

Simulation Challenges

Nevertheless, simulations present problems of their own. Some of these we anticipated before conducting the study, and some we learned while doing it. The major challenge did not involve procedures for creating the simulation program. Rather, our major problem turned out to be specifying the conceptual model to be simulated. We spent many hours reading and reviewing literature and arguing about how HR systems actually operate.

Progress was made when we began to work outward from a decision to contrast employee outcomes of merit with bonus systems. This decision was influential in how the rest of the simulation model was constructed: It led us to study middle-level managers and professionals, largely because they experience both types of pay systems. Characteristics of merit pay and bonus systems in these types of internal labor markets are well known, as are characteristics of performance measurement systems (Auster & Drazin, 1987; Gerhart & Milkovich, 1989; Kahn & Sherer, 1988; Medoff & Abraham, 1980, 1981).

This choice also was fortuitous because substantial descriptive information is available on other HR rules governing these sorts of employees in large, bureaucratically administered organizations. Such organizations are often arranged according to internal labor markets, where new members enter from the external market at the bottom of the hierarchy; openings at higher levels are filled through internal promotion when possible (Althauser & Kalleberg, 1981; Osterman, 1994). This sort of information helped us model promotion rules and procedures to account for turnover.

We experienced more difficulty where institutional knowledge was lacking. As noted, we did not find much information directly on the stability of employee performance over time. In response, we simply established two different levels to study. The results thus suggest an impact of variation in performance stability on pay–performance relationships. They do not, however, tell us what might be expected in field studies of actual organizations.

We also found little information on relationships between pay and probable future performance at the time of hire. Consequently, some of our most difficult modeling problems involved establishing relationships between pay and performance in the first time period of the simulation and for employees that entered organizations from the external labor market in subsequent time periods.

Lacking a better alternative, we modeled initial pay–performance and human capital relationships consistent with results obtained from earlier cross-sectional research as noted. This had the advantage of linking our simulation to evidence from the field. Our simulation results are arguably tenable if the HR practices we studied were implemented in organizations with "typical" pay–performance and human capital relationships. They may be less tenable in other situations, such as in organizational start-ups. Furthermore, results from the study made it clear that the relationships initially specified were important to observed pay–performance relationships, even at the end of the simulation. Thus, in retrospect, it would have been desirable to vary initial employment conditions in order to study their consequences on our dependent variables.

In sum, we found it advantageous in our modeling efforts to draw from knowledge already generated about organizations. In this sense, simulations and traditional empirical research on organizations are complementary. We encountered greater difficulty when empirical evidence was difficult to obtain; the problems we experienced suggested empirical research topics that could be useful. In addition, the outcomes of simulation research can have value in identifying needed empirical research; for example, we learned that stability of performance through time is clearly important to how some HR systems operate.

Presentation Problems

A problem we did not anticipate involved how to communicate the study and its results. We became aware of this difficulty when we presented initial versions of the simulation at conferences sponsored by the National Bureau of Economic Research, first at Cambridge, Massachusetts, in 1988 and then again at Cornell University in 1989.

The methodology, not the analysis or results, proved most difficult to describe in an understandable manner. Conference participants had difficulty grasping how we "created" labor forces and how we "subjected" the labor forces to variation in HR practices. We felt that the believability of our results suffered accordingly.

We were only partly successful in overcoming this problem in our published summary of the study. Papers that cite it often report only that we performed a study on pay systems. We suspect our study has not been explained more thoroughly because reviewers have difficulty understanding it. Several papers that have tried to summarize our findings have done so incorrectly.

Our novice status as simulators may have contributed to this problem; nevertheless, we raise the issue for others who may consider performing simulations. No matter how skillfully performed, a simulation will have little impact if readers are unable to understand it. At least in our experience, communicating simulations clearly presents a challenge.

With the wisdom of hindsight, we believe that the more one can make the description of a simulation analogous to a description of conventional empirical research, the better the readers will understand it. Readers of organizational simulation research are more likely to be conventional empiricists for the foreseeable future. We revised our written summary to parallel the description of a conventional experiment, complete with the terminology of experimentation.

Suggestions for Simulation Research

Simulations of organizational processes are widely applicable, as suggested by other chapters in this volume; many issues can usefully be addressed by the methodology. Several research suggestions in this section are based on a simulation model that resembles ours. The suggestions are designed in part to show the breadth of issues to which simulations may bring useful insights.

Extensions

Earlier we noted difficulty in deciding how to model initial pay–performance and human capital relationships. These problems occurred in modeling organizational employees in the first time period of the simulation and for new entrants to organizations during the simulation.

It would be particularly interesting to study the consequences of variation in pay increase practices for existing employees (as we did) and variation in pay practices for new entrants. Pay policies for these two groups of employees often are not coordinated. As an extreme example, faculty merit raise decisions at the University of Wisconsin are determined at the legislative level. State macroeconomic and political conditions influence the size of merit raises. Alternatively, departments within the university have substantial discretion in determining pay levels for new entrants. Consequently, pay structures can take widely different forms, depending on the relative rates at which the two sources of pay level change. Research that models the consequences of changes in both pay systems could render valuable recommendations for administrative practices.

Our simulation investigated the implications of random error in the measurement of performance. Evidence suggests that random error is pervasive in performance measurement (Borman, 1978) and that simulation is particularly suitable for studying it. However, systematic errors also are prevalent in performance measurement (for a review, see Murphy & Cleveland, 1991). With minor modifications, our simulation could be used to model systematic error.

Other Research Issues

Examples just described could use the same dependent variables we used, namely, relationships between pay and performance. The general organizational model developed, however, could be used to study other dependent variables and, hence, issues. The following two examples illustrate possibilities and address a limitation of our study.

In our simulation, employee performance was modeled to increase deterministically, as a function of increasing experience, and randomly, as a function of error. Turnover was modeled to decrease deterministically, as a function of increasing time in the organization, and randomly, as a function of error. The formulations are a limitation of the model, because they violate our expectation that behavior is also a function of motivation. A useful extension of our model also would model those behaviors as a function of the consequences of differing pay–performance relationships. For example, the model could be modified so that performance also was made a function of motivation, as hypothesized in expectancy (Vroom, 1964) or equity (Adams, 1963) theory.

A second extension illustrates how our model could be used to address a very different issue. Specifically, a large body of empirical research exists on gender and race differentials in pay (e.g., Blau & Kahn, 1992). Most of this research has been designed to investigate discrimination in pay setting. Methodologically, the studies typically develop some sort of earnings equation whereby pay is regressed on gender, race, human capital, and other types of control variables. Various techniques have been developed to ascertain the degree of discrimination, if any (Oaxaca, 1973). This research is controversial: Researchers disagree about the amount of specification error, the implications of measurement error, and the like. In short, there is disagreement over whether the statistical models actually capture gender or race discrimination that may be present.

A simulation model such as ours could address this issue and turn it around. Discrimination in various forms could be embedded in the pay relationships constructed as a part of the simulation. Alternative statistical methods for identifying discrimination could then be evaluated by seeing how accurately they identify the discrimination already known to be present.

In summary, organizational simulation models such as ours may be of value for a variety of research issues. The methodological framework allows researchers to modify characteristics at an organizational level—the "context" described by recent calls for innovative HR and OB research. Although we restricted the degree to which employee behavior was endogenous, such restriction is not required. Employee behavior can be made endogenous using any behavior models a researcher chooses. Furthermore, the method is suitable for studying a variety of employee outcomes, including performance, attendance, and retention.

References

Adams, J. S. (1963). Wage inequities, productivity, and work quality. *Industrial Relations, 3,* 9–16.

Althauser, R. P., & Kalleberg, A. L. (1981). Firms, occupations and the structure of labor markets. In I. Berg (Ed.), *Sociological perspectives on labor markets* (pp. 119–149). New York: Academic Press.

Auster, E. R., & Drazin, R. (1987). *The persistence of sex inequality at higher levels in the hierarchy: An Intraorganizational perspective.* Unpublished manuscript, Columbia University.

Blau, F., & Kahn, L. (1992). Race and gender pay differentials. In D. Lewin, O. Mitchell, & P. D. Sherer (Eds.), *Research frontiers in industrial relations and human resources* (pp. 381–416). Madison, WI: IRRA.

Borman, W. C. (1978). Exploring upper limits of reliability and validity in job performance ratings. *Journal of Applied Psychology, 63*(2), 135–144.

Cappelli, P., & Sherer, P. D. (1991). The missing role of context in OB: The need for a meso-level approach. *Research in Organizational Behavior, 13,* 55–110.

Gerhart, B. A., & Milkovich, G. T. (1989). Salaries, salary growth, and promotions of men and women in a large private firm. In R. T. Michael & H. I. Hartmann (Eds.), *Pay equity: Empirical inquiries* (pp. 23–43). Washington, DC: National Academy Press.

Jackson, S. E., & Schuler, R. S. (1995). Understanding human resource management in the context of organizations and their environments. *Annual Review of Psychology, 46,* 237–264.

Kahn, L., & Sherer, P. (1988, August). *How does merit pay induce higher performance? A test of expectancy and efficiency wage theories.* Paper delivered at the National Academy Meetings, Anaheim, CA.

Lawler, E. E. (1971). *Pay and organizational effectiveness.* New York: McGraw-Hill.

Lawler, E. E. (1981). *Pay and organization development.* Reading, MA: Addison-Wesley.

MacDuffie, J. P. (1995). Human resource bundles and manufacturing performance: Organizational logic and flexible production systems in the world auto industry. *Industrial and Labor Relations Review, 48,* 197–221.

Medoff, J. L., & Abraham, K. G. (1980). Experience, performance, and earnings. *Quarterly Journal of Economics, 95*(4), 703–736.

Medoff, J. L., & Abraham, K. G. (1981). Are those paid more really more productive? The case of experience. *Journal of Human Resources, 16*(2), 186–216.

Milkovich, G. M., & Newman, J. M. (1996). *Compensation* (5th ed.). Chicago: Irwin.

Mowday, R. T., & Sutton, R. I. (1993). Organizational behavior: Linking individuals and groups to organizational contexts. *Annual Review of Psychology, 44,* 195–229.

Murphy, K. R., & Cleveland, J. N. (1991). *Performance appraisal: An organizational perspective.* Boston: Allyn & Bacon.

Oaxaca, R. (1973). Male–female wage differentials in urban labor markets. *International Economic Review, 14,* 693–709.

Osterman, P. S. (1994). Internal labor markets: Theory and change. In C. Kerr & P. D. Saudohar (Eds.), *Labor economics and industrial relations: Markets and institutions* (pp. 303–339). Cambridge, MA: Harvard University Press.

Rousseau, D. M. (1985). Issues of level in organizational research: Multi-level and cross-level perspectives. *Research in Organizational Behavior, 7,* 1–37.

Schuster, R., & Zingheim, P. K. (1992). *The new pay: Linking employee strategy and organization performance.* New York: Lexington Books.

Schwab, D. P. (1999). *Research methods for organizational studies.* Hillsdale, NJ: Erlbaum.

Schwab, D. P., & Olson, C. O. (1990). Merit pay practices: Implications for pay–performance relationships. *Industrial and Labor Relations Review, 43,* 237–255.

Vroom, V. H. (1964). *Work and motivation.* New York: Wiley

Whicker, M. L., & Sigelman, L. (1991). Computer simulation applications: An introduction. *Applied Social Research Methods Series* (Vol. 25, pp. 48–52). Newbury Park, CA: Sage.

COMMENT:

Consequences of Organizational Reward Systems

John R. Hollenbeck

Schwab and Olson (Chapter 6) present an analysis of the implications of two different pay policies in terms of their long-term effects on the relationship between pay and performance. Specifically, they examine the long-term implications of adopting merit systems versus bonus systems. Although I have conducted several Monte Carlo studies, I have been involved in only one study that I would call a simulation study (i.e., in which a dynamic system is modeled over time). Although the peer review process has never been overly kind to me, I thought that trying to publish this simulation study was a particularly frustrating experience. Since then, as an editorial board member and editor of *Personnel Psychology*, I have witnessed other authors of simulation studies go through the peer review process at many of the traditional applied psychology outlets. Based on this experience, I have come to the conclusion that it is difficult to get traditional empirical researchers to accept simulation studies.

In fact, I would go as far as to say that this lack of peer acceptance stands as the single biggest impediment to the development of simulation methodology in the applied behavioral and social sciences. When Schwab and Olson discuss the liberating aspects of simulation research (e.g., eliminating problems associated with gaining organizational access and control over manipulations, randomly assigning people to conditions, dealing with human subjects committees, missing data, and traveling to research sites), it sounds so good that it is hard to believe more researchers are not conducting more simulation studies. The reality, however, is that most simulation research is difficult to conduct and meets with a great deal of criticism (both legitimate and otherwise). These two features may explain why it is so rarely seen in applied behavioral and social sciences journals. Because I perceive lack of peer acceptance as a major problem, I will organize this review around that issue. Specifically, I will focus on four features that authors of simulation studies should build into their research in order to enhance peer acceptance by traditional empirical researchers.

Start With a Critical and Crystallized Problem and Dependent Variable

Given that most reviewers will inevitably raise a number of methodological issues with a simulation study, it is important that the problem being addressed and the dependent variable being simulated are easy to appreciate (i.e., the nature of the issue needs to be concrete and of obvious importance). With respect to the Schwab and Olson chapter, many people outside the area of compensation may not recognize how critical an analysis of merit versus bonus systems is, given the changing nature of pay policies in the 1990s. This decade has witnessed a major shift away from traditional merit systems to bonus systems, and few firms that have made this shift have thought seriously about the long-term implications for worker motivation. Thus, the problem is important, but it also is crystallized in the sense that it is a recurring, routine, and well-structured problem that eventually calls for a specific policy decision.

Thus, Schwab and Olson take on a good problem. If authors could have improved on this aspect of the work in one single way, it would have been to give a deeper explanation of how their dependent variable relates to the primary outcome of applied interest. That is, in the real world, the effect of compensation systems is generally measured in terms of individual worker attitudes and behaviors or in terms of firm-level performance and labor costs. The ultimate dependent variable in this simulation study, however, is the correlation between performance and pay over time. Since most reviewers will have never seen a correlation like this used as a dependent variable in an empirical study, its use begs the question of how this correlation relates to worker attitudes and behaviors or to firm-level performance and labor costs.

For example, one conclusion is that the correlation of pay with performance over 10 years is higher for merit (r = .558) relative to bonus systems (r = .394). Perhaps because these r's were calculated to the third decimal, one might wonder whether such a difference, developing over a 10-year period, would actually be perceptible to employees. If the difference is not perceptible, then it would probably not lead to differences in attitudes and behaviors, and thus the appropriate conclusion is that the choice of merit raises versus bonuses is unimportant. If the difference is perceptible, then one comes to the conclusion that merit raises are preferable to bonuses. Thus, whereas the problem is definitely critical and crystallized, the relevance of the specific findings to the problem would be enhanced if one could more cleanly reason from the simulated dependent variable (the pay–performance correlation) to the real constructs of interest (worker attitudes and behaviors or firm performance or labor costs). Without help, it is hard to be sure which of those two mutually exclusive conclusions is actually correct.

Model Dynamic Systems Over Repeated Cycles

It also is hard to deny the value of simulation research when it allows one to examine the implications of dynamic systems over long time periods and multiple cycles. Traditional empirical researchers have mastered the cross-sectional study and the analysis of self-reports. Indeed, despite numerous admonitions against the practice (see Campbell, 1982), most research can still be characterized in this fashion. Traditional empirical researchers consider a simple before-and-after design with a control group as a longitudinal study; although this design may be true in some sort of technical sense, it does not come close to capturing the type of effects one might see in a truly dynamic system over time.

The Schwab and Olson chapter examines the dynamic effect of two compensation systems over what is basically a 10-year (or 10-cycle) time period. The authors look at 640 different organizations over time and control all meaningful factors, both between organizations and within organizations. One could wait for the actual empirical study that does this, but one might wait for a long time. Thus, one is in the position of "looking for the next best thing"; from this position, the type of simulation presented here is highly valuable and can result in a number of meaningful insights that would have not been obvious in advance.

For example, it is fair to say that a great deal of research in the area of applied psychology has been directed at assessing and eliminating unreliability in the performance appraisal process. Most of this research has been either cross-sectional or of the before–after variety, and most of it is self-validating in the sense that the negative effects of unreliable ratings can be documented. One of the nonintuitive findings from the simulation study, however, is that if one examines this issue over a long period, the effect of unreliability in the rating process is trivial, despite nontrivial differences from year to year. Thus, by simulating the process in a more dynamic fashion over a longer time period, this study does a good job of examining an issue that is difficult, if not impossible, to assess using traditional empirical research methods.

Again, in the spirit of trying to improve a generally good study, one single feature that could be added to this study would deal with treating performance as an endogenous variable. Although this study is dynamic in the sense that previous bonuses and raises are figured into future salary, one outcome that is not truly modeled in a dynamic sense is performance. Because the whole theory being tested here implies that the pay–performance relationship is important because of its effects on worker motivation, the fact that the level of this correlation has no effect on subsequent performance is a limitation.

For example, a person who is rated unreliably in this simulation is treated as a fairly congenial person. That is, the reliability of the low rating condition is in the .30s, and thus deviations from the true score in either direction are likely to be quite large. Yet, despite being grossly underrated (and essentially docked pay in a context in which some other person received a large and totally undeserved rating with subsequent pay enhancement), our unreliably rated worker still comes back to work next year and gives us the standard .10 increment in performance attributable to experience. This seems somewhat inconsistent in a study that places so much emphasis on the need to keep pay and performance in line for fear of what misalignment does in terms of worker motivation. Someone who dedicated a large part of his or her research career to enhancing the reliability of the rating process might use this aspect of the simulation to discount the conclusion that unreliability in the process is not a concern over the long run. Of course, as noted earlier, the beauty of simulation research is that different types of reactions to unreliable ratings could be built into future simulations, and this is exactly what Schwab and Olson suggest should be done in future studies.

Start With a Narrow Focus and a Minimum of Assumptions

As illustrated above, perhaps the easiest thing for a reviewer of a simulation to do is to come up with some additional factor that should have been included in the design. However, probably the most difficult thing for an author of a simulation study to do is to anticipate in advance the form such additions are likely to take. Reviewers are tempted to do this in all research, but with empirical field studies, reviewers sometimes restrain themselves from completely redesigning the study, because they recognize that the data are already collected and they cannot reasonably ask the authors to go back in time. This type of restraint is rarely lavished on authors of laboratory studies, and it is virtually never reserved for authors of simulation studies because "it's so easy" to simply go back and add another factor to the design.

This discrepancy between what looks easy in theory but is actually difficult in practice is another major factor limiting the volume of simulation studies in the applied behavioral and social sciences. As currently configured, the research presented in the Schwab and Olson chapter simulates 640 organizations, each having 100 employees, over 10 yearly cycles. This is basically a 640,000-entry database. If one "merely" asks for an addition of two new conditions (e.g., the one suggested earlier, whereby the pay–performance correlation affects future performance, and a condition in which ratings are biased rather than unreliable), we quickly move from 640,000 entries to more than 2.5 million entries (if we completely cross the two new factors). This data matrix would call the bluff of most researchers. Given that reviewers are inevitably going to ask for expansions of the design that will be hard to anticipate, it seems like a good idea to start small, with intentions to grow, as opposed to starting out large, in a vain hope to cover all bases.

The simulation described in this chapter, for example, was framed as a 2 × 2 × 2 × 2 × 10 design and, at least as currently written up, may have had two factors too many. The logic and underlying rational for the "pay system" factor and the "measurement error" factor were well described. The need for the 10 within-organization observations over time also is straightforward, because we are primarily interested in the dynamic effects over time. As I read this chapter, however, I never appreciated the reasons why promotional rules and performance stability were components of this simulation.

Regardless, once these were included, it would have be useful to fully report the results for all factors. The authors themselves note that it is helpful in communicating studies such as these to present them like empirical experiments. Framing the study as a 2 × 2 × 2 × 2 × 10 design and laying out a heuristic representation of the data matrix is helpful for gaining an appreciation for the structure of the simulation. It also would have been easier to appreciate all the results of the simulation if they had been framed in terms of an ANOVA or regression of the five factors on the dependent variables, complete with cell means and effect sizes for different factors. Such a table was provided as part of the original article that presented this study, but it was not included in this chapter because of length considerations. One gets a much better feel for these data as a whole from the earlier article.

Keep the Focus on Normative Theory Testing

Research can be exploratory and directed toward theory building, or highly deductive and directed toward theory testing. In addition, a theory can be either descriptive, in the sense that it describes "what is," or it can be normative, in the sense that it describes "what should be." In general, I suspect that simulations will be evaluated more positively when they are deductively testing normative theories.

Mook (1983) made this same point with respect to laboratory studies, suggesting that the authors want to be able to say that (a) there is nothing currently specified by the theory that would state why it would not work in this laboratory context and, thus, this context serves as a meaningful test of the theory, and (b) the claim is not being made that the real world is veridical to what goes on in the laboratory context, but rather that the real world should be more veridical to what goes on in the laboratory context. Substituting the words "simulation study" for "laboratory context" makes Mook's observations equally valid.

The simulation presented in this chapter is clearly normative. It tries to uncover how pay "should" be distributed. As a test of pure theory, however, it is limited by the imprecise nature of the theories we have in the applied behavioral and social sciences. Many theories can be used to get to the general prescription that "pay should be related to performance," but few speak directly to the many manifestations that could exist under the general heading "pay related to performance." Both merit raises and bonuses link the two, but it is difficult to predict which of the two forms is better from existing theories. Thus, what we have here is not a test of any specific theory; rather, it is a looser test of "well, there are at least two ways to link pay to performance," and this tests one versus the other. Whereas there is some real value to the latter, the ability to meaningful contribute to cumulative theory building is restricted.

Again, this is not the authors' fault. There should be a law preventing one from publicly stating a theory that one has absolutely no intention of ever empirically testing him- or herself. Theorizing, undisciplined by the constraints that go along with operationalizing and testing the theory, will often lead to undesirable outcomes. Perhaps there should be an amendment to this law restricting theorists even further to only those theories that can be meaningfully modeled (or perhaps, operationalized well enough to be expressed as a computer program—see Simon, 1992). Because such a law and amendment are unlikely to be enacted, the best we can hope for is a better dialogue between theory builders, modelers, and empirical researchers. To date, theory builders and empirical researchers have dominated the conversations in the applied behavioral and social sciences. Schwab and Olson, along with the other authors in this book, may bring more balance to the dialogue.

References

Campbell, J. (1982). Some remarks from the outgoing editor. *Journal of Applied Psychology, 67,* 691–701.

Mook, D. G. (1983). In defense of external invalidity. *American Psychologist, 48,* 1379–1387.

Simon, H. A. (1992). What is an explanation of behavior? *Psychological Science, 3,* 150–161.

CHAPTER 7

Information Distribution, Participation, and Group Decision

Explorations with the DISCUSS and SPEAK Models

Garold Stasser

Social cognition means two different things. A long-standing meaning is cognition about other humans; in this sense, "social" refers to the content of the cognition (Fiske & Taylor, 1984). Another, more recently emerging meaning is cognition in and by groups of people (Fiske & Goodwin, 1994; Hinsz, Tindale, & Vollrath, 1997; Larson & Christensen, 1993). Hinsz et al. (1997) reviewed an extensive literature that fits the "groups as information processors" theme and claimed that it is useful to organize the group performance literature by processes that are ordinarily ascribed to individual thinkers: information acquisition, encoding, storage, retrieval, and manipulation. This movement is not an effort to revive the old concept of a "group mind" but rather recognizes that cognitive activity often occurs in social contexts and that groupwork requires coordinated and interactive cognition (Resnick, Levine, & Teasley, 1991; Wegner, 1987, 1995). In this sense, social cognition is a complex and dynamic interaction among individual minds. Communication is the most accessible form of social cognition, but it is not the only form. For example, people may seek and retain certain types of information because of what they know about their coworkers (Liang, Moreland, & Argote, 1995; Wittenbaum, Stasser, & Merry, 1996). In another example, people may distrust or discount information that is not validated by another as accurate (Hinsz, 1990; Stewart & Stasser, 1995).

On the one hand, if cognition is frequently a social process, then understanding cognition requires a theoretical perspective that incorporates interacting and reacting "minds." On the other hand, if group process and performance are highly cognitive, then understanding what groups do requires understanding how members' minds work together. One approach to capturing the complexities of social cognition is to build a working model of the individual mind and then fuse several of the individual

Support for the preparation of this chapter was provided by National Science Foundation grant SBR-9410584 to Garold Stasser.

minds into an interacting system. This fusing of minds can be accomplished in several ways, but computer simulation is well suited to such an endeavor. Once theoretical propositions and empirical findings can be expressed as computational steps, they can potentially be linked together in a set of interacting computations to explore combined and emergent properties of the whole system. Thus, a working model of the mind can, in principle, lead to a model of minds working together.

This chapter reviews the development of DISCUSS, a model of group decision making. Indeed, "development" is an apt term because DISCUSS has grown, sometimes slowly and sometimes in spurts, over several years. Throughout its development, however, the idea of "interacting minds" has been a guiding metaphor. This chapter aims to present DISCUSS as a theoretical statement for those who are interested in group decision making and to illustrate the use of computational modeling as a tool for theorizing. The chapter also describes other ways that DISCUSS could have evolved and the strengths and shortcomings of the way that it did evolve.

The first section of the chapter briefly reviews the research findings and attendant theoretical questions that motivated the development of DISCUSS. The second section presents an overview of DISCUSS in its elementary form and an example of a simulation study designed to explore alternative interpretations of empirical results—a retrospective simulation. The final section presents a more recent version of the model, DISCUSS–P, and illustrates the roles that computer simulation can play in going beyond existing data—a prospective simulation.

Groups as Faulty Information Processors

DISCUSS was conceived to answer questions about collective information processing in the context of group decision making. The questions were prompted by some surprising empirical results. Stasser and Titus (1985) asked four-person teams of university students to consider three candidates for president of the student government. The candidates were hypothetical and were represented by personal attributes and political positions that had been identified as desirable, neutral, or undesirable in a survey of students. One candidate ("Best") was given eight desirable, four neutral, and four undesirable traits. The other two, "Okay" and "Ohum," each had four desirable, eight neutral, and four undesirable traits. Thus, Best was designed to be the most popular candidate. Indeed, when group members received complete profiles of the candidates (the completely shared condition), 67% chose Best before meeting in their groups (see Figure 7.1). Okay and Ohum split the remaining 33% of the pregroup votes. Moreover, when members were fully informed before discussion, 83% of the four-person groups chose Best (see Figure 7.2). Thus, the initially most popular choice among individuals become even more popular with groups—a finding reminiscent of group polarization effects (Myers & Lamm, 1976).

Stasser and Titus (1985) were more interested, however, in what happened when members were not fully informed before discussion. They created two partially

FIGURE 7.1

Percentage of individuals choosing each of the candidates

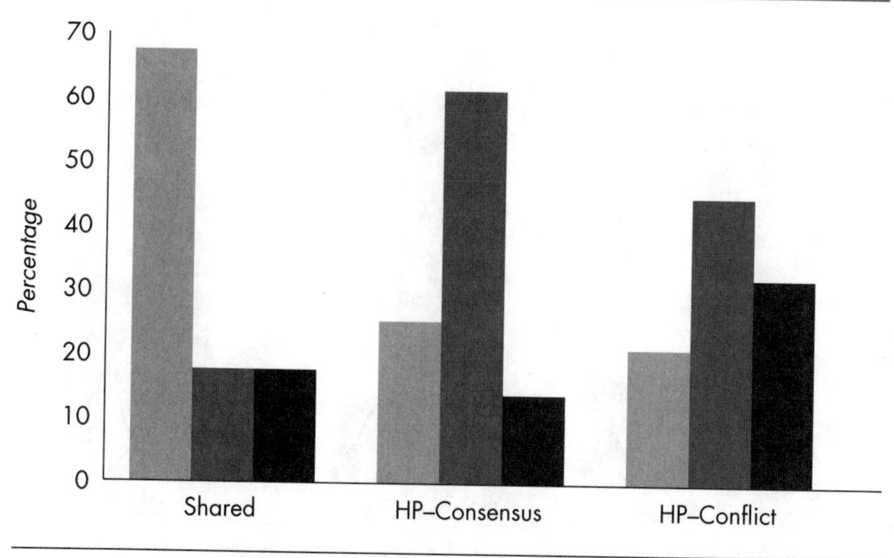

Legend: Best Okay Ohum

Source: Data adapted from Stasser, G., & Titus, W. (1985). Pooling of unshared information in group decision making: Biased information sampling during discussion. *Journal of Personality and Social Psychology, 48,* 1467–1478. Adapted with permission.

informed conditions by distributing information among the four members of a group before discussion in one of two ways. In the hidden-profile/consensus (HP–consensus) condition, they shifted pregroup support from Best to Okay by giving each member only two of the desirable traits for Best and only one of the undesirable traits for Okay. Thus, from the perspective of any one member, Okay appeared to have more positive and fewer negative traits than did Best. Nonetheless, the group as a whole had complete information, and by exchanging unshared information, members could have ascertained that Best was better than Okay. In the hidden-profile/conflict (HP–conflict) condition, Stasser and Titus (1985) used the same strategy of selectively distributing information to shift support from Best, but in this case, two members received a pattern favoring Okay and the other two received a pattern favoring Ohum. The intent was to create conflict over Okay and Ohum, perhaps setting the stage for the group to discover that Best was really the best. As Figure 7.1 illustrates, distributing information in these ways had the intended effect on prediscussion opinions. In both HP conditions, Best received fewer than one fourth of the initial votes, Okay was clearly the favorite in the HP–consensus condition, and Okay and Ohum both were more popular than Best in the HP–conflict condition.

FIGURE 7.2

Percentage of groups choosing each of the candidates

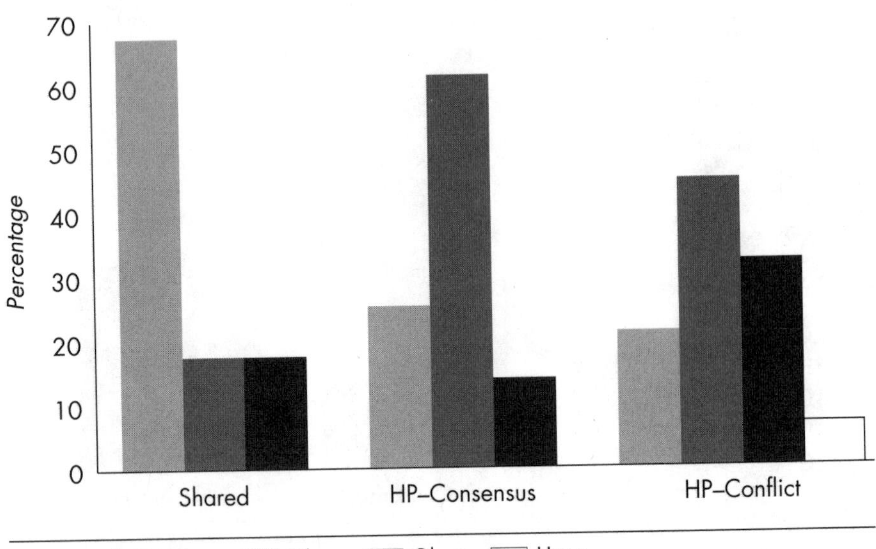

Source: Data adapted from Stasser, G., & Titus, W. (1985). Pooling of unshared information in group decision making: Biased information sampling during discussion. *Journal of Personality and Social Psychology, 48,* 1467–1478. Adapted with permission.

The question of interest is, What happened when groups discussed and collectively chose a candidate? The HP conditions represent decision contexts in which pooling information could dramatically shift sentiment. That is, exchange of unshared information during group discussion would reveal the superior profile of Best relative to the other candidates. However, as the group decision results in Figure 7.2 document, group discussion did not serve this corrective function. For example, in the HP–consensus condition, a higher proportion of groups (71%) than individuals (61%) selected Okay. Even though members had ample opportunity to give each other reasons to favor Best over Okay, Okay tended to gain rather than lose support during the course of discussion. On the face of it, these results support a normative rather than informational view of social influence: What matters is how many people support a position at the onset of discussion, not what is said during discussion (Burnstein & Vinokur, 1977; Festinger, 1954; Gigone & Hastie, 1993; Kaplan, 1989; Myers & Lamm, 1976). Ancillary recall data from Stasser and Titus (1985) and subsequent work (e.g., Stasser, Taylor, & Hanna, 1989; Stasser & Titus, 1987), however, suggested a less tidy but more interesting explanation: It is not necessarily the case that group members were unresponsive to discussion content, but it is possible that many of the unshared items of information were not mentioned during discussion.

Stasser and Titus (1985, 1987) identified two reasons that unshared information may be omitted from discussion. First, members may be predisposed to mention items that support or justify their initial opinions. If that were the case, the information supporting Best as the best choice would emerge only if some members supported him at the onset of discussion. Second, information that is widely available before discussion has a sampling advantage over information that is available only to one or a few people. For example, suppose that all four members of a group knew that Okay promised to safeguard the popular practice of providing "study days before finals week," but only one knew that Best held an equally popular position of advocating for "a trimester calendar." In that scenario, any one of the four could mention the "study days" issue in support of Okay, but only one could mention the "trimester" issue in support of Best. In other words, because it was more widely disseminated before discussion, the study days issue also was more likely to enter discussion than was the trimester issue. Subsequent empirical work has supported both of these possibilities (see, for example, Hollingshead, 1996; Larson, Christensen, Abbott, & Franz, 1996; Larson, Foster-Fishman, & Keys, 1994; Stasser, Taylor, & Hanna, 1989; Stewart & Stasser, 1995).

Nonetheless, it is reasonable to ask whether differences in the sampling rates of shared and unshared information can account for the clear failure of groups in Stasser and Titus (1985) to discover the superiority of Best in the face of a hidden profile. That is, are the results incompatible with an information-processing view of group decision making? Moreover, is it necessary to assume that members were advocates, biasing their contributions to the discussion to support their initial opinions, or does the sampling advantage to shared information provide a sufficient explanation? The answers to such questions are difficult, if not impossible, to intuit or to obtain by verbal reasoning. Additionally, many related questions of both applied and theoretical interest concern how the distribution and access to information among group members affects group discussion and decision making. DISCUSS was developed to address such questions.

DISCUSS: A Model of Collective Information Processing

Overview

Figure 7.3 presents an abbreviated flowchart of DISCUSS. It simulates group decision making in two distinct phases. First, during *prediscussion*, members individually acquire information and form initial preferences based on their knowledge. Second, during *discussion*, members discuss (exchange information), vote, and decide. The discussion phase consists of speaker cycles: a speaker is selected, the speaker

FIGURE 7.3

Abbreviated flowchart for DISCUSS

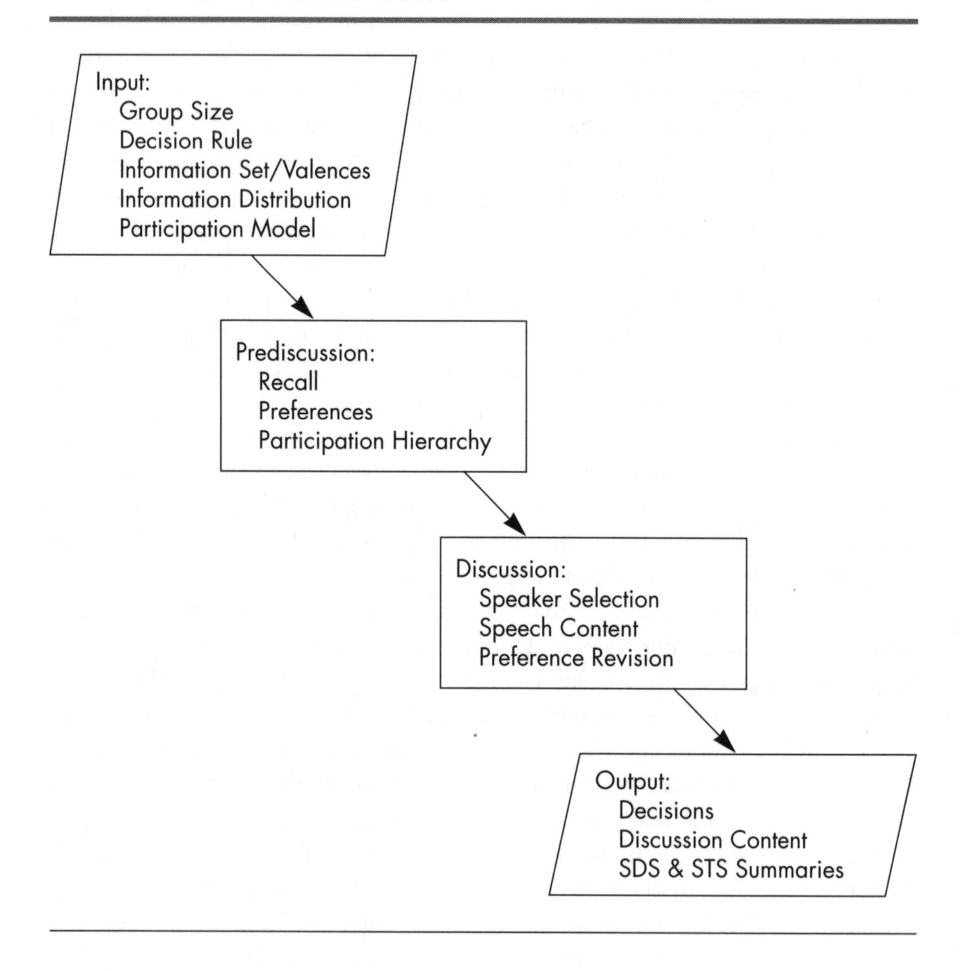

retrieves an item from memory to contribute and, if the information is new to other members, they add the item to their memory and reassess their preferences. At the end of each speaker cycle, a "vote" is taken to see if a required consensus (i.e., majority or unanimity) has been reached.

Input

Input to the program occurs in two forms. *Control* input specifies features of the simulation run, such as the number of groups to be simulated and the type of output desired. Of more interest here are the elements of *substantive* input, listed in Figure 7.3, which define essential characteristics of the group, its task, and its interaction. Group size is the number of members, and the decision rule is the number that must agree to reach a decision.

Each item in the *information set* is linked to a decision alternative and has a valence. The sign of the valence indicates whether the item supports (+) or opposes (–) the decision alternative, and the absolute value of the valence determines its weight (relative to other items) in the evaluation of alternatives. Consider, for example, an information-impoverished decision task with two alternatives: Alternative A is defined by the information set (1, 1, 0, –.5), and B is defined by the set (2, 1, 0, –2). Both alternatives have two positive, one neutral, and one negative attribute. However, B has two relatively important attributes, one positive and one negative. In default mode, DISCUSS treats item valences as constant across individuals; everyone evaluates and weighs information in the same way. However, DISCUSS also accepts a *valence disparity* parameter value, and for each member it samples a set of item valences from a population of values normally distributed around the specified valence, with standard deviation equal to the value of the disparity parameter. This latter option is more realistic for most social judgment tasks, in which natural variation occurs in how people evaluate information.

The *information distribution* can be thought of as a two-dimensional array: One dimension is defined by group members, and the other is defined by items of information in the information set. If an element of the array contains a one, then the member represented by the row can access the item represented by the column; if the entry is zero, the member does not have access to that item.

The information set and its distribution among group members define the essential characteristics of the task environment in the model. Other input determines features of the individual and collective information processing and the social interaction, which are process input variables that will be described later in this chapter.

Prediscussion Simulation

The prediscussion simulation determines what information, preferences, and relative participation rates members will bring to the group interaction. Members have limited but elastic recall capacity. As the number of items to be recalled increases, the probability of recalling any one item decreases. However, the functional relationship between recall probability and information-set size is calibrated to yield more items recalled, on average, as set size increases (see Stasser, 1988, for an elaboration). For each member, DISCUSS counts the number of items accessed (as specified in the information distribution array), computes the probability of recalling single items, and steps through the accessible items, using a Monte Carlo procedure to determine whether each item is retained in the member's long-term memory. If a nonzero value of the disparity parameter was input, DISCUSS also samples item valences for each item for each member.

Once the contents of memory and members' evaluations of information are determined, preferences are computed. DISCUSS represents people as information averagers (Anderson & Graesser, 1976). For each decision alternative, an evaluation is formed by averaging the valence for remembered items associated with that alternative. The alternative with the largest (signed) average is the preferred alternative.

Because the discussion phase is simulated as a series of speaker cycles, patterns of participation in group discussions are of interest. Members' participation rates determine the number of opportunities for disseminating the contents of their memories. Modeling participation in small-group discussion has a long history that dates back to the work of Bales (1953) and Stephan and Mishler (1952; see Stasser & Vaughan, 1996, for a review). Stephan and Mishler (1952) proposed that the distribution of participation rates can be described by a power function of the form:

$$P_i = [r^i] / [3^{N}_{j=1} r^j] \quad \textbf{(7.1)}$$

where P_i is the proportion of speaking turns taken by the *i*th most talkative members of the group ($i = 1, 2, 3, \ldots, N$; where N is group size), and r is the proportional change in speaking rates between adjacent ranks ($0 < r \leq 1$). Note that if $r = 1$ in this expression, each member takes $1/N$ of the speaking turns. As r decreases, participation rates become less evenly distributed within the group. DISCUSS accepts as input the value of r. Empirical estimates of this value obtained from groups of various sizes typically range from .5 to .8 (for more detail, see Stasser, 1988; Stasser & Taylor, 1991). Using the input value of the participation parameter, *r, and group size, DISCUSS computes a vector of participation rates and randomly assigns members to those rates.*

To illustrate, suppose that $N = 5$ and $r = .7$. DISCUSS generates a vector, *P,* of participation rates (proportions) using Equation 7.1. In this example, this operation yields $P = \{.36, .25, .18, .12, .09\}$. That is, the top participator in the group is expected to take more than one third of the speaking turns, and the top two participators, more than 60% of the turns. DISCUSS then randomly distributes members across the positions in the participation hierarchy. Note that this strategy assumes that what members know, how much they know, or what they prefer is unrelated to their participation rates.

By the end of the prediscussion phase, DISCUSS has constructed the number of group members indicated by group size. Members are represented by the contents of their memories, their preferences, the valences that they individually attach to items of information, and their relative participation rates. These member characteristics are the raw material for the discussion phase of the model.

Discussion

As Figure 7.3 summarizes, discussion is simulated as a sequence of speaker turns; each turn involves selecting a speaker, selecting from the speaker's memory the content of the speech, and then updating others' memories and preferences. Figure 7.4 gives a more detailed depiction of these events.

First, DISCUSS identifies a speaker using the vector of participation rates generated during the prediscussion phase. More specifically, DISCUSS forms a cumulative probability distribution over the participation ranks. Using the previous example for $N = 5$, $r = .7$, and $P = \{.36, .25, .18, .12, .09\}$ yields $P_{cum} = \{.36, .61, .79, .91, 1.0\}$. The program samples a pseudorandom number, X, in the range of 0 to 1 and identifies the speaker by finding the first entry in P_{cum} that exceeds X. For example, suppose that X were .85: The speaker for that cycle would be the one that was assigned the fourth location in the speaking hierarchy during the prediscussion phase.

FIGURE 7.4

Flowchart of discussion phase of DISCUSS

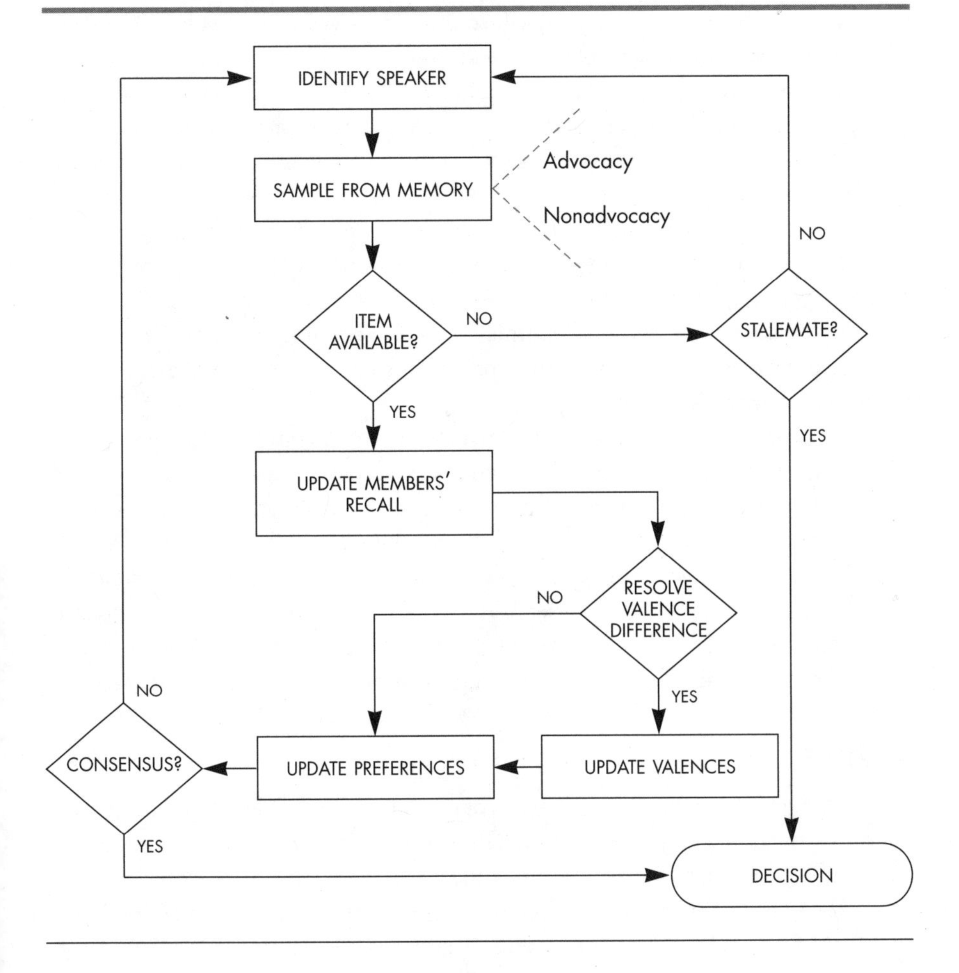

Second, DISCUSS samples an item from the identified speaker's memory. The program does not include repetitions of items; thus, the selection is restricted to items that have not already been mentioned. DISCUSS allows the speaker's preference to bias this selection process to various degrees, as determined by the value of an advocacy parameter, a. In the extreme cases, if $a = 0$ (nonadvocacy), an item is selected at random from the available set or, if $a = 1$ (advocacy), only items that are consistent with the speaker's current preference are considered. Intermediate values of a result in preference-opposing items being less likely than supporting items to be selected.

Third, assuming that a new item has been contributed to the discussion, this item is added to each member's memory. That is, DISCUSS members are never inattentive, nor do they discount or ignore information. If members are permitted disparate evaluations of items, a valence adjustment (va) parameter determines whether, how, and to what degree such disparities are resolved when an item is mentioned. In the extremes, if $va = 1$ (norm), members converge on a shared evaluation of the item or, if $va = 0$ (nonnorm), the disparity in item valences remains. Intermediate values of va result in a reduction, but not an eradication, of the disparity. In the event that disparities are completely or partially removed, DISCUSS also permits specification of two convergence points. One convergence point (the default option) is the valence that the speaker attaches to the item. That is, members move toward the speaker's interpretation of the information. The other convergence point is the average item valence across members. Once members' memories are updated (and valences are adjusted, depending on the version), members' preferences are recomputed.

Finally, the speaker cycle is completed by determining whether the required number of members agree, given the updated preferences. If so, the discussion is terminated. Otherwise, the next speaker cycle starts.

One detour from the above route deserves brief mention: DISCUSS groups can reach a stalemate. The only way that a group can move toward consensus in DISCUSS is for speakers to add new information to the discussion. If a sequence of speakers fails to add anything new, then the group is declared "hung." The number of consecutive "no new news" speaker cycles that is tolerated can be controlled by input. However, if no number is specified, DISCUSS sets the number to group size. In this default case for a group of six, DISCUSS will record a no-decision outcome if six consecutive speakers produce no new information.

Output

DISCUSS aggregates across various types of output across simulated groups, including the distributions of prediscussion preferences and group decisions, the proportion of times that items are recalled pre- and postdiscussion, and the proportion of times that items are mentioned during discussion. Optional output includes social-decision scheme (SDS; Davis, 1973) and social-transition scheme (STS; Kerr, 1981) summaries. An SDS summary is a matrix whose columns represent the decision alternatives and whose rows represent the various ways in which members of a group can distribute their preferences over the decision alternatives. The entries in the SDS matrix give the relative frequencies of each decision as a function of the initial distribution of preferences within the group. An STS summary is a matrix whose columns and rows are defined by the possible distributions of members over the decision alternatives. The entries in an STS matrix give the relative frequencies of movement from one distribution of preferences to another over time. (See Davis, 1973; Kerr, 1981; and Stasser, Kerr, & Davis, 1989, for a more extensive discussion and examples of SDS and STS matrices.)

Retrospective Simulation: Hidden Profiles Revisited

One function of a theoretical statement is to account for existing data and, in doing so, to provide alternative or refined ways of understanding past results. Stasser (1988) used the DISCUSS model to simulate the decision task and information distributions used by Stasser and Titus (1985). The general goal was to ascertain whether the group decision processes as represented in DISCUSS could produce preference and decision results close to those obtained in the empirical study (see Figures 7.1 and 7.2). As already mentioned, the more specific conceptual issues were whether collective information processing could account for the failure of groups to discover a hidden profile and, if so, whether one needs to assume that members biased their contributions to the discussion to support their initial preferences.

In setting up the DISCUSS simulation, Stasser (1988) made extensive use of unreported pilot data collected by Stasser and Titus (1985) to construct the candidate profiles. Recall that candidate Best was given eight positive, four neutral, and four negative attributes, whereas the other candidates (Okay and Ohum) were assigned four positive, eight neutral, and four negative items. Thus, in the DISCUSS simulation, each of the three decision alternatives was represented by 16 information items. Pilot data showed that the positive items were typically rated about 1.5 points above a neutral point on a 7-point scale, which was anchored by "very undesirable" and "very desirable." Negative items were 1 point below the neutral point, on average. Additionally, the most positively rated items were given to Best. To capture these patterns, Stasser (1988) assigned four of the eight positive items for Best the value 2.0, the remaining positive items for Best and the other candidates the value of 1.5, the neutral items 0, and the negative items –1.0.

The information distribution patterns that defined the experimental conditions in Stasser and Titus (1985) were reproduced as input in the information distribution arrays of DISCUSS. Stasser (1988) obtained six versions of DISCUSS by crossing two discussion styles ("advocacy" versus "nonadvocacy" information selection) with three ways of treating item valences: constant valences across members; variable valences with no resolution of disparities (nonnorm); and variable valences, with convergence on speakers' evaluation of information when it is mentioned during discussion (norm). Only the norm versions of the model closely reproduced the distributions of preferences and group decisions obtained by Stasser and Titus (1985). Assuming that members evaluated information in the same way from the onset failed to reproduce prediscussion preferences, and allowing disparities in evaluation to remain for mentioned information led to too many stalemates.

Interestingly, however, the advocacy and nonadvocacy versions of the DISCUSS-norm model yielded nearly identical results across Stasser and Titus's (1985) information distribution conditions. Moreover, both versions closely reproduced the empirical results. To illustrate, Figures 7.5 and 7.6 compare the simulated results (Pred) from the nonadvocacy-norm DISCUSS model with the observed results (Obs) for prediscussion preferences and group decisions. The comparable figures for the

FIGURE 7.5

Observed (Obs) and predicted (Pred) percentage of individuals choosing each candidate

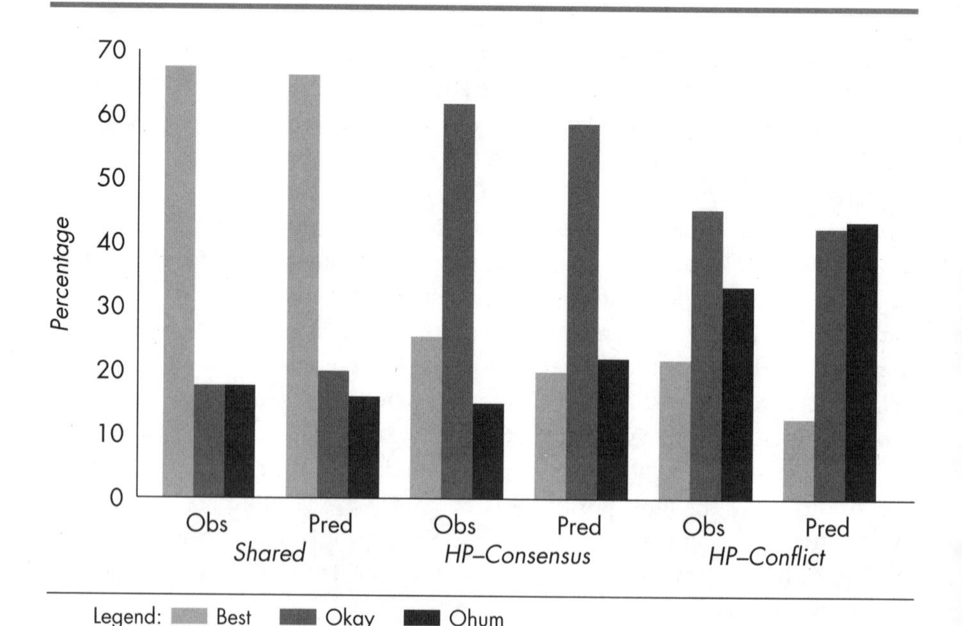

Legend: Best Okay Ohum

Sources: Observed data from Stasser, G., & Titus, W. (1985). Pooling of unshared information in group decision making: Biased information sampling during discussion. *Journal of Personality and Social Psychology, 48,* 1467–1478. Model predictions from Stasser, G. (1988). Computer simulation as a research tool: The DISCUSS model of group decision making. *Journal of Experimental Social Psychology, 24,* 393–422. Adapted with permission.

FIGURE 7.6

Observed (Obs) and predicted (Pred) percentage of groups choosing each candidate

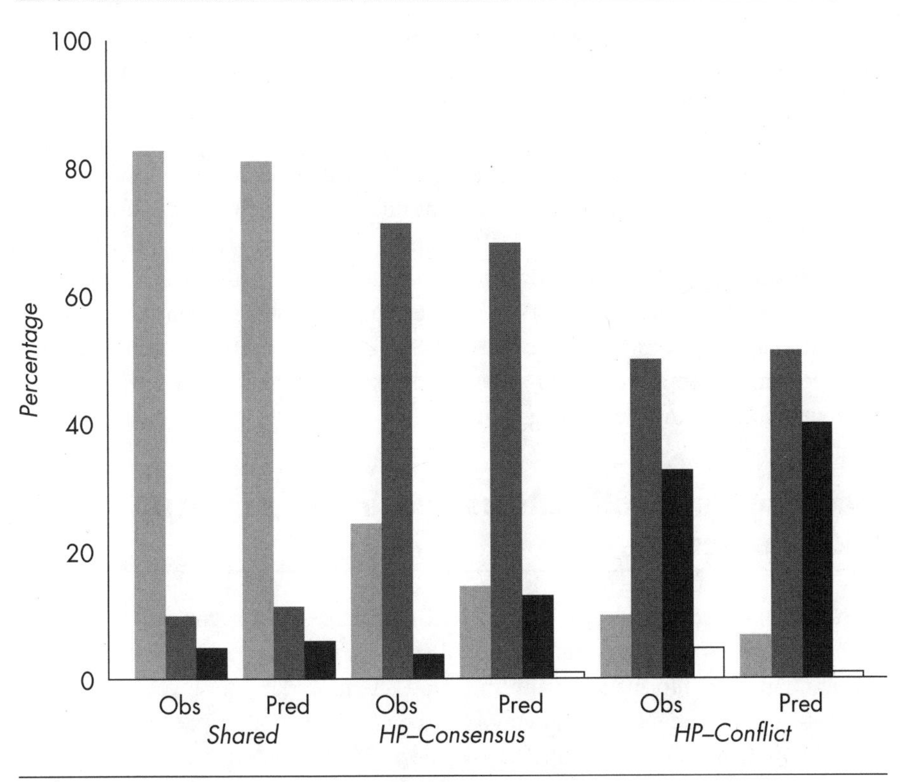

Legend: Best Okay Ohum Hung

Sources: Observed data from Stasser, G., & Titus, W. (1985). Pooling of unshared information in group decision making: Biased information sampling during discussion. *Journal of Personality and Social Psychology, 48,* 1467–1478. Model predictions from Stasser, G. (1988). Computer simulation as a research tool: The DISCUSS model of group decision making. *Journal of Experimental Social Psychology, 24,* 393–422. Adapted with permission.

advocacy-norm DISCUSS simulation are omitted but are virtually identical to Figures 7.5 and 7.6.

Returning to the original questions, collective information sampling and exchange as represented in DISCUSS can account for the failures of groups in Stasser and Titus (1985) to discover hidden profiles. That is, one need not assume that the groups were ignoring information or that normative processes, such as conformity and acquiescence, were the dominant modes of social influence. Moreover, the fact that the simulation of advocacy and nonadvocacy information exchange produced nearly identical results suggests that it would have mattered little whether members edited their contributions to the discussions to maintain consistency with their preferences. Both preference-consistent and unbiased selection of communication would have produced nearly the same outcome in the situations that Stasser and Titus (1985) studied. In other words, even an unbiased exchange of information does not ensure that groups will effectively pool their diverse sets of information and reveal a hidden profile if it exists.

As Stasser (1988) cautioned, however, one should not conclude that advocacy and nonadvocacy discussion styles always produce the same outcomes. Indeed, subsequent simulations that examined different information distributions and tracked output variables other than group decisions have documented marked differences in the results of advocacy and nonadvocacy simulations (Stasser, 1988; Stasser, Kerr, & Davis, 1989; Stasser & Vaughan, 1996). For example, Stasser, Kerr, and Davis (1989) showed that the advocacy version of DISCUSS produces patterns of opinion change and decision process (as captured by STS and SDS summaries) that are characteristic of groups deciding matters of judgment, whereas the nonadvocacy version does not.

Modeling Participation Rates: Simplicity, Complexity, and Parsimony

DISCUSS takes several shortcuts in modeling group decision making, opting for "good enough" approximations to psychological and social processes. For example, the simulation of information acquisition and retention does not incorporate much of what is known about human memory (except that memory capacity is represented as limited and elastic). No attempt has been made to incorporate a "biologically plausible" model of memory, an enterprise that is thriving in the cognitive sciences. The medium of computer modeling certainly allows for the possibility of incorporating more advanced models of memory at this step. The limiting factors are the resources (computing capacity, time, expertise, creativity) allocated to the modeling effort. Pragmatically, one must decide where to take such shortcuts. These decisions are not just pragmatic ones, however, and they depend on a number of factors: judged adequacy of the approximations, state of theory, centrality of the process to the model, and so forth.

Participation is central to DISCUSS, and its speaker selection procedure is straightforward, easy to program, and computationally efficient. Moreover, it is conceptually simple. It suggests that people import stable levels of talkativeness into the group and that the tendency to talk has nothing to do with one's knowledge or preference. In the end, though, the question is not so much whether the representation is too simple—indeed, simplicity can be a another term for parsimony, a positive attribute of theoretical propositions. More to the point, the question is whether the simplicity is acceptable, or even desirable, given one's modeling objectives.

Addressing acceptability depends partly on articulating the limitations of a shortcut and considering alternative instantiations. For example, one can imagine decision contexts in which talkativeness depends on such task-related characteristics as expertise. In those cases, it does not make sense to assign participation rates randomly. Rather, it could make more sense to assign higher participation rates to members who know more or who have access to more information. One advantage of the medium of computer language for articulating theory and building models is that it allows—even invites—the addition of such complexities. As others have noted (Abelson, 1968; Stasser, 1990), however, danger lurks in this invitation to complexity. Among other things, complexity increases the difficulty of using the model (e.g., more parameters to set and more computing capacity and time required) and may complicate the interpretation of simulation findings. More important, unnecessary complexity compromises the theoretical crispness and clarity of the model. In sum, one should add complexity judiciously.

DISCUSS–P: DISCUSS + SPEAK

Because the flow of information and its impact on the evaluation of alternatives is at the heart of DISCUSS, who speaks and when are important considerations. Recent work examining participation patterns in small groups documents not only inequality in participation across members but also an uneven distribution of each member's contributions over time (Dabbs & Ruback, 1987; Parker, 1988; Stasser & Taylor, 1991). For example, a low participator may have a brief period of frequent contributions, and a high participator may not speak at all during that time.

Stasser and Taylor (1991) developed SPEAK, a computational model of the progression of speaking turns during face-to-face discussion in small groups. SPEAK uses the idea of a speaking hierarchy as embodied in Equation 7.1, but it adds a cyclical component that produces megaturns (i.e., periods of high activity superimposed on a stable base rate of participation). More specifically, when a member speaks, SPEAK increments the probability that this member will take the next available turn also. If the member does not take the next turn, this increment in speaking probability starts to decay, and it gradually returns to a baseline if the member remains silent for several turns. Using this routine, Stasser and Taylor (1991) were able to reproduce many features of the speaking patterns that they observed in six-person mock juries and that Parker (1988) had observed in four-person conversational groups.

SPEAK, like the speaking hierarchy routine in DISCUSS, is based largely on empirically derived relationships. It does not attempt to mimic processes that may underlie the formation of speaking hierarchies or the waxing and waning of speech over the course of discussion. Stasser and Vaughan (1996) discussed several social and psychological processes that may account for such regularities in speaking, but they found none that were sufficiently comprehensive, tractable, and coherent to model computationally. A promising approach views speaking hierarchies as arising from social queues (Horvath, 1965) that are based on stable characteristics (e.g., status, dominance, or competence; Ridgeway, 1984) and cyclical patterns as arising from implicit, context-specific rules of interaction (Parker, 1988). Nonetheless, the present state of theory does not support a more process-oriented model of discussion, and emulating distinctive features of the patterns of speaking in small groups is, for many purposes, an adequate solution.

Stasser and Vaughan (1996) developed DISCUSS–P by adding the SPEAK model to the discussion phase of the DISCUSS model, thereby permitting a more realistic simulation of the speaking-turn allocations during group deliberation. DISCUSS–P accepts input that adjusts the size of the increment in speaking likelihood based on recent participation and the rate of decay of this increment when subsequent turns are not taken. Additionally, DISCUSS–P incorporates the option of assigning locations in the speaking hierarchy based on task-relevant characteristics, such as amount of information (either accessed or remembered) or strength of preference. Finally, DISCUSS–P also includes a "round-robin" option that simply passes speaking turns around the group and thus generates participation that is spread evenly over members and time. The round-robin option not only provides a baseline process against which to evaluate the impact of more complex processes but also simulates an aspect of many procedural interventions that are aimed at equalizing participation in discussion and decisions.

Prospective Simulation: Hidden Profiles Again

One distinct benefit of computational modeling is that it encourages one to explore territory that is not covered by existing data (for examples and added discussion of this point, see Abelson, 1968; Hastie, 1988; Ostrom, 1988; Stasser, 1990). Davis and Kerr (1986) noted that this is a particularly attractive feature of formal models because of the "sparseness" of data that address fundamental issues in group process and organizational behavior. Whereas retrospective simulation attempts to account for existing data (often with the aim of validating a model), prospective simulation goes beyond existing data.

Prospective simulation may have any of several objectives. One aim is to gauge the extent to which past findings are invariant across features of the social and task environments (e.g., group size, information load). A related aim is to fill the gaps between or to extrapolate beyond existing data sets. Finally, prospective simulation can be a valuable tool for planning empirical research by bracketing probable effect sizes, identifying levels and combinations of variables that are promising to examine, and providing a working model of planned interventions.

To illustrate how simulation serves some of these functions, consider a simulation reported by Stasser and Vaughan (1996). Having reviewed the literature on patterns of participation in face-to-face discussions, they asked whether, or under what conditions, different patterns of participation might materially affect group decisions. They reasoned that two conditions seemed to be necessary for speaking patterns to matter. First, some members would need to access different sets of information (as in a hidden profile). If members were sampling from the same information pool, who spoke first or most frequently would not systematically alter the content of discussion. Second, speaking rates would need to be related to some task-relevant attribute of members, such as the amount of information remembered or the certainty of preference. Otherwise, variability across groups in speaking patterns would produce "noise" but not systematically change the content or outcomes of discussions.

They explored these questions with a simulation study using three different participation submodels with DISCUSS–P: random (all members equally likely to participate at any time), round-robin (participation passed systematically around the group), and a full SPEAK version that incorporated speaking hierarchies and megaturns. In addition, two variants of SPEAK were implemented. In one variant, locations in the speaking hierarchy were assigned randomly (as in the earlier versions of DISCUSS). In the other variant, members who remembered more information (i.e., retained more items in their long-term memory) at the end of the prediscussion phase were assigned higher participation ranks. Simulated groups of sizes four, six, or twelve decided between two alternatives: Alternative A, with twelve positive, eight neutral, and four negative attributes versus Alternative B, with eight positive, eight neutral, and eight negative attributes. In some cases, all members of a group had access to all information before discussion (shared condition), whereas in the remaining cases, only two members had complete access (informed minority) and the remaining members (ill-informed majority) received a hidden profile of information that made B appear better than A. Minority influence was a subtheme to the simulation: Under what conditions would the informed minority successfully prevail and convince the ill-informed majority of the superiority of option A? Finally, both advocacy and nonadvocacy discussion styles were simulated.

The results showed that when all members could access all information before discussion, nearly all groups chose A regardless of size, participation pattern, or discussion style (i.e., advocacy or nonadvocacy). However, when a hidden profile was implemented, support for A was substantially reduced, particularly in larger groups. In the HP conditions, the informed minority was more likely to prevail when participation rates were related to the amounts of information remembered and an advocacy discussion style ensued. Somewhat counterintuitively, enforcing equal participation through a round-robin procedure reduced the minority's effectiveness. From a research design or intervention perspective, it is informative to note that the largest effects of participation model and discussion style occurred for 12-member groups. Even though it is tempting to opt for smaller groups when designing research, this simulation suggested that it may be counterproductive when examining issues of minority influence and discussion style.

As a final note on prospective simulation, it would be virtually impossible to run an empirical study of the magnitude of this simulation study. Without the benefit of the simulation, one would most likely opt for a study of much smaller dimensions—perhaps two levels of discussion style (advocacy and nonadvocacy) and two levels of participation style (round-robin and unconstrained), using groups no larger than six. The largest predicted difference for six-person groups in this reduced design was about 30 percentage points (30% of round-robin, nonadvocacy groups chose A compared with 60% of unconstrained, advocacy groups). To have a reasonable chance of detecting this difference in a planned contrast (80% power, .05 alpha level, one-tailed), one would need more than 40 groups per condition. In the group performance literature, sample sizes are typically smaller, ranging from 10 to 15 per condition. If the sample size were 15, the statistical power for detecting the predicted difference of 30 percentage points at the conventional .05 level is less than .5. Moreover, this analysis yields a conservative estimate of the needed sample size because manipulations in a computational simulation can be cleanly implemented (i.e., all groups "instructed" to adopt a nonadvocacy style do so perfectly), whereas interventions in interacting groups are typically "noisy." The point is that small-sample group studies are frequently high-risk studies, particularly when examining outcome data such as decisions. Simulation studies provide one way of assessing the degree of such risk.

Computational Modeling: Why Do It?

Computational modeling is a labor-intensive and thoughtful undertaking. What appears to be a straightforward computing problem can become unexpectedly difficult. The translation of ideas into computational steps often reveals ambiguity, vagueness, and incompleteness. Sometimes ideas simply unravel when one tries to patch them into a computer program. Even if the translation of theoretical notions into programming statements is successful, the output of the computational steps may bear faint resemblance to empirical results or be inconsistent with established theory, forcing the modeler "back to the drawing board" (Shiffrin & Nobel, 1997). The tidy and concise presentations of mature computational models rarely hint at their troubled youths. So, why bother?

The difficulty of expressing theoretical notions in computational steps can be frustrating, but it gives rise to two related benefits of computational modeling. One is that model development frequently reveals gaps and inconsistencies in verbally stated theories, forcing one to refine and elaborate theoretical propositions. The other is that a computational model's representation of a process is clear (sometimes painfully so) to those who care to examine its contents carefully. Such clarity often highlights areas that need attention. For example, discomfort about the way in which speaking turns were allocated in DISCUSS prompted both an empirical study

(Stasser & Taylor, 1991) and an extensive review of the literature (Stasser & Vaughan, 1996). Those efforts, in turn, informed the model, leading to a refinement of the speaker selection routine. Nonetheless, even this refinement is not entirely satisfactory. It relies heavily on empirically derived relationships that describe participation patterns but do not illuminate the social and psychological mechanisms involved. Clearly, there is room for more work here.

Also, it is clear that DISCUSS has bitten hard on the lure of an information-processing view of people and of communication among people. Whereas the information-processing view is a useful perspective, one cannot easily dismiss the role of normative social influence in group decision making. Undoubtedly, tasks and decision contexts exist in which normative considerations are quite important (Deutsch & Gerard, 1955; Kaplan, 1989). For example, Hastie and Pennington (1991) suggested that opinion change during jury deliberation may involve two parallel processes: One is an assessment of the likelihood of the various positions prevailing in the group, and the other is an assessment of the merits of the alternatives based on evidence (information). A theoretical challenge is to articulate how the two processes work together in sufficient detail and completeness to permit the translation into computational steps.

In sum, computational modeling serves numerous functions ranging from exploring alternative interpretations of existing data to assessing the adequacy of planned experiments. The most important function, however, is the refinement and advancement of theory. As Ostrom (1988) argued, computer language is a symbolic system, along with natural language and mathematics, that we can use to articulate theories. He further noted that computer language offers the precision of mathematical expression and the flexibility of natural language, making it a particularly attractive medium in the social and behavioral sciences.

References

Abelson, R. P. (1968). Simulation of social behavior. In G. Lindzey & E. Aronson (Eds.), *Handbook of social psychology* (Vol. 2, pp. 274–356). Reading, MA: Addison-Wesley.

Anderson, N. H., & Graesser, C. (1976). An information integration analysis of attitude change in group discussion. *Journal of Personality and Social Psychology, 34,* 210–222.

Bales, R. F. (1953). The equilibrium problem in small groups. In T. Parsons, R. F. Bales, & E. A. Shils (Eds.), *Working papers in the theory of action* (pp. 444–476). Glencoe, IL: Free Press.

Burnstein, E., & Vinokur, A. (1977). Persuasive argumentation and social comparison as determinants of attitude polarization. *Journal of Experimental Social Psychology, 13,* 315–332.

Dabbs, J. M., Jr., & Ruback, R. B. (1987). Dimensions of group process: Amount and structure of vocal interaction. In L. Berkowitz (Ed.), *Advances in experimental social psychology* (Vol. 20, pp. 123–169). San Diego: Academic Press.

Davis, J. H. (1973). Group decisions and social interaction: A theory of social decision schemes. *Psychological Review, 80,* 97–125.

Davis J. H., & Kerr, N. L. (1986). Thought experiments and the problem of sparse data in small group research. In P. Goodman (Ed.), *Designing effective work groups* (pp. 305–349). San Francisco: Jossey-Bass.

Deutsch, M., & Gerard, H. B. (1955). A study of normative and informational social influences upon individual judgment. *Journal of Abnormal and Social Psychology, 51,* 629–633.

Festinger, L. (1954). A theory of social comparison processes. *Human Relations, 7,* 117–140.

Fiske, S. T., & Goodwin, S. A. (1994). Social cognition research and small group research, a West Side Story or. . . ? *Small Group Research, 25,* 147–171.

Fiske, S. T., & Taylor, S. E. (1984). *Social cognition.* New York: Random House.

Gigone, D., & Hastie, R. (1993). The common knowledge effect: Information sampling and group judgment. *Journal of Personality and Social Psychology, 65,* 959–974.

Hastie, R. (1988). A computer simulation of person memory. *Journal of Experimental Social Psychology, 24,* 423–447.

Hastie, R., & Pennington, N. (1991). Cognitive and social processes in decision making. In L. B. Resnick, J. M. Levine, & S. D. Teasley (Eds.), *Perspectives on socially shared cognition* (pp. 308–327). Washington, DC: American Psychological Association.

Hinsz, V. B. (1990). Cognitive and consensus processes in group recognition memory performance. *Journal of Personality and Social Psychology, 59,* 705–718.

Hinsz, V. B., Tindale, R. S., & Vollrath, D. A. (1997). The emerging conceptualization of groups as information processors. *Psychological Bulletin, 121,* 43–64.

Hollingshead, A. B. (1996). The rank-order effect in group decision making. *Organizational Behavior and Human Decision Processes, 68,* 181–193.

Horvath, W. (1965). A mathematical model of participation in small group discussions. *Behavioral Science, 10, 164–166.*

Kaplan, M. F. (1989). Task, situational, and personal determinants of influence processes in group decision making. In E. E. Lawler & B. Markovsky (Eds.), *Advances in group process* (Vol. 6, pp. 87–105). Greenwich, CT: JAI Press.

Kerr, N. L. (1981). Social transition schemes: Charting the road to agreement. *Journal of Personality and Social Psychology, 41,* 684–702.

Larson, J. R., Jr., & Christensen, C. (1993). Groups as problem-solving units: Toward a new meaning of social cognition. *British Journal of Social Psychology, 32,* 5–30.

Larson, J. R., Jr., Christensen, C., Abbott, A. S., & Franz, T. M. (1996). Diagnosing groups: Charting the flow of information in medical decision making teams. *Journal of Personality and Social Psychology, 71,* 315–330.

Larson, J. R., Jr., Foster-Fishman, P. G., & Keys, C. B. (1994). Discussion of shared and unshared information in decision-making groups. *Journal of Personality and Social Psychology, 67,* 446–461.

Liang, D. W., Moreland, R., & Argote, L. (1995). Group versus individual training and group performance: The mediating role of transactive memory. *Personality and Social Psychology Bulletin, 21,* 384–393.

Myers, D. C., & Lamm, H. (1976). The group polarization phenomenon. *Psychological Bulletin, 83,* 602–627.

Ostrom, T. M. (1988). Computer simulation: The third symbol system. *Journal of Experimental Social Psychology, 24,* 382–392.

Parker, K. (1988). Speaking turns in small group interaction: A context-sensitive event sequence model. *Journal of Personality and Social Psychology, 54,* 956–971.

Resnick, L. B., Levine, J. M., & Teasley, S. D. (1991). *Perspectives on socially shared cognition.* Washington, DC: American Psychological Association.

Ridgeway, C. L. (1984). Dominance, performance and status in groups: A theoretical analysis. In E. J. Lawler (Ed.), *Advances in group process* (Vol. 1, pp. 59–93). Greenwich, CT: JAI Press.

Shiffrin, R. M., & Nobel, P. A. (1997). The art of model development and testing. *Behavior Research Methods, Instruments, & Computers, 29,* 6–14.

Stasser, G. (1988). Computer simulation as a research tool: The DISCUSS model of group decision making. *Journal of Experimental Social Psychology, 24,* 393–422.

Stasser, G. (1990). Computer simulation of social interaction. In C. Hendrick (Ed.), *Review of personality and social psychology: Vol. 11. Research methods in personality and social psychology* (pp. 120–141). Newbury Park, CA: Sage.

Stasser, G., Kerr, N. L., & Davis, J. H. (1989). Models of influence in decision-making groups. In P. B. Paulus (Ed.), *Psychology of group influence* (2nd ed., pp. 279–326). Hillsdale, NJ: Erlbaum.

Stasser, G., & Taylor, L. A. (1991). Speaking turns in face-to-face discussions. *Journal of Personality and Social Psychology, 60,* 675–684.

Stasser, G., Taylor, L. A., & Hanna, C. (1989). Information sampling in structured and unstructured discussions of three- and six-person groups. *Journal of Personality and Social Psychology, 57,* 67–78.

Stasser, G., & Titus, W. (1985). Pooling of unshared information in group decision making: Biased information sampling during discussion. *Journal of Personality and Social Psychology, 48,* 1467–1478.

Stasser, G., & Titus, W. (1987). Effects of information load and percentage of shared information on the dissemination of unshared information during group discussion. *Journal of Personality and Social Psychology, 53,* 81–93.

Stasser, G., & Vaughan, S. I. (1996). Models of participation during face-to-face unstructured discussions. In J. H. Davis & E. Witte (Eds.), *Understanding group behavior: Consensual action by small groups* (Vol. 1, pp. 165–192). Hillsdale, NJ: Erlbaum.

Stephan, F. F., & Mishler, E. G. (1952). The distribution of participation in small groups: An exponential approximation. *American Sociological Review, 17,* 598–608.

Stewart, D. D., & Stasser, G. (1995). Expert role assignment and information sampling during collective recall and decision making. *Journal of Personality and Social Psychology, 69,* 619–628.

Wegner, D. M. (1987). Transactive memory: A contemporary analysis of the group mind. In B. Mullen & G. Goethals (Eds.), *Theories of group behavior* (pp. 185–208). New York: Springer-Verlag.

Wegner, D. M. (1995). A computer network model of human transactive memory. *Social Cognition, 13,* 319–339.

Wittenbaum, G. M., Stasser, G., & Merry, C. J. (1996). Tacit coordination in anticipation of small group task completion. *Journal of Experimental Social Psychology, 32,* 129–152.

COMMENT:

The DISCUSS and SPEAK Models

Lessons on the Value of Linking Theory, Empirical Research, and Computer Simulation

M. Anjali Sastry

Garold Stasser's DISCUSS computational model, in various versions, offers the researcher a tool for understanding group decision making that complements more traditional methods. His experience with it offers the reader a variety of lessons to guide the design and use of computational modeling research. This commentary first reviews Stasser's (Chapter 7) research approach, framing his key contributions here as lessons for researchers. It then offers some thoughts on the questions his research has set out to explore, taking into consideration substantive issues about group decision making that Stasser's work raises. It concludes by reflecting on some of the larger questions about modeling social systems that arise from considering the modeling issues Stasser and his colleagues have tackled.

Tracing the development of the DISCUSS model, Stasser shows how he and his colleagues used the model to explore some questions generated by contrasting existing theories and by considering puzzling empirical results. The chapter presents a convincing case for computational modeling as a third approach for building understanding in social science, one that complements empirical studies and verbal theorizing by allowing the researcher to explore questions that would be difficult, perhaps impossible, to resolve by experiment and verbal reasoning alone. In fact, others (e.g., Sterman, 1994) have argued that verbal reasoning can be so flawed by systematic biases and cognitive limitations, particularly in situations involving dynamic complexity, that researchers need such formal methods as computational modeling to ensure that inferences are correctly drawn and that explanations are internally consistent. Thus, we can expand on Stasser's notions of retrospective and prospective simulation, adding that computer models can be used to develop explanations that are sufficient, that address gaps in the existing theory, and that generate predictions that are consistent with the assumptions of the theory (Carley, 1995).

By sketching the steps involved in the evolution of DISCUSS, Stasser gives us a sense of how computational models can be used to explore tentative explanations for observed empirical results and to resolve conflicts between alternative theoretical perspectives of the phenomena. A hallmark of this approach—the back-and-forth, alternating work on empirical, theoretical, and modeling fronts—underscores the importance of closely connecting computational modeling to the real-world phenomena and existing theories that motivate the modeler's research. Without such connections, computational models may seem irrelevant to others, and the field could miss an important opportunity to build cumulative research.

Framing the empirical puzzle as the tendency of groups to omit from consideration data that are not shared by all group members, Stasser establishes a clearly defined research question that DISCUSS was built to explore. Here we see another lesson for others interested in using computational modeling for social science research: Define the research goal carefully and clearly—even narrowly. Without a well-defined research question, it would be difficult to judge the performance of the model and difficult to establish model boundaries and level of analysis. For instance, without existing empirical data to provide a benchmark against which model results can be evaluated, Stasser's task of building and exploring DISCUSS would be complicated considerably.

Acknowledging limitations and discussing drawbacks of the model provide a third lesson for would-be modelers. Not only are such acknowledgments important for establishing credibility—a modeler who anticipates criticism and addresses it is more likely to attract the support of others—but they also provide the modeler with ideas about the next steps in refining and extending the model, part of the often messy and time-consuming process of revisiting and improving any computational model of a social system. In this chapter, Stasser acknowledges constraints on his study, cautioning us about extending inferences drawn from the DISCUSS simulations to other situations (e.g., the idea that advocacy and nonadvocacy discussion styles produce similar results). He also notes points on which the model could be critiqued: Memory is explicitly represented only in a most basic fashion, and participation is modeled with a simple formula. Discussing alternatives to his choices, he helps the reader think about how participation could be modeled differently, for instance, by accounting for the speaker's expertise. The discussion of how participation is modeled sets the stage for the next refinement to the model, which represents cyclical turn-taking. Thus, one of the limitations of the first version of DISCUSS is addressed in the next model, DISCUSS–P.

Our fourth lesson concerns the value of simplicity, particularly in initial model tests. In fact, like many computational modelers (e.g., see Carley & Lin, 1997), this research uses stylized tasks as means to develop and test theories and models. Such a stylized task allows the researchers to assess a baseline case against which more elaborate scenarios can be tested; it also may be more amenable to empirical exploration in experimental settings, allowing the correspondence between the model and the real world to be tested. As noted, Stasser introduces the development of DISCUSS with a relatively simple decision task that has already been explored empirically; in introducing the model, he also presents default cases, which are the simplest assumptions for a range of model options. For instance, one default assumption is that all group members assign the same valence to a given decision alternative; that assumption can be relaxed to allow valence disparities among group members in subsequent simulations. Similarly, participation rates are modeled by a simple and tractable power function, for which Stasser finds supporting evidence in the literature, but which he later refines.

Although Stasser's chapter offers us a variety of general lessons on how to use computational modeling as a theory-refining tool that can build on and guide empirical studies, it also presents some intriguing ideas about group decision making. We turn briefly to such substantive issues next, and as we shall quickly see, questions about the theoretical explanations for the phenomena Stasser has set out to investigate are closely tied to questions about his modeling approach.

Questions Concerning the Modeling Approach

How would real-world agents behave if they followed the steps simulated in DISCUSS? The answer was not always clear. For instance, in the nonnorm condition, the model allows for the group to converge on a valence value that is the average of its members. How would this happen in a real group? Would all members have to speak in order for others to learn of their valences? If not, what is the means by which convergence takes place? Asking such questions can be a useful way of figuring out whether the assumptions that are necessary to make the model tractable also make sense as representations of the real world. Not all modeling assumptions accurately capture the underlying processes, as Stasser is careful to point out, and the modeler must live with such shortcuts in order to build a model that works. Nevertheless, it is useful to step back and assess the realism as well as the empirical and theoretical support of processes and mechanisms in the model.

Another key question to consider in interpreting the simulation results is, What assumptions about group decision making most influence the model results? Although we know that, like all models, DISCUSS, SPEAK, and DISCUSS–P contain simplifications, omissions, and shorthand representations of real-world phenomena, and we learn what some of them are (the representation of participation, for instance), we do not have a good sense of the relative importance of the simplifying assumptions. Is the omission of expertise as a determinant of participation rates more influential than the effects of recent participation captured by the turn-taking modification described in the chapter? Might advocacy matter, after all, if status, dominance, or competence were accounted for? Of course, no single study—or set of studies—could possibly examine all assumptions and their effects, but there is room for the modeler to try using sensitivity tests to determine which parameters and assumptions are most important. This is precisely what Stasser does in testing six versions of DISCUSS with different assumptions for advocacy and valence. Yet, the reader would appreciate a more detailed explanation of why some conditions, and not others, were chosen for extensions and modifications. Perhaps an opportunity exists to explain how this set of DISCUSS simulation tests was designed with existing empirical and theoretical puzzles in mind. In other words, what is the support for the particular choices of model extensions that are explored in the chapter?

A third question, which links the substantive with the methodological, concerns the initial goal of the research presented in this chapter: to explore and contrast the normative and informational views of social influence theory, along with the information-sharing explanation developed by Stasser and Titus (1985, 1987). When we come to the description of model tests, however, it is not clear that DISCUSS explicitly represents each of the rival explanations. Is there a version of the model that captures a normative explanation and a version of the model that captures an informational perspective? Although the model simulations were set up to explore the relative effect of sampling bias and advocacy on results—aspects of the model that earlier empirical work by Stasser and Titus (1985) highlighted—we are not told whether other adjustments to the model would shed light on the theoretical debate that frames this chapter. For instance, it also might have been of interest to explore the behavior of two "ideal-type" versions of DISCUSS, each representing the extremes of normative and informational perspectives. Every model parameter that would be different under the two cases could then be presented and explained with reference to the existing theory and any relevant empirical results. Such an approach might not have changed the results Stasser reports here, but it could have served a valuable pedagogical purpose.

In the end, every modeler must decide which parameters or assumptions to explore. The data the model builder draws on to make such a decision are, by definition, incomplete, and it would clearly be impossible to test all combinations of assumptions and parameters. A researcher with Stasser's extensive empirical experience may be at an advantage in such a situation, because he or she can rely on his experience, unreported data from past studies, and intuition to figure out what the most interesting and important model tests and extensions are likely to be.

A further question any computational modeler must tackle is, How are we to judge results? Stasser asks whether the DISCUSS results were "close to" those obtained empirically, and he offers graphs of the results as evidence. But how are we to evaluate whether the two sets of results are close enough? What tests could we conduct to convince ourselves? One solution, which is Stasser's approach, is to look for the same patterns in results across treatment conditions. As he argues, simulations that cannot produce the same pattern can be eliminated as candidate explanations. A next step beyond this criterion would be to establish tests of significance.

The last point concerns an issue Stasser mentions near the end of his chapter, where he is critical of the omission, in DISCUSS and SPEAK, of the social and psychological mechanisms that shape speaker selection, which are clearly of central importance to the model results. One must not fault the models too severely on those grounds. Surely any model falls short of representing the underlying processes at some point—empirically derived relationships and patterns enter all models at some level, standing in for a fuller representation of the processes that generate them. Yet every modeler must figure out where to draw the line—whether the omission of a particular process or mechanism will compromise the simulation results. This concern is not trivial: research on complex adaptive systems suggests that understanding behavior at one level of analysis may require an explicit focus on emergence, which is the interaction of lower level processes to generate higher-level behaviors (Holland, 1998). Researchers studying organizations (e.g., Carley, 1995) have recently joined physical and biological scientists in exploring how to capture such emergence and select appropriate levels of analysis. With Stasser's work on group decision making, we now have another important contribution in the social sciences. And the fact that DISCUSS and its successors raise as many questions as they help to answer gives us a sense of how generative computational modeling can be.

References

Carley, K. M. (1995). Computational and mathematical organization theory: Perspectives and directions. *Computational and Mathematical Organization Theory, 1*, 39–56.

Carley, K. M., & Lin, Z. (1997). A theoretical study of organizational performance under information distortion. *Management Science, 43*, 976–997.

Holland, J. H. (1998). *Emergence: From chaos to order.* Reading, MA: Addison-Wesley.

Stasser, G., & Titus, W. (1985). Pooling of unshared information in group decision making: Biased information sampling during discussion. *Journal of Personality and Social Psychology, 48*, 1467–1478.

Stasser, G., & Titus, W. (1987). Effects of information load and percentage of shared information on the dissemination of unshared information during group discussion. *Journal of Personality and Social Psychology, 53*, 81–93.

Sterman, J. D. (1994). Learning in and about complex systems. *System Dynamics Review, 10*, 291–330.

CHAPTER 8

Computational Modeling with Petri Nets

Solutions for Individual and Team Systems

Michael D. Coovert
David W. Dorsey

Those who seek to understand behavior have at their disposal a wide variety of research tools. Most of the methodologies come from two traditional disciplines—study of individual differences or experimentation. Inferential strategies, such as correlation and analysis of variance, have emerged from these disciplines and, serving us well, have led to advances in the scientific basis for understanding behavior.

Yet, there are situations in which we cannot apply a suitable traditional methodology. A major emphasis of this chapter is to describe one such problem—the need to model a system at several levels of abstraction and to carry those models across time—and our solution, which involves the application of Petri nets. After providing a brief overview of Petri nets, the chapter gives a detailed description of the problem encountered when modeling individuals and teams across time. A formal definition of Petri nets is provided in the appendix.

A Brief Overview of Petri Nets

Conventional tools, such as flow diagrams, narrative descriptions, and timeline analysis, are useful for a variety of modeling problems; however, they impose constraints on the representation and therefore are not powerful enough for certain types of tasks. Specifically, those tools make it difficult to expose critical time dependencies, task concurrencies, and behavior that is event driven. Petri nets are a useful and powerful modeling tool and overcome these shortcomings.

This research was supported in part by Contract No. DAAL03-86-D0001, Delivery Order 2212, of the Scientific Services Program. The views, opinions, and/or findings contained in this chapter are those of the authors and should not be construed as an official Department of the Army position, policy, or decision, unless so designated by other documentation.

C. A. Petri (1962) proposed the methodology as a general-purpose tool for modeling systems with distributed, asynchronous, concurrent, and stochastic properties. Furthermore, Petri nets can model parallel activities (and conflict) as well as aggregates of individuals.

Petri nets have both graphical and mathematical properties. Their graphical representations provide an excellent communication medium. As a mathematical tool, Petri nets establish algebraic equations, state equations, or other mathematical models that control the behavior of the system. The mathematical underpinnings of the nets allow for rigorous analysis.[1] The mathematics of Petri nets here are beyond the scope of this chapter; for more information, see Reutenauer (1990) and Desel and Silva (1998).

Basic Components

Consider the everyday task of driving a car. While in control of the car, the driver performs many activities, such as checking the environment for traffic signs and traffic lights as well as controlling the car by steering, providing gasoline to the engine, and applying the brakes. This simple "model" of driver behavior has activities, such as pressing the gas pedal to provide gasoline, pressing the brake pedal, and the cognitive activity of observing and interpreting the street signs and stoplights. Some of these activities are performed in parallel, such as pressing the gas pedal and steering. Other activities are serial, such as observing a streetlight changing from green to red and pressing the brake to stop the car. The model also contains elements to signify that one activity has ended and another can begin. Consider the driver observing the stoplight changing from green to red. As the driver prepares to stop the car, his or her foot needs to be removed from the gas pedal. Once off the gas pedal, the driver can move the foot over and apply pressure to the brake. This model of driver behavior has elements that represent both active and passive states of the driver. Active states include such behaviors as steering, pressing the gas and brake, and the cognitive activity of determining whether the stoplight is red, yellow, or green. Passive states in the model are used to signify the end of one activity (e.g., pressing the gas pedal) and enable the start of a new activity (e.g., pressing the brake).

Building a Petri net model of driver behavior is straightforward, because Petri nets have only three basic elements. Active components, the first element, are used to represent agents or events and are generally referred to as *transitions;* they are depicted as rectangles or squares (▯ □). Passive components are the second system type, and they are represented as circles or ovals (○). Passive components also represent channels, preconditions, or postconditions and are generally referred to as *places;*

---

[1]A good overview of recent developments and extensions of Petri nets can be found in the book edited by Jensen & Rozenberg (1991). Readers interested in special issues are encouraged to explore the literature (see Jensen and Rozenberg, 1991; Peterson, 1981; Reisig, 1992) on the topic of interest and to use various software packages for the analysis of their models (see Alphatech, 1992; Chiiola, 1989; Metasoftware, 1992; Perceptronics, 1992).

they typically represent a state in which one activity has ended and another can begin. Connections between the active and passive system components are made through arrows (→←), with the direction of the arrow indicating the direction of the relationship (e.g., the flow of information). For example, an active component connected to a passive component and the passive connected to a subsequent active one are represented as □→○→□.

Figure 8.1 presents a model of driving behavior built from these three elements. We see the active elements of driving: determining if a stoplight is red, yellow, or green, and applying the brakes or providing gasoline. Places are used to represent that activities can begin.

Two additional components include a weight function (W) that can be used to assign probabilities (or likelihoods) to an arc, and a marking associated with the places (M) to denote the current state of the net. In Figure 8.1, notice that two arcs lead from the yellow light: one to apply the brake and the other to provide gas. Our model can represent a conservative driver, who 85% of the time will brake when a light turns yellow and only 15% of the time will provide gas to speed through. A model of an aggressive driver would have those likelihoods reversed. The marking of the net in Figure 8.1 shows the driver just beginning. Across time, the state of the net will change as the driver provides gas, checks the color of the light, and so on. So the marking of a net allows us to say what exactly is happening at any specific time in this dynamic representation.

Petri nets can be excellent tools for communication because of their graphical nature, but these nets go beyond flow charts and block diagrams in that they incorporate *tokens,* which are used to simulate dynamic and concurrent activities of a system. Tokens reside in places and move throughout the net as the transitions "fire." The firing of a transition is controlled by rules associated with the transition. In the simplest case, a transition is enabled and fires as soon as a token resides in the place that precedes it. Tokens are used to represent abstract or nonabstract entities within a model and are usually depicted as a solid circle ●. In our example (see again Figure 8.1), we are using a small car as a token. As the driver performs different activities, the model represents it by the token (our car) moving throughout the Petri net model.

Summary

In the simplest case, only three elements are used to construct a Petri net model: (a) Transitions reflect active model components, (b) places represent passive components, and (c) directed arcs add structure through linkages between places-to-transitions and transitions-to-places. Tokens represent the current state of the system (i.e., wherever a token resides, that activity is being performed or that place is being occupied). In our work described in this chapter, we use a slightly richer representation with the weight functions and the markings. The weight functions are useful, because we need to control behavior within a net when more than one arc can be traversed at any particular decision point. The markings allow us to determine characteristics of

FIGURE 8.1

Petri net model of a car driver's behavior when approaching a stoplight

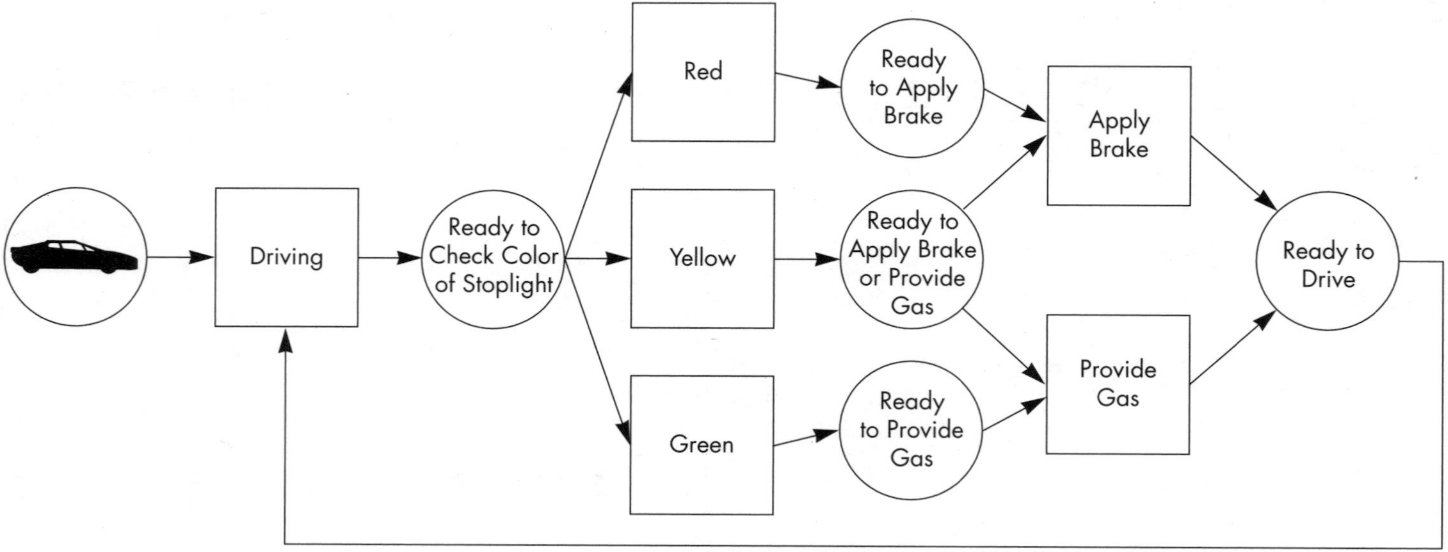

Driving
Ready to Check Color of Stoplight
Red
Yellow
Green
Ready to Apply Brake
Ready to Apply Brake or Provide Gas
Ready to Provide Gas
Apply Brake
Provide Gas
Ready to Drive

the net (e.g., the amount of work load) at any particular time. Mathematics underlies the graphical structure and controls the behavior of the system.

Modeling Individual and Team Performance in a Dynamic Decision-Making Environment

During the late 1980s, the U.S. Navy was involved in several incidents that had unfortunate and grievous consequences. The best known of these incidents involved the Aegis-class guided-missile cruiser Vincennes. Out of these tragic incidents grew several research programs whose goal is, in part, to aid understanding of human performance in complex decision-making environments. Such an understanding can contribute to development of interventions (such as training) and decision aids to augment human performance for individuals and teams in these environments.

Early work by the first author (Coovert, Campbell, Dorsey, Rametta, & Craiger, 1992) demonstrated that Petri nets provide a useful modeling capability for representing people as they interact with various computer and control systems in combat information centers. That is, we can represent, in a graphical manner, individuals performing various tasks and duties. This chapter extends that effort by (a) providing analytical evidence regarding the advantages of Petri nets as a diagnostic tool in assessing human performance in a dynamic team environment, (b) using Petri net modeling and computer simulation as a means for testing psychological theories of decision making, and (c) demonstrating how specific variables of interest (i.e., expertise) can be modeled and analyzed using simulations.

Method

Jobs

The three jobs modeled in this study are the Tactical Information Coordinator, Identification Supervisor, and Electronic Warfare Supervisor. These jobs are a subset of the larger combat information center (CIC) team on board U.S. Navy Aegis ships. The Tactical Information Coordinator is responsible for all air and surface tracking and identification. The Identification Supervisor is responsible for establishing and entering identification parameters, monitoring the assignment of identification to tracks, and resolving identification conflicts. The Electronic Warfare Supervisors oversee the operation of certain radars and sensors to ensure, among other things, the proper reporting, correlation, and triangulation of tracks. (A track is any contact identified by the various radars and sensors.)

Specification of Behaviors

To determine what actions, behaviors, or decisions might occur in each of the three positions for a given event, a declassified version of a scenario entitled "Desert

Shriek" was used. This scenario includes 122 discrete identifiable events that are important to the team. The information comes in the form of radar data, voice reports, link data (from other platforms), or electronic warfare data. Figure 8.2 provides a general overview of some of these events in the form of a timeline.

Subject-matter experts provided us with the list of appropriate behaviors that each operator should perform for each event throughout the scenario. This information included (a) how critical the event is within the scenario (e.g., a missile launch toward one's own ship is more critical than a friendly merchant ship fading from radar), (b) the pre- and postevent behaviors that occur for each event (e.g., before a hostile aircraft changes course, the Tactical Information Coordinator should be observing the radar screen; after the hostile aircraft changes course, the Tactical Information Coordinator should immediately update all information on that aircraft), and (c) the likelihood that an expert would engage in the described behavior and the likelihood that a novice would do the same thing.

For example, on the timeline in Figure 8.2 at time 24 minutes and 00 seconds is an event in which two hostile aircraft change course toward one's own ship. The experts provided a criticality index for the event; the behaviors that each operator (Tactical Information Coordinator, Identification Supervisor, Electronic Warfare Supervisor) should be performing, given what had happened up to that point in the scenario; and the likelihood that an expert and novice, respectively, would engage in the appropriate behavior for that event. We used this information to build the models of operator behavior for the simulations.

Apparatus

Percnet/HSI software (Perceptronics, 1992) was used, and the simulations were executed on a SUN SPARCstation. *Percnet* is a graphical computer simulation environment and uses modified Petri nets as the primary modeling tool. It also allows for expert-system information. The model builder can incorporate strategies commonly used in expert systems to represent knowledge, such as frames and production rules. These capabilities are important for modeling the amount of work load experienced by the teams. Issues related to work load will be presented shortly.

Procedure

Subsequent to gathering the data from the subject matter experts, Petri net models of each of the three positions in the team were built with *Percnet*. The specific architecture of these models will be discussed shortly. After constructing the basic net structures, control structures were added that allowed the manipulation of independent variables such as level of expertise (i.e., novice versus expert) and informational ambiguity. Dependent measures, including behavioral duration (i.e., time), behavioral frequencies, and work load measures, were collected based on simulation runs of the different conditions.

FIGURE 8.2

Timeline of scenario events

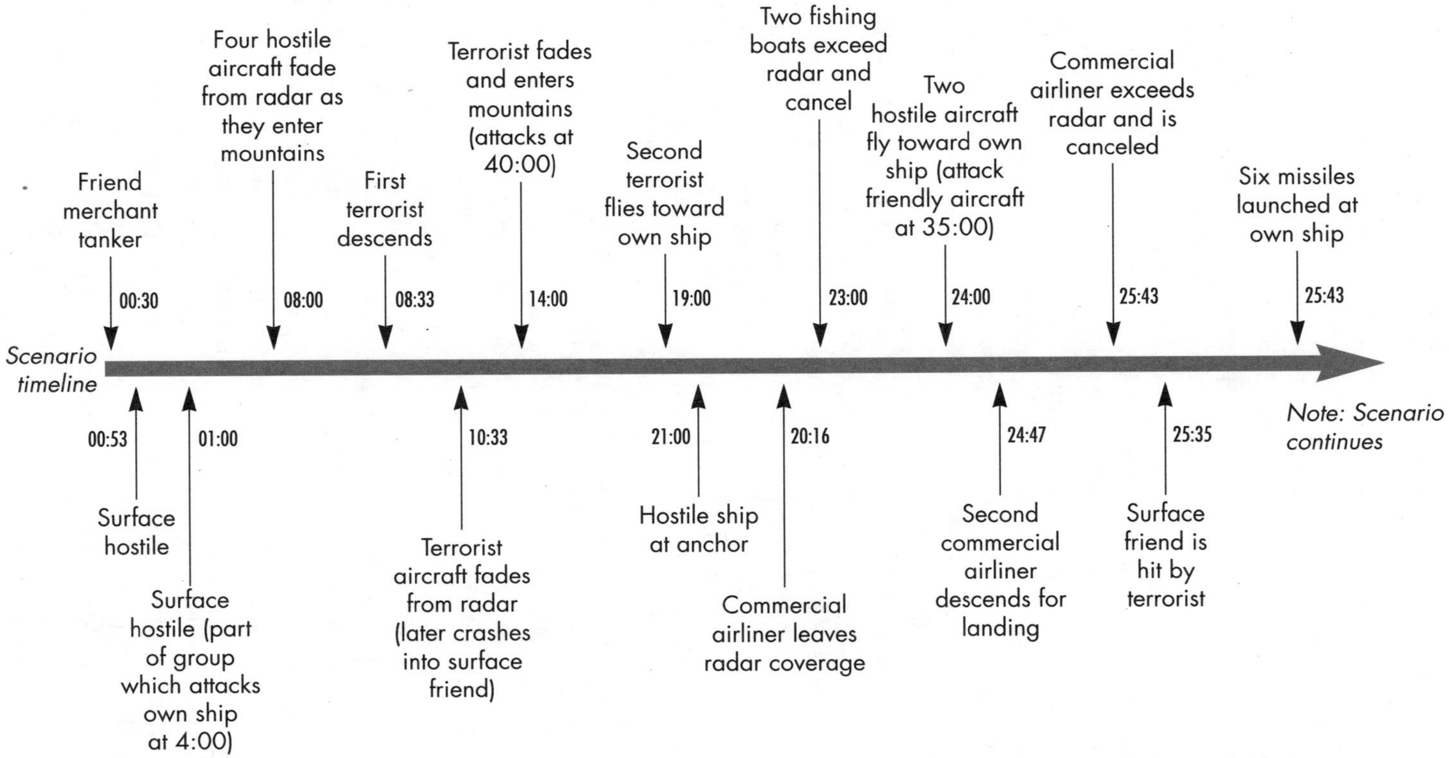

Friend merchant tanker
00:30

Four hostile aircraft fade from radar as they enter mountains
08:00

First terrorist descends
08:33

Terrorist fades and enters mountains (attacks at 40:00)
14:00

Second terrorist flies toward own ship
19:00

Two fishing boats exceed radar and cancel
23:00

Two hostile aircraft fly toward own ship (attack friendly aircraft at 35:00)
24:00

Commercial airliner exceeds radar and is canceled
25:43

Six missiles launched at own ship
25:43

Scenario timeline

00:53
Surface hostile

01:00
Surface hostile (part of group which attacks own ship at 4:00)

10:33
Terrorist aircraft fades from radar (later crashes into surface friend)

21:00
Hostile ship at anchor

20:16
Commercial airliner leaves radar coverage

24:47
Second commercial airliner descends for landing

25:35
Surface friend is hit by terrorist

Note: Scenario continues

Independent and Dependent Variables

The independent variables chosen for manipulation were expertise and the ambiguity of information. The two variables are a small representation of the variables that probably play a role in CIC performance, but subject-matter experts agreed that they are among the most important ones. Expertise was operationally defined in terms of a dichotomy based on amount of experience, either expert or novice. For our purposes, an expert model is based on the behavior of a trainer at the naval facility who instructed and trained incoming teams for Aegis cruisers. Novice models are based on the behaviors of individual sailors who are trained by the expert trainers. *Informational ambiguity* is defined and manipulated as a set of events involving conflicting or vague information. An illustration of informational ambiguity is the degree of unreliable identification or sensor data resulting from adverse atmospheric conditions. In the simulations, informational ambiguity corresponded to a delay in operator behavior as well as to an increase in the probability of performing a nonoptimal behavior. Graphically, these consequences are illustrated in one of two ways. The first is as an individual proceeding down an incorrect arc in a network of possible behaviors. The second class of problems would be a key decision transition not firing (or being significantly delayed) and would be illustrated as a token not proceeding throughout the network. Both expertise and informational ambiguity are hypothesized to be key factors in dynamic, naturalistic, decision-making environments (Klein, 1989).

The dependent variables generated from the simulation include behavior duration (i.e., mean duration of activities—how long it takes a person to perform a task), behavioral probability (frequency of behavior—the probability that an operator performed the correct behavior in reaction to a scenario event), and the amount of individual operator and team work load. Work load is defined according to the Multiple Resource Model (MRM) of Wickens, Kramer, Vanasse, and Donchin (1983). This is an information-processing perspective of work load, and it makes certain assumptions about how difficult it is to perform tasks concurrently (colloquially known as "how to walk and chew gum at the same time"). A more relevant example involves the process of learning to drive a car. Most people find it fairly easy to sit in the seat, look out the windshield, and understand what is going on around them. However, coordinating the movement of the hands and arms to steer the car and of the legs and feet to accelerate and brake take additional resources (increased work load). Increased speed of the car and an increased number of cars around that of the driver will increase the amount of cognitive work and overall work load. Adding the processing of auditory information by listening and talking on a cellular phone will take further cognitive resources and result in increased work load. Of course, individual levels of expertise will affect the amount of work load. A novice driver will experience greater levels of work load while driving on a busy interstate highway during rush hour, whereas someone who has been driving in rush hour traffic every day for a few years will be under less work.

Wickens's model is as follows.

$$W_T = \sum_{i=1}^{m} \sum_{t=1}^{n} a_{t,i} + \sum_{i=1}^{m} \sum_{t=1}^{m} c_{i,j} \sum_{t=1}^{n-1} \sum_{s=t+1}^{n} (a_{t,i} + a_{s,j}) \tag{8.1}$$

where W_T = instantaneous work load at time T, $i,j = 1 \ldots m$ are the resource channels (e.g., audio, visual), $t,s = 1 \ldots n$ are the operator activities, $a_{t,i}$ = loadings on channel i to perform activity t (e.g., the amount of effort to process visual information), and $c_{i,j}$ = conflict between channels i and j (e.g., if processing visual information, the amount of conflict to simultaneously listen to information). This model of work load measures the individual demands on a series of resource channels (e.g., visual processing; auditory processing; verbal processing; spatial processing; continuous physical, or motor, activity; and discrete motor activity) and also takes into account concurrent activities in terms of resource conflict. Subject-matter experts determined individual resource demand values for each activity.

Design of the Operator Nets

Figure 8.3 depicts the basic architecture for the models of CIC operator behavior. The upper panel of the figure represents the general architecture, and the lower panel presents a specific example. The scenario events themselves are not being modeled; rather, the behavioral or "problem" space of the operators is the object of the modeling (Anderson, 1993). As the figure illustrates, the modified Petri nets in the *Percnet* implementation are similar to traditional Petri nets.

The activities (noted as circles or ovals) represent a specific activity taking place. In the *Percnet* implementation, the events (rectangles) mark the end of specific activities, and the events fire to denote that a specific event has taken place (Perceptronics, 1992). Along the top of each net is a series of two behaviors (labeled "Effective behavior 1" and "Effective behavior 2" in the general net) that an operator might engage in after having receiving cues that a specific event has just occurred. These acts can be thought of as the appropriate actions needed in response to the event. In the lower panel of the figure, the event is "Terrorist 2 flies toward own ship," and the two correct[2] behaviors that the Tactical Information Coordinator should take are first, to "gather kinematics on terrorist 2," and second, to "communicate information" with the team.

Also, inspection of the generic net indicates that instead of engaging in the appropriate series of acts, the operator might make an error, either at the first or second step in the series, and engage in another generic behavior (labeled "Error 1 behavior" and "Error 2 behavior"). These represent nonoptimal performance, or behavior performed in response to a scenario event that was specified as nonoptimal by the subject-matter experts. In the specific example provided in the lower panel of

[2]The data collected from the subject-matter experts outlines what each of the appropriate actions should be.

FIGURE 8.3

Petri net architecture of operator behavior

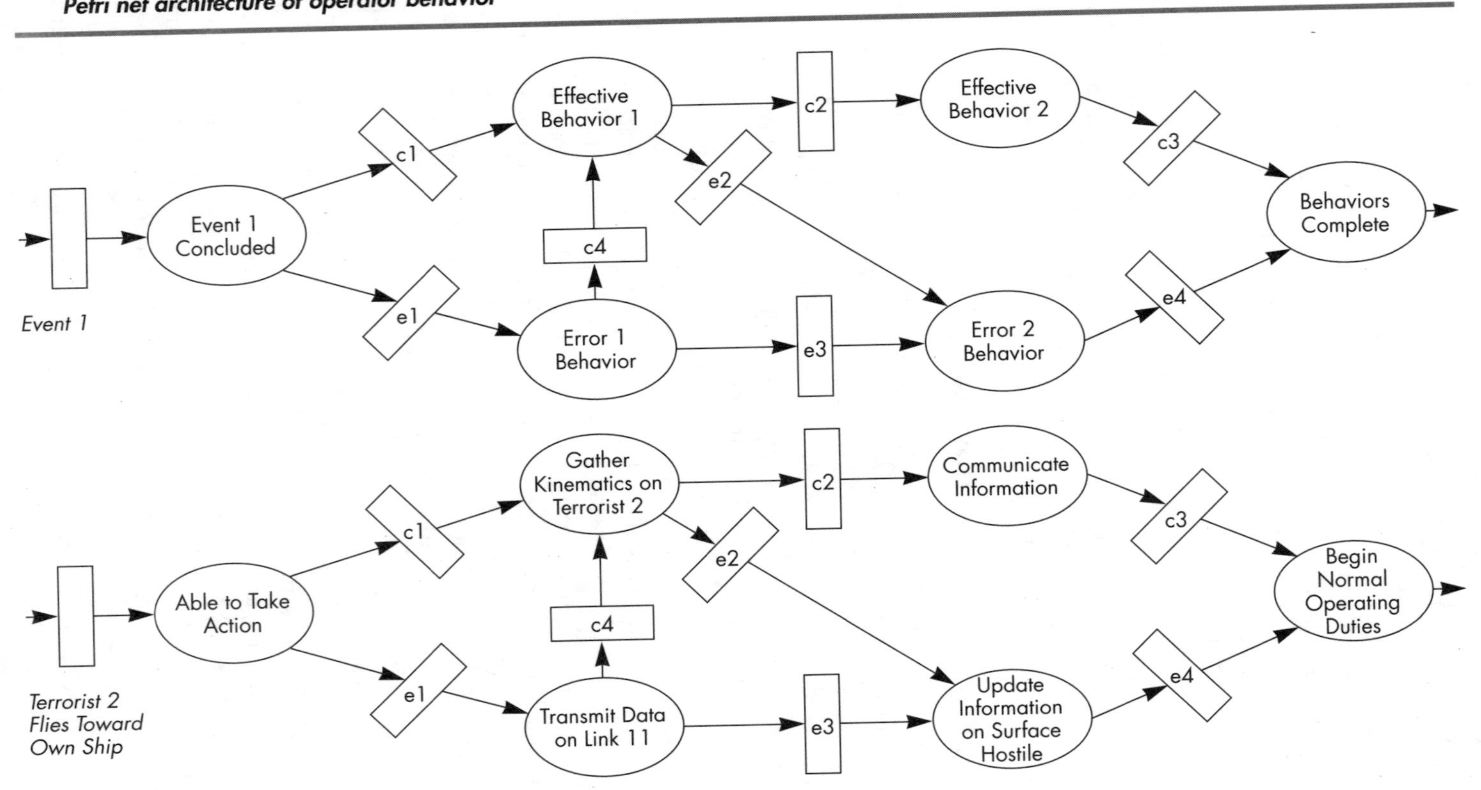

Note: The upper panel depicts generalized behavior, and the lower panel provides specific examples. c1 through c4 are correct actions, whereas e1 through e4 are errors.

Figure 8.3, the first error is to "transmit data on link 11," and the second error is to "update information on the hostile surface ship." These behaviors are modeled as a function of the independent variables discussed earlier. For example, the probability that any of the events labeled with an e1 through e4 in the figure will fire might be low for an expert (e.g., .01) and high for a novice (e.g., .70).

Also, note that even if an operator does make a mistake initially, he or she might still engage in the next appropriate behavior. For example, operators who initially make a mistake and transmit data on link 11 might recover and take corrective action (c4) and proceed to gather kinematic information on terrorist 2. Similarly, after gathering kinematic information on the terrorist, they might make the subsequent correct action (c2) and communicate, or they might perform an incorrect behavior, such as updating information on a hostile surface ship (e2).

Hierarchical Modeling

Petri nets allow the measurement of performance at different levels of a system hierarchy, such as team, position, duty, or task. Figure 8.4 provides an example of how the Petri net model for the Electronic Warfare Supervisor operator is constructed in a hierarchical fashion. Each of the dotted-line arrows indicates that the net in the level below is a subnet, or elaboration, of the original net. The activities with the double circles indicate that the net contains a subnet.

The top portion of Figure 8.4 corresponds to the overall team, with the three positions. The center portion is the *duty*[3] level, and is the level of our main focus. The bottom portion of the figure corresponds to the *task* level; the nets could go even further down to elemental levels of operator behavior corresponding to such actions as specific button pushes. (We have, in fact, constructed nets at this high level of detail for other purposes, such as to model human–computer interaction with the Command and Decision, Weapons Control, and radar systems.) We choose the duty level as the main level of focus for performance measurement because it most clearly indicates the outcomes of operator decision making. The task level is basically the sequential steps that the operator has to take in order to complete a specific activity.

Results

This section presents some highlights from our simulation results (more detailed results are available in Coovert & Dorsey 1994, and Dorsey, 1993). We describe select findings based on work load, behavioral frequency (i.e., what the operator is doing), and behavioral duration (i.e., how long it takes the operator to perform the action).

---

[3]*Duty* is used here as it is used in traditional job analysis: a job is composed of a series of duties that can be further broken into tasks.

FIGURE 8.4

Petri net model of a three-member team elaborated to duties and elaborated to tasks

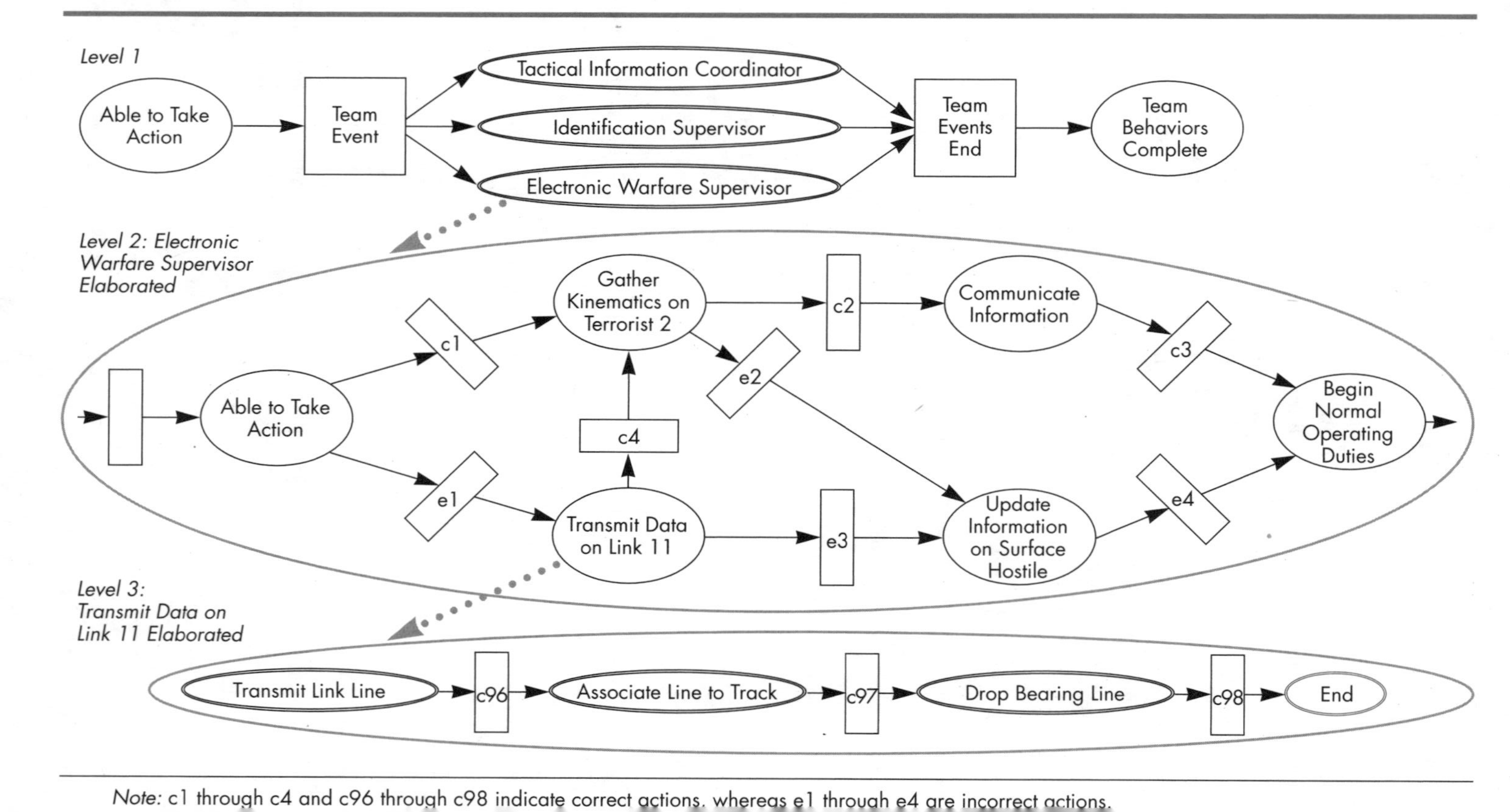

Note: c1 through c4 and c96 through c98 indicate correct actions, whereas e1 through e4 are incorrect actions.

Each measure is really a function of behavior taken in response to some type of informational event in the scenario: voice, link, or other sensor data (see Figure 8.2).

Based on Wickens et al.'s (1983) MRM model, work load measures for both an expert and a novice Tactical Information Coordinator were computed. Total time to complete the scenario, the overall work loads, the point where the work load was the highest, and the activities that caused the highest work loads all were identified.

As expected, the expert Tactical Information Coordinator completes the scenario in the least time and has a slightly higher work load. The activities causing the highest levels of work load are, however, the same for the expert and novice Tactical Information Coordinator. Interestingly, the novice operator reaches those high levels of work load much later in the scenario, most likely because the operator "got behind" and was unable to accomplish the correct tasks in the correct order and in a timely manner.

The same information was computed for the Identification Supervisor and Electronic Warfare Supervisor positions. Interestingly, except for the experts having a higher overall work load than the novices, the Tactical Information Coordinator pattern of results does not hold for the other two positions. First, there is little time difference in the total length of time to perform the duties for the experts and novices. Also, the time for the highest level of work load is slightly longer for the experts than for the novices. The point that causes the highest levels of work load is different for the novices than for the experts. These differences from the Tactical Information Coordinator position perhaps result from the novices spending more time than the experts did in "error" activities.

A second dependent measure is the frequency (or probability) that a correct behavior occurred in response to the stimulus event. The frequency patterns generated from the Petri net models can be statistically compared to determine whether they are different from one another. For example, even though the numbers look much different for the Tactical Information Coordinator novice and expert operator, are those differences large enough to be statistically significant? We compared those values for each operator using a nonparametric chi-square test, and the results are presented in Table 8.1.

A final point of interest regarding behavioral differences at the individual operator level is the considerable difference in the amount of time the various operators spent in activities that the subject-matter experts indicated were nonoptimal, given the context of the scenario. Table 8.2 presents this information; as expected, the novices spent much more time in nonoptimal activities than did the experts.

Team-Level Analysis

The same information examined for the operators also can be analyzed for the team as a whole. Again, this is one of the strengths of the approach—being able to model and analyze behavior from multiple levels of abstraction. Our modeling revealed

TABLE 8.1

Nonparametric chi-square comparisons of activity–frequency values for experts versus novices

OPERATOR	NO. OF ACTIVITIES	CHI-SQUARE
Tactical Information Coordinator	50	$\chi^2_{49} = 138.2, p < .01$
Identification Supervisor	15	$\chi^2_{14} = 8.7$, NS
Electronic Warfare Supervisor	23	$\chi^2_{22} = 37.9, p < .02$

TABLE 8.2

Total time in error activities (seconds)

OPERATOR	EXPERT TEAM (% OF TOTAL TIME)	NOVICE TEAM (% OF TOTAL TIME)
Tactical Information Coordinator	496.14 (40)	1,495.72 (86)
Identification Supervisor	143.05 (21)	232.68 (36)
Electronic Warfare Supervisor	0.00 (0)	82.74 (13)

that, in the aggregate, the expert team can perform each behavior elicited by the scenario events much more quickly than the novice team. The work load levels are higher for the expert team, both for the average work load and for the highest work load. As would be expected, the behaviors the individual operators engage in during the periods of highest work load are different for the experts and novices.

Activity frequencies in terms of work load range can also be compared for the two team types. Figure 8.5 presents a graph of the different work load ranges for the expert and novice teams, respectively, at different time segments of the scenario. The patterns are quite different from one another, indicating the different levels of work load affecting operators of the expert and novice teams. Statistically, the activity frequencies can be evaluated with the chi-square test to determine if they are significantly different; and they are, based on 88 team activities $\chi^2_{87} = 185, p < .01$.

A final result is that the expert team spent, on average, 20% of its time in nonoptimal behaviors, whereas the novice team spent 45% of its time in nonoptimal behaviors.

Conclusion

The purpose of our present work has been to introduce a powerful modeling tool to researchers and practitioners and describe how it can be used for problems with various levels of complexity. Our work demonstrates that Petri nets provide a useful

FIGURE 8.5

Comparison of work load levels experienced by expert and novice teams

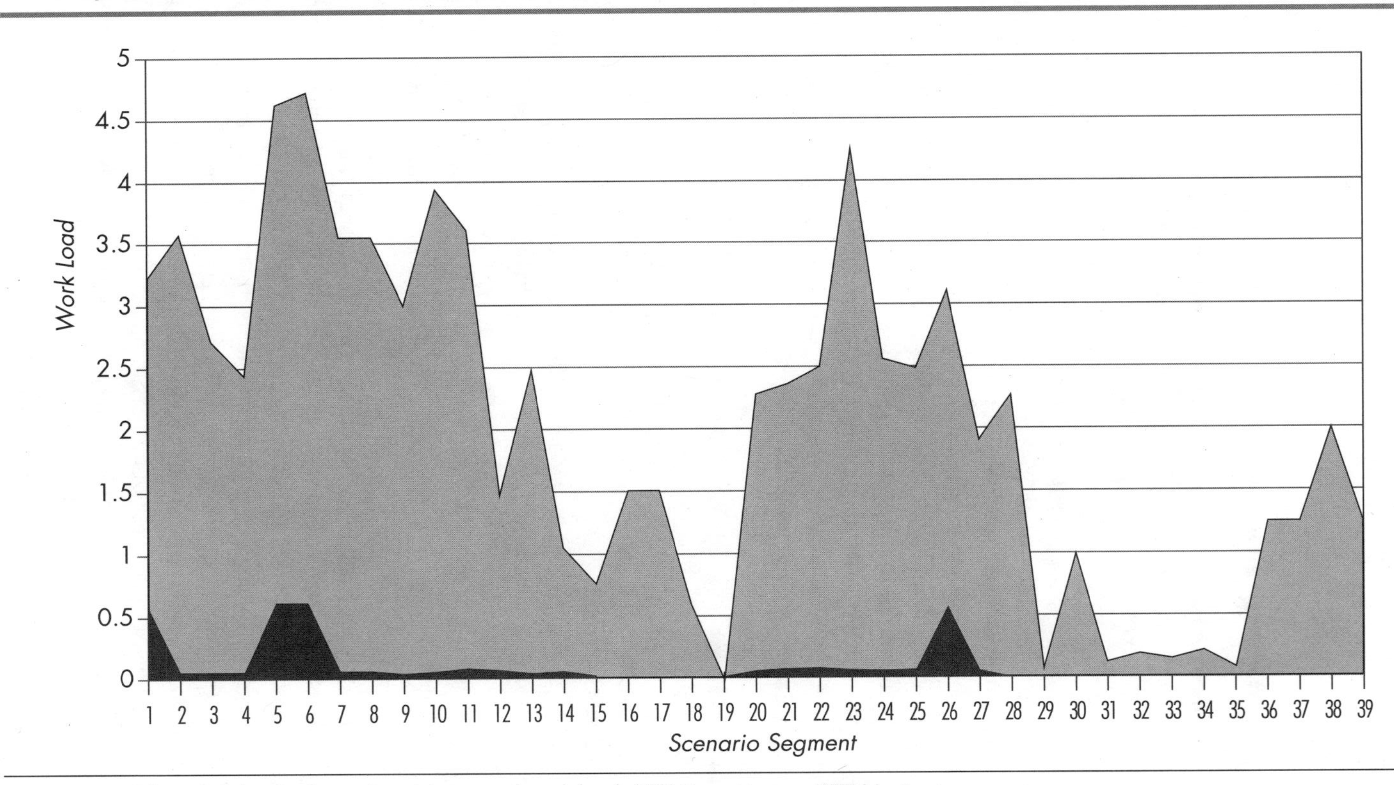

Note: Higher work load value indicates increased work load. Expert team Novice team

tool for modeling human performance in dynamic decision-making environments. Furthermore, models can be constructed to determine the impact of various individual-difference variables, such as expertise, on the performance of individual operators as well as teams.

Generalizing the Nets

Another important aspect of the Petri net approach, which we have already briefly mentioned, is its ability to represent individuals within a system. A common extension to basic Petri nets is what are called *colored Petri nets* (Jensen, 1992). These nets incorporate tokens that may be differentiated by color, with various colors indicating arbitrary data values. This is a key development for modeling complex systems and is useful in many applications. The implication is that tokens may inherit and carry properties in the network, thereby changing their color or data values and altering the possible net spaces along which the tokens travel. Because of this feature, we can simulate individual attributes such as knowledge, skills, or abilities (or even the acquisition of knowledge, skills, or abilities after entering training activities); tenure; individual performance measures; group membership; and a host of other individual or group differences. By assigning data attributes to tokens, complex and seemingly unmanageable issues can be represented and modeled.

Limitations

The question remains, however, as to what extent the mapping between our Petri net representation and the real-world problems is useful. We briefly address two aspects of this issue.

First, it is obvious that the model's validity and the computer simulation results depend heavily on real-world data, which serve to frame the model and drive the accompanying simulations. This is essentially the "garbage in–garbage out" problem familiar to all researchers working with computer-based models. Only to the extent that the subject matter experts provide veridical information can the simulations generate useful information.

The second issue is how to handle the growth of complexity within a network model. We need to capture enough detail in the model so that all critical parameters are represented, but in a complex environment, where many individuals are interacting with several different computer systems, the model rapidly becomes very large. This question relates to Bonini's paradox (Lewandowski, 1993), which asks the question: Does the simulation or model turn out to be no easier to understand than the real-world processes (Dutton & Starbuck, 1971)?

From a less pessimistic perspective, it is clear that variables such as expertise can be manipulated and tested in Petri net models. This capability is promising for hypothesis testing and modeling specific theories as well as for generating hypotheses.

For example, in this study we generated some interesting questions concerning the levels of work load experienced by both experts and novices. Is it possible that the types of errors made by novices affect work load, and might this have an overall effect on performance?

Similarly, the growth of complexity in building network-based simulation models should not be viewed as a fatal flaw in representing real-world systems. Because of advancements being made in technologies such as object-oriented modeling and intelligent agents, it may be possible to manage the complexity of computer-based models and simulations by combining modeling approaches (e.g., object-oriented Petri nets).

The flexibility of Petri nets to allow both global and local performance measurement is a clear advantage of our approach. One can consider the measures related to a specific event–activity pairing or consider the overall picture of activity within a set of nodes. This type of data also can address problems related to the flow of work behavior. For example, is there a specific activity in which operators are taking too much time in terms of relaying information, thus creating a bottleneck for the entire team's performance? Also, a given vector of node measures could be validated against some criterion measure (e.g., a vector of the same activities as performed by an expert team on an important outcome criterion). Some preliminary work indicates that certain approaches hold promise, including linear statistics (Mahalanobis distance) and nonlinear analyses (neural networks).

Another question we might address with these models concerns team composition: How does a team with a mix of both expert and novice operators react compared with a team entirely composed of expert operators? Other more directly applied issues indicate the need for advanced modeling tools. For example, how can one concurrently measure such aspects of team performance as communication, psychomotor activities, work load fluctuations, and information flow? Also, how are errors propagated throughout the team's information-processing network? The Petri net modeling and simulation hold great promise for addressing these types of issues. If researchers hope to address the dynamic nature of behavior, measurement techniques have to move away from conventional analytic approaches to techniques that address the moment-to-moment interdependencies that exist in a system.

Decisions concerning the implementation of any advanced technology should ultimately be an issue of costs versus benefits. There is little doubt that computational modeling efforts may require extensive resources in terms of time, expertise, and information. However, when planning efforts involve systems as complex as many organizational systems are, tools may be needed that reinforce systems thinking and ultimately lead to improved action programs. Petri nets and the associated graphical language approach to computational modeling offer such a tool.

References

Alphatech, Inc. (1992). *Modeler.* Burlington, MA: Author.

Anderson, J. R. (1993). Problem solving. *American Psychologist, 48,* 35–44.

Chiiola, G. (1989). *GreatSPN.* Torino, Italy: University di Torino.

Coovert, M. D., Campbell, G. E., Dorsey, D., Rametta, L., & Craiger, J. P. (1992). *Quantifying team decision making performance through the use of Petri net models* (Vol. 1, Technical Report). Tampa, FL: University of South Florida, Department of Psychology and Institute for Human Performance, Decision Making, and Cybernetics.

Coovert, M. D., & Dorsey, D. W. (1994). Simulating individual and team expertise in a dynamic decision making environment. In A. Verbraek, H. G. Sol, & P. W. G. Bots (Eds.), *Proceedings of the fourth international working conference on dynamic modelling and information systems* (pp. 187–204). Delft, The Netherlands: Delft University Press.

Desel, J., & Silva, M. (1998). *Application and theory of Petri Nets 1998* (Proceedings of the 19th International Conference). Lisbon: Springer.

Dorsey, D. (1993). *Modeling human performance with Petri nets.* Unpublished master's thesis. Tampa: University of South Florida.

Dutton, J. M., & Starbuck, W. H. (Eds.). (1971). *Computer simulation of human behavior.* New York: Wiley.

Jensen, K. (1992). *Coloured Petri nets, Volume 1: Basic concepts.* Berlin: Springer-Verlag.

Jensen, K., & Rozenberg, G. (Eds.). (1991). *High-level Petri nets: Theory and application.* Berlin: Springer-Verlag.

Klein, G. A. (1989). Recognition-primed decisions. In W. B. Rouse (Ed.), *Advances in man–machine systems research* (Vol. 5, pp. 47–92). Greenwich, CT: JAI Press.

Lewandowski, S. (1993). The rewards and hazards of computer simulations. *Psychological Science, 4,* 236–243.

Metasoftware. (1992). *Design CPN.* Boston: Author.

Perceptronics. (1992). *Percnet/hsi user's manual.* Woodland Hills, CA: Author.

Peterson, J. L. (1981). *Petri nets and the modeling of systems.* Englewood Cliffs, NJ: Prentice Hall.

Petri, C. A. (1962). *Kommunikation mit automaten.* Schriften des IIM Nr. 2, Institute fur Instrumentelle Mathematik, Bonn. English Translation: Communicating with automata. Technical Report RADC-TR-65-377 (1966). New York: Griffiss Air Force Base.

Reisig, W. (1992). *A primer in Petri net design.* Berlin: Springer-Verlag.

Reutenauer, C. (1990). *The mathematics of Petri nets.* Hartford, England: Prentice Hall.

Wickens, C., Kramer, A., Vanasse, L., & Donchin, E. (1983). Performance of concurrent tasks—A psychophysiological analysis of the reciprocity of information processing resources. *Science, 221,* 1080–1082.

Appendix

Formally, the structure of a Petri net is a bipartite directed graph, $G = [P, T, F, W, M]$, where $P = \{p_1, p_2, \ldots, p_n\}$ is a set of finite places, $T = \{t_1, t_2, \ldots, t_m\}$ is a set of finite transitions, and $F = \{P \times T\} \cup \{T \times P\}$ is a set of directed arcs. The set of input places of a transition (t) is given by $I(t) = \{p|(p,t) \in F\}$, and the set of output places of transition (t) is given by $O(t) = \{p|(t,p) \in F\}$. The weights are specified as $W{:}F\ \{1, 2, 3, \ldots\}$ delineating the weight function for each arc. Finally, the marking of the places with tokens and the number of tokens are given by $M{:}P\ \{1, 2, 3, \ldots\}$.

COMMENT:

Getting Tangled in One's Own (Petri) Net

On the Promises and Perils of Computational Modeling

Norbert L. Kerr

Coovert and Dorsey's chapter nicely illustrates both some of the strengths of computational modeling as a method of inquiry—that is, the promise of the method—and some of its weaknesses—that is, some of the common perils of computational modeling. Below I consider a few of each.

On the Promise of Computational Modeling

The Promise of Accounting for Complexity

Perhaps the best rationale for developing and applying computational models is that they enable one to tackle complex systems. Coovert and Dorsey suggest that Petri nets provide a general conceptual and mathematical tool that can be used to analyze and model many complex systems, including performance teams and organizational entities. Indeed, the reader begins to get a feel for the power and flexibility of this tool through the authors' description of the basic components of Petri nets and their presentation of a Petri net model of a particular system (that of a warship combat information center [CIC]). One begins to appreciate how many complex real systems might be fairly represented in terms of the movement of tokens—or people or products or information—through a network of interconnected nodes. Particularly appealing in this regard is the power of this approach to capture the complexities of dynamic systems, with actions at one point having implications for subsequent (and, with feedback loops, previous) stages in the system.

For example, in reading the chapter, I was led to imagine adapting the Petri net logic to the operation of a decision-making group of special interest to me—the criminal jury. The subtasks of jury deliberation (e.g., choosing a foreperson, identifying alternative plausible stories or scenarios, reaching consensus on a most plausible version of the facts, deciding on whether the necessary elements of a crime are supported by the evidence, setting a functional standard of proof) have been modeled in isolation or in partial combinations (see Penrod & Hastie, 1979, or Hastie, Penrod, & Pennington, 1983, for reviews). However, one can, in principle, conceive of a Petri net model that combines these and other disparate and complex subtasks into a single model.

The Promise of Illuminating Pictures

Coovert and Dorsey also emphasize the special advantage of a modeling tool—like Petri nets—that can provide a meaningful graphical representation, a picture of the system. It is easier to explain and understand such visually rich models. It also is easier to see weaknesses and alternative versions of such models—one can question the necessity and utility of old or new links by exploring and modifying the graphs.

The Promise of Thought Experimentation

Computational models of group behavior offer the promise of exploring the effects of altering task, group, or member variables without actually manipulating these variables in situ. Elsewhere (Davis & Kerr, 1986), this has been called thought experimentation—experimenting with variables through simulation. When the groups in question are large, unwieldy, and difficult-to-access organizations, this promise is particularly attractive.

In their application of Petri nets, Coovert and Dorsey illustrate the potential of their computational model for such thought experimentation. For example, they note that one might explore the consequences (for working time, down time, decision quality, etc.) of varying how many and which CIC roles were filled with novices versus experts.

On the Perils of Computational Modeling

The intrepid user and popularizer of computational models should avoid certain perils, however. The perils are not as troublesome when the modeler's task is to present his or her latest work to those well versed in and convinced of the utility of modeling in general or of their specific modeling approach (e.g., Petri nets) in particular. But when the task is not to preach to the choir but to win new converts, one must be especially cautious. Coovert and Dorsey, I fear, have failed to avoid several of these all-too-common perils.

The Peril of Presenting a "Black Box" Model

If the rationale for developing and applying a computational model is to aid in understanding a complex behavioral setting, the model itself must not be as unclear and shrouded in mystery as the setting it is designed to illuminate. As Coovert and Dorsey have noted, users of computational models should keep in mind "Bonini's paradox" (i.e., that simulation complexity can sometimes match or even exceed the complexity of the actual behavioral system under study). But the same caution must hold when one is describing one's model. It is not essential that the model be a simple one; indeed, if it aspires to describe a complex set of phenomena, it is likely that it will itself be rather complex. But it is essential that the model be comprehensible not only to its users but also to the audiences with whom those users would communicate (e.g., we, the readers of Coovert and Dorsey's chapter). Without a clear, detailed, and comprehensive description of the model and its operation, audiences cannot assess the psychological plausibility of the model's assumptions, develop their own hypotheses about how the model might be most fruitfully applied or modified, or fairly evaluate the results of applying the model. In short, if the model is presented in a sketchy, piecemeal fashion, the reader cannot intelligently understand and evaluate it. It becomes a "black box," whose workings are shrouded in mystery and whose purported accomplishments must be accepted largely on faith.

Coovert and Dorsey introduce us to the most basic building blocks of Petri nets, but then quickly jump to the final black box model, with only a sketchy outline of the crucial intervening construction work. For example, we learn that there are three key players in the CIC team, that they each have to make a number of judgments, that one can simulate scenarios of interest (e.g., using the vaguely described "122 discrete identifiable events" [p. 167] sampled in Figure 8.2), that one can (in principle) construct Petri nets modeling their interconnected series of tasks, and so on. However, we are provided only (in Figures 8.3 and 8.4) a description of an isolated portion of the full net, without a detailed description of the particulars of the model's construction (e.g., starting assumptions, how probabilities of various transitions were estimated, how the actions of different team members are connected, what the full structure of the net is). Likewise, in the reported application of the model to the CIC team, key variables are sketchily defined (e.g., the "loadings" and "conflicts" that go into the computation of the key workload statistic are not defined).

It is a common failing of human communication to presume that one's listener will fill in the gaps in one's presentation. But when one is presenting computational models and wants the listener to both understand and appreciate the utility of one's model, this is a perilous failing.

The Peril of Promising Too Much

As Coovert and Dorsey note, computational models are, in principle, powerful tools. The best way to persuade those who do not currently use those tools (e.g., most scholars of organizational behavior) is to demonstrate explicitly that one can learn something that was unknown and not self-evident using the tool. Conversely, few will be persuaded of the power of computational models if their applications only serve to state the obvious or to restate the structure of the model itself.

Joe McGrath (1981) offers the following bit of doggerel on the user of computer simulations:

> He's got a big computer
> He runs it every day.
> It formulates, and calculates,
> And simulates away.
> He inputs it, stochastically,
> It outputs back in kind;
> Cause what it gives is what it's got;
> It's the echo of his mind.

This is not the "garbage in–garbage out" problem mentioned by Coovert and Dorsey. That refers to the fact that the results of a simulation can be no better than the parameter estimates and starting assumptions that it begins with. We are focusing on a rather different problem here. Necessarily, the consequences of a computational model are "built in"; what comes out must be the "echo" of the creator's mind. However, the most useful of these models also lead us to conclusions that were not implicit in the creator's initial assumptions. Lewandowski (1993) offered good illustrations from cognitive psychology. I can offer a few from my own subdiscipline of social psychology:

- Both theory and intuition suggest that increasing the benefits or decreasing the costs of cooperation should raise cooperation levels. Messick and Liebrand (1997) used a computational model of cooperation to demonstrate that under plausible social processes (viz., one cooperates when one's current outcomes compare favorably with those of nearby others and refuses to cooperate when they do not), cooperation levels will be relatively insensitive to the explicit benefits and costs of cooperation.
- Hastie et al. (1983) developed a computer simulation of the jury decision-making process that not only accurately predicted behavioral criteria, which were foremost in the model's formulation (e.g., overall rates of conviction and acquittal), but also successfully predicted a number of other behaviors which were essentially by-products of the model's calculations (e.g., deliberation times and rates of reversals of large factions).
- Both intuition and much social influence work suggest that opinion minorities cannot endure indefinitely—the demonstrated powers of opinion majorities to both pressure and persuade should eventually eliminate such minorities. However, Nowak, Szamrej, and Latané (1990) presented a dynamic model of social influence that demonstrated that under plausible

> assumptions about social influence, local geographic clusters of minority opinion can persist indefinitely.

In contrast, the key results of Coovert and Dorsey's application of Petri nets to CIC teams seem little more than a restatement of the model's assumptions. If a model assumes that novices considering ambiguous information are more likely to make incorrect choices and to take longer to make their choices than experts considering less ambiguous information, will we be surprised or impressed when the resulting model finds that where there are differences, experts are faster than novices and spend less time in nonoptimal activities?[1] How does such a computational model add to or deepen our understanding of the effects of team member experience or information ambiguity? What plausible model would make any different predictions?

I am not saying that Petri net models cannot lead to novel and useful insights. Indeed, in the latter sections of their chapter, Coovert and Dorsey suggest several nonobvious (but still largely unexplored) implications of such a model of a CIC (e.g., locating bottlenecks). Rather, if one is going to try to win converts to a new analytic approach, it is important that the tangible fruits of that new approach be nontrivial and that they bear some reasonable resemblance to what is promised. The latter brings us to a final unavoided peril.

The Peril of Asserting (Versus Demonstrating) Utility

Coovert and Dorsey assert the superiority of computational models over more traditional analytic tools. For example,

- Conventional tools . . . are not powerful enough for certain types of tasks. Specifically, those tools make it difficult to expose critical time dependencies, task concurrencies, and behavior that is event driven. Petri nets are a useful and powerful modeling tool and overcome these shortcomings. (p. 163)
- Our work demonstrates that Petri nets provide a useful tool for modeling human performance in dynamic decision-making environments. (pp. 176–178)
- If researchers hope to address the dynamic nature of behavior, measurement techniques have to move away from conventional analytic approaches to techniques that address the moment-to-moment interdependencies that exist in a system. (p. 179)
- [W]hen planning efforts involve systems as complex as many organizational systems are, tools may be needed that reinforce systems thinking and

[1]The work load results are potentially more interesting, but without both a clearer explanation of what work load is and a more detailed description of the full model, it is difficult for a reader to determine this.

ultimately lead to improved action programs. Petri nets and the associated graphical language approach to computational modeling offer such a tool. (p. 179)

The argument seems to be that conventional methods (which at various points are identified with such methods as individual-difference studies, experimentation, correlation, and analysis of variance) are (a) too limited; (b) inadequate to the task of analyzing complex dynamic systems; (c) particularly inadequate when the costs of decision errors are high; and (d) are, at least in certain corporate settings, the wave of the future.

But simply asserting the superiority of any new approach (including computational modeling) is unlikely to convince the uninitiated of this approach's utility—much less its superiority over better established and proven analytic tools. Rather, such utility needs to be demonstrated, preferably in explicit and detailed applications of the new approach. Unfortunately, the CIC application does little to demonstrate Petri nets' utility, nor is such utility established by passing and oblique reference to other novel techniques (such as "object-oriented modeling," "linear statistics," or "neural networks").

The most unfortunate aspect of this situation is that the authors' enthusiasm for Petri nets in particular and computational modeling in general is well justified. But they (and we fellow enthusiasts) will need to make much better conceptual and empirical cases if we hope to infect others with our enthusiasm.

References

Davis, J. H., & Kerr, N. (1986). Thought experiments and the problem of sparse data in small-group performance research. In P. Goodman (Ed.), *Designing effective work groups* (pp. 305–349). New York: Jossey-Bass.

Hastie, R., Penrod, S., & Pennington, N. (1983). *Inside the jury*. Cambridge, UK: Cambridge University Press.

Lewandowski, S. (1993). The rewards and hazards of computer simulations. *Psychological Science, 4*, 236–243.

McGrath, J. E. (1981 March). The judgment call follies or research and all that jazz. Presentation at the Conference on Innovations in Methodology for Organizations, Center for Creative Leadership, Greensboro, NC.

Messick, D., & Liebrand, W. (1997). Levels of analysis and the explanation of the costs and benefits of cooperation. *Personality and Social Psychology Review, 1*, 129–139.

Nowak, A., Szamrej, J., & Latané, B. (1990). From private attitude to public opinion: A dynamic theory of social impact. *Psychological Review, 97*, 362–376.

Penrod, S., & Hastie, R. (1979). Models of jury decision making: A critical review. *Psychological Bulletin, 86*, 462–492.

CHAPTER 9

Pressures to Uniformity and the Evolution of Cultural Norms

Modeling Dynamic Social Impact

Bibb Latané

Once upon a time, just 50 years ago, social analysts had the peculiar idea that the big problem in the brave new postwar world was going to be an overabundance of time. We had solved the wars in Europe and the Pacific by learning to produce vast quantities of guns and planes efficiently. Now, we could apply the same efficiency to making enough peacetime goods to satisfy everyone's need for material comfort. The problem would be to find something for people to do with all the leisure time that would be freed up by the new technology that would drive the new economy and shape the new society.

Educators, of course, had an answer—more and better education. Universities geared up to admit a higher proportion of high school students and to expand their programs in continuing education, adding new departments of recreation and leisure studies to the curriculum and beefing up their offerings in the liberal arts. Educating well-rounded, informed citizens through an emphasis on the liberal arts, universities would enable people to solve the problem of how to occupy their minds by teaching them how to create and appreciate art and culture. By teaching history as well as science, poetry as well as epistemology, ethics as well as engineering, universities would produce not only better human beings but also more competent citizens and voters, with the side benefit of producing a more perfect democracy.

The reality, of course, has been far different. People complain, not about too much free time, but about stress from too much work. Harvard economist Juliet Schor's (1991) book, *The Overworked American: The Unexpected Decline of Leisure,* presents extensive evidence that, compared with 50 years ago, the average person in this country works an additional month every year. Both men and women work longer, despite a doubling of labor productivity that could have allowed us to enjoy the same material standard of living on a 20-hour work week.

Why do people work so hard? Some experts blame capitalism. Because of the high costs of hiring, training, and insuring new workers, large companies find it cheaper to induce people to work overtime. Others blame advertising. Slick television spots with beautiful people driving glamorous cars drive us to work harder to share the image. Swedish economist Staffan Lindner (1970) blames increased productivity itself. His book, *The Harried Leisure Class,* suggests that time-intensive leisure activities, such as love, poetry, and home cooking, all suffer as people find that the only way to make an hour of free time worth as much as an hour of work is to book expensive vacations and buy expensive gear, leading to a vicious cycle of needing more and more money to enjoy less and less free time.

Berkeley sociologist Arlie Hochschild (1997) blames workers themselves. Her book *The Time Bind—When Work Becomes Home and Home Becomes Work* suggests that people choose to work longer hours because they find satisfaction in their jobs, rather than seeing their jobs only as a way of paying for satisfaction. According to this view, although they complain, people may be willingly complicit in an emotional bargain, trading reduced involvement with their homes, their families, their communities, and their nation for greater involvement with their jobs.

Whatever the cause, society seems to have decided collectively that it is more important to spend time at work rather than at home. Starting from the premise that such collective decisions reflect long-term and large-scale social influence, this chapter has three purposes. One is methodological—to demonstrate how simple spreadsheets can be used to model the complex dynamics of social influence. The second is didactic—to use these spreadsheets to illustrate dynamic social impact theory, a new approach to understanding the temporal evolution and regional differentiation that characterize the emergence of norms in groups of all sizes, from organizations to nations. The third is theoretical—to show that social norms of appropriate work effort could result from dynamic social comparison processes as people in groups try to decide how much time to spend at work, and that these processes could lead to an escalation of effort.

Self-Organizing Systems: How Pressures to Uniformity Create Subcultures in Groups

To cope with an influx of returning veterans after World War II, the MIT Housing Bureau commissioned Kurt Lewin's newly established Research Center for Group Dynamics to survey residents of Westgate, a married-student housing project. The survey asked whom residents talked to and what they thought about a proposed tenants' council; it found, first, that people talked most to their neighbors and, second, that opinions clustered within courtyards. One courtyard might be gung-ho about the Council, another might be favorable but passive, and a third might be negative. Each courtyard seemed to have developed its own subculture. The explanation for this result became the title of the classic 1950 book by social psychologists Leon Festinger, Stanley Schachter, and Kurt Back, *Social Pressures in Informal Groups.*

Over the next few years at the University of Michigan, these investigators produced an impressive body of laboratory research on groups and individuals in an attempt to provide microlevel psychological explanations for macrolevel social phenomena. This research effort produced theories of pressures to uniformity, social comparison, and cognitive dissonance. Groups create a social reality by imposing a shared viewpoint on their members (Festinger, 1950). The power of the group is proportional to its cohesiveness or to the net attractiveness of the group to its members (Back, 1951). Social pressures produce uniformity by leading people faced with disagreement to attempt to change themselves (Festinger, Gerard, Hymovitch, Kelley, & Raven, 1952), to change others (Festinger & Thibaut, 1951), and to reject deviates (Schachter, 1951). Pressures to uniformity originate in a drive in the human organism to evaluate opinions and abilities by a process of social comparison (Festinger, 1954). If comparison results in disagreement, especially about important relevant issues for which there is little physical reality, dissonance (Festinger, 1957) is aroused, leading to additional cognitive effort.

Thus, theory begat theory, each time not as a derivation from the preceding theory, but as a new, lower level explanation for another higher-level phenomenon, with each stage of theory development always referring to but encompassing more phenomena than the previous stage.

This process of developing individual psychological explanations for the social phenomenon of clustering in groups was extremely fruitful in opening all sorts of other phenomena to investigation, but it would have been even more satisfying had the researchers completed the circle by proving that group diversity paradoxically results from pressures to uniformity. Unfortunately, it became increasingly difficult for these researchers to do large-scale group research after leaving the Big Ten university environment, and this part of the research agenda was dropped.

Societal Consequences of Individual Action

Sociologists and other global theorists often assail the search for psychological explanations for social phenomena as reductionistic, scientistic, and driven by physics envy. They claim that group-level properties must be understood at the level of groups, without reference to the individuals who participate in them. According to a slogan attributed to Durkheim, "every time a social phenomenon is directly explained by a psychological phenomenon, we may be sure that the explanation is false."

Nevertheless, people keep trying, and with increasing success. According to Adam Smith, the separate choices of people acting in their own interest creates an economy—a self-organized division of labor in which people with different expectations and choices contribute to the common welfare. Classical economies are local, emerging from the choices of individuals, rather than global, commanded from above. According to Serge Moscovici (1984), conversations among people in bar rooms and at the dinner table create social representations—socially shared ideas that help people make sense of the world. Social representations are local, emerging from the conversations of everyday people, rather than global, being passed down by wise elders like Durkheim's collective representations.

According to biologist Stewart Kauffman (1995), economists Joshua Epstein and Robert Axtell (1996), mathematician John Casti (1994), physicist Per Bak (1996), political scientist Robert Axelrod (1984), and psychologist John Holland (1995), an interdisciplinary group of scientists associated with the Santa Fe Institute, the blind and invisible hand of local interaction creates emergent complexity in an amazing variety of physical, biological, and social contexts—from avalanches to revolutions, from mass extinctions to stock market crashes, from new species to new strategies for cooperation. Loosing this hand in a computer can lead not just to new forms of intelligence, but to new forms of life (Levy, 1992).

These theories describe self-organizing systems in which order grows from the bottom up, emerging from the interactions of lower level entities reacting to their local environment. The theories are local, rather than global, in that order emerges among entities with no links to any central nervous system or world capital. They are democratic, rather than totalitarian, in that policy is provided through the trial and error of the many and not through the dictates of the few. They are congregational, rather than episcopal, in that truth emerges from within the group and is not handed down from an anointed higher authority. Although coming from a different scientific tradition, dynamic social impact theory shares these characteristics.

Social impact theory (Latané, 1981) originated as an attempt to integrate a large body of research suggesting that human attributes such as emotions, traits, habits, and beliefs can be changed as a consequence of interactions with other people. These changes reflect a variety of processes, but whatever their mechanism or form, individuals will generally be affected in proportion to a multiplicative function of the strength, immediacy, and number of other people influencing them. The basic idea of dynamic social impact theory (Latané, 1996a, 1997; Nowak, Szamrej, & Latané, 1990) was to take this well-established psychological law and apply it iteratively and recursively to a group of interacting people. As we shall see, dynamic social impact theory leads to surprising predictions of four emergent group-level phenomena—the consolidation, clustering, continuing diversity, and correlation of individual attributes. Collectively, these phenomena constitute the development of subcultures.

Deriving the Social Implications of Psychological Theory

Social scientists have a tough time linking processes at the level of individual human beings with their consequences for groups, organizations, and societies. Rather than attempting rigorous derivations, sometimes it seems the best we can do is apply loose analogies from experiments on individuals or small groups to large-scale social entities. We collect some data, wave our hands, and try to convince ourselves that the psychology of individuals tells us something about group dynamics, that small groups have some bearing on larger social systems, and that such reductionistic approaches may help us understand a society as a whole.

Formal mathematical analysis can sometimes produce nonobvious implications that seem plausible and may even be testable. Often, however, especially with respect to complex systems like societies, they may not be convincing. Even experts may find it difficult to check the validity of the derivations, which to nonexperts are, literally, Greek. When people cannot read for themselves, they must depend on the mathematical equivalent of bishops to read for them. When it comes to mathematics, however, even the Pope is not infallible, because derivations often depend on simplifying assumptions that may turn out to be unrealistic. For example, it is often necessary to assume that outcomes are strictly proportional to inputs to get rich and powerful analytical solutions. Unfortunately, strict linearity is usually implausible in the real world, and even a slight degree of nonlinearity can have dramatic effects on system dynamics (Latané & Nowak, 1997).

Just as it is difficult to evaluate or even understand the results of mathematical analysis, many reasons exist to be dubious about the results of computer simulation. Everyone knows that computers produce garbage from garbage, but they also can turn even the most delicious theoretical idea into trash. Even worse, they may produce a sanitized form of refuse that looks superficially like a fine feast.

The hardware, although extremely complex, is not the problem. We may not be able to observe what goes on inside the beige box of a computer, but we trust that given the same input, the machine will do the same thing, right or wrong, every time. We also trust that the mass adoption of personal computers will lead to the swift identification of cases in which the hardware does it wrong (even an obscure Pentium-chip problem took less than 2 years to discover). The key to anything involving computers is testing, testing, and more testing, and the massive but unplanned testing provided by the marketplace provides an invaluable adjunct to the systematic, planned testing that should be part of any program of simulation.

The real problem comes with the software—the code in which the simulation is written. Computer code is hard to read and harder to evaluate. Experts in programming argue about whether C++, Delphi, Pascal, Smalltalk, or Visual Basic is the best language for composing computer simulations. Despite often being the cleanest and fastest way of saying something, such low-level programming languages, like mathematical notation, can obscure rather than convey meaning by intimidating or stultifying a large part of the audience. Often, simulators avoid such problems simply by not presenting their code—but this not only leaves us at their mercy, it leaves them at the mercy of their human fallibility, deprived of an important opportunity for catching errors. Like the hardware, special-purpose software is not usually open for inspection. Unlike the hardware, it has not usually had the benefit of massive testing.

Computer simulations are an important tool for understanding dynamic processes, but often, as with mathematical equations or the Latin Bible, they are written in a language that few people can understand, and so we depend on experts or priests to explain them to us. Consequently, many of us are a bit dubious and not always religious about our belief in their revelations. One goal of this chapter is to show that computer simulations can be written in English so that we can read these scriptures ourselves and see what divine wisdom is revealed by this tool, without the intermediation of bishops.

Multiagent Simulation, Cellular Automata, Object-Oriented Programming, and Dynamic Social Impact

The effort to produce artificial intelligence long ago passed beyond developing brute-force chess programs to attempting to incorporate specialized mental skills. The multiagent approach to computer simulation incorporates subprograms that interact to produce a division of intellectual labor. For some computer scientists, these agents represent different modules, aspects, or faculties of an individual human mind, but they also can be taken to represent different people, each endowed with the ability to receive information, process it, and produce a response that can be communicated to other agents. Perhaps because of their origin in an engineering subculture, agents tend to be complex entities with many rules and procedures.

A second tradition derives from John von Neumann's (1966) attempt to create conceptual entities that could reproduce and evolve without the guidance of a Higher Being. The simplest cellular automata are one- or two-dimensional arrays in which the values of individual cells are determined by their four or eight nearest neighbors. John Conway's intriguing Game of Life popularized cellular automata as an esoteric mathematical recreation in which interacting cells following their own rules produce astonishing patterns without outside intervention (Poundstone, 1985). The rule defining the Game of Life is particularistic and unlikely to have much relevance to real-world social systems, but the discovery that complex behavior can result from simple rules has stimulated intense interest in other rule systems. Investigators of cellular automata, perhaps because of their own subculture, tend to treat rules as arbitrary entities—cataloguing them or allowing them to evolve—rather than as scientific laws in their own right.

Object-oriented programming (Decker & Hirschfield, 1995) represents a conceptual movement or paradigm as much as a tradition or set of procedures. Unlike structured, list-processing, or procedural programming, components of computer code are encapsulated as autonomous entities that can interact with other computer "objects." Such modularity can lead to programs that are more robust, easier to maintain, change, or reuse, with less chance of leaving residues of orphaned and unclaimed code. Objects can be anything from an icon on a computer screen to an abstract concept. In the language of object-oriented programming, each object has both attributes and procedures and is responsible for its own behavior. The attributes or values of each object constitute its content. The procedures of an object represent things it can do, methods by which it interacts with its environment. Computer objects also have ways of communicating among themselves by sending messages back and forth and systems of inheritance by which children can be created from parents.

Object-oriented programming techniques would seem useful for designing cellular automata and multiagent simulations and especially appropriate for simulating dynamic, self-organizing social systems composed of human beings with individual attributes and procedures. Like computer objects, people are encapsulated, semiautonomous entities that communicate with other objects in their environment, changing their attributes according to specifiable procedures. Perhaps we should think of ourselves as objects in an object-oriented program running on a large computer designed to study the possible emergence of intelligent life in the universe.

Dynamic social impact theory differs from these approaches in that it starts with simple psychological laws and then looks for their social consequences. Unlike multiagent simulations with their collections of ad hoc rules and cellular automata with their relative deemphasis on rule content, dynamic social impact theory is based on a carefully formulated, research-based set of psychological principles.

Spreadsheets as Social Theories

Only 25 years ago, few people thought personal computers had much of a future in a world dominated by mainframe computers. The application that got personal computers onto business desktops was not so much the word processor as the spreadsheet. This ingenious application allowed users to insert formulas into a matrix of cells to compute values based on other cells. Executives were happy to leave typing to their secretaries, but they loved being easily able to put together and play with numbers using such programs as Visicalc, Lotus 1-2-3, and Quattro. These programs enabled executives and people from academia alike to draw up budgets, keep track of grades, and even do some rudimentary data analysis.

Although it is not common to think of them that way, spreadsheets can be considered as rudimentary object-oriented programming environments. The cells in a spreadsheet correspond to objects, the values to attributes, and the formulas to procedures. This chapter suggests that spreadsheets also may be useful tools for social simulation, serving as derivation machines for understanding the social consequences of psychological laws:

- A spreadsheet can be defined to represent a social system. Each cell or range of cells can be considered to correspond to an individual human being.
- Cell values can be considered to represent individual attributes, such as beliefs, values, or behaviors. Some attributes may be relatively transitory, like

a momentary emotional state, and others may be relatively enduring, like a long-lasting psychological trait; cell values indicate how angry you are at the moment or how optimistic you tend to be in general.

- Cell formulas can be taken to represent psychological laws. Formulas tell how a cell's attributes are determined from its previous value and the values of the other cells in its environment.
- Different cells or ranges of cells can be seen as representing different people. For example, each person in a group might correspond to a different column, with different rows representing different points in time or different attributes.
- Spreadsheets can be three-dimensional or layered, so that, for example, if columns represent people and rows represent attributes, then sheets can represent time periods.
- Cells communicate with one another through their formulas, pulling information from specifiable other cells and processing it in specifiable ways. Thus, almost any type of communication pattern can be represented.
- Cells have a great degree of flexibility in how they can respond to each other. For example, the value of one cell can be set to equal the average of some other cells, and this relation can be made conditional on the value of still other cells through the use of IF statements.
- Cell references are automatically corrected when formulas are copied from one cell to another, reducing clerical effort and associated probability of error.
- Spreadsheet routines can be automated simply by stepping through a series of commands to produce a macro or program in a language like Visual Basic. Although many programmers prefer other languages, Visual Basic is intuitive, easy to read, and even easy to write.
- Results can be easily displayed by creating indices and graphs. These can measure not only individual averages but also group-level characteristics.
- Commercial spreadsheets are well tested. Literally millions of people are out there banging away at them every day, discovering bugs and flaws. Although the underlying code is extremely complicated, it has gone through many cycles of rigorous testing and error correction. Although there may be undiscovered errors, especially in lesser used features, the risk is certainly lower than with special-purpose, homemade software.
- The structure and formulas of a specific spreadsheet can be made visible. Other people can check what you have done and change it if they want to. You can refer to cells and ranges with names, to make formulas easier to understand. Finally, you can comment on them. Files can even be posted to the Web as open documents, completely accessible to peer review. These features help guard against errors in programming the simulation.

Spreadsheet Models of Dynamic Social Impact

The remainder of this chapter describes in detail a set of four simple spreadsheets designed to simulate opinion change in small groups. The spreadsheets were composed in Excel 97, a component of the Microsoft Office 97 application suite; however, similar procedures could be conducted, perhaps more easily, with other widely available products. The chapter describes simulation formulas and procedures in detail, so the reader can duplicate and modify them at his or her pleasure. The set of spreadsheets is available on the World Wide Web at www.humanscience.org.

Figure 9.1: A Linear Model of Group Opinion Change

Figure 9.1 simulates a linear change model of opinions in a group of 24 people arranged as though they were sitting around a large table with a big floral centerpiece, able to talk only with the people to their immediate left and right. Row 4 shows the addresses of each of the 24 people, with the entries in Rows 5 through 8 representing the addresses of the 4 people with whom they exchanged messages. Thus, Person C communicated with A, B, D, and E; Person A communicated with W, X, B, and C; and so forth. This geometry, termed a *ribbon* by Latané and L'Herrou (1996) because people are arranged in a line with the two ends connected to form a circle, is equivalent to a simple one-dimensional cellular automaton. One could define any other network simply by changing the addresses in Rows 5 through 8.

Opinions are coded as numbers between 0 and 1, representing the range of possible choices on each round of discussion. Conditional formatting allows the font, background color, or other aspects of the display of each cell's information to be automatically adjusted to reflect its value. In this case, cell backgrounds were formatted so that any cell with a value less than .3 is colored yellow, any cell with a value greater than .7 is blue, and any cell with a value in between is green. In a black-and-white reproduction, the colors show up as different shades of gray, graduated from lighter to darker.

Initial prediscussion opinions are shown in Row 10. To make initial opinions random, the formula for each cell in Row 10 consists of the functions = ROUND(RAND)(, 0), which return a random number rounded off to either 0 or 1. In this case, Persons C, G, L, and 6 others happened to adopt the minority choice.

Opinion Change

In this simple linear model, an individual's opinions at any time are a simple average of the opinion of everybody in the local environment at the previous time. Each cell in Rows 11 through 45 of Column A contains the identical formula:

$$
\begin{aligned}
= \text{AVERAGE (INDIRECT (A\$4 \& (ROW( ) – 1)),}\\
\text{INDIRECT (A\$5 \& (ROW( ) – 1)),}\\
\text{INDIRECT (A\$6 \& (ROW( ) – 1)),}\\
\text{INDIRECT (A\$7 \& (ROW( ) – 1)),}\\
\text{INDIRECT (A\$8 \& (ROW( ) – 1)))}
\end{aligned}
\tag{9. 1}
$$

Although this formula may seem intimidating, it is a simple combination of three functions. For example, INDIRECT (A$5 & (Row( ) – 1)) looks for the value in the cell at the intersection of the column designated in cell A5 and the preceding row. This value represents one of the neighbor's opinions in the preceding time period. The AVERAGE function combines this value with those of the other 3 neighbors and the person's own previous opinion, which are found in a similar fashion. For example, the formula for the cell representing Person B looks up to discover that X, A, C, and D are its neighbors and averages their opinions with Person B's own previous opinion to determine the new opinion.

This model could be made somewhat more complicated by allowing people to weigh their own opinions differently from their neighbors, as in Norman Anderson's (1968) weighted-averaging models of information integration, except that here, each unit of information represents a different person's opinion. This is a traditional linear attitude change model of the class treated analytically by Abelson (1964).

Written in this fashion, the formula can be copied directly to the other columns, reducing the possibility of clerical errors. Address elements with a dollar sign ($), such as the row numbers, are absolute and will not be altered when the formula is copied—other elements, such as the column labels, are relative and will be automatically converted to the appropriate value.

Each cell formula can be considered as a simple psychological law showing how one person might react to his or her attitudinal environment. The question is, What will happen to the climate of opinion in a group as a number of people react interactively to one another in this way over time? Two forms of self-organization, consolidation and clustering, result from this simple linear model.

Consolidation

The mean opinion on every trial is always within the previous range, and opinions quickly converge toward the average of the original opinions. Initial values, all zeros and ones in Row 10, quickly converge toward the mean of the initial distribution, which in this case is 9/24 or .375. This result can be called *consolidation,* standing for the reduction in diversity that results from social influence. Consistent with Abelson's (1964) mathematical proof, consolidation seems to be a ubiquitous outcome of linear averaging models in fully connected networks, in which every person is connected to every other by at least one path, whatever its length.

FIGURE 9.1

Simple linear averaging model of group opinion formation

	A	B	C	D	E	F	G	H	I	J	K	L	M	N	O	P	Q	R	S	T	U	V	W	X
1																								
2																								
3	*Addresses of Group Members and Their Neighbors*																							
4	a	b	c	d	e	f	g	h	i	j	k	l	m	n	o	p	q	r	s	t	u	v	w	x
5	w	x	a	b	c	d	e	f	g	h	i	j	k	l	m	n	o	p	q	r	s	t	u	v
6	x	a	b	c	d	e	f	g	h	i	j	k	l	m	n	o	p	q	r	s	t	u	v	w
7	b	c	d	e	f	g	h	i	j	k	l	m	n	o	p	q	r	s	t	u	v	w	x	a
8	c	d	e	f	g	h	i	j	k	l	m	n	o	p	q	r	s	t	u	v	w	x	a	b
9	*Simulated Discussion: Linear Averaging Model*																							
10	1.0	1.0	.0	1.0	1.0	1.0	.0	1.0	1.0	1.0	1.0	.0	1.0	1.0	1.0	1.0	1.0	.0	.0	1.0	.0	.0	.0	.0
11	.4	.6	.8	.8	.6	.8	.8	.8	.8	.8	.8	.8	.8	.8	1.0	.8	.6	.6	.4	.2	.2	.2	.2	.4
12	.5	.6	.6	.7	.8	.8	.8	.8	.8	.8	.8	.8	.8	.8	.8	.8	.7	.5	.4	.3	.2	.2	.3	.4
13	.5	.6	.6	.7	.7	.8	.8	.8	.8	.8	.8	.8	.8	.8	.8	.7	.6	.5	.4	.3	.3	.3	.3	.4
14	.5	.6	.6	.7	.7	.7	.8	.8	.8	.8	.8	.8	.8	.8	.8	.7	.6	.5	.4	.4	.3	.3	.4	.4
15	.5	.5	.6	.7	.7	.7	.8	.8	.8	.8	.8	.8	.8	.8	.7	.7	.6	.5	.5	.4	.4	.4	.4	.4
16	.5	.5	.6	.7	.7	.7	.8	.8	.8	.8	.8	.8	.8	.8	.7	.7	.6	.5	.5	.4	.4	.4	.4	.4
17	.5	.5	.6	.6	.7	.7	.7	.8	.8	.8	.8	.8	.8	.7	.7	.7	.6	.5	.5	.4	.4	.4	.4	.5
18	.5	.5	.6	.6	.7	.7	.7	.8	.8	.8	.8	.8	.8	.7	.7	.6	.6	.5	.5	.5	.4	.4	.4	.5
19	.5	.5	.6	.6	.7	.7	.7	.8	.8	.8	.8	.8	.7	.7	.7	.6	.6	.6	.5	.5	.5	.4	.5	.5
20	.5	.6	.6	.6	.7	.7	.7	.7	.8	.8	.8	.8	.7	.7	.7	.6	.6	.6	.5	.5	.5	.5	.5	.5
21	.5	.6	.6	.6	.7	.7	.7	.7	.8	.8	.8	.7	.7	.7	.7	.6	.6	.6	.5	.5	.5	.5	.5	.5
22	.5	.6	.6	.6	.7	.7	.7	.7	.7	.8	.8	.7	.7	.7	.7	.6	.6	.6	.5	.5	.5	.5	.5	.5
23	.5	.6	.6	.6	.7	.7	.7	.7	.7	.7	.7	.7	.7	.7	.7	.6	.6	.6	.5	.5	.5	.5	.5	.5
24	.5	.6	.6	.6	.7	.7	.7	.7	.7	.7	.7	.7	.7	.7	.7	.6	.6	.6	.5	.5	.5	.5	.5	.5
25	.5	.6	.6	.6	.7	.7	.7	.7	.7	.7	.7	.7	.7	.7	.7	.6	.6	.6	.5	.5	.5	.5	.5	.5
26	.6	.6	.6	.6	.6	.7	.7	.7	.7	.7	.7	.7	.7	.7	.7	.6	.6	.6	.6	.5	.5	.5	.5	.5
27	.6	.6	.6	.6	.6	.7	.7	.7	.7	.7	.7	.7	.7	.7	.7	.6	.6	.6	.6	.5	.5	.5	.5	.5
28	.6	.6	.6	.6	.6	.7	.7	.7	.7	.7	.7	.7	.7	.7	.7	.6	.6	.6	.6	.5	.5	.5	.5	.5
29	.6	.6	.6	.6	.6	.7	.7	.7	.7	.7	.7	.7	.7	.7	.6	.6	.6	.6	.6	.6	.5	.5	.5	.6
30	.6	.6	.6	.6	.6	.7	.7	.7	.7	.7	.7	.7	.7	.7	.6	.6	.6	.6	.6	.6	.6	.5	.6	.6
31	.6	.6	.6	.6	.6	.7	.7	.7	.7	.7	.7	.7	.7	.7	.6	.6	.6	.6	.6	.6	.6	.6	.6	.6
32	.6	.6	.6	.6	.6	.7	.7	.7	.7	.7	.7	.7	.7	.7	.6	.6	.6	.6	.6	.6	.6	.6	.6	.6
33	.6	.6	.6	.6	.6	.7	.7	.7	.7	.7	.7	.7	.7	.7	.6	.6	.6	.6	.6	.6	.6	.6	.6	.6
34	.6	.6	.6	.6	.6	.7	.7	.7	.7	.7	.7	.7	.7	.7	.6	.6	.6	.6	.6	.6	.6	.6	.6	.6
35	.6	.6	.6	.6	.6	.7	.7	.7	.7	.7	.7	.7	.7	.7	.6	.6	.6	.6	.6	.6	.6	.6	.6	.6
36	.6	.6	.6	.6	.6	.6	.7	.7	.7	.7	.7	.7	.7	.7	.6	.6	.6	.6	.6	.6	.6	.6	.6	.6
37	.6	.6	.6	.6	.6	.6	.7	.7	.7	.7	.7	.7	.7	.6	.6	.6	.6	.6	.6	.6	.6	.6	.6	.6
38	.6	.6	.6	.6	.6	.6	.7	.7	.7	.7	.7	.7	.7	.6	.6	.6	.6	.6	.6	.6	.6	.6	.6	.6
39	.6	.6	.6	.6	.6	.6	.7	.7	.7	.7	.7	.7	.7	.6	.6	.6	.6	.6	.6	.6	.6	.6	.6	.6
40	.6	.6	.6	.6	.6	.6	.7	.7	.7	.7	.7	.7	.7	.6	.6	.6	.6	.6	.6	.6	.6	.6	.6	.6
41	.6	.6	.6	.6	.6	.6	.6	.7	.7	.7	.7	.7	.7	.6	.6	.6	.6	.6	.6	.6	.6	.6	.6	.6
42	.6	.6	.6	.6	.6	.6	.6	.7	.7	.7	.7	.7	.6	.6	.6	.6	.6	.6	.6	.6	.6	.6	.6	.6
43	.6	.6	.6	.6	.6	.6	.6	.7	.7	.7	.7	.7	.6	.6	.6	.6	.6	.6	.6	.6	.6	.6	.6	.6
44	.6	.6	.6	.6	.6	.6	.6	.6	.7	.7	.7	.7	.6	.6	.6	.6	.6	.6	.6	.6	.6	.6	.6	.6
45	.6	.6	.6	.6	.6	.6	.6	.6	.7	.7	.7	.6	.6	.6	.6	.6	.6	.6	.6	.6	.6	.6	.6	.6

Clearly, this result differs from the distribution of opinions in the Westgate housing community, where people in different courtyards persisted in holding different opinions.

Clustering

A second noticeable feature of Figure 9.1 is clustering. Neighbors quickly become more similar than strangers. Although the two choices were randomly located to begin with, the group becomes separated into regions where everybody leans toward one position and other regions where everybody leans toward the other. This clustering is transitory, because the differences between regions erode at their borders and the clusters soon fade away into a sea of uniformity. Perhaps this is why such incipient subcultures have not received much attention from students of group dynamics.

Despite the emergence of two group-level phenomena, there is nothing particularly remarkable about the results of Figure 9.1, except that they miss some of the most important dynamics. Making the model nonlinear provides some surprises.

Figure 9.2: Linear and Nonlinear Models Compared

Figure 9.2 is designed to allow a comparison between the traditional linear formula of Figure 9.1 and a nonlinear version that incorporates a threshold for change: Unless somebody is persuaded to change all the way, they will not change at all. This model is nonlinear because outputs are no longer proportional to inputs.

The design of Figure 9.2 is identical to that of Figure 9.1 in all but four respects: First, it adds a second, nonlinear model of opinion change. This is done simply by converting the linear formula to an IF statement so that a person's new opinion will be 0 or 1, according to whether the linear average of previous opinions is below or above .5. The first argument of an IF statement sets a condition, the second determines what happens if the condition is met, and the third determines what happens if the condition is false. Thus, the core formula becomes:

IF (AVERAGE (five opinions) < .5, 0, 1) **(9.2)**

In this case, the IF formula results in an opinion of 0 if there is any leaning in the direction (AVERAGE(...) < .5) and an opinion of 1 otherwise.

Second, each model is traced for only eight time periods. Although this is not sufficient to achieve full consolidation for the linear averaging model, it does reveal the important differences between the two.

Third, indices of consolidation and clustering are calculated and displayed at the bottom. Consolidation is shown simply as a decrease in the variance of opinions over time. Clustering is also a function of variance—in this case, the ratio of the total variance to the average variance among neighbors. This statistic can be evaluated

FIGURE 9.2

Two models of opinion formation in groups

Addresses of Group Members and Their Neighbors

a	b	c	d	e	f	g	h	i	j	k	l	m	n	o	p	q	r	s	t	u	v	w	x
w	x	a	b	c	d	e	f	g	h	i	j	k	l	m	n	o	p	q	r	s	t	u	v
x	a	b	c	d	e	f	g	h	i	j	k	l	m	n	o	p	q	r	s	t	u	v	w
b	c	d	e	f	g	h	i	j	k	l	m	n	o	p	q	r	s	t	u	v	w	x	a
c	d	e	f	g	h	i	j	k	l	m	n	o	p	q	r	s	t	u	v	w	x	a	b

Simulated Discussion: Linear Averaging (New Opinion = Neighborhood Average)

.0	.0	1.0	1.0	.0	.0	.0	1.0	.0	.0	.0	1.0	.0	1.0	1.0	1.0	1.0	.0	1.0	.0	.0	.0	1.0	1.0
.6	.6	.4	.4	.4	.4	.2	.2	.2	.4	.2	.4	.6	.8	.8	.8	.8	.6	.4	.2	.4	.4	.4	.4
.5	.5	.5	.4	.4	.3	.3	.3	.2	.3	.4	.5	.6	.7	.8	.8	.7	.6	.5	.4	.4	.4	.4	.5
.5	.5	.4	.4	.4	.3	.3	.3	.3	.3	.4	.5	.6	.6	.7	.7	.6	.6	.5	.4	.4	.4	.4	.4
.5	.5	.4	.4	.4	.3	.3	.3	.3	.4	.4	.5	.6	.6	.6	.6	.6	.6	.5	.5	.4	.4	.4	.4
.4	.4	.4	.4	.4	.3	.3	.3	.3	.4	.4	.5	.5	.6	.6	.6	.6	.6	.5	.5	.5	.4	.4	.4
.4	.4	.4	.4	.4	.4	.3	.3	.4	.4	.4	.5	.5	.6	.6	.6	.6	.6	.5	.5	.5	.5	.4	.4
.4	.4	.4	.4	.4	.4	.4	.4	.4	.4	.4	.5	.5	.6	.6	.6	.6	.6	.5	.5	.5	.5	.4	.4
.4	.4	.4	.4	.4	.4	.4	.4	.4	.4	.4	.5	.5	.5	.6	.6	.6	.5	.5	.5	.5	.5	.5	.4

Simulated Discussion: Nonlinear Change (0 if Neighborhood Average < .5, 1 Otherwise)

.0	.0	1.0	1.0	.0	.0	.0	1.0	.0	.0	.0	1.0	.0	1.0	1.0	1.0	1.0	.0	1.0	.0	.0	.0	1.0	1.0
1.0	1.0	.0	.0	.0	.0	.0	.0	.0	.0	.0	.0	1.0	1.0	1.0	1.0	1.0	1.0	.0	.0	.0	.0	.0	.0
.0	.0	.0	.0	.0	.0	.0	.0	.0	.0	.0	.0	1.0	1.0	1.0	1.0	1.0	1.0	.0	.0	.0	.0	.0	.0
.0	.0	.0	.0	.0	.0	.0	.0	.0	.0	.0	.0	1.0	1.0	1.0	1.0	1.0	1.0	.0	.0	.0	.0	.0	.0
.0	.0	.0	.0	.0	.0	.0	.0	.0	.0	.0	.0	1.0	1.0	1.0	1.0	1.0	1.0	.0	.0	.0	.0	.0	.0
.0	.0	.0	.0	.0	.0	.0	.0	.0	.0	.0	.0	1.0	1.0	1.0	1.0	1.0	1.0	.0	.0	.0	.0	.0	.0
.0	.0	.0	.0	.0	.0	.0	.0	.0	.0	.0	.0	1.0	1.0	1.0	1.0	1.0	1.0	.0	.0	.0	.0	.0	.0
.0	.0	.0	.0	.0	.0	.0	.0	.0	.0	.0	.0	1.0	1.0	1.0	1.0	1.0	1.0	.0	.0	.0	.0	.0	.0
.0	.0	.0	.0	.0	.0	.0	.0	.0	.0	.0	.0	1.0	1.0	1.0	1.0	1.0	1.0	.0	.0	.0	.0	.0	.0

			TIME PERIOD								
	ISSUE	INDEX	*0*	*1*	*2*	*3*	*4*	*5*	*6*	*7*	*8*
Consolidation	1	σ^2 1	.26	.04	.02	.02	.01	.01	.01	.01	.00
(Decrease in variance)	2	σ^2 2	.26	.23	.20	.20	.20	.20	.20	.20	.20
Clustering	1	*F1*	1.0	1.9	2.6	3.1	3.5	4.0	4.5	5.0	5.4
(Increase in F ratio)	2	*F2*	1.0	1.5	2.3	2.3	2.3	2.3	2.3	2.3	2.3

by reference to standard tables of the *F* distribution, in this case with 5 and 23 degrees of freedom.

Finally, to avoid clutter, the row and column labels are hidden.

To simplify comparison, both models were set to start with the same initial opinions, but they produce very different results, not only for individuals but also for groups. Consolidation and clustering change in nature and are joined by a new property—continuing diversity.

Consolidation

The two models depicted in Figure 9.2 start with the same neighbors and initial opinions, but they differ in the nature and degree of consolidation. In the linear case, although diversity is reduced, minority members influence the final group mean in proportion to their numbers. The mean stays the same—only the variance is reduced. In the nonlinear case, individual opinions cannot converge and consolidation takes the form of a reduction in minority size. Because minorities, by definition, receive less social support and therefore greater pressure to change than majorities, they almost always suffer at the expense of the majority. The case illustrated in Figure 9.2 started with 11 people in the minority and ended with only 6. For nonlinear change, consolidation involves not only a reduction in variance but a change in mean—with the average opinion shifting toward the majority position as fewer people hold the minority position.

Clustering

Clustering results from both models, but it is more persistent and sharply defined with the nonlinear version. Clustering in the linear model is ephemeral and soon disappears. In the nonlinear case, people will maintain their previous opinions if they have at least two neighbors who agree with them. Thus, in a ribbon geometry such as this, a cluster will be stable if it consists of at least 3 people in a row. These clusters represent identifiable subgroups and provide the seeds for continuing diversity.

Continuing Diversity

In the linear model, change continues until there is no further disagreement. Minority members have a proportional effect on the final group mean, but the initially identifiable minority position disappears.

In the nonlinear model, change continues only until clustering is successful in segregating the minority from the majority. By being segregated, the minority is protected against adverse influence and can continue. Even those people located at the edge of a cluster have as much support as opposition and everyone, even in a sharply divided group, can be in a local majority. Groups can stabilize at a Nash equilibrium, in which no person has any further reason to change despite continuing disagreement. Minority positions may become less prevalent, but identifiable minority factions persist and diversity is maintained. Continuing diversity is made possible by the fact that in a nonlinear system, clustering trumps consolidation.

Which Model When?

Obviously, the two models are different, but which is right? It may be that both are—but for different kinds of attributes. For example, a new catastrophe theory (Harton & Latané, 1997; Latané & Nowak, 1994) suggests that whereas the distribution of attitudes on unimportant issues tends to be continuous, attitudes on important issues tend to be extreme or categorical. Perhaps the former exhibit linear, and the latter exhibit nonlinear change rules. If so, increasing the perceived importance of an issue might paradoxically decrease the chance of reaching agreement on it—even for people eager to conform to the majority view.

Both models exhibit consolidation and clustering, but in somewhat different forms. The nonlinear model adds continuing diversity to the mix of emergent system properties. Figure 9.3 illustrates a fourth property, correlation, and shows it in a richer influence structure, such as that found in organizational work groups.

Figure 9.3: The Emergence of Correlation in a Work Group Structure

Some theorists believe that every organizational work group is unique (Levine & Moreland, 1991) and that work groups have a stronger influence than organizations on the behavior of most employees (Moreland & Levine, in press). According to such views, work groups represent subcultures, each with a different approach to organizational life (Baba, 1995; Gregory, 1983; Rentsch, 1990; Sackman, 1992; Van Maanen & Barley, 1985). Employees from different work groups in the same organization often think, feel, and act in distinct ways, and work group norms are good predictors of employee behaviors (Baratta & McManus, 1992; Blau, 1995; Markham & McKee, 1995; Martocchio, 1994; Mathieu & Kohler, 1990; Nicholson & Johns, 1985). The existence of work group subcultures becomes especially dramatic when work group norms and organizational values conflict (Bearman, 1991; Homans, 1950; Roethlisberger & Dickson, 1939).

Figure 9.3 was designed with two goals: first, to show that self-organization occurs in the complex influence structures that characterize work groups in organizations, and second, to illustrate a fourth form of self-organization, namely, correlation.

As can be seen from the new addresses of message recipients in the top rows of Figure 9.3, the group is now divided into 6 subgroups of 4 people, each member of which exchanges messages with the other 3, as well as with 1 person from a neighboring subgroup. Thus, this structure is like a set of 6 families living around a circular cul-de-sac, each with a mother, father, son, and daughter, each talking with the other members of their own family as well as with one of their counterparts next door. Alternatively, this structure can be seen as similar to work groups in an organization, with workers spending most of their time communicating internally but having a friend in a neighboring work group.

The nonlinear change model of Figure 9.2 is applied to three different issues, each of which is separately randomized with respect to initial position, ensuring that opinions are unrelated at the start. Because the change formula for one issue makes no reference to positions on the other issues, there would seem to be no way in which positions on different issues could affect each other.

FIGURE 9.3

The emergence of correlation in a work group structure

Addresses of Group Members and Their Neighbors

a	b	c	d	e	f	g	h	i	j	k	l	m	n	o	p	q	r	s	t	u	v	w	x
b	a	d	c	f	e	h	g	j	i	l	k	n	m	p	o	r	q	t	s	v	u	x	w
c	d	a	b	g	h	e	f	k	l	i	j	o	p	m	n	s	t	q	r	w	x	u	v
d	c	b	a	h	g	f	e	l	k	j	i	p	o	n	m	t	s	r	q	x	w	v	u
w	x	e	f	c	d	i	j	g	h	m	n	k	l	q	r	o	p	u	v	s	t	a	b

Simulated Discussion: Issue 1

a	b	c	d	e	f	g	h	i	j	k	l	m	n	o	p	q	r	s	t	u	v	w	x
1.0	.0	.0	.0	.0	.0	.0	1.0	.0	1.0	.0	.0	1.0	1.0	.0	.0	1.0	1.0	1.0	1.0	.0	.0	1.0	1.0
.0	.0	.0	.0	.0	.0	.0	.0	.0	.0	.0	.0	.0	.0	1.0	1.0	1.0	1.0	1.0	1.0	1.0	1.0	1.0	.0
.0	.0	.0	.0	.0	.0	.0	.0	.0	.0	.0	.0	.0	.0	1.0	1.0	1.0	1.0	1.0	1.0	1.0	1.0	1.0	1.0
.0	.0	.0	.0	.0	.0	.0	.0	.0	.0	.0	.0	.0	.0	1.0	1.0	1.0	1.0	1.0	1.0	1.0	1.0	1.0	1.0
.0	.0	.0	.0	.0	.0	.0	.0	.0	.0	.0	.0	.0	.0	1.0	1.0	1.0	1.0	1.0	1.0	1.0	1.0	1.0	1.0

Simulated Discussion: Issue 2

a	b	c	d	e	f	g	h	i	j	k	l	m	n	o	p	q	r	s	t	u	v	w	x
1.0	1.0	1.0	.0	.0	.0	1.0	1.0	.0	1.0	1.0	1.0	1.0	1.0	1.0	1.0	.0	1.0	1.0	.0	.0	.0	1.0	.0
1.0	1.0	1.0	1.0	1.0	.0	.0	1.0	1.0	1.0	1.0	1.0	1.0	1.0	1.0	1.0	1.0	1.0	.0	.0	.0	.0	.0	.0
1.0	1.0	1.0	1.0	1.0	1.0	1.0	1.0	1.0	1.0	1.0	1.0	1.0	1.0	1.0	1.0	1.0	1.0	.0	.0	.0	.0	.0	.0
1.0	1.0	1.0	1.0	1.0	1.0	1.0	1.0	1.0	1.0	1.0	1.0	1.0	1.0	1.0	1.0	1.0	1.0	.0	.0	.0	.0	.0	.0
1.0	1.0	1.0	1.0	1.0	1.0	1.0	1.0	1.0	1.0	1.0	1.0	1.0	1.0	1.0	1.0	1.0	1.0	.0	.0	.0	.0	.0	.0

Simulated Discussion: Issue 3

a	b	c	d	e	f	g	h	i	j	k	l	m	n	o	p	q	r	s	t	u	v	w	x
1.0	.0	1.0	1.0	1.0	1.0	.0	1.0	.0	.0	1.0	1.0	1.0	.0	.0	1.0	1.0	.0	1.0	1.0	.0	.0	.0	1.0
1.0	1.0	1.0	1.0	1.0	1.0	1.0	1.0	.0	1.0	1.0	.0	1.0	1.0	1.0	.0	1.0	1.0	1.0	1.0	.0	.0	.0	.0
1.0	1.0	1.0	1.0	1.0	1.0	1.0	1.0	1.0	1.0	1.0	1.0	1.0	1.0	1.0	1.0	1.0	1.0	1.0	1.0	.0	.0	.0	.0
1.0	1.0	1.0	1.0	1.0	1.0	1.0	1.0	1.0	1.0	1.0	1.0	1.0	1.0	1.0	1.0	1.0	1.0	1.0	1.0	.0	.0	.0	.0
1.0	1.0	1.0	1.0	1.0	1.0	1.0	1.0	1.0	1.0	1.0	1.0	1.0	1.0	1.0	1.0	1.0	1.0	1.0	1.0	.0	.0	.0	.0

	ISSUE	INDEX	TIME PERIOD 0	1	2	3	4
Consolidation	1	σ^2 1	.26	.24	.25	.25	.25
(Decrease in variance)	2	σ^2 2	.24	.23	.20	.20	.20
	3	σ^2 1	.25	.22	.14	.14	.14
Clustering	1	*F*1	1.00	2.45	3.04	3.04	3.04
(Increase in *F* ratio)	2	*F*2	1.05	1.55	2.35	2.35	2.35
	3	*F*3	.94	1.26	2.17	2.17	2.17
Correlation	1 & 2	$\|r\|$ 12	.19	.37	.68	.68	.68
(Increase in absolute	1 & 3	$\|r\|$ 13	.10	.26	.53	.53	.53
value of *r*)	2 & 3	$\|r\|$ 23	.13	.32	.77	.77	.77

Consolidation, Clustering, and Continuing Diversity

Consolidation is even more pronounced in the work group structure than with the ribbon for reasons detailed more fully by Latané and Bourgeois (1996), leading to a greater frequency of unification, especially if the initial minority is smaller than 33%. Clustering, however, is still pervasive, with the borders of clusters often but not always coinciding with work group borders, and diversity is usually maintained.

Correlation

Because issues are defined arbitrarily and scores could have easily been reversed, a positive correlation means the same as a negative one. Therefore, Figure 9.3 displays correlation coefficients in terms of their absolute value. The average correlation coefficient rises from .14 at the beginning to .66 at the end, with a coefficient of .30 being statistically significant.

Correlation reflects the degree to which clusters of opinions overlap or coincide on different issues. As the number of independent opinions decreases and cluster size gets larger, correlation emerges. In effect, it is a product of the reduction in degrees of freedom caused by clustering. Correlations bear no relation to content; they have nothing to do with any possible underlying semantic or substantive similarity among issues. They do, however, provide the seeds for identifiable subcultures.

Repeating the simulation with different initial opinions would produce somewhat different patterns, but the general result is usually the same: consolidation, clustering, correlation, and continuing diversity.

Simulation and Reality

Human cultures can be viewed as temporally evolving, regionally differentiated bundles of beliefs, values, and behaviors. In the present simulations, temporal evolution takes the form of consolidation, regional differentiation represents clustering, and bundling represents correlation. The simulations show the emergence of subcultures in groups as small as 24 people, but the same process may account for similar phenomena in larger groups.

Westgate Courtyards as Subcultures

The subcultures emerging from Figure 9.3 are similar in form to, if smaller in scale than, the Westgate courtyards studied by Festinger et al. (1950), validating their hypothesis that group differences in attitudes toward a tenants' council could have resulted from pressures to uniformity. Thus, the new tool of spreadsheet simulation supports a simple explanation for an old research finding—the spatial segregation of opinions. The discovery of emergent correlation extends that finding—it is likely that courtyards differed in more respects than their attitudes toward a tenants' council and that these differences were correlated, although not necessarily logically connected.

Electronic Discussion Groups as Subcultures

More impressively, the simulation outcomes also closely resemble the results of recent laboratory studies designed to test dynamic social impact theory (Latané & Bourgeois, 1996; Latané & L'Herrou, 1996). In the course of this 4-year series of experiments, 864 college students were organized into 36 groups, each consisting of 24 people who spent 2 1/2 weeks communicating by electronic mail. Among other tasks, they exchanged messages on a variety of relatively uninvolving topics, such as "which painter, Klee or Kandinsky, do you think the majority of this group will prefer?" and were given a small reward for each correct answer. Thus, there was a considerable motive for being responsive to information from the other participants and a consequent high degree of social influence. Not only do these studies report highly significant degrees of consolidation, clustering, continuing diversity, and correlation in three different geometries of social space, but the differences among topics, groups, and even individuals can be successfully predicted from theory-based simulations (Bourgeois & Latané, in press).

But How Can Subcultures Evolve New Norms?

How can we explain the 50-year change in American work effort? Both the linear averaging version of Festinger's (1950) pressures to uniformity and its nonlinear equivalent predict that subgroup norms should settle down at either the initial mean or at the majority position. How could we explain a norm that progressively evolves toward greater work effort? Perhaps a second theory developed from the line of research stimulated by the original Westgate findings might apply—the theory of social comparison.

Figure 9.4: A Social Comparison Model of Work Group Effort

According to social comparison theory (Festinger, 1954), in the absence of direct physical evidence, people compare with one another to evaluate their opinions and abilities. A basic assumption of the theory is that people will seek to compare with others who are similar to themselves. In addition, people are assumed to have a unidirectional drive upward. Therefore, the model assumes that people will prefer to compare with someone who is doing just a little better or making just a little bit more money.

Imagine an organizational work group in which each member is trying to decide how many hours to stay at his or her desk. On the one hand, each wants to be well regarded, especially when it comes time for promotions and raises. On the other hand, each does not want to work excessively hard, especially if it makes other people uncomfortable. So what do they do? They compare their job success with other people in their work group to help them decide how hard to work. Some potential dimensions for comparison are hidden—it can be hard to distinguish the results of luck from those of skill. Others are open—outcomes in the form of salary or space allocation, effort in the form of number of hours at work. As each person is influenced by the others, a norm emerges.

The basic idea behind Figure 9.4 is to see what would happen to work norms if people compare outcomes in order to decide how much effort to put in, adjusting

FIGURE 9.4

Emergence of work group norms

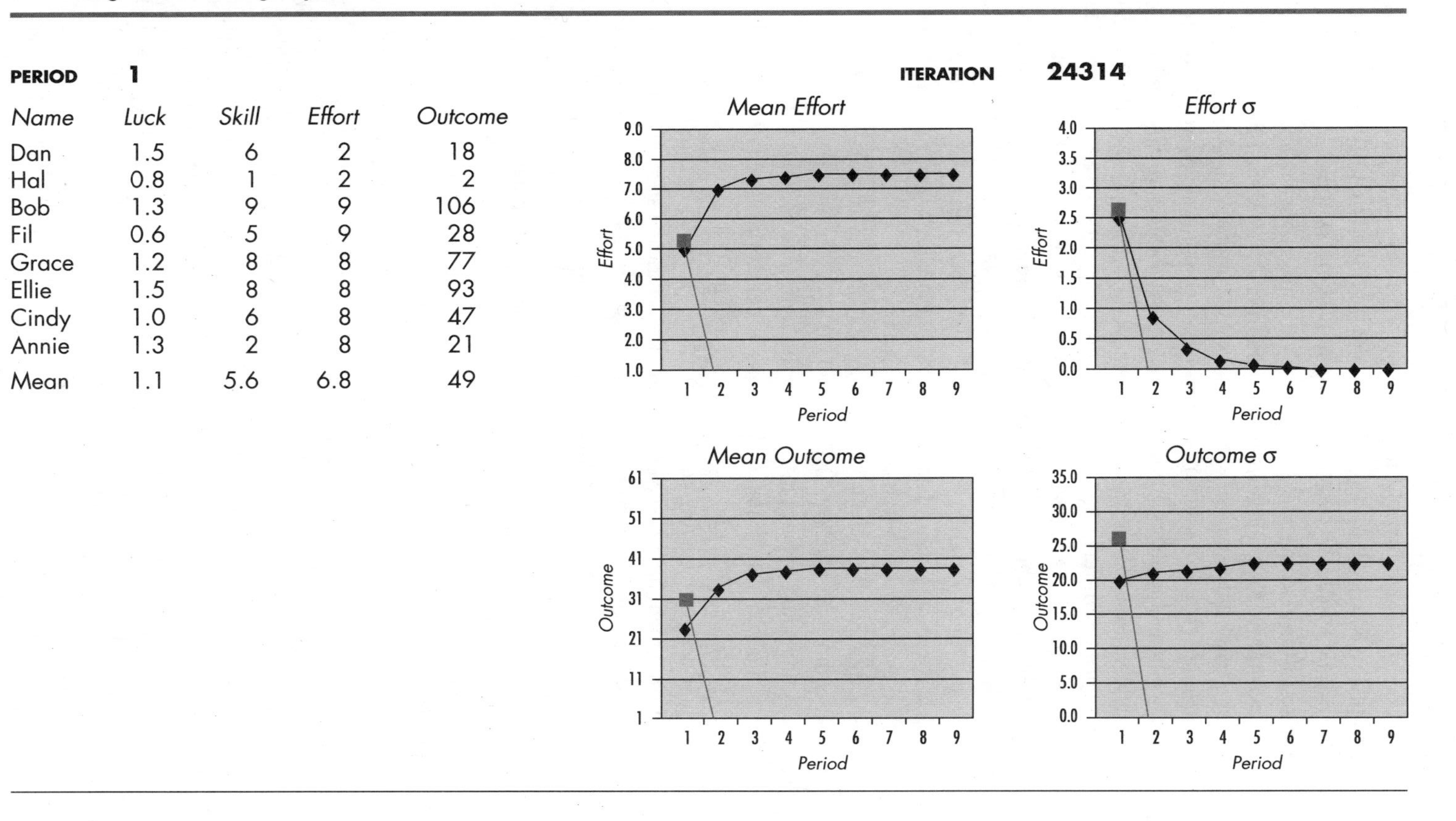

PERIOD **1**

Name	Luck	Skill	Effort	Outcome
Dan	1.5	6	2	18
Hal	0.8	1	2	2
Bob	1.3	9	9	106
Fil	0.6	5	9	28
Grace	1.2	8	8	77
Ellie	1.5	8	8	93
Cindy	1.0	6	8	47
Annie	1.3	2	8	21
Mean	1.1	5.6	6.8	49

their effort to match that of the person with the next higher outcome. That is, the appropriate level of effort is determined not by emulating the boss but by trying to work just as hard as the person with the next higher outcome. What will be the resulting norm?

Figure 9.4 incorporates a simple model of job success—outcomes are a multiplicative result of luck, skill, and effort. Luck represents the entire set of variables, externally determined, outcome-related factors, such as whether you happen to be on duty when a big client drops in. Luck, recalculated for each person for each day, is a random number between .5 and 1.5 and is thus equally likely to produce benefit and harm. Skill reflects the relatively enduring set of externally controlled outcome-related abilities and resources that people bring to their jobs. Not just IQ and stamina, but also whether your spouse is well connected in the community, skill is randomly determined at Period 0 and can have a value between 1 and 9. Effort represents the set of variables, self-controlled attributes that affect outcomes. Effort, which also can range from 1 to 9, is initially rationalized—on subsequent periods, it is hypothesized to result from social comparison.

Taking advantage of automatic range names, the formula for outcome can be written simply as "LUCK × SKILL × EFFORT." Even an undergraduate should be able to understand it, since it is written in English, rather than Latin. In this simple model, outcomes can be taken either as an index of productivity (the value of the employee to the company) or reward (the extent to which the organization recognizes productivity by giving back a high salary). It would be interesting to model situations in which these two elements are not identical, especially with regard to job satisfaction. As a result of being a multiplicative result of three factors, outcomes are highly skewed, with many people near the bottom and few at the top (the only way you can achieve a high outcome is to be high on everything). In this respect, the model is consistent with American society, where we also have a highly skewed distribution of outcomes.

Simulation

Figure 9.4 represents 8 members of a work group, showing their respective levels of luck, skill, effort, and outcome. For each of a series of 8 time periods, the sheet is sorted by outcome and recalculated. (The program must be set for manual rather than automatic recalculation.) Pressing Ctrl+r sets the process in operation by invoking a simple macro written in Visual Basic. A macro is used to control a sequence of events; in this case, the list of workers is first sorted in descending order of their outcomes and the sheet is recalculated, with workers each adjusting their effort to match the level of effort of the worker immediately above. The new level of effort for each person is calculated by a simple IF statement: "If the outcome of the next higher person is greater than one's own, adopt that person's effort, otherwise retain one's previous level of effort." Then, the dice of Luck are thrown again, a new set of outcomes is determined, and the Period and Iteration counters are updated. The computations are so fast that we found it necessary to add a wait interval every period in order to make it easier to observe the changes.

Two cells function as counters. The period counter uses the formula IF(period = 8, 0, period + 1) to increment itself by one every time the macro executes, starting again at 0 with new levels of skill and initial effort whenever the period counter gets to 8. The Iteration counter increments only when Period = 0.

Results

The social comparison model differs from the previous ones in that the sources of influence vary over trials and are not fixed neighbors. Nonetheless, it represents a social influence process in which people adjust themselves to match other people. Therefore, one might expect that the four forms of self-organization—consolidation, clustering, correlation, and continuing diversity—also would show up here, but between, not within, groups.

Consolidation, Clustering, and Continuing Diversity

Because everybody can compare with anybody else, no spatial factor shapes influence within groups. Consequently, although consolidation should be powerful, no possibility exists of clustering within groups. The absence of internal clustering, in turn, precludes continuing diversity within groups, each of which should adopt its own work norm. In the simulations, groups quickly came to equilibria, in which the variation of effort approached zero, reflecting the absence of internal clustering or continuing diversity within groups.

These phenomena, however, were quite pronounced between groups, with different levels of effort in different groups. Thus, although each group developed its own norm, different groups developed different norms. Furthermore, the norms evolved in the direction of greater effort.

Effort

If a skilled but lazy person happens to be lucky at the beginning, he or she will set the norm for the group, and it will converge on a low level of effort. However, if the group includes at least one reasonably skilled hardworking person, everyone else is soon inspired to work equally hard. The net result is an increase in the average level of effort from its initial random value of 5, with many groups topping out at 9 and the mean rising to 7.5. There was also a notable decrease in variance as people become more similar to one another.

Outcomes

The mean outcome also increased, presumably because of the increase in effort. Surprisingly, there was no change in the variance of outcomes. Reduced variance in effort leads to less variance in outcomes, because the former is a component of the latter, but increases in mean effort multiply with luck and skill to create more variance in outcomes.

I do not claim that this model duplicates typical American work groups in the last half of the 20th century or that its results are the reason we work so much harder than we used to. Rather, I suggest that such a spreadsheet model provides a powerful aid to intuition in assessing the group-level effects of psychological processes. The model could easily be extended to incorporate judgments of fairness, job satisfaction, or other job-related attributes. Outcome models might vary the relative weighting of luck, skill, and effort. We also might want to include ways of representing the race, age, and gender of the individuals in this workplace, so that some individuals might choose to compare only with those of their own category. Spreadsheets may help us understand the dynamic consequences of whatever modification we might choose to make.

Conclusions

Using Spreadsheets for Simulation

My first purpose was to show that computer simulation is not necessarily a mysterious thing practiced only by people who speak Greek. With the investment of a few hours, even someone who is not a computer expert can create a simulation with results that allow him or her to test any number of hypotheses and compare them with real data. Like translating the Bible into English, Excel allows almost anyone the opportunity to come to their own conclusions. One does not need a programmer or a priest to explain what is going on or have to take a course, go off to school, or work for three weeks to understand it. Just as with the Bible, simulations are not necessarily unambiguous, but one can draw one's own conclusions.

The word "simulation" is sometimes taken to mean "lying," and many people are appropriately skeptical of simulations because they can be jiggled in almost any way. Although simulation is difficult (see Latané, 1996b), spreadsheets reduce the difficulty and danger of error. Spreadsheets are not a panacea, however. Compared to more advanced, special purpose programs such as SITSIM (Latané & Nowak, 1997; Nowak & Latané, 1994), they can become cumbersome, especially with large numbers, continuous distances, and shifting partners.

Spreadsheets might become valuable as part of a computerized teaching laboratory. Students could work with the models—changing formulas, geometries, and key parameters—and thereby see the consequences for consolidation, clustering, continuing diversity, and correlation. Mastering spreadsheets is valuable in its own right, and the payoff in intuition also should be high. Seeing the connection between cells in the spreadsheet and people in society might help convey an understanding of how the character of nations can be shaped from below by social interactions among individual citizens.

Illustrating Dynamic Social Impact Theory

My second purpose was to illustrate dynamic social impact theory through the use of simulations. Simulations are useful in determining which assumptions or aspects of a psychological law make a difference at the group level and which do not. Even if a certain assumption is important for understanding individual functioning, it may not be worth worrying about if it does not affect the behavior of the social system as a whole. A large-scale program of systematic simulation has shown that dynamic social impact theory is remarkably robust or general with respect to theoretical assumptions, parameter values, system characteristics, and initial conditions (Latané & Nowak, 1997). Several elements are critical—linearity, individual differences, the nature of social space, and even the degree of randomness in the determination of change or temperature. One of the fascinating results from simulation is that increasing the "temperature," or randomness of the model leads to more organization in the form of greater consolidation, clustering, and correlation—up to a point, of course. These results suggest that when it comes to dynamic social processes, details may not make such a difference after all.

Such simple models as those I have presented here seem obviously too primitive to capture the actual history of specific social systems. However, Bourgeois and Latané (in press) have shown that similar simulations can track the evolution of specific groups at several levels, predicting not only the general degree of consolidation, clustering, and correlation but the specific norms emerging in different groups and even the specific beliefs of different individuals.

Explaining the Evolution of Work Norms

This brief chapter spans the changing research focus in social psychology over the past 50 years of research, completing a cycle from the original group-level Westgate finding of clustering, through individual-level processes such as social comparison and dissonance, and back to group-level phenomena such as the four Cs of dynamic social impact. It also spans societal changes from a time when we thought the problem was too much leisure time to one in which the problem is too little. My third purpose in this chapter was to see whether a model growing out of the former set of changes could account for the latter—the remarkable increase in how long Americans work.

The present simulations show that under some conditions, social comparison processes could lead work groups to adopt increasingly higher norms for how hard to work. Other research stimulated by social impact theory under the rubric "social loafing" has found that people often work less hard in groups (Latané, Williams, &

Harkins, 1979; Latané, 1986), in part because of a diffusion of responsibility. Is there a contradiction? I don't think so. The key difference may be identifiability—social loafing is promoted by the fact that individual contributions to group efforts are not identifiable (Williams, Harkins, & Latané, 1981), whereas the results described in this chapter depend on people being able to observe the levels of effort adopted by their colleagues.

With their role of training future generations of citizens, educators are charged with the responsibility of predicting the future demands that society will require in the way of skills, values, and knowledge. Perhaps simulations may enable our present generation of educators to do a better job than our predecessors of the 1950s. On the other hand, educators are subject to the same social processes as other people and even we have been caught up in the move to longer hours. Most of my colleagues now teach summers as well as winters, and sabbaticals at half pay no longer seem so attractive.

Our research has also been affected: In social psychology, at least, the average length of articles in our key journals more than doubled in the 20 years following the 1950s, and the amount of time spent in the editorial process, at least as measured by the number of reviewers and the amount of correspondence, increased even more (Jackson & Latané, 1978; Latané & Jackson, 1978). Whether this temporal change, which seems to have continued over the last 20 years, has led to better science, or even whether it resulted from social comparison processes in the peculiar subculture of social psychology, is debatable. However, social processes are reversible, and if we understand them through the application of systematic research and theory, we may be able to nudge them in the direction of a more satisfying science and a better society.

References

Abelson, R. P. (1964). Mathematical models of the distribution of attitudes under controversy. In N. Frederickson & H. Gulicksen (Eds.), *Contributions to mathematical psychology* (pp. 141–160). New York: Holt, Rinehart, & Winston.

Anderson, N. H. (1968). A simple model for information integration. In R. P. Abelson, E. Aronson, W. J. McGuire, T. M. Newcomb, M. J. Rosenberg, & P. H. Tannenbaum (Eds.), *Theories of cognitive consistency: A sourcebook* (pp. 731–743). Chicago: Rand McNally.

Axelrod, R. (1984). *The evolution of cooperation.* New York: Basic Books.

Baba, M. L. (1995). The cultural ecology of the corporation: Explaining diversity in work-group responses to organizational transformation. *Journal of Applied Behavioral Science, 31,* 202–233.

Back, K. W. (1951). Influence through social communication. *Journal of Abnormal and Social Psychology, 46,* 9–23.

Bak, P. (1996). *How nature works: The science of self-organized criticality.* New York: Springer-Verlag.

Baratta, J. E., & McManus, M. A. (1992). The effect of contextual factors on individuals' job performance. *Journal of Applied Social Psychology, 22,* 1702–1710.

Bearman, P. S. (1991). Desertion as localism: Army unit solidarity and group norms in the U.S. Civil War. *Social Forces, 70,* 321–342.

Blau, G. (1995). Influence of group lateness on individual lateness: A cross-level examination. *Academy of Management Journal, 38,* 1483–1496.

Bourgeois, M., & Latané, B. (in press). Simulating dynamic social impact: Four levels of prediction.

Casti, J. L. (1994). *Complexification: Explaining a paradoxical world through the science of surprise.* New York: HarperCollins.

Decker, R., & Hirschfield, S. (1995). *The object concept.* Boston: PWS.

Epstein, J. M., & Axtell, R. (1996). *Growing artificial societies: Social science from the bottom up.* Cambridge, MA: MIT Press.

Festinger, L. (1950). Informal social communication. *Psychological Review, 57,* 271–282.

Festinger, L. (1954). A theory of social comparison processes. *Human Relations, 7,* 117–140.

Festinger, L. (1957). *A theory of cognitive dissonance.* Evanston, IL: Row Peterson.

Festinger, L., Gerard, H. B., Hymovitch, B., Kelley, H. H., & Raven, B. (1952). The influence process in the presence of extreme deviates. *Human Relations, 5,* 327–346.

Festinger, L., Schachter, S., & Back, K. (1950). *Social pressures in informal groups: A study of human factors in housing.* Palo Alto, CA: Stanford University Press.

Festinger, L., & Thibaut, J. (1951). Interpersonal communication in small groups. *Journal of Abnormal and Social Psychology, 46,* 92–99.

Gregory, K. L. (1983). Native-view paradigms: Multiple cultures and culture conflicts in organizations. *Administrative Sciences Quarterly, 28,* 359–376.

Harton, H. C., & Latané, B. (1997). Information- and thought-induced polarization: The mediating role of involvement in making attitudes extreme. *Journal of Social Behavior and Personality, 12,* 271–300.

Hochschild, A. R. (1997). *The time bind: When work becomes home and home becomes work.* New York: Henry Holt.

Holland, J. H. (1995). *Hidden order: How adaptation builds complexity.* Reading, MA: Addison-Wesley.

Homans, G. C. (1950). *The human group.* New York: Harcourt Brace.

Kauffman, S. (1995). *At home in the universe: The search for the laws of self-organization and complexity.* New York: Oxford University Press.

Jackson, J., & Latané, B. (1978). On the displacement of authors by editors. *Personality and Social Psychology Bulletin, 4,* 381–383.

Latané, B. (1981). The psychology of social impact. *American Psychologist, 36,* 343–365.

Latané, B. (1986). Responsibility and effort in organizations. In P. S. Goodman (Ed.), *Designing effective work groups* (pp. 277–304). San Francisco: Jossey-Bass.

Latané, B. (1996a). Dynamic social impact: The creation of culture by communication. *Journal of Communication, 46*(4), 13–25.

Latané, B. (1996b). Dynamic social impact: Robust predictions from simple theory. In R. Hegselmann, U. Mueller, & K. Troitzsch (Eds.), *Modeling and simulation in the social sciences from the philosophy of science point of view* (pp. 287–310). Dordrecht, The Netherlands: Kluwer Theory and Decision Library.

Latané, B. (1997). Dynamic social impact: The societal consequences of human interaction. In C. McGarty & A. Haslam (Eds.), *The message of social psychology: Perspectives on mind and society* (pp. 200–220). Oxford, England: Blackwell.

Latané, B., & Bourgeois, M. J. (1996). Experimental evidence for dynamic social impact: The emergence of subcultures in electronic groups. *Journal of Communication, 46*(4), 35–47.

Latané, B., & Jackson, J. (1978). Editors finally outnumber authors. *Personality and Social Psychology Bulletin, 4,* 195–196.

Latané, B., & L'Herrou, T. (1996). Social clustering in the Conformity Game: Dynamic social impact in electronic groups. *Journal of Personality and Social Psychology, 70,* 1218–1230.

Latané, B., & Nowak, A. (1994). Attitudes as catastrophes: From dimensions to categories with increasing involvement. In R. Vallacher & A. Nowak (Eds.), *Dynamical systems in social psychology* (pp. 219–249). New York: Academic Press.

Latané, B., & Nowak, A. (1997). Self-organizing social systems: Necessary and sufficient conditions for the emergence of consolidation and clustering. In G. Barnett & F. Boster (Eds.), *Progress in communication sciences: Advances in persuasion* (pp. 43–74). Norwood, NJ: Ablex.

Latané, B., Williams, K., & Harkins, S. (1979). Many hands make light the work: Causes and consequences of social loafing. *Journal of Personality and Social Psychology, 37,* 822–832.

Levine, J. M., & Moreland, R. L. (1991). Culture and socialization in workgroups. In L. B. Resnick, J. M. Levine, & S. D. Teasley (Eds.), *Perspectives on socially shared cognition* (pp. 257–279). Washington, DC: American Psychological Association.

Levy, S. (1992). *Artificial life: The quest for a new creation.* New York: Pantheon.

Linder, S. B. (1970). *The harried leisure class.* New York: Columbia University Press.

Markham, S. E., & McKee, G. H. (1995). Group absence behavior and standards: A multilevel analysis. *Academy of Management Journal, 38,* 1174–1190.

Martocchio, J. J. (1994). The effects of absence culture on individual absence. *Human Relations, 47,* 243–262.

Mathieu, J. E., & Kohler, S. S. (1990). A cross-level examination of group absence influences on individual absence. *Journal of Applied Psychology, 75,* 217–220.

Moreland, R. L., & Levine, J. M. (in press). Socialization in organizations and workgroups. In M. Turner (Ed.), *Groups at work: Advances in theory and research.* Hillsdale, NJ: Erlbaum.

Moscovici, S. (1984). The phenomenon of social representations. In R. M. Farr & S. Moscovici (Eds.), *Social representations* (pp. 1–42). Cambridge/Paris: CUP/ Maison des Sciences de L'Homme.

Nicholson, N., & Johns, G. (1985). The absence culture and the psychological contract: Who's in control of absence? *Academy of Management Review, 10*, 397–407.

Nowak, A., & Latané, B. (1994). Simulating the emergence of social order from individual behavior. In N. Gilbert & J. Doran (Eds.), *Simulating societies: The computer simulation of social phenomena* (pp. 63–84). London: University College London Press.

Nowak, A., Szamrej, J., & Latané, B. (1990). From private attitude to public opinion: A dynamic theory of social impact. *Psychological Review, 97*, 362–376.

Poundstone, W. (1985). *The recursive universe: Cosmic complexity and the limits of scientific knowledge.* Chicago: Contemporary Books.

Rentsch, J. R. (1990). Climate and culture: Interaction and qualitative differences in organizational meanings. *Journal of Applied Psychology, 75*, 668–681.

Roethlisberger, F. J., & Dickson, W. J. (1939). *Management and the worker.* Cambridge, MA: Harvard University Press.

Sackman, S. A. (1992). Culture and subcultures: An analysis of organizational knowledge. *Administrative Science Quarterly, 37*, 140–161.

Schachter, S. (1951). Deviation, rejection, and communication. *Journal of Abnormal and Social Psychology, 46*, 190–208.

Schor, J. B. (1991). *The overworked American: The unexpected decline of leisure.* New York: Basic Books.

Van Maanen, J., & Barley, S. R. (1985). Cultural organization: Fragments of a theory. In P. J. Frost, L. F. Moore, M. R. Louis, C. C. Lundberg, & J. Martin (Eds.), *Organizational culture* (pp. 31–53). Beverly Hills, CA: Sage.

Von Neumann, J. (1966). *Theory of self-reproducing automata.* Urbana: University of Illinois Press.

Williams, K., Harkins, S., & Latané, B. (1981). Identifiability and social loafing: Two cheering experiments. *Journal of Personality and Social Psychology, 40*, 303–311.

COMMENT:

Simulations on the Cheap

The Latané Approach

James H. Davis

The Latané chapter aims to achieve three goals: (a) to show how simple spreadsheets can be used to model the complex dynamics of social influence; (b) to illustrate the approach, using dynamic social impact theory, and understand better the temporal and structural evolution of subcultures within various kinds of groups; and (c) to demonstrate how social norms of appropriate work effort might develop from simpler interpersonal processes (i.e., social-comparison processes) and, consequently, how effort might "naturally" escalate. Although all three aims are realized, and well, the most notable is the first, a methodological offering. Why this might be so, is itself of interest.

First, it is important to confront the puzzle of why the conceptual simulation of social behavior has not been a particularly popular activity, despite the increasing availability of tools that would simplify the task—most notably, a decades-long growth of cheap and friendly computing power. It is not that social researchers lacked fair and early warning of the tools to come, a description of their potential, or an ample array of exemplars to emulate. For example, Abelson (1968), in a piece specifically tailored to social psychologists' needs, not only laid out the specifics of simulation and its potential role in social research but also described explicitly how the digital computer might serve as the vehicle. Oft-cited and widely admired, Abelson's paper had virtually no effect on the mainstream of actual social research, either basic or applied. Twenty years later, Davis and Kerr (1986) even avoided the word "simulation" (preferring instead the camouflage of "thought experiment," a special construal of a term having a somewhat different connotation in physical science), while actually advocating simulation as an especially important instrument in applied settings in which data are sparse. To be sure, in the years following Abelson's prophetic discussion, the computer was increasingly exploited for the statistical analysis of empirical data, but even that use was largely limited to a few special cases of the general linear model, for which computational recipes had become highly standardized and widely available. The examples afforded by, say, atmospheric physicists modeling the atmosphere and running specific computer simulations to observe outcomes under particular conditions (parameter values), or aeronautical engineers simulating various airframes on the computer, before even building a prototype, somehow did not induce social researchers to engage in simulations for similar purposes. Why should this be so?

At least part of the answer may lie in the nature of the theory that dominates social and much of organizational psychology. Consider a sample of popular theories that continue to attract attention and currently stimulate research on social behavior: cognitive dissonance (Festinger, 1957), groupthink (Janis, 1982), and equity theory (Adams, 1965). Dissimilar in many respects, these theories resemble each other in that they are highly informal constructions, use the natural language system, are rich in metaphor, and use lavishly nuanced statements about social behavior. The problem is not that these theoretical notions were initially less precise than their conceptual counterparts that were written as computer programs or algebraic statements, but that they continued to be so. Few people inspired by these ideas went on to develop specific models for the special case applications of the research at issue. Instead, the original "word theories" were called up time and again in their original form, unchanged for the particular research application.

The conceptual mechanics of the matter were addressed in depth more than two decades ago by Harris (1976) in a paper with the revealing title "The Uncertain Connection Between Verbal Theories and Research Hypotheses in Social Psychology." (Perhaps even more informative was the title of an earlier, preliminary piece by Harris, 1974, "This Is a Science? Social Psychologists' Aversion to Knowing What Their Theories Say.") Harris noted that theoretical terms were not well defined, boundary conditions were unspecified, and so on. He then showed that under various plausible interpretations of assumptions, conditions, terms, and so forth, several well-known theories contained contradictions and inconsistences or, at least, could reasonably be represented in a variety of ways. One conclusion that may be drawn from Harris's demonstrations is that the various theoretical notions he analyzed were incomplete. That cognitive dissonance theory, for example, was a valuable aid to understanding many heretofore puzzling social phenomena is undeniable, and it was clearly a spur to much important research. Without further development, however, such a theory could not support explicit extrapolations and inferences through simulation as Latané (and others in this book) have described the enterprise. Thus, there has been little theoretical basis in the field at large for simulation work.

Clearly, simulation requires a strong theoretical model that exists in a suitable form. One must have something with which to simulate! Something must be computed, and there must be a vehicle for accomplishing that. It is this conceptual precondition that Latané did not emphasize in his chapter, but he might well have done so. To be sure, a spreadsheet is a wonderful tool. An explicit theory must exist in a simulation-friendly form or be capable of being put into such a form. In other words, it was the existence of social impact theory (and the body of empirical research that documents its value) that enabled a spreadsheet model to be constructed, thereby not only illustrating computational modeling through such a program but also allowing something interesting to be said about social behavior as well.

Thus, given the style of theory that has long predominated in social research, there has been little call for social researchers to serve as their own "priests and bishops," as Latané colorfully labels those who understand the special "Latin" (i.e., mathematics and computer code) of simulation. His offering of an English-speaking spreadsheet as intermediary is, consequently, especially merciful, and by boldly posting his theses (his prose is not timid), he may indeed provoke a reformation of sorts. However, earlier similar proposals also were of considerable merit, and these have been ignored (e.g., Abelson, 1968; Davis & Kerr, 1986). The difference is that the spreadsheet approach just might be simple enough, yet powerful enough, to be unavoidably appealing.

Individual to Group

It is possible to conclude, then, that there exists a considerable store of widely appreciated social theory, not now simulation-friendly, that could be developed for computer simulation studies. Recall that Harris (1976), in his critique of theory in social psychology, undertook to provide supplemental assumptions and plausible explicit interpretations of what a theory could be interpreted to mean, and then proceeded to deduce the consequences. Latané did much the same in his chapter, using Festinger's (1954) social comparison theory (SCT). Notably, the focus of SCT (like most theory in social psychology) is the individual, not large or small groups. Latané's idea was to see what the large-scale effects, over time, might be of playing out the social comparison notions (made explicit for this case) at the individual level.

The result was a "social comparison model of work group effort" (p. 206), that produced a number of group-level consequences that were not intuitively apparent without the computer simulation. Indeed, Latané emphasizes that the model is incomplete as a duplication of American work groups, but he argues that nonetheless, "such a spreadsheet model provides a powerful aid to intuition in assessing the group-level effects of psychological processes" (p. 210). Such simulations are indeed a powerful vehicle for drawing inferences from existing data, extrapolating between pieces of available evidence, or deducing implications that now rest largely, if not solely on (clinical) intuition.

An earlier essay by Schelling (1978), appropriately entitled, "Micromotives and Macrobehavior" advanced a similar thesis. Like Latané, Schelling attempted (among other things) to show how relatively simple individual-level processes can produce rather complex phenomena at the group level but that these system-level consequences are not the result of some simple aggregation function. (Schelling also warned against the hazards of deducing individual-level motives and other cognitive phenomena from observations of the aggregate—giving especially compelling examples concerning race, crowds, and organizations, among others.) Although Latané has added to the discussion an important tool—and a highly accessible tool at that (namely, the spreadsheet)—many theoretical analyses of individual-to-group questions, of course, will continue to require more complicated quantitative engines than spreadsheet models.

Summary and Conclusion

The Latané chapter, like much of this book, can be viewed as much as a call to simulation arms as a report of findings from conceptual analyses using simulation techniques. There have been earlier such calls (again, see Abelson, 1968; Davis & Kerr, 1986). Latané, like the earlier prophets, has generously illustrated the value of simulation as an aid to intuition by producing concrete results in table and graph format. Unlike the others, however, he also has included a clear description of a simple and inexpensive method for researchers to do their own simulations, using widely available spreadsheet programs for desktop computers. Will this most recent sermon succeed in producing significant numbers of converts?

References

Abelson, R. P. (1968). Simulation of social behavior. In G. Lindzey & E. Aronson (Eds.), *Handbook of social psychology* (Vol. 2). Reading, MA: Addison-Wesley.

Adams, J. S. (1965). Inequity in social exchange. In L. Berkowitz (Ed.), *Advances in experimental social psychology* (Vol. 2). New York: Academic Press.

Davis, J. H., & Kerr, N. L. (1986). Thought experiments and the problem of sparse data in small group research. In P. Goodman (Ed.), *Designing effective work groups* (pp. 305–349). San Francisco: Jossey-Bass.

Festinger, L. (1954). A theory of social comparison processes. *Human Relations, 7*, 117–140.

Festinger, L. (1957). *A theory of cognitive dissonance.* Evanston, IL: Row Peterson.

Harris, R. J. (1974, October). This is a science? Social psychologists' aversion to knowing what their theories say. In R. J. Harris (Ed.), Two comments on the uncertain connection between theory and data in social psychology. *Social Psychology Bulletin, 74*(2).

Harris, R. J. (1976). The uncertain connection between verbal theories and research hypotheses in social psychology. *Journal of Experimental Social Psychology, 12*, 210–219.

Janis, I. L. (1982). *Groupthink.* Boston: Houghton-Mifflin.

Schelling, T. C. (1978). *Micromotives and macrobehavior.* New York: W. W. Norton.

CHAPTER 10

Modeling Change in Fields of Organizations

Some Simulation Results

J. Miller McPherson

This chapter describes the results of a computer simulation of the general theory of voluntary associations and other less formal groups, on which I have been working since the early 1980s (McPherson, 1981, 1983). The essence of the theory is that these groups operate in a multidimensional property space I now call *Blau space,* because Peter Blau (1977) has given us the clearest view of how the variables that make up this property space work to structure society.

The essence of the Blau space idea is that certain dimensions of social life organize the frequency and intensity of social contact among people in society. If we could closely study a simple society, we would observe that individuals make relatively few systematic distinctions among each other—primarily those of age, gender, and physical capabilities. As society grows in size and scope, however, the scale of the system requires that other dimensions of social life, such as education, income, wealth, esteem, and so forth, come to organize social interaction. As I have argued elsewhere (McPherson & Ranger-Moore, 1991), the four main stages of societal complexity correspond to four distinctive configurations of Blau space. In hunting-and-gathering societies of 20 to 50 people, relatively few differences exist among individuals, because the accumulation of wealth is problematic in groups that need to move all their belongings every few weeks. The few differences in social rank are also small. In horticultural societies of up to several thousand people, there is usually a single individual of high social rank, but this position is based on achievement, rather than inheritance and transmittal through social institutions. The difference between the "big man" and most of the ordinary members of society is large, but it is not transmitted intergenerationally. In agricultural societies of several million people,

The National Science Foundation supported data collection for this chapter with grants SES-8120666, SES-8319899, SES-8821365, and SBR-9308326, Miller McPherson, Principal Investigator. I thank Lynn Smith-Lovin for comments on an earlier draft of this chapter and David Richmond for programming assistance.

the form of social differentiation leads to large correlations of wealth, rank, and kinship with the ruling elite. Thus, although several gradations in social rank exist, these gradations are correlated with each other: Nobles are likely to have high social rank, high wealth, high power, close kinship ties to the king, and so forth. Finally, when we reach the industrial stage, the dimensions have a great deal of variation, and they are less correlated with each other. The occupied locations in Blau space are diverse, so that social differentiation in Blau space can become extreme. The development of the middle class means that a large number of people with intermediate statuses are in the system and that these statuses may be based on inconsistent values of wealth, social rank, and the other Blau dimensions. The presence of intellectuals (moderately high social rank, relatively low material wealth) as a meaningful social category allows a major contrast with the self-made millionaire, who may have high material wealth but little of the social capital that comes from a high-status background. The weaker correlations among the dimensions imply that a large number of actors with inconsistent values exist on the multiple dimensions of Blau space.

Not only are the people in Blau space distributed more widely in industrial society, but more dimensions make a difference. Consider the research that suggests that height, weight, manners, and many other dimensions act to condition social interaction. As social psychologists have shown convincingly, physical beauty alone can be successfully translated into social status (Webster & Driskell, 1978). As the size and scale of the social system increase, the number of dimensions increases and the correlations among them decrease, leading to greater diversity in the system as a whole but allowing the development of distinctive regions that may be less connected with the rest of the system. The greater the distance between locations in this space, the greater the social differences among the people who occupy those locations, and the more likely they are to have different lifestyles, attitudes, beliefs, and so forth.

The basic socioeconomic variables of age, gender, race, education, and others are important Blau dimensions, along with the equally fundamental properties of space and time. In Blau's book *Inequality and Heterogeneity* (1977), the variables that define this space are the dimensions of social life that shape the associations people have with one another. A key aspect of Blau's theory, and one which is essential to this chapter, is that social contact among people in society is a declining function of distance in Blau space. Direct social contacts are not likely to reach out far across Blau space.

The thesis in my 1983 paper (McPherson, 1983) on this topic was that organizations are localized in Blau space; they occupy niches in that space because the people making up each organization are limited in the range of the Blau dimensions they span. The organizations are localized because they recruit through social networks; that is, membership in these groups comes about almost exclusively through direct social contacts among people (see Booth & Babchuk, 1969). Because the contacts span short distances in Blau space, the organization can recruit only people who are close by in the space to the already existing members of the group; that is, only people who are similar to the existing members in the Blau dimensions will become members. In network terms, the potential recruits for the group are the aggregate of the ego nets (the social contacts of a person) of the current members.

The empirical result of this network recruitment is that groups are arrayed in localized regions of Blau space. The niche of the group is centered on the mean of the characteristics of the members, and it extends away from the mean to form a hyperbox in multidimensional Blau space. The conception of competition in the 1983 paper was that when the organizations overlapped in the space, they were competing for the same kind of people as potential members. In other words, when the niches of two groups intersected, the overlapping area was a region in which the two groups were competing for exactly the same resource—a particular kind of person, defined by that region of Blau space. When the shipping distribution center for a mail-order business and the buildings and grounds department of the university have people in the same geographic region who are interchangeable in Blau space, then the two groups are competing for the same resource. If the two groups are near enough in the time dimension in addition to the social dimensions, then the competition will become quite literal, and the prospective member in the contested region will be able to affiliate with only one of the groups.

But this ecological competition does not depend simply on scheduling difficulty in time. The underlying imagery supposes that groups exact resources from people generally and that these resources are finite. When two groups focus on the same kind of people, and both require substantial resources, the model suggests that either the groups will accommodate each other by adjusting their niches or one of the groups will fail.

One of the most frequent responses that people have made to this idea is skepticism that the groups actually compete with each other. People have remarked that they have difficulty with the idea that even trivial groups, such as bridge clubs or hobby groups, could have detectable effects on anything, much less on other trivial groups. Some of my most recent work with voluntary groups has been directed toward this criticism. As Popielarz and McPherson (1995) show, people exit voluntary groups at different rates when they are located at different places in the niche. Members who are in the center of the niche will stay in the group much longer, on average, than members at the edge of the niche. And members in zones where there is intense overlap with the niches of other groups will exit the group at a higher rate. This latter finding, the *niche overlap effect,* is a basic feature of the simulation model I present here.

Another related response I have encountered from others is that the groups are too fluid to pin down. That is, the flow of people through these groups is likely to be so random and subject to such historically particular circumstances that one cannot really model such ephemeral events. As our 1996 paper (McPherson & Rotolo, 1996) shows, these ephemeral events are quite systematic: We were successful in predicting the time path of several populations of voluntary groups over a 15-year period. We successfully predicted each type of group's track through Blau space over time as well as changes in the group's dispersion over time.

Now we ask ourselves two questions. First, what is the systematic source of movement or stability in the system? Second, what potential mechanism could account for the relative positions of the groups over time? To answer these questions, we need to consider the mechanisms by which an organization can move around in the space. Clearly, the only way the group can change its position is through systematic changes in the composition of the group. If the group gains new members in one direction and loses them in another, it will change its position. Adaptation of the group to a new location in the space will occur when members are lost and gained in such a way as to move the entire distribution of the group. The group could change its location in any dimension of Blau space by systematic selection in one or more directions. Thus, groups can move about in Blau space in response to opportunities or costs in their vicinity. In addition, the groups could generalize or specialize in Blau space by recruiting increasingly heterogeneous or homogeneous members, or the groups could grow or decline in membership in response to changing conditions.

The reader will no doubt be struck by the similarity of this model to the biological model of species evolution (see Ricklefs, 1979; Wright, 1931). This analogy is not accidental. Biotic populations adapt to contingencies in the environment by selection of individual organisms; that is, the process of natural selection occurs when less fit members of a species die at a higher rate and do not reproduce themselves successfully. Relatively small changes in the mortality rates in different parts of the niche will produce major shifts in the overall population over time. Similarly, when one of our groups has been exposed to systematic changes in the membership through systematic attrition of members, systematic attraction of new members, or a combination of both, then the group has adapted in Blau space.

Now, a crucial question and the immediate topic of this chapter is, What underlying forces drive the stability or change in the membership composition over time? A major force toward stability, as we have already suggested, is the fact that social contacts occur through limited ranges in Blau space; that is, social contacts are homophilous. There is a force toward conservatism in the character of the group—new members will tend to be like the old ones. Yet, at the edges of the group, one would expect that the group could attract new members, like the outliers in the group, and these new outliers could recruit new and even more different members, and so forth. Empirical evidence tells us that the groups are relatively stable in both their means and variances over time; they do not move about much. What is producing this result?

The answer offered by the McPherson (1983) paper is that groups do not operate in isolation; that is, they compete with each other for members. The model that I discuss in this chapter deals with the problem of competition in two fundamental ways. First, I explicitly model all competitors in the same domain. If the domain of organization is voluntary associations, the simulation represents all sorts of voluntary associations that theoretically can compete with each other. The explicit interactions of these groups with each other produce dynamic movement in the system. The second feature of the simulation is that the effects of competition from other kinds of entities—such as families, governments, sustenance organizations, and the like—are excluded from the model. I isolate the system from these effects. The assumption here is that the other entities do not interfere systematically in such a way as to increase the fitness of particular groups and decrease the fitness of others. This heroic assumption allows me to proceed to model the competitive interactions on which I am directly focusing.

The goal of this chapter is to explore the consequences of various mixes of competition and homophily on a number of system outputs: the number of groups; their size, age, dispersion, and overlap; and the stability of the social ties that bind actors together.

The Simulation

Why Simulate?

I first want to show why simulation is an essential exercise at this stage of the project. First, temporal variation in the crucial parameters that govern the behavior of these systems is likely to be small for any given system. Because gathering data on groups like these is so extraordinarily expensive, I have been able to look at only two examples over time in any detail. The first example was the entire United States, as represented in the General Social Survey data from 1972 to 1987. The second system was a sample of roughly 2,800 groups from a Great Plains state from 1974 to 1989 (McPherson, Popielarz, & Drobnic, 1992). Although the results from these applications are encouraging, they still are only two cases. What one would need in order to evaluate the effects of several parameters at once on the model would be, at the very least, dozens of systems. I would like to have the tens of millions of dollars needed to gather these data, but they are not forthcoming at present. The only way to get more than a handful of cases for study is to generate them myself.

Second, simulation allows me to study the behavior of these hypothetical systems over arbitrarily long time periods. The two empirical studies mentioned above only cover about a 15-year time period, whereas some of the groups in them have been around for many decades. Thus, simulation results allow us to get a better understanding of the long-term process.

Probably the most important reason to simulate is that we can systematically study the effects of the forces of homophily and competition on the size and number of groups, their dispersion, and their overlap. These parameters are really at the heart of the model; they probably do not vary significantly among any of the model's empirical applications because these studies are so bounded in time and space.

Finally, the simulation results will ultimately allow us to get some insight into the relationships among output variables in the system. Looking ahead a bit, we will see that there are some systematic connections among variables such as the average size of groups, their turnover, dispersion, and so forth.

Assumptions

The most fundamental assumption for the model is that groups gain and lose adherents through social contact. That is, the model assumes that people are introduced to groups through connections with people already associated with the group. A significant amount of empirical research suggests that this assumption is correct (Snow, Zurcher, & Eckland-Olson, 1980, and especially McPherson et al., 1992). In fact, the evidence is strong enough that I actually use empirical estimates for the effect of each social contact on the probability of joining and leaving a given group (see also Popielarz & McPherson, 1995). Explicitly, I assume that each individual has a heightened probability of joining a group when that person has social contact with a member of the group (see Feld, 1981). Conversely, social contacts outside the group will increase the probability that a given member will leave the group. I do not vary the strength of the parameter governing the effects of these contacts in this report; the parameters are set at their estimated values based on empirical research.

The second important assumption for the simulation is that social ties in Blau space are homophilous. The probability of social contact between people is a declining function of distance in Blau space. Once again, the evidence for this assumption is quite strong (Marsden, 1987, 1988; Yamaguchi, 1990; and the extensive review in McPherson & Smith-Lovin, 1986). In the simulation, actors will generate social contact probabilistically with one another; the probability of contact declines with Blau distance. Homophily bias is generated by varying the probability of tie formation between actors as a function of Blau distance. Actors close together in Blau space will have a heightened probability of social contact; the probability of contact declines monotonically (logistically) with distance. I vary the strength of the homophily bias parameter in this report.

I next assume that new social contact occurs at a higher rate inside groups. One could regard this assumption as simply an extension of the definition of social group. In the simulation, common membership in a group heightens the probability that two actors will initiate social contact in future rounds of interaction. The empirical evidence for this assumption is not as strong as for the first assumption, but indirect evidence from McPherson et al. (1992) allows us to estimate this effect. This parameter is not varied in the current simulation.

The final important assumption contained in the simulation is that groups compete with each other for the time and other resources of individuals. The concrete embodiment of this assumption is that membership in multiple groups heightens the probability of exit from any one of the groups. Fairly convincing empirical support for this assumption is presented in Popielarz and McPherson (1995), who have shown that the rate of exit from a group is strongly affected by memberships in other groups. This parameter is varied in the simulation.

To summarize, the parameters varied in this report include those governing the strength of homophily and the amount of competitive interaction between groups.

Parameters governing the effect of each social contact on the probability of joining or leaving groups are set at their empirically estimated values. The size of the system for this report is 50 actors. Studies of significantly larger groups, limited because of computer capacity, suggest that the general conclusions from size 50 are not different in a theoretically important way from the results reported here. Further study of the relationship between system size and the variables reported here is under way.

Outcomes Studied

Three general categories of outcomes shape the population of groups. The first are the dynamics of ties themselves, where ties are connections or links between people. Thus, I track the stability of ties. This variable measures the extent to which ties between people persist. Because ties form inside groups with heightened probability, the distribution, overlap, and persistence of groups, in addition to the input parameters, can affect the stability of ties.

The second category of outcomes has to do with characteristics of the groups for given combinations of parameters. I study the relationship between the input parameters and the number, size, and dispersion of surviving groups at any given time; I also track the persistence of groups as indicated by mean group age at a given time.

The third class of outcomes has to do with the entire population of groups at any time. I track the membership overlap—the extent to which actors in the system are members of multiple groups simultaneously. In empirical research, this characteristic has been frequently studied in the form of the mean number of memberships held by the people in the system. Many studies have studied this variable at the individual level (see Knoke, 1990; extensive reviews of the early literature are available in Smith, 1975, and Smith & Freedman, 1972), but none have tried to establish any connection between the mean number of groups to which people belong and system characteristics. Results from the bioecological literature suggest that competition significantly reduces the overlap in niche space.

Program

The core device in the simulation is the $N \times N$ ties matrix, which is a matrix of zeros and ones. When the *i*th person has a social network tie to the *j*th person, there is an entry of "1" in the *i*th row, *j*th column of the matrix. When two people are not connected, there is an entry of "0." There are zeros on the main diagonal, and the matrix is symmetric. Social contacts are probabilistically generated as a function of (a) the homophily principle and (b) common membership in groups. The homophily principle dictates that people nearby in Blau space are more likely to be connected, whereas those distant from each other are less likely to be connected. When the ties matrix is ordered by distance in Blau space (i.e., rows near each other in the matrix represent people similar to one another on the Blau characteristic), the homophily principle generates a clustering of ones near the main diagonal (top left to bottom right) of the matrix. In the simulation, people who are members of the same group are given a heightened probability of developing a network tie.

The people-by-groups matrix models the relationship between actors and groups. The rows are people, the columns are groups. In each simulation, the number of people is fixed, and the formation and dissolution of groups leads to variability in the number of columns in the matrix. An entry of 1 indicates that the *i*th person is a member of the *j*th group. The formation of groups occurs through social contact; when a social contact survives one complete round of interaction, a group of size 2 is formed. The group can either grow, stay constant, or decline after formation. Growth occurs through the addition of new members, which results from ties between the current members of the group and the potential new member. Decline occurs when current members are pulled out of the group probabilistically or through their ties to nonmembers.

Results

Figure 10.1 shows the multivariate relationships among competition, homophily, and mean group age. When competition is low, a clear and substantial increase in group survival occurs as the homophily bias increases. The mean group age nearly doubles as the homophily bias parameter moves from the lower limit to the upper limit. The mechanism through which homophily bias produces more durable groups is through the increase in tie stability discussed above. The relatively strong effect of homophily on group survival disappears when the stability of network ties is controlled, as shown in Table 10.1, column 1. Thus, the restriction of actors' social world through

FIGURE 10.1

Effects of homophily on system outcomes

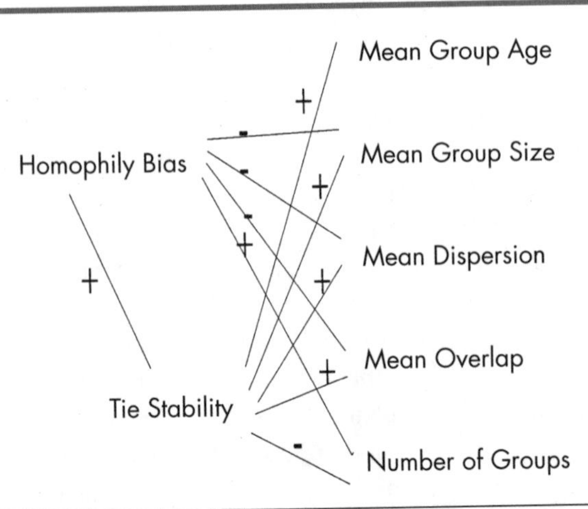

TABLE 10.1

The linear, additive effects of homophily, competition, and tie stability on the output variables (N = 650)*

	MEAN AGE		MEAN OVERLAP		MEAN DISPERSION		MEAN SIZE		NUMBER OF GROUPS	
DEPENDENT VARIABLE	**B**	**SE**	**B**	**SE**	**B**	**SE**	**B**	**SE**	**B**	**SE**
Constant	15.945	1.396	60.374	2.587	0.526	0.016	–0.454	0.016	16.184	1.065
Homophily bias	–0.084	0.108	–1.660	0.201	–0.014	0.001	–1.504	0.162	0.432	0.083
Competition	–24.218	1.365	–64.772	2.530	–0.454	0.016	–53.080	2.044	3.108	1.041
Tie stability	17.751	0.917	10.545	1.699	0.055	0.011	16.788	1.372	–12.636	0.699
Multiple regression	0.849		0.826		0.710		0.862		0.796	

*Unstandardized regressions, performed on results from simulations of size 50 over 50 time periods.

increased homophily leads to more stability in their social ties, which leads to more persistent social groups.

The relatively strong effect of homophily on tie stability acts to suppress the relationship of homophily bias with other output variables. Once the indirect effects of homophily through tie stability are taken into account, homophily has a strong and negative effect on group overlap, group size, and group dispersion, as columns 2, 3, and 4 in Table 10.1 reveal. Homophily has a positive effect on the number of groups once tie stability is taken into account.

Thus, the apparently weak relationship of homophily bias to the output variables actually occurs because tie stability acts in strong and opposite fashion to the direct effects of homophily. Homophily is shown to have substantial direct and indirect effects on the output variables once this suppressor variable is controlled. This result is apparent in summary Figure 10.2, which emphasizes the fact that the effect of homophily on the mean age of groups is completely indirect, through tie stability, while tie stability itself acts as a suppressor variable, producing indirect effects of opposite sign than the direct effects on the other output variables. The weak zero-order relationship between homophily and the output variables is produced by the strong effect of homophily on tie stability and that variable's subsequent relationship to the other output variables.

The effects of competition are straightforward: Competition decreases the mean age, overlap, dispersion, and size, and it increases the number of groups. Competition fragments the system into smaller and smaller groups, with less dispersion, shorter duration, and less overlap.

Discussion

This discussion is organized around each of the output variables.

FIGURE 10.2

Effects of competition on system outcomes

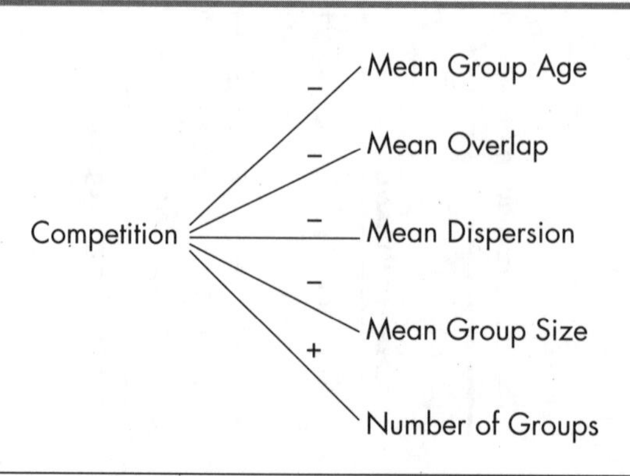

Tie Stability

The multivariate relationships among homophily, competition, and tie stability are strongly curvilinear. The effect of increased homophily is always to increase tie stability, but competition shows a clear curvilinear relationship to tie stability. Tie stability is at a maximum when competition is in the middle range. Extremely high or low competition suppresses tie stability, because high competition kills off the groups that foster tie stability, and low competition creates overlapping groups, which produces competing demands on the limited number of ties that a person may possess. Tie stability is intimately connected with the survival of groups, as discussed below.

Mean Age

This variable compactly summarizes the survival rate of groups. Configurations of parameters with high rates of organizational death will have low mean ages, and vice versa. Heightened competition leads to drastic increases in organizational death rates at high levels of competition. At high levels of competition, groups last for only one round of the simulation, whereas at low levels of competition and high levels of homophily, groups last indefinitely. Although homophily has an extremely strong effect on group survival at low levels of competition, it has none whatsoever at high levels of competition. These complex homophily effects are produced, it appears, by the indirect effect of homophily through tie stability.

Systems with low levels of competition and high levels of homophily, then, will be likely to have groups that are moderately persistent, but systems with low homophily and low competition will have stable, long-lasting groups. This pattern is consistent with societies with well-developed stratification systems. One would expect little change in such systems without outside perturbation. Under this regime, groups will last longer, on average, than individuals and will produce enduring group culture and stable institutional arrangements.

Group Overlap

Both homophily and competition suppress group overlap. Systems with high competition and high homophily will produce disjoint groups, whereas lowered competition and homophily will encourage overlap. Overlapping groups have been historically associated with lowered social conflict, heightened cooperation, the development of democratic institutions, and stable political arrangements (see Kornhauser, 1962). The intersection of social circles that is characteristic of low levels of homophily at the individual level produces overlapping groups at the system level.

When groups are heavily overlapped in a system, individuals are subjected to influences from many directions simultaneously, with no single force able to monopolize a person's resources (see Babchuk & Edwards, 1969). Groups such as cults, which are able to isolate individuals from the influence of other groups, in contrast, are able to control individual actors to a greater degree. At the system level, when society is carved up into disjointed sets of mutually disconnected actors, the development of distinctive local culture, norms, and identities (tribalism) may lead to conflict among groups.

Group Dispersion

Both homophily and competition decrease the dispersion of groups in social space. Under a regime of high homophily and high competition, groups will have members who are very similar to one another. Groups will expose individual members to few differences among other members, leading to heightened commonality of experience and outlook. Group membership under such conditions reinforces similarities among members, rather than exposing them to more cosmopolitan connections to diverse others. When groups are both overlapped and dispersed, society is integrated by the ties created through the system of intersecting groups.

Group Size

The size of groups is the most powerful force shaping group structure. Large groups, which derive from lower competition and lowered homophily bias, will have increased internal differentiation, heightened inequality of power relations, tendency toward oligarchical political structure, and other structural patterns that tend to differentiate members from one another (Mayhew, 1983). Smaller groups, however, tend to have heightened participation, greater member involvement, more intimacy, and greater cohesiveness. Both competition and homophily bias tend to reduce group size, although the indirect effect of homophily through tie stability is to make larger groups, leading to a total effect of near zero for homophily.

Number of Groups

The obverse of the reduction in the size of groups is an increase in their frequency. Both competition and homophily increase the number of groups, although the indirect effect of homophily through tie stability is to decrease number, leading to a total effect near zero.

In summary, Figure 10.3 presents the overall picture of the relationships among the inputs and outputs for the system. As systems move from high homophily and high competition to low values of those variables, there is a general trend toward larger, more stable, longer lasting, and more encompassing groups. Homophily acts as a stabilizing force in the system when competition is low, but it can be overpowered by high levels of competition. The most stable configuration occurs when both homophily and competition are low. Under these conditions, groups grow to encompass the entire system and are completely overlapped. At high levels of homophily

FIGURE 10.3

Homophily, competition, and overall system outcomes

Competition		Homophily: HIGH	Homophily: LOW
	HIGH	Many small groups with high death rates, low overlap, low dispersion	Many small groups with high death rates, moderate overlap and dispersion
	LOW	Moderate numbers of medium-size groups, low death rates, moderate overlap and dispersion	Some old, large, heavily overlapped, highly dispersed groups and some younger groups

and low levels of competition, one or two groups establish primacy, and other groups that are formed later come and go quickly. The most unstable configurations occur under high competition, when groups come and go at an extremely rapid pace. If, in addition, there exists high homophily bias, these groups will be isolated from one another and relatively homogeneous. Under these chaotic conditions, society would be an extremely problematic environment for individuals. At the other extreme, society would be coherent and stable but would probably be relatively unresponsive to individual input. The most palatable middle ground appears to be the condition of high homophily and low competition.

References

Babchuk, N., & Edwards, J. N. (1969). Voluntary associations and the integration hypothesis. *Sociological Inquiry, 35,* 149–162.

Blau, P. M. (1977). *Inequality and heterogeneity.* New York: Free Press.

Booth, A., & Babchuk, N. (1969). Personal influence networks and voluntary association affiliation. *Sociological Inquiry, 39,* 179–188.

Feld, S. L. (1981). The focused organization of social ties. *American Journal of Sociology, 86,* 1015–1035.

Knoke, D. (1990). *Organizing for collective action.* New York: Aldine de Gruyter.

Kornhauser, W. (1962). Social bases of political commitment. In A. M. Rose (Ed.), *Human behavior and social processes* (pp. 321–339). Boston: Houghton-Mifflin.

Marsden, P. V. (1987). Core discussion networks of Americans. *American Sociological Review, 52,* 122–131.

Marsden, P. V. (1988). Homogeneity in confiding relations. *Social Networks, 10,* 57–76.

Mayhew, B. H. (1983). Hierarchical differentiation in imperatively coordinated associations. In S. Bacharach (Ed.), *Research in the sociology of organizations* (pp. 153–229). Greenwich, CT: JAI Press.

McPherson, J. M. (1981). A dynamic model of voluntary affiliation. *Social Forces, 59,* 705–728.

McPherson, J. M. (1983). An ecology of affiliation. *American Sociological Review, 48,* 519–532.

McPherson, J. M., Popielarz, P., & Drobnic, S. (1992). Social networks and organizational dynamics. *American Sociological Review, 57,* 153–170.

McPherson, J. M., & Ranger-Moore, J. (1991). Evolution on a dancing landscape: Organizations and networks in dynamic Blau space. *Social Forces, 70,* 19–42.

McPherson, J. M., & Rotolo, T. (1996). Testing a dynamic model of social composition: Diversity and change in voluntary groups. *American Sociological Review, 61,* 179–202.

McPherson, J. M., & Smith-Lovin, L. (1986). Sex segregation in voluntary associations. *American Sociological Review, 51,* 61–79.

Popielarz, P., & McPherson, J. M. (1995). On the edge or in between: Niche position, niche overlap, and the duration of voluntary association memberships. *American Journal of Sociology, 101,* 698–720.

Ricklefs, R. E. (1979). *Ecology.* New York: Chiron Press.

Smith, C., & Freedman, A. (1972). *Voluntary associations: Perspectives on the literature.* Cambridge, MA: Harvard University Press.

Smith, D. H. (1975). Voluntary action and voluntary groups. In A. Inkeles, J. Coleman, & N. Smelser (Eds.), *Annual review of sociology* (Vol. 1, pp. 247–270). Palo Alto, CA: Annual Reviews.

Snow, D. A., Zurcher, L. A., Jr., & Eckland-Olson, S. (1980). Social networks and social movements: A microstructural approach to differential recruitment. *American Sociological Review, 45,* 787–801.

Webster, M. A., Jr., & Driskell, J. E., Jr. (1978). A status generalization: A review and some new data. *American Sociological Review, 43,* 220–236.

Wright, S. (1931). A evolution in Mendelian populations. *Genetics, 16,* 97–159.

Yamaguchi, K. (1990). Homophily and social distance in the choice of multiple friends: An analysis based on conditionally symmetric log-bilinear association models. *Journal of the American Statistical Association, 85,* 356–366.

COMMENT:

The Formation, Continuation, and Dissolution of Informal Groups

Jeffrey R. Edwards

As eloquently argued by McGrath (1982), simulations are an important tool in the arsenal of methods available to social sciences researchers. Simulations can be used to capture critical elements of complex social systems and to model longitudinal phenomena that would require years of data collection to investigate empirically. Simulations also can accommodate ranges of values for population parameters, including values not observed in a particular sample, thereby allowing researchers to conduct sensitivity analyses and explore "what if" scenarios. Finally, simulations can be used to evaluate the logical integrity and consistency of theoretical models in the absence of data collection (Sastry, 1997).

The simulation conducted by McPherson (Chapter 10) aptly illustrates these advantages. It examines the effects of competition and homophily (i.e., the tendency of people to affiliate with similar others) on the formation, continuation, and dissolution of informal groups. The simulation is part of a larger research program conducted by McPherson that includes extensive empirical research. Thus, McPherson's work demonstrates the use of multiple methods to converge on answers about the nature of important phenomena (McGrath, 1982).

The following comments on McPherson's research, and on his simulation work in particular, are organized by substantive and methodological issues. As the comments indicate, McPherson's simulation and its underlying research base suggest several interesting avenues for future research on informal and formal groups. The methods used in the simulation serve as a model for future simulation research and at the same time may be extended in several ways.

Substantive Issues

Meaning of Similarity

A key variable in McPherson's simulation is homophily, which refers to the principle that interpersonal similarity increases the likelihood of group membership. Similarity is viewed as a function of distance in Blau space, which captures the positioning of people relative to one another with regard to various sociodemographic dimensions and categories. Although similarity is commonly used as a summary concept to compare two individuals, it may obscure important information regarding interpersonal differences and their effects on outcomes. This information may be framed as a series of questions that may be addressed in future simulations like McPherson's.

First, of the dimensions in Blau space on which individuals may differ, which ones are most important to the effects of homophily? As argued by Cronbach and Gleser (1953), "*similarity is not a general quality. It is possible to discuss similarity only with respect to specified dimensions*" (italics in original; p. 457). Accordingly, the forces behind a general homophily effect may be clarified by examining the simultaneous effects of dissimilarity on specific Blau space dimensions, using a multivariate approach (Edwards, 1993). Not only would this approach capture the overall effects of homophily but also it would reveal whether the Blau space dimensions encompassed by homophily produce different effects.

Second, are the effects of dissimilarity symmetric, such that being above another individual on a Blau space dimension has the same effects as being below that individual? Although the concept of homophily apparently assumes symmetric effects, it is likely that differences on some Blau space dimensions may yield asymmetric effects. For example, people who desire upward mobility (Harlow, 1973) may be more attracted to groups of higher social rank than to groups of lower social rank.

Third, does absolute position on a Blau space dimension influence the probability of joining a group? For instance, assuming education level is normally distributed, people with average education have ample opportunity to interact with others with similar education, because people with average education are prevalent in society. For them, similarity on education level would be an unlikely basis on which to create an informal group. In contrast, for those with higher education levels, education may provide an important impetus for group formation, because affiliation with others with similar education would otherwise not occur.

Similarity Versus Complementarity

The concept of homophily is based on a similarity–attraction principle. Although this principle has received extensive empirical support, people also may gravitate to one another not because they are similar, but because they fulfill each other's needs. This phenomenon is manifested in marital relationships, in which dissimilar spouses may fulfill distinct needs of one another (Saint, 1994). Analogously, teams may form not because each member possesses the same skills, but because each member contributes different skills that collectively help the group function. The distinction between similarity and complementarity has been examined in the person–environment fit literature (Muchinsky & Monahan, 1987), and this distinction may be useful to research on the development of informal groups.

Extensions to Work Organizations

Although McPherson's research focuses on voluntary informal groups, his research may have important implications for other types of groups, such as formal work organizations. Some possible extensions of the research to work organizations are suggested below.

Attraction, Selection, and Attrition

An extensive body of research has examined employee attraction, selection, and attrition (Landy, Shankster, & Kohler, 1994). This research has been guided by two general perspectives on why employees join and remain in organizations. One perspective, which embodies the homophily principle, states that employees and organizations are attracted to one another based on similarity in such attributes as beliefs and values (Schneider, 1987). Following this perspective, attraction, selection, and attrition create organizations with members who are homogeneous over time. An alternative perspective suggests that employees join organizations that satisfy their needs, desires, and values; analogously, organizations select employees for their ability to meet work requirements (Dawis & Lofquist, 1984). According to this perspective, organizations do not gravitate toward homogeneity (i.e., homophily) but instead may become homogeneous or heterogeneous, depending on which configuration best fulfills employee needs and organizational requirements. Following McPherson's work, these two perspectives could be modeled simultaneously to determine how each view explains the composition of organizations over time.

Downsizings

Because McPherson's work focuses on voluntary membership in groups, it does not address situations in which people are forced to leave a group. Forced departures, however, are common in work organizations, as manifested by organizational downsizings. Using McPherson's simulation approach, downsizings could be modeled as intermittent shocks, and the effects of those shocks on various outcome variables may be examined. For example, do downsizings increase or decrease the likelihood that people will subsequently join an organization, and does this likelihood depend on the characteristics of the displaced people in Blau space? Is there a critical mass for the number of displaced people, such that when this number is exceeded, the probability of organizational survival is diminished? Do large, sporadic downsizings yield the same effects as a series of smaller downsizings? Answers to such questions have theoretical and practical relevance, and the conceptual and methodological approaches used by McPherson may help generate these answers.

Promoting Diversity

Through proactive hiring and retention practices, many organizations have attempted to create diverse work forces. These practices intentionally create heterogeneity and therefore operate against the effects of homophily identified by McPherson's research. Thus, the promotion of diversity and the principle of homophily represent countervailing forces that influence the demographic composition of work organizations. The effects of those forces over time may be modeled through simulations that specify parameters representing various hiring and retention practices and different degrees of homophily. Such simulations may yield answers to important questions, such as which approaches to diversity are most likely to yield a work force with proportional representation of employees in relevant demographic groups, and whether certain approaches may produce unintended shifts in work force composition.

Methodological Issues

From a methodological standpoint, McPherson's work has several important strengths, many of which are manifestations of the complementary advantages of simulations relative to empirical methods. Other strengths arise from the care with which the simulation was designed and the logic used to interpret its findings. For example, although the homophily bias exhibited weak effects on the outcome variables, McPherson decomposed those effects into substantial relationships of opposite sign. He also judiciously avoided tests of statistical significance, which can be easily manipulated in simulation research by merely increasing the number of cases simulated. Given the strengths of this simulation, the following observations should be viewed as suggested methodological extensions and enhancements.

System Isolation

As McPherson notes, his simulation restricted its focus to voluntary membership in informal groups. By imposing this restriction, the simulation did not capture the effects of competition for group membership from other groups, such as families and work organizations. This restriction was useful from a pragmatic standpoint because it kept the simulation manageable in scope. In reality, however, most adults must constantly juggle the competing demands of multiple roles, such as work, family, and social groups (Burke & Greenglass, 1987). By modeling these competing demands, the external validity of a simulation such as McPherson's may be enhanced. Of course, some simplification of reality is necessary because each factor added to a simulation exponentially increases its complexity.

Parameter Values

The simulation varied two parameters (i.e., homophily bias and the number of groups to which a person belonged) and held two parameters constant (i.e., the probability that social contact with group members will prompt a person to join a group and the probability that membership in the same group will initiate future social contact). The values of these parameters were based on previous empirical research, which represents an important strength of this simulation. Nonetheless, the fact that only two parameters were varied raises the question of how the results of the simulation would be affected if all four parameters were varied. Admittedly, the complexity of a simulation increases with the number of parameters varied, and the value of the information gained by varying additional parameters must be weighed against the cost of the additional complexity introduced. Perhaps an iterative procedure could be used, in which parameters that are varied but have little effect are subsequently held constant. For example, this simulation found that variation in the homophily bias parameter had little effect on several of the outcomes examined. In future simulations, this parameter may be fixed at some value (e.g., its mean), and other parameters may be allowed to vary. Of course, this approach presumes that only main effects of parameters are of interest (i.e., there are no interactions among variables represented by the parameters), such that researchers can meaningfully examine the effects of variation in one parameter without regard to the values of other parameters.

Conclusion

McPherson's research on the formation, continuation, and dissolution of informal groups has yielded important findings relevant to a variety of fields, and his simulation work represents a careful and informative application of this method. By positioning this method within a program of research that includes theory development and empirical work, McPherson has aptly demonstrated the value of multiple methods to the accumulation of knowledge.

References

Burke, R. J., & Greenglass, E. (1987). Work and family. In C. L. Cooper & I. T. Robertson (Eds.), *International review of industrial and organizational psychology* (pp. 273–320). New York: Wiley.

Cronbach, L. J., & Gleser, G. C. (1953). Assessing the similarity between profiles. *Psychological Bulletin, 50,* 456–473.

Dawis, R. V., & Lofquist, L. H. (1984). *A psychological theory of work adjustment.* Minneapolis: University of Minnesota Press.

Edwards, J. R. (1993). Problems with the use of profile similarity indices in the study of congruence in organizational research. *Personnel Psychology, 46,* 641–665.

Harlow, D. N. (1973). Professional employees' preference for upward mobility. *Journal of Applied Psychology, 57,* 137–141.

Landy, F. J., Shankster, L. J., & Kohler, S. S. (1994). Personnel selection and placement. In L. W. Porter & M. R. Rosenzweig (Eds.), *Annual review of psychology* (Vol. 45, pp. 261–296). Palo Alto, CA: Annual Reviews.

McGrath, J. E. (1982). Dilemmatics: A study of research choices and dilemmas. In J. E. McGrath, J. Martin, & R. A. Kulka (Eds.), *Judgment calls in research* (pp. 69–102). Beverly Hills, CA: Sage.

Muchinsky, P. M., & Monahan, C. J. (1987). What is person–environment congruence? Supplementary versus complementary models of fit. *Journal of Vocational Behavior, 31,* 268–277.

Saint, D. J. (1994). Complementarity in marital relationships. *Journal of Social Psychology, 134,* 701–703.

Sastry, M. A. (1997). Problems and paradoxes in a model of punctuated organizational change. *Administrative Science Quarterly, 42,* 237–275.

Schneider, B. (1987). E = f(P,B): The road to a radical approach to person–environment fit. *Journal of Vocational Behavior, 31,* 353–361.

CHAPTER 11

Organizational Adaptation in Volatile Environments

Kathleen M. Carley

Theories of organizational adaptation address the value of exploration, flexibility, and change. However, exploration, flexibility, and change are not without cost. Thus, theories of adaptation also address the need to balance the forces for change against the costs of change and the benefits of exploiting current expertise. Most arguments for change assume that organizational adaptation is the result of balance at a single level (strategic or operational) or of a single type of learning (individual or group). My argument, however, is that this balance is not at a single level but is the result of maneuvering within an ecology of learning in which change is occurring at many levels—individual, organizational, and environmental. Thus, adaptation is not so much a matter of balance as it is of finding the right evolutionary path and of trading change in one dimension for stability in another.

This chapter uses a computational model, ORGAHEAD, to illustrate this way of thinking about organizational adaptation (Carley, 1998; Carley & Svoboda, 1996). Computational theorizing is an important tool for developing an understanding of the complex systems referred to as *organizations*; it enables the researcher to think through (in a computer-assisted fashion) the interactions of dynamic, nonlinear processes. Using ORGAHEAD, this chapter explores the types of maneuvers that result in adaptation and maladaptation for organizations faced with environments that range from stable to highly volatile. ORGAHEAD can be thought of as the embodiment of a theory about how organizations change. Analysis of the results generates a series of theoretical predictions about organizational adaptation.

This work was supported in part by the Office of Naval Research, U.S. Navy Grant No. N00014-97-1-0037, by the National Science Foundation NSF IRI9633 662, by the Institute for Complex and Engineered Systems at Carnegie-Mellon University (CMU), and by the center for Computational Analysis of Social and Organizational Systems at CMU. The views and conclusions contained in this document are those of the author and should not be interpreted as representing the official policies, either expressed or implied, of the Office of Naval Research, the National Science Foundation, or the U.S. government.

Theoretical Basis of ORGAHEAD

ORGAHEAD can be thought of as an operationalized grounded theory. Its basis is the body of empirical and theoretical research on organizational learning and design as well as several theories of different aspects of organizational behavior. From the information-processing tradition comes a view of organizations as information processors composed of collections of intelligent individuals. Each individual is boundedly rational and is constrained in actions by the nature of access to information in the current organizational design (e.g., rules, procedures, authority structure, communication infrastructure) and by his or her own cognitive capabilities. Organizations are seen as capable of changing their design (DiMaggio & Powell, 1983; Romanelli, 1991; Stinchcombe, 1965a) and as needing to change if they are to adapt to changes in the environment or the available technology (Finne, 1991). Different organizational designs are seen as better suited than others to some environments or tasks (Hannan & Freeman, 1977; Lawrence & Lorsch, 1967). Aspects of the model have been tuned to reflect the findings of various empirical studies related to these theories. The theories, which are unified into a single computational theory of organizational behavior, interact in complex fashions to determine the overall level of organizational performance. The aspect of organizational performance of concern here is accuracy: Given a set of tasks, will the organization make the correct decision for each task? A number of theories attempt to explain the impact of learning on organizational performance or accuracy. Herein, the concern is with two such theories—one focused on experiential learning and the other on strategic learning.

Experiential Learning Perspective

According to this perspective, organizations learn as the people within them perform tasks and accumulate experience. People gain experience as they face a series of similar or identical tasks over time and receive feedback on how well they are doing. Experiential learning results in large initial gains in performance but in decreasing gains over time as the individuals gain familiarity with the task (the S-shaped experience curve). Experiential learning on the part of personnel can benefit organizations, and those with highly trained and experienced personnel are usually expected to perform better than organizations with less highly trained and experienced personnel. Individual experience, however, does not always translate directly into organizational experience (Darr, Argote, & Epple, 1995). Rather, the organization's design serves as a procedure for combining or aggregating the experience of individual workers (Carley, 1992; Cohen, March, & Olsen, 1972). Thus, if we could clone personnel, two organizations with different designs but the same personnel would exhibit different performance.

Strategic Learning Perspective

According to this perspective, organizations learn by exploring new ways of doing business, but organizations also become more staid and do less exploration as they age. In this case, organizational learning results from a process in which strategic planning—by the CEO or some central unit—about how to position the firm to achieve high future performance leads to changes in procedures, reassignments of personnel, and reengineering of the workforce.[1] Over time, such factors as institutional norms, sunk costs, traditions, and emergence of stable social networks gradually increase the cost and decrease the value of and likelihood of exploration. Such strategic learning, which can be observed as changes in the organization's design, can benefit the organization. That is, organizations that adopt designs that are forecast to improve their performance are expected to perform better, unless the forecasts are wrong. To be sure, individuals, such as CEOs, or groups, such as executive committees, engage in the strategic-planning exercise. However, the CEO or executive committee's actions are realized as embedded changes in the organization's design (just as the interactions among friends become embedded in underlying social network). The organization's design and the myths about changing it (such as stories about what worked previously) become, in effect, a long-term social memory, external to any one individual but something that can be more or less relied on when contemplating future decisions. In the context of social memory or distributed cognition, change to the organization's design is an act of organizational learning.[2]

The interaction between experiential and strategic learning is complex and nonlinear. Strategic changes in the organization's design may mitigate or enhance the value of experience. Thus, it is difficult to predict the joint impact of both types of learning on organizational performance. In ORGAHEAD, experiential and strategic learning are simultaneously active. We can use this computational model to theorize about how the interactions between these two types of learning influence overall

---

[1]Clearly, change to the organization's design is not always strategic. Sometimes forces beyond managerial control result in alternative designs. However, the focus of this chapter is on strategic change, because for many organizations, such changes are more sweeping. Nonstrategic design changes, like the strategic changes, are likely to interact with experiential learning, individual performance and, possibly, organizational performance (Krackhardt, 1992). Thus, the observations in this chapter about change at the individual and structural levels are likely to have some relevance even to cases of nonstrategic design change.

[2]Underlying both experiential and strategic learning is the idea that all types of learning result in changes in the connections among different pieces or sets of information. For people, these connections occur within the brain as new ideas become interconnected to old. Artificial systems, such as organizations, also have the same capacity to learn by creating connections among information. For organizations, the pieces of information exist as a variety of knowledge bases, such as the minds of individuals, file systems, job descriptions, databases, or artificial agents (e.g., webbots).

organizational performance (measured as accuracy). ORGAHEAD is a procedural theory of organizational performance; the relationship between performance and learning is determined by a series of processes, such as how decisions are made, how the organization's structure is changed, and how people learn. (These processes will be described later in this chapter.)

Factors in Organizational Performance

At any point in time, each organization's performance is uniquely related to the task, the organization's design, the experience of all personnel, the impact of previous designs on the experience garnered by personnel, and the processes by which personnel learn and the design changes. Because we can characterize various aspects of the organization's design and various aspects of individuals as a set of factors, we can, at any point in time, explore the relationship between these factors and the organization's performance. In fact, we can think of the organization as simultaneously operating in two spaces—design and experience. An important point to keep in mind is that no small set of factors exists that uniquely captures all aspects of design or experience (this is true both for the model and the real world). Thus, a high number of dimensions may be needed to capture all salient aspects of the design space and the experience space. Another important point to keep in mind is that in a process model, these factors are not simple inputs; rather, they shift their values dynamically over time, and all factors are interrelated in complex ways.

We can think of the relation of performance to these various factors as the performance surface. Figure 11.1 illustrates graphically the expected performance of an organization given two elements of design: size and work load. The surface can be

FIGURE 11.1

Illustrative performance landscape

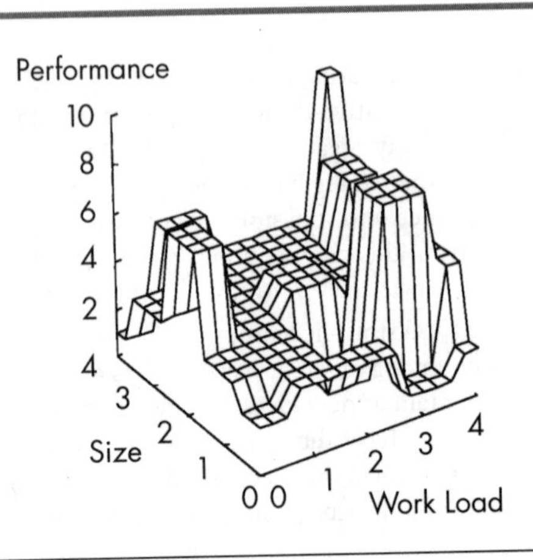

thought of as a landscape. All organizations are, over time, trying to find the optimal form. In the experience space, this search for the optimal form is carried out, in part, by personnel doing tasks and gaining experience. In the design space, the search is carried out, in part, by the CEO (or some executive committee) sequentially altering the organization's design. For real organizations and for ORGAHEAD, design and experience are functions of more than two variables and the performance surface is even "messier" than that illustrated.

Several important points must be made about the performance surface. First, the processes that result in organizations exhibiting a certain level of performance at a certain point in time also result in a systematic relationship between performance and a large number of design and individual factors, such as size, density, span of control, work load, average experience, and retention. These relationships, though systematic, are rarely linear. For example, in Figure 11.1, an organization that tries to climb this surface by either just increasing size or just increasing work load will often suffer drops rather than increases in performance, even though to be a top performer, the organization will need to be high in both size and work load. Second, the large number of factors means that it is not possible to graphically display the performance surface relative to all factors (for design, experience, or both). Third, the performance surface is the space of possibilities; that is, it shows the expected relationship between performance and design (or experience) for all possible designs (or experiences). In a world in which there are only a few organizations (real or simulated), there may not be an organization at each point in the space. Over time, organizations may come to cluster in certain regions of this landscape. Fourth, the trajectory of any one organization over time is unlikely to be linear. One implication of this point is that although maladaptive organizations may be lower or higher on some dimensions than adaptive organizations, if the maladaptive organizations change in the direction of the adaptive organizations, they may not see a performance gain.

For both real organizations and simulated ones, the performance surface is not necessarily stable. The environments that organizations face can change for a number of reasons (e.g., technology, legislation, change in cultural norms, and change in availability of resources). Changes in the environment often are changes in either the task, the way in which organizations can redesign themselves, or the way in which personnel learn and make decisions. Environmental shifts can fundamentally alter the performance surface, particularly as perceived by the organization. Consequently, the relation between performance and design may change. Figure 11.2 illustrates the change over time in the performance surface as a function of two possible dimensions of organizational design.

When is change good? To answer this question, it is important to distinguish change from adaptation. *Change* is defined as any difference between an organization at one time and the next. Change may or may not represent learning. *Adaptation* is defined as those changes that enable the organization to maintain or improve its performance. Because different designs are better in different circumstances,

FIGURE 11.2

Illustration of changing performance landscapes

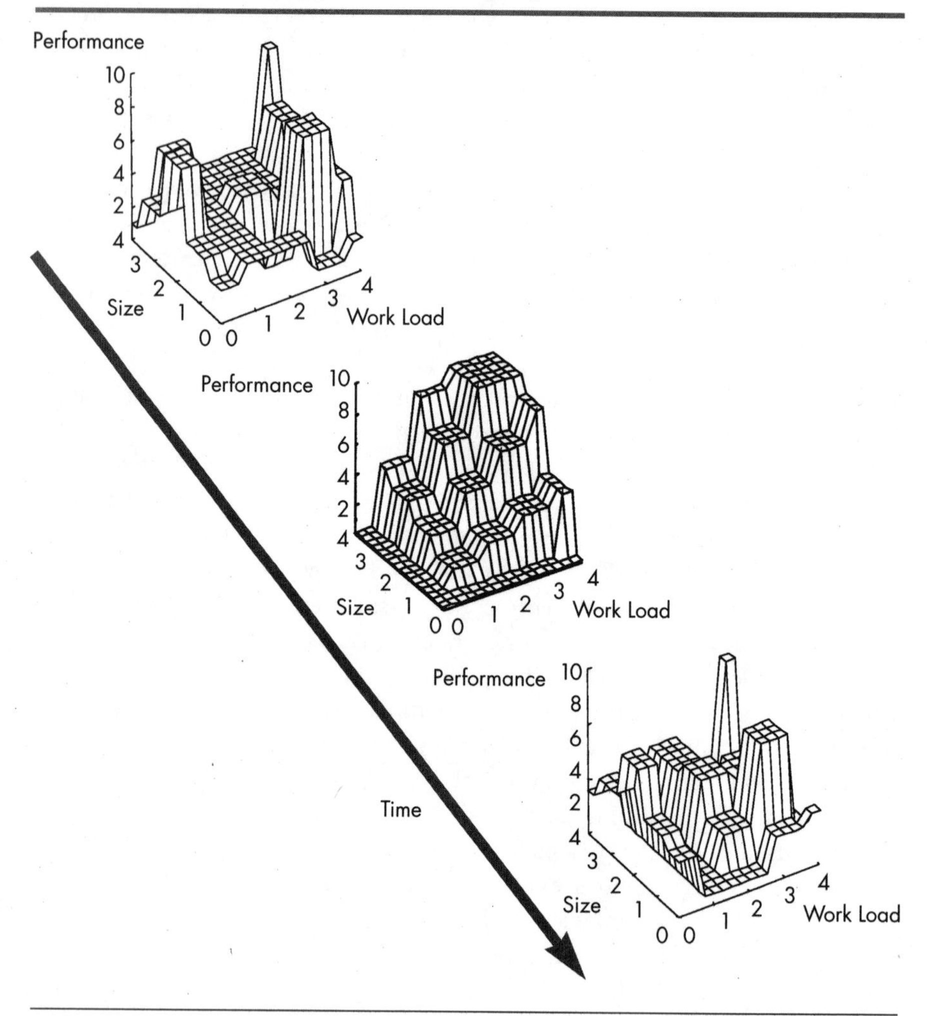

adaptation can be thought of as the successful result of a process of searching for the optimal—or at least better—design for the environment confronting the organization, given that the organization itself is altering its behavior as the people within the organization garner experience. Adaptive organizations, then, are those that end up situated on the higher peaks.

Change, or exploration, by an organization enables but does not guarantee adaptation. Change in design enables the organization to walk around a performance surface and move toward a peak. Change has at least two potential drawbacks: First, if the performance surface is volatile, then the organization runs the risk of moving to a new point in design space that, although a "peak" at Time 1, is actually a "valley" at Time 2. Second, for most organizations, performance improvements are often garnered by staying at the same point in the design space and exploiting current talents, knowledge, and skills of personnel. Indeed, March (1996) discussed continuity as being critical for true adaptation. Levinthal and March (1993) have suggested that organizational learning, because it involves balancing exploration and exploitation, can result in various types of learning myopias. For example, experiential learning can result in a tendency to exploit knowledge (i.e., to keep doing what one does well) and thereby overlook or discount the future, what others are doing, and contradictory information or failures. They conclude that despite these myopias, learning is still advantageous to the firm.

Why are myopias advantageous? This chapter provides a partial answer: Because organizational learning occurs at many levels, myopia at one level may be countered by and, possibly, even encourage a broader view at another level. Moreover, without learning, the chance of finding a better design is low. At the same time, however, the chance of finding a better design is nonzero for several reasons. Essentially, the organization can benefit from fortuitous accidents. At the strategic level, selective retention or random actions on the part of the CEO or the executive committee can result in the organization moving to a better design. At the operational level, selective retention or random actions on the part of personnel can result in the organization with a particular design appearing to be better or worse than it is when all personnel are acting perfectly. This would engender a misperception of the relationship between that design and the organization's performance, which may then discourage or encourage the CEO's or executive committee's search for a new design.

Learning is advantageous to the firm precisely because the organization is engaged simultaneously in multiple types of learning. As previously noted, the concern in this chapter is with two types of learning, experiential and strategic. Experiential learning, which resides largely in the individual, is seen as resulting from the process of trial and error and from feedback. Strategic learning, which resides largely in the linkages or connections among people, is seen as resulting from organizations' processes of planning, reorganization, and reengineering. Such change is strategic because reorganization generally is expected (e.g., by the CEO) to improve performance (Butler, 1993; Kilmann & Covin, 1988). The value of these two types of learning may depend on the environment. For example, in a stable environment experiential learning should be quite effective because the lessons of experience should remain valid. In a volatile environment, hard-won experience may be less valuable because the jobs of tomorrow may not be the jobs of today. In a stable environment there may be little to strategize about, and the organization may quickly lock onto the right structure; in contrast, in a volatile environment the ability to anticipate the future may be critical. But is this really the case? We can use computational theorizing to begin to address questions like these about the dynamics of organizational life, structure, and learning.

Organizational Adaptation Model

ORGAHEAD is a computational theory of strategic organizational behavior as a search through the problem space of potential organizational designs. ORGAHEAD was designed to reflect basic realities of organizational life. As in any organization, a task or set of tasks is being done; each personnel member occupies a particular role in the organization, reporting to others, doing tasks, and gaining experience; and a strategic or management function tries to anticipate the future, assigns personnel to tasks, and determines who reports to whom. These fundamental features of organizations are captured in Figure 11.3, which serves as a top-level view of the ORGAHEAD model.

From a learning perspective within ORGAHEAD, organizations are characterized at two levels—operational and strategic. At the operational level, the organization is

FIGURE 11.3

Top-level view of ORGAHEAD

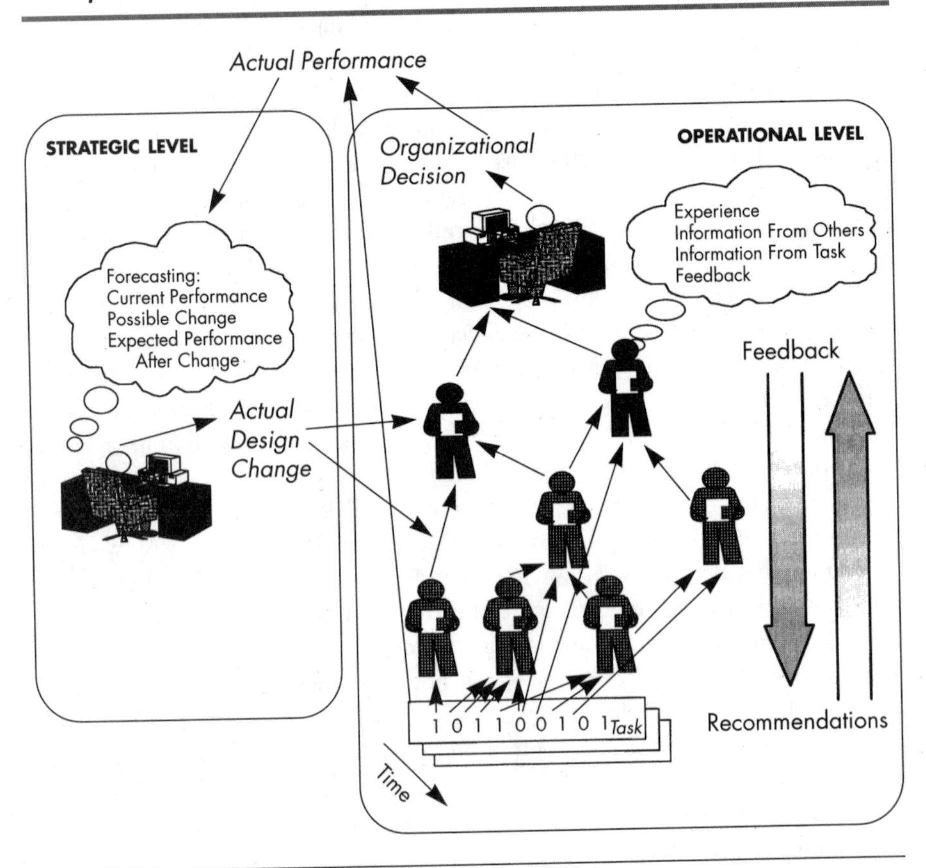

characterized using ACTS theory (Carley & Prietula, 1994); each organization is characterized in terms of a set of *A*gents who are *C*ognitively capable, *T*ask oriented, and *S*ocially situated. At the strategic level, the organization is characterized as a purposive actor; that is, a CEO or executive committee tries to forecast the future and decides how to change the organization to meet the projected needs. The following sections describe each of the three primary components within ORGAHEAD—the task model, the operational model, and the strategic model.

Task and Task Environment

In ORGAHEAD, the organization faces a sequence of tasks. Each task has associated with it a "correct decision." This correct decision is not known, a priori, by anyone within the organization. For each task, the CEO must make the organization's decision. This decision may or may not match the correct decision. Organizational performance is a function of how often this decision matches the correct decision (i.e., of the organization's accuracy).

Organizations can engage in many tasks. A common one is the classification task, which has the following properties. An item exists that needs to be classified as being of a certain type. The item can be characterized as having a set of attributes, according to which it is classified. Examples of classification tasks include diagnosis, situation assessment, and multiple-choice tests. A simple version of the classification task is the binary-choice task. In the binary-choice task the objective is to determine whether a given binary string is of Type A or B (a string cannot be both A and B). For each string there is a correct decision. Of course, the decision maker may not correctly classify the string (i.e., the decision maker may misclassify an A string as a B string or vice versa). The specific task used in the ensuing analysis is a nine-bit binary classification task. Classification tasks in general, and the binary-choice task in particular, have been extensively studied by researchers interested in team and organizational performance (see, for example, Carley, 1992, 1998; Hollenbeck, Ilgen, Sego, et al., 1995; Hollenbeck, Ilgen, Tuttle, & Sego, 1995; Lin & Carley, 1997; Pete, Pattipati, & Kleinman, 1993; Tang, Pattipati, & Kleinman, 1992).

Environments can be thought of as task environments (i.e., the set of tasks faced by an organization). For example, when the task is the binary-choice task, the environment might be the set of binary strings of length N that must be classified by the organization. Environments have various characteristics, such as bias and stability or volatility. (Another interpretation of bias is as a niche environment.) One way of thinking of bias is as a greater-than-chance likelihood of one particular outcome. For example, in the binary-choice task, the environment is unbiased if all outcomes (whether the string is of Type A or B) are equally likely, given a set of strings. The more likely one outcome is than the other, given a set of strings, the higher the bias is of that environment. The binary-choice task is unbiased if a string is of Type A (i.e., if there are more ones than zeros in the set of task features) or B; otherwise, all strings of length N are possible, and the probability that any task feature is a one is .5. Under these conditions, neither outcome (A or B) is more likely to occur.

Environments also can vary in their stability. Hannan and Freeman (1977, p. 952) characterized environmental instability as an oscillating sequence of "patches." Seasonal markets, such as lawn care, have this oscillatory nature. Environmental instability is a function of both the frequency and the degree of the shift. We can operationalize instability as oscillations between one class of tasks and another (e.g., between an unbiased and a biased task).[3] The degree of shift is operationalized as the difference in the bias between the two classes of tasks; the greater the difference in bias, the greater the degree of the shift. Frequency of shift is the number of tasks of a specific class that the organization faces before it shifts to a different class of tasks. In a stable environment, all tasks are chosen from the same distribution. In an unstable environment, the tasks are chosen from different distributions, both unbiased and biased, in an oscillatory fashion.

The specific task largely determines the specific optimal structure and may constrain the level of performance (Carley, 1992). Thus, unless one is interested in finding the organizational design for a specific task, the issue is not what design is found, but what factors affect differences in the designs that are found or in the rate at which the optimal design is found. In the ensuing analysis, the focus is not on what structures are found but on what causes different structures to be found and whether they are found in both stable and volatile environments.

Operational Level

In ORGAHEAD each person in the organization works on, at most, part of the task (no individual sees the whole string). The operational part of ORGAHEAD is built out of the CORP model (Carley, 1992; Carley & Lin, 1995, 1997). CORP is an information-processing model of organizational performance in which organizational performance results from aggregating the performance of individuals. All individuals are boundedly rational in terms of organizational access to information and cognitive ability to process information (Carley & Newell, 1994; Simon, 1955, 1956). Individuals are limited cognitively; they cannot do the task by themselves and can handle only a maximum of seven pieces of information. They forget, have primacy and recency biases (they remember only the first 500 tasks and the most recent 500 tasks they have seen), remember general trends rather than particular tasks, and are overconfident in their decisions. Individuals are limited structurally as well: They cannot access all information, the information they can access depends on their role in the organization, and they often must act not on the basis of actual task information but on the interpretation of that information as forwarded by others in the organization. Their roles are a function of the authority structure (who reports to whom)

---

[3]For an alternative operationalization using formal logic, see Bruggeman (1997).

and the resource access structure (who has access to what resources or information). Individuals can learn from their experience over time. In each time period in which they receive information, they report whether they think (on the basis of that information) the overall task is of Type A or B, and then they find out whether or not the task really was of Type A or B. They learn by keeping track of the likelihood that when they see pattern *X*, the task will be of Type A or B. Each individual, regardless of his or her position in the organization, acts as an experiential learner, acquires information, classifies the pattern of information that he or she sees, recommends the choice that was most often correct in the past for that pattern to his or her superior, receives feedback as to whether the task was really of Type A or B, and increments his or her memory. If the individual has no previous experience, he or she simply guesses. The pattern of information seen by an individual can be raw information on this specific task, the recommendations of other individuals for this task, or both.

The process of pattern classification, recommendation, and reporting up through the authority structure is the organizational process by which individual-level decisions are aggregated into a single organizational decision—the decision made by the CEO (see Figure 11.3). At the apex of the organization is a single superior, or CEO. Below the CEO is a network that connects individuals into a single organizational structure. We can think of this network as a directed graph, *S*, showing who reports to whom. Overlaying this authority structure is a second network that connects individuals to raw task information. We can think of this as a directed graph, *R*, showing which information on the task is observed, monitored, or handled by which individual. This second graph is the resource access structure. Each piece of information is a resource for the organization. The resource access structure determines which part of the task is observed by which individual. In each time period, there is a single task for which the organization collectively makes a classification; this is the decision made by the CEO. Each time period, the flow of information (and opinions) is from the task to the CEO, as filtered by the two networks—the authority structure, *S*, and the resource access structure, *R*. The organization's design can be formally characterized by the joint structure–design *(S,R)*.

Organizational performance is measured as accuracy, or the percentage of problems in a window of opportunity that the organization correctly classifies. The organization is faced with a sequence of tasks, and replacement tasks are drawn at random from the population of tasks. Each time period *(t)*, the organization, as represented by the CEO, must make a decision for the current task. Of the *N(t)* individuals who are collectively processing *I(t)* pieces of information, some individuals are processing raw information on the task and reporting their opinions to other individuals. Other individuals are processing these opinions, and still others may be processing both raw task information and opinions. Who is doing what and who reports to whom depends on the organizational design. An organization may comprise anywhere from 2 to 45 individuals organized in one to three tiers below the CEO, with a maximum of 15 individuals per tier. An additional, or first, tier is composed of a single CEO. As noted, the organizational decision is the CEO's decision. By convention, the CEO is referred to as Level 1 and the tier furthest removed from the CEO as Level 4.

Strategic Level

At the strategic level, organizational performance is affected by the ability of the CEO or central unit to anticipate the future and take the appropriate strategic actions to alter the organization's design in response to environmental cues. Change at this level is determined by the organization's change strategy. The change strategy[4] has three parts: (a) the changes to the current design that are allowable, (b) the conditions under which changes are made, and (c) the likelihood of the various changes.

Recall that the organization's design is characterized in terms of the authority structure and the resource access structure. Change in design involves changing these structures. Four types of changes are possible, regardless of the change strategy:

1. *Downsizing*—drop n individuals (such that $1 \leq n \leq N_o(t)$).
2. *Upsizing*—add n individuals (such that $1 \leq n \leq N_{max} - N_o(t)$).
3. *Redesigning*—delete the tie between individual i and j (i reports to j) and reassign individual i to report to individual k.
4. *Reengineering*—delete the tie between individual i and piece of information s and add a tie between individual j and piece of information s.

Exactly how many changes of a particular type occur at a time is given by a Poisson distribution.[5] Changing connections through redesign and reengineering moves connections and will not lead to an absolute increase or decrease in personnel.

---

[4]A strategy is a set of moves and their individual statistical distributions, which determine the probability that a given move will be chosen. Different strategies can be defined either by altering what moves are possible or by altering the underlying distributions. Conceptually, however, some researchers might be more comfortable thinking of changes in the underlying distribution, particularly small changes, as perturbations of a single strategy. For example, imagine the two following strategies. In strategy 1, the only moves possible are hires and fires, and the probability of each is determined with a Poisson distribution with a mean of 0.2. In strategy 2, the only moves possible are hires and fires, and the probability of each is determined with a Poisson distribution with a mean of 0.3. For some researchers, this second strategy will represent a new strategy; for others, it will represent only a perturbation on an existing strategy.

[5]ORGAHEAD is a discrete event simulator. Thus, the number of personnel or connections that can be added or dropped each period is a positive integer. Poisson is a standard distribution used when x (in this case the number of changes) can take on only positive integer values.

Changes in personnel, through upsizing and downsizing, cause changes in all the ties associated with those personnel.

The organization begins with a particular design (*S*(0),*R*(0)) and proceeds to process 500 tasks. After this, regardless of the change strategy, the organization continuously cycles through the following actions: (a) make decisions for a sequence of tasks, (b) evaluate performance, (c) propose a change to the structure, and (d) change the structure. The strategies vary in the time in which they move from the decision phase to the structural change phase and in the way in which they decide on a possible new design. The four strategies are stable (no change), random, procedural, and strategic.

Organizations with a stable change strategy do not alter their design over time; this is the baseline case against which to evaluate the extent to which change is adaptive. Organizations with a random change strategy randomly alter their design every time the organization's performance changes by 5% or more. The level at which change occurs in the organizational structure and the type of change is random. After a change occurs, the organization remains "dormant" long enough for new people (and old) to get used to the new organizational design. Change was equally likely at all levels (25%), and there was a 25% probability that no change would occur.

Organizations with a procedural change strategy hired personnel when things were going well (5% or more improvement in performance) and fired personnel when things were going poorly (5% or more drop in performance). Under this strategy, change was more likely at lower levels in the organization. Specifically, the probability of change at level 4 was 50%, 30% at level 3, and 5% at level 2. Again, there was a 25% probability that no hiring or firing would occur when the efficiency warranted it.

Under the "strategic" strategy, the organization used strategic planning to determine whether to make a change; whether a change actually was made depended on expectations. Over time, the organization learned what types of changes were effective and became increasingly averse to making changes that were not expected to improve performance. This scenario was implemented through *simulated annealing.*

Simulated annealing is a heuristic approach to optimization (Kirkpatrick, Gelatt, & Vecchi, 1983; for an overview, see Rutenbar, 1989). In an annealer, the system tries to optimize some function by moving through states sequentially, and the path through those states is constrained by the set of ways of altering the current state. A move is chosen from the set of possibilities, and its potential impact is evaluated before it is accepted (or not) by the Metropolis criteria. According to the Metropolis criteria, nonrisky moves are always accepted, and risky moves are sometimes accepted but with a decreasing likelihood over time. This rate of decrease is controlled in part by the "temperature" of the system, which determines its excitation; thus, as the temperature drops, the system becomes more rigid and less capable of change. The result is an heuristically based optimization process that tends to locate better states but is not guaranteed to locate the best state.

Similarly, the organization moves through a series of organizational designs, one at a time. Over time, the organization attempts to optimize its design, given some cost function (such as minimizing salary, maximizing the number of widgets produced, or maximizing decision accuracy). The CEO or central unit has a set of possible strategies (i.e., move set) that dictates which designs are possible given the current design. The CEO does not compare all strategies but simply evaluates a strategy by trying to anticipate the future (Allison, 1971; Axelrod, 1976; Cohen & March, 1974). Strategic adaptation requires the CEO to have knowledge about which individuals in the organization have what information and which capabilities. Consequently, the organization's optimization process is imperfect. Strategic change moves the organization closer to the goal but may not achieve it (March & Simon, 1958; Simon, 1944). Organizations gamble on redesigns that might possibly "increase costs," and they are much more prone to this kind of risky behavior when they are new (Stinchcombe, 1965b). With maturation the organization becomes staid and trapped by its own competency (Levitt & March, 1988).

The goal of the strategic change process as implemented herein is to find the organizational design that maximizes performance. In other words, the goal is to alter the organization's design sequentially so as to locate the tallest peak shown in Figure 11.1. For the strategic approach, first the organization's performance for 100 tasks is calculated. Then the CEO chooses one change from the set of possible changes, thereby suggesting a new organizational design. This design is evaluated (using a limited "lookahead" of 100 tasks). Then the forecast performance of the proposed design is compared with the previous performance of the current organization, and a strategic decision is made as to whether to accept the change. Finally, if the change is accepted, the organization's design is altered, and the process begins again. If the change is not accepted, the process begins again with the unchanged organization. Performance at time *t* for the current organization is the percentage of the most recent 500 tasks that the organization correctly classified before time *t*.

The probability of accepting the new design is determined using the Metropolis criteria. Specifically, the change is always accepted if the forecast performance for the hypothetical organization is better than the known performance of the current organization. Furthermore, when the forecast is poorer the change may still be accepted. In fact, we can think of the probability of accepting the "bad" design as resulting from the impact of the organization's risk aversiveness on its decision. This probability is calculated, using the Boltzman equation, as

$$P = P_0 e^{\Delta cost(t)/T} \qquad \textbf{(11.1)}$$

such that $cost(t) = 0 - performance(t)$, and P_0 is the initial probability of accepting a "bad" design. This probability decreases as the temperature decreases. We can think of temperature as the organization's current level of risk aversion. Herein, temperature drops every 100 tasks (time periods) as $T(t + 1) = \alpha \times T(t)$, where α can be thought of as the rate at which the organization becomes risk averse.

Summary

ORGAHEAD predicts organizational performance (measured as accuracy in doing a task) from the task, the operations needed to perform the tasks (individual actions and experience), and the strategic changes to alter the organization to do the task better (refer to Figure 11.3). All aspects of ORGAHEAD are dynamic. That is, in each time period the specific task individuals and the organization face is different. Over time, the environment of tasks may be changing. At the operational level, individuals learn through experience as they do the task, but what they do and what they learn is a function of their position in the organization's design. At the strategic level, attempts at anticipating the future often result in changes in this design.

Virtual Experiment

Using ORGAHEAD, a series of virtual experiments were run to examine the impact of change strategies on performance and adaptability in a changing environment. In each experiment, two or more initial conditions were considered, and then for each condition, the behavior over time of a large number of organizations was simulated using Monte Carlo techniques.

As with human experiments, it is not possible to explore all variations given the proposed model. Thus, hypotheses in the literature were used to give guidance as to what factors are important to observe and when we are most likely to observe differences in organizational performance.

The first experiment examined two environments: (a) a stable environment under an unbiased task condition and (b) a volatile environment oscillating between an unbiased and a highly biased task every 1,000 tasks. For the highly biased task, the outcome was an A if there were three or more ones in the string; otherwise, the outcome was a B. The second virtual experiment examined three environments for organizations that changed strategically: stable (no shifts), low volatility (shifts every 5,000 tasks), and high volatility (shifts every 1,000 tasks). It is reasonable to expect that the strategy the CEO follows in deciding which change to make to the organization's design should affect the organization's ability to adapt to the different environments. Thus, for both experiments, this chapter examines four change strategies: stable (no change), random, procedural, and strategic.

In both experiments, for each initial condition 1,000 organizations were generated randomly in a Monte Carlo fashion. The initial size of the organization (2 to 45 individuals), the number of levels below the CEO (1 to 3), the initial reporting structure ($S(0)$), and the initial resource access structure ($R(0)$), all were chosen randomly with replacement from the set of possibilities. Each organization was simulated for 2,000 time periods (after the initial 500).

The goal of the analysis was to gain insight into strategic adaptation to a dynamic environment. One approach is to see what characterizes the organizations that are adaptive (i.e., end up on the peaks in the long run) from those that are maladaptive (i.e., end up in the valleys in the long run) in the various environments. As previously noted, the performance surface is multidimensional, even in the design space. To contain the analysis, only three aspects of design are examined here: size, density, and work load. Size is the number of individuals in the organization, density is the fraction of possible connections in the reporting structure that actually exist, and work load is the average number of items of information that each employee needs to handle to make a decision. The higher the work load, the greater the information-processing requirements on the individuals and the more slowly they are likely to learn. Because the concern is with adaptation, only the long-term performance of the organizations is considered. Moreover, organizations begin with individuals who have no experience, initial organizational performance is approximately 50%. The adaptiveness of the organization can thus be seen by measuring its performance at a later time period, such as the last 500 tasks. Because strategic learning is relatively slow compared with experiential learning, looking at organizational performance during later (rather than earlier) time periods provides a more complete understanding of the effects of strategic change on the organization. Finally, as a result of speed and space considerations, full data are available only for the 50 most adaptive and 50 least adaptive organizations in all the conditions. Consequently, it is generally not possible to display the performance surface even relative to just size and work load for all cells in these experiments. For a few cells, the full surface was generated (not shown).

Determinants of Adaptivity

A series of questions about adaptability were raised (e.g., Under what conditions is change beneficial? Why is learning advantageous? Does strategic learning provide greater advantage in a volatile environment, and experiential learning greater advantage in a stable environment?). The following sections examine these and other questions about organizational adaptation. To make clear the determinants of adaptation, the focus is on a comparison of the relatively adaptive and maladaptive organizations. *Adaptive* organizations are defined as the 50 organizations (out of the 1,000 simulated) that exhibited the highest level of performance at the end of the 2,000 trials. *Maladaptive* organizations are defined as the 50 organizations that exhibited the lowest performance at the end of the trials. By examining differences and similarities in the organizations that are relatively more adaptive or maladaptive, a series of lessons about organizational adaptation can be garnered.

Lesson 1: Change Is Not Adaptive

In general, change was not adaptive. To highlight the findings, the average amount of change for several types of change for adaptive and maladaptive organizations is shown in Table 11.1. These results suggest that in a stable environment, change is typically maladaptive. In Table 11.1 we see that in a stable environment, maladaptive organizations end up changing more than adaptive organizations do. Downsizing is maladaptive if it eliminates the organizational knowledge residing in the minds of the personnel—both knowledge about the task and knowledge about people. Furthermore, in an oscillatory or volatile environment, the need for that type of knowledge returns periodically. Consequently, these results suggest that adaptive firms should downsize less often, regardless of the environment. In contrast, upsizing is more valuable in a volatile than in a stable environment. Finally, in a stable environment, the simulated organizations taking the strategic approach to change tend to change more than their nonstrategic counterparts; however, their final performance is comparable to those which change either randomly or procedurally.

These results also suggest that in high-volatility environments, more change is needed than in stable environments to achieve a reasonable level of performance. Interestingly, the adaptive organizations in a volatile environment tend to perform, on average, as well as or better than the adaptive organization in a stable environment. In stable environments, simulated organizations tend to lock into structural competency traps. That is, they lock into a particular way of doing things, a particular structure. Locking into structural competency traps leads the organization to cease strategic learning and to exploit experiential learning.

One question is whether the observed differences in top (adaptive) and bottom (maladaptive) performers hold more generally. As was previously noted, given the size and complexity of this computationally generated database, full data are not available for each cell, and so all correlations cannot be provided. Thus, to address this issue, the available full data for the 1,000 organizations with a random change strategy were examined (see Table 11.2). All correlations are in the expected direction in Table 11.2, the most significant ones of which are those between performance and downsizing. Although the correlations are as expected, the relationship between amount of change and performance is not linear. In these results there is evidence both of diminishing returns to change and of cases in which moderate performers change more or less than either the adaptive or maladaptive organizations.

The lesson, from both the current study and this earlier study, is that change is not necessarily adaptive. Whether or not change helps the organization maintain or improve its performance depends on the strategy used for selecting changes, the type of environment, and the type of change. Future work should explore whether it also matters when the changes are made.

TABLE 11.1

Average number of changes made by adaptive and maladaptive organizations

	ADAPTIVE				MALADAPTIVE			
ENVIRONMENT/CHANGE	REDESIGN	REENGINEER	UPSIZE	DOWNSIZE	REDESIGN	REENGINEER	UPSIZE	DOWNSIZE
Stable								
Random	2.38	0.94	1.22	0.52	5.98	2.72	1.62	1.48
Procedural	1.70	1.00	1.02	0.40	6.02	3.24	1.38	1.68
Strategic	54.98	29.92	25.28	14.32	63.30	31.80	15.98	23.44
Volatile								
Random	31.38	12.70	12.48	6.48	30.32	15.40	10.58	7.44
Procedural	30.04	16.24	12.70	6.84	24.94	18.96	10.66	7.18
Strategic	56.78	31.90	11.12	7.60	64.38	33.20	10.10	14.38

TABLE 11.2

Correlation between amount of change* and performance by environment

ENVIRONMENT	REDESIGN	REENGINEER	UPSIZE	DOWNSIZE
Stable	–0.21	–0.19	–0.15	–0.27
Volatile	0.01	–0.06	0.16	–0.13

*Random change strategy.

Lesson 2: History Matters

As was just seen, each of the change strategies leads to a different level of change but results in structures that are comparable in terms of performance. Do the same organizational structures emerge regardless of which strategy is used? If so, the strategy that causes the least change could be considered the most efficient one. The point here is not to find the optimal structure for this task. The optimal structure is idiosyncratic to the task and, as such, is not particularly interesting. The point is to see whether the same structure emerges regardless of which change strategy is used.

Another way of asking this question is, Regardless of change strategy, do organizations tend to converge on the same peaks in the performance surface? In other words, do differences in change strategy cause organizations to migrate to different locations in the performance surface in the same amount of time? This question can be addressed in many ways; one is to look at the performance surfaces. Another way is to look at the different positions of the adaptive and maladaptive organizations given each of the change strategies. This question is addressed using computational analysis.

First, what do the performance surfaces look like? If, for 1,000 simulated organizations that change either randomly or strategically, we compare the organizational structure of high performers (organizations that have a final performance level greater than 85%) with that of the other simulated organizations, we find that high performers differ in their structure, often quite dramatically. In terms of a performance surface, we would say not only that is this not a single-peak surface, but also that all peaks in performance are not clustered in the same region. Second, these results indicate that some high performers are trapped on peaks that are far from the area of maximal peak density. These organizations have distinct structures (e.g., a group whose size is small [10] and work load low). Third, moderate performers are in regions that border high performers and sometimes are even surrounded by high performers. Thus, for some of these moderate-performing organizations, moving up in size will improve performance, and for others, moving down in size will improve performance. Fourth, there is a general trend: Low performers (the maladaptive organizations) tend to be lower in size and work load than do the high performers (the adaptive organizations). Finally, although it is not shown here, for these simulated organizations this surface changes with the change strategy of the organization and with the type of environment.

Figure 11.4 shows the final size, density, and work load for the organizations by change strategy and environment. As can be seen in the figure, the design of the adaptive organizations differs by environment and change strategy. We cannot simply say that one strategy is more efficient than another, because all change strategies lead to different final organizational designs. For example, in this study adaptive organizations are smaller and less dense in stable than in volatile environments. Strategy and environment interact. Adaptive organizations that change randomly tend to be smaller and more dense, with lower work load than their strategic counterparts in the stable environment; they have a higher work load than their strategic counterparts in the volatile environment. In contrast, organizations that change strategically exhibit similar final designs in both the stable and volatile environments.

In the foregoing analysis we examined only the adaptive organizations and saw that the change strategy affected the shape of the adaptive organizations. As organizational theorists, we might ask, does the change strategy also affect the shape of the maladaptive organizations? Figure 11.5 shows that the change strategy among the simulated organizations leads to different organizations emerging in both the maladaptive and the adaptive arena. In particular, when the change strategy is random or procedural, the organizations that emerge as maladaptive tend to be larger and less dense and possess lower work loads than those emerging as adaptive. In contrast, under a strategy of strategic change, this study suggests that maladaptive organizations are smaller and more dense and have lower work loads than their adaptive counterparts.

Regardless of the change strategy, given the same set of tasks, organizational theorists might expect that two organizations with the same design will exhibit the same performance if the employees within the organization have the same knowledge. The results displayed in Figures 11.4 and 11.5, however, suggest that two organizations with the same design and different change strategies actually are making different decisions and thereby achieving different levels of performance. How can this be?

First, in this study the structures that emerge under the different change strategies—even when they have the same size, density, and work load—are somewhat different in configuration. Size, density, and work load do not capture all the nuances of the design. In other words, design matters—the exact configuration of the organization affects its performance. Second, as was noted, two organizations with identical configurations will perform the same only if the employees are also identical. The change strategy, however, affects what the employees know. The change strategy determines what employees learn and when they learn it as well as the context of that learning. Thus two employees who "grow up" in organizations with different change

FIGURE 11.4

Impact of change strategy and environment on design of adaptive organizations

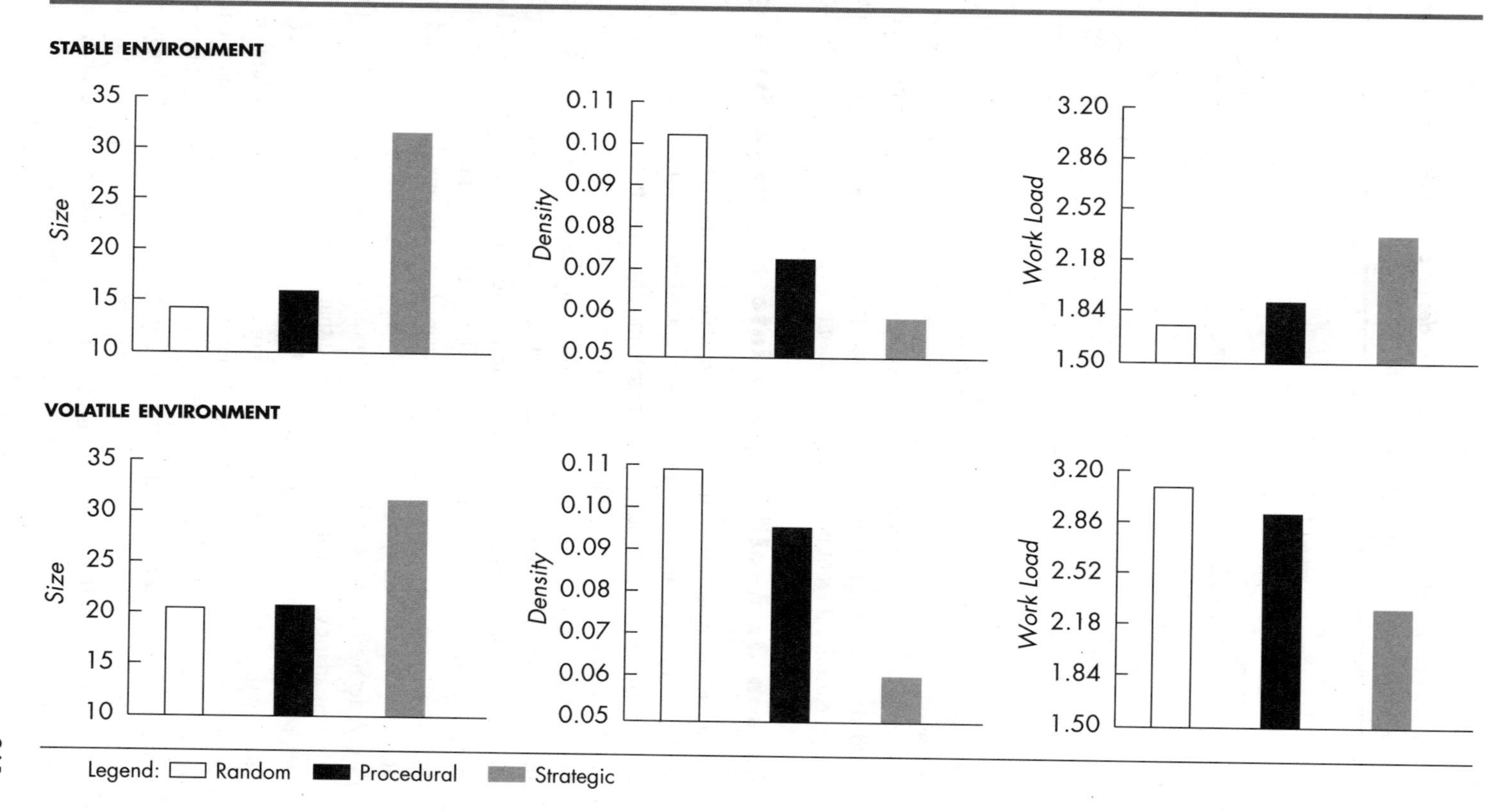

FIGURE 11.5

Impact of change strategy on the relative design of maladaptive and adaptive organizations in a volatile environment

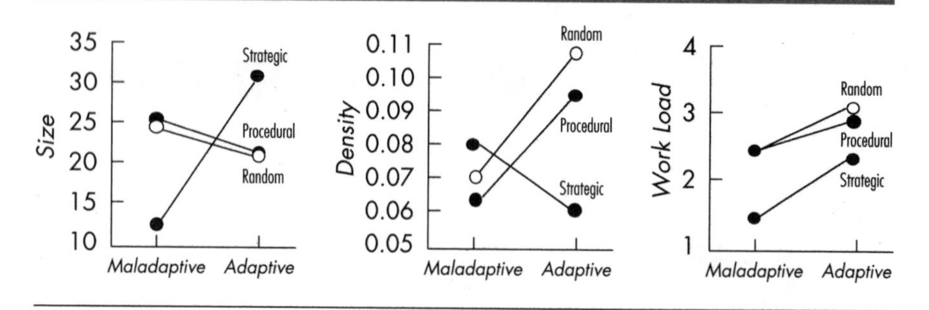

strategies will learn different things, even when those organizations are faced with the same set of tasks. History matters: The path by which an organization reaches a particular design determines the effectiveness of that design. Consequently, this study demonstrates that adaptive and maladaptive organizations with the same final design exhibit different performance because they got there by different routes.

Lesson 3: Avoid Locking into a Change Strategy

Consider the organizations that in the end are either adaptive or maladaptive. In this study, organizational change results in increased variation in organizational design (see Figure 11.6). To be sure, on average some difference initially exists in the simulated organizations. This difference grows over time, however—an important fact. Maladaptive organizations using a procedural or random strategy tend to overshoot in size and undershoot in density and work load. In contrast, in this study maladaptive organizations acting strategically tend to undershoot in size and work load and not to decrease far enough in density. These results demonstrate that the same change strategy can move the adaptive organizations in one direction and the maladaptive organizations in another.

A detailed analysis of the behavior over time of simulated organizations that ended up as adaptive or maladaptive suggested that organizations get locked into certain ways of changing. These cases suggest that organizations develop a metalearning strategy that constrains future behavior. For example, one highly adaptive strategic organization began with initially high levels of hiring; over time, when it changed, it only changed connections (i.e., who was doing what and who reported to whom). As another example, a maladaptive strategic organization began small, downsized even more, and then got locked into a cyclical pattern of hiring and firing. Thus, it appears from these results that organizations can get locked into spirals of behavior, which involve not just poor or good performance but also organizational designs and

FIGURE 11.6

Change in design over time

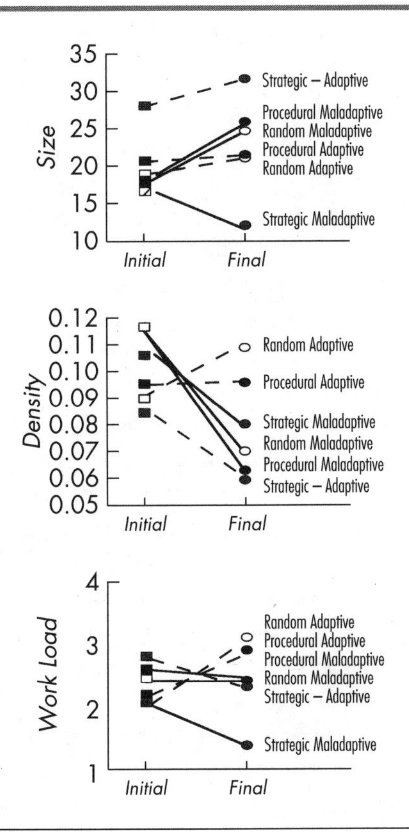

approaches to changing it that further serve to degrade or improve performance. Over time this pattern of behavior causes initial differences between the organizations to grow. In this sense, being adaptive involves locking into the right pattern of change, given the chosen change strategy. Maladaptive organizations appear to be the ones that lock into a way of changing that causes them to overshoot or undershoot their objectives, or to reenforce their current negative tendencies. Future work is needed on the trajectories and patterns of change over time.

The Value of Learning

This chapter presents a conception of organizations as information processors and search engines. From this theoretical conception of organizations, it follows that ultimate performance is a function of where they start and the path they follow, that learning is necessary but not sufficient for adaptation, that change is not adaptation, and that the path to success depends on factors both internal and external to the organization. Many paths to success therefore exist. This chapter also characterizes organizations as being capable of learning at many levels. Learning at one level can interfere with or support learning at another level. Thus, organizations with identical designs but different histories will perform differently as the structural learning affects what is learned experientially and as the experiential learning affects changes in the organization's structure.

This work is only one step in looking at organizational adaptation in different environments. The environments examined herein are volatile only in a simple sense—the same class of task is not always being done. But what of environments in which the organization is periodically faced with a truly novel task, where over time the organization sees many different tasks, rather than just cycling between two known tasks? Would such novelty affect the answers reached herein? In those situations, we might expect that the negative effects of downsizing would be less pronounced and, in fact, that downsizing might even be advantageous. Along these lines, in this analysis change was seen as costless, apart from information-processing costs. If additional costs were added for change, then, again, the value of change might be less. Clearly, other potentially relevant factors also have not been considered in this analysis. If additional relevant factors were included, they would alter the specific results—that is, that large low-density organizations are most adaptive in stable environments for organizations that change strategically. However, they are not likely to change the critical results—that the designs that are adaptive stem from the environment and the change strategy, that change is not necessarily adaptive but becomes more so in a volatile environment, that history matters, and so on. Finally, one of the values of formal theorizing is that it allows the theorist to incrementally incorporate additional factors and work through the implications of those factors in a rigorous and consistent manner. In this way, insights about design, performance, and change build up incrementally.

Hannan and Freeman (1984) proposed a structural theory of organizational inertia suggesting that although uncommon, change was related to organizational survival. In an empirical study, however, Kelly and Amburgey (1991) found that organizational change was not necessarily related to either environmental change or to survival. Their argument was that inertia was not lack of change but change in the old ways. The theoretical conception that this chapter presents can be viewed as a refinement of both arguments. In keeping with structural inertia theory, this work suggests that although change is necessary for survival, it is not sufficient. Kelly and Amburgey argued that for organizations, continuing to change as they have in the past (i.e., extrapolation), even in the face of environmental shifts, may be dysfunctional. Unlike Kelly and Amburgey, however, I would suggest that extrapolation can be beneficial. The point is that whether extrapolation is beneficial depends on whether the organization is moving along the correct path. Likewise, the key to survival is neither change nor extrapolation but determining whether the organization is on the right path. In a sense, this is a much harder search problem. Future research should be directed at determining how to determine which path is the correct one and how to jump between paths.

A possible mechanism for jumping between paths is to change how one changes (i.e., strategic change). Consider how the organizations are changing in the preceding analysis. Over time, the organizations that pursued a random or procedural change strategy did not change how they changed; only organizations that changed strategically changed how they changed. A closer examination of the strategically changing organizations suggests that for those organizations, adaptation was a matter of fine-tuning. The organizations appeared to begin by getting the right number and set of people (initial judicious upsizing and downsizing). Over time, however, the amount of personnel changeover dropped precipitously, and the amount of reassignment and retasking increased. This pattern suggests that the organizations were first assembling the right set of people and then tuning themselves by altering the people with whom they were working or the tasks on which they were working.

Eccles and Crane (1988) argued that over time, organizations indeed act as annealers. This study suggests that annealing may be a valuable learning mechanism for organizations. If learning does occur within the organization at many levels, then multiple types of learning need to be considered. If learning at one level can interfere with or support learning at another level, then understanding the conditions under which different types of learning interact with each other and the ways in which the different types of learning are manifested becomes critical for understanding and predicting organizational adaptivity. The possibility of multilevel learning switches the focus of attention from whether organizations learn to the conditions under which different types of learning prevail and adaptation occurs. In particular, the interplay between strategic and experiential learning appears to be quite important. At the strategic level, learning is manifested in the linkages among personnel and tasks, but such learning can interfere with individual experiential learning. Consequently, being able to dynamically change how change is made in these linkages may be critical if organizations are to adapt. The analysis presented in this chapter suggests that organizations that anneal and tune their designs over time have this capability.

References

Allison, G. (1971). *Essence of decision.* Boston: Little, Brown.

Axelrod, R. M. (1976). *Structure of decision: The cognitive maps of political elites.* Princeton, NJ: Princeton University Press.

Bruggeman, J. (1997). Niche width theory reappraised. *Journal of Mathematical Sociology, 22,* 201–220.

Butler, R. (1993). The evolution of the civil service: A progress report. *Public Administration, 71,* 395–406.

Carley, K. (1992). Organizational learning and personnel turnover. *Organization Science, 3*(1), 20–46.

Carley, K. M. (1998). Organizational adaptation. *Annals of Operations Research, 75,* 25–47.

Carley, K. M., & Lin, Z. (1995). Organizational designs suited to high performance under stress. *IEEE Transactions on Systems, Man, and Cybernetics, 25,* 221–230.

Carley, K. M., & Lin, Z. (1997). A theoretical study of organizational performance under information distortion. *Management Science, 43,* 976–997.

Carley, K., & Newell, A. (1994). The nature of the social individual. *Journal of Mathematical Sociology, 19*(4), 221–262.

Carley, K., & Prietula, M. (1994). ACTS theory: Extending the model of bounded rationality. In K. Carley & M. Prietula (Eds.), *Computational organization theory* (pp. 55–87). Hillsdale, NJ: Erlbaum.

Carley, K. M., & Svoboda. D. (1996). Modeling organizational adaptation as a simulated annealing process. *Sociological Methods and Research, 25*(1), 138–168.

Cohen, M. D., & March, J. G. (1974). *Leadership and ambiguity: The American college president.* New York: McGraw-Hill.

Cohen, M. D., March, J. G., & Olsen, J. P. (1972). A garbage can model of organizational choice. *Administrative Science Quarterly, 17*(1), 1–25.

Darr, E., Argote, L., & Epple, D. (1995). The acquisition, transfer, and depreciation of knowledge in service organizations: Productivity in franchises. *Management Science, 41,* 1750–1762.

DiMaggio, P. J., & Powell, W. W. (1983). The iron cage revisited: Institutional isomorphism and collective rationality in organizational fields. *American Sociological Review, 48,* 147–160.

Eccles, R. G., & Crane, D. B. (1988). *Doing deals: Investment banks at work.* Boston: Harvard Business School Press.

Finne, H. (1991). Organizational adaptation to changing contingencies. *Futures, 23,* 1061–1074.

Hannan, M. T., & Freeman, J. (1977). The population ecology of organizations. *American Journal of Sociology, 82,* 929–964.

Hannan, M. T., & Freeman, J. (1984). Structural inertia and organizational change. *American Sociological Review, 49,* 149–164.

Hollenbeck, J. R., Ilgen, D. R., Sego, D. J., Hedlund, J., Major, D. A., & Phillips, J. (1995). The multi-level theory of team decision making: Decision performance in teams incorporating distributed expertise. *Journal of Applied Psychology, 80,* 292–316.

Hollenbeck, J. R., Ilgen, D. R., Tuttle, D., & Sego, D. J. (1995). Team performance on monitoring tasks: An examination of decision errors in contexts requiring sustained attention. *Journal of Applied Psychology, 80*, 685–696.

Kelly, D., & Amburgey. T. L. (1991). Organizational inertia and momentum: A dynamic model of strategic change. *Academy of Management Journal, 34*, 591–612.

Kilmann, R. H., & Covin, T. J. (Eds.). (1988). *Corporate transformation: Revitalizing organizations for a competitive world* (Vol. 1. Jossey-Bass Management Series). San Francisco: Jossey-Bass.

Kirkpatrick, S., Gelatt, C. D., & Vecchi, M. P. (1983). Optimization by simulated annealing. *Science, 220*, 671–680.

Krackhardt, D. (1992). The strength of strong ties: The importance of philos in organizations. In N. Nohira & R. G. Eccles (Eds.), *Networks and organizations: Structure, form, and action.* Boston: Harvard Business School Press.

Lawrence, P. R., & Lorsch, J. W. (1967). *Organization and environment: Managing differentiation and integration.* Boston: Harvard University, Graduate School of Business Administration.

Levinthal, D. A., & March, J. G. (1993). The myopia of learning. *Strategic Management Journal, 14*, 95–112.

Levitt, B., & March, J. (1988). Organizational learning. *Annual Review of Sociology, 14*, 319–340.

Lin, Z., & Carley, K. M. (1997). Organizational response: The cost–performance tradeoff. *Management Science, 43*, 217–234.

March, J. G. (1996). Continuity and change in theories of organizational action. *Administrative Science Quarterly, 41*, 278–287.

March, J. G., & Simon, H. (1958). *Organizations.* New York: Wiley.

Pete, A., Pattipati, K. R., & Kleinman, D. L. (1993). Distributed detection in teams with partial information: A normative descriptive model. *IEEE Transactions on Systems, Man, and Cybernetics, 23*, 1626–1648.

Romanelli, E. (1991). The evolution of new organizational forms. *Annual Review of Sociology, 17*, 79–103.

Rutenbar, R. A. (1989). Simulated annealing algorithms: An overview. *IEEE Circuits and Devices Magazine, 5*, 12–26.

Simon, H. A. (1944). Decision-making and administrative organization. *Public Administration Review, 4*, 16–31.

Simon, H. A. (1955). A behavioral model of rational choice. *Quarterly Journal of Economics, 69*, 99–118.

Simon, H. A. (1956). Rational choice and the structure of the environment. *Psychological Review, 63*, 129–138.

Stinchcombe, A. (1965a). Organization-creating organizations. *Transactions, 2*, 34–35.

Stinchcombe, A. (1965b). Social structure and organizations. In J. G. March (Ed.), *Handbook of organizations* (pp. 153–193). Chicago: Rand McNally.

Tang, Z., Pattipati, K. R., & Kleinman, D. L. (1992). A distributed binary hypothesis testing problem with correlated observations. *IEEE Transactions on Automatic Control, 37,* 1042–1046.

COMMENT:

Modeling Structures of Organizations

David Krackhardt

Theory building has a long and, often, noble tradition in the field of organizations. Whereas publishing (and career survival) depend largely on empirical work, when we think about the most prominent people in our field, such as Karl Weick, Jim March, or Jeff Pfeffer and Gerry Salancik, we think of their theories, not their *t* tests. The publication of the *Academy of Management Review* in 1976 legitimized this role for the rest of us mortals by providing a serious outlet for theory building.

The primary problem with theory building as an enterprise is that quality control is difficult. Consensus on what separates high-quality theory from mediocre theory is hard to come by. The "good theory" seems to have fallen into the same category as the famous Supreme Court dictum on pornography: I may not be able to define it, but I know it when I see it. With the tastes for different theories as numerous as the number of organizational scholars themselves, even the Supreme Court's guideline is not particularly useful.

To discuss the quality of a theory, at a minimum we must start with some criteria that we are willing to apply generally. In this regard, I have found two prominent scholars' comments to be useful: Weick's (1979) general–accurate–simple (GAS) model and Dubin's (1978) work on theory building itself. Weick argued that theories have three desirable qualities:

1. They should be general; that is, they should apply to a wide range of social phenomena or number of contexts.
2. They should be accurate; that is, their predictions about relationships among variables and outcomes should be borne up under empirical scrutiny.
3. They should be simple or parsimonious in their explanation.

He further articulated why it is almost impossible to do all three simultaneously, postulating that theories will tend to accomplish two of the three goals, at the expense of the third. For example, case studies often provide us with a theory of what happened in a particular firm, yielding an accurate and relatively simple explanation but one that does not easily generalize outside the boundaries of the specific organization being studied. Armchair theorizing often yields elegantly simple and general explanations of phenomena but often does not predict accurately. Finally, Weick noted that sophisticated computer models, such as those of the weather, can yield highly accurate predictions and can be applied to a wide set of conditions, but their structure is often impenetrable to the human mind. They therefore do not provide us with nice, simple explanations of phenomena.

Weick (1979) did not pontificate about which combination is supreme; instead, he argued, all three types of theories have their place. It is instructive, however, that relatively few theories in organizational theory can be categorized as sacrificing simplicity for the sake of accuracy and generality.

Dubin (1978), in contrast, places more emphasis on the building blocks of theorizing. In his award-winning book, he argued that developing theory is a logical process. The guts of a theory—the propositions and their attendant hypotheses—are derived, not made up, from a set of clearly articulated premises. He goes into great detail about where these premises come from, because they drive the theory-building process. The four necessary building blocks are as follows:

1. "units," or variables (concepts, objects) that can take on particular values
2. "laws of interaction," or a set of statements describing how the units relate to one another
3. specifications on the "boundary conditions" within which the laws of interaction will apply
4. a description of the various "system states" the model can go through (Dubin argued that this last point is important in specifying how systems change).

Dubin readily acknowledged that some theories are better than others, but his primary concern is that many claims pass as theory when, in fact, they do not meet even the minimum requirements to be a theory. That is, they have not been logically thought through sufficiently to qualify as serious theory.

If we combine Weick's (1979) and Dubin's (1978) perspectives, we see that we are faced with a formidable task. To create theories that are both complex enough to deal with the real world and accurate enough to be useful and interesting (thereby, as Weick suggested, necessarily sacrificing some of their parsimony), we face the even more difficult task of meeting Dubin's reasonable but demanding requirements of working through the logical implications of the theoretical premises.

Precedent exists for this formidable task, however. For more than 40 years, the systems dynamics group at MIT has been producing computer models that show

how organizational systems behave in complex ways (see George Richardson's [1996] two-volume review of the field). The systems dynamics group, however, especially under the auspices of its founder, Jay Forrester, has applied its craft not to the development of theory but rather to solving organizational problems directly, such as how to create a policy that will control corporate inventory levels or reduce urban blight. Nonetheless, the systems dynamics group has taught us two important lessons about systems in general (Senge, 1990). First, systems—even the simplest feedback systems—are humanly impossible to grasp in their behavior. Thus, it is impossible to produce an armchair theory of a system that will be even close to accurate and general. Second, the structure of a system, especially the location of the feedback loops and delays, has a far greater impact on the behavior of the system as a whole than do the levels and flows within the system. These are two general principles of systems theory that seem to apply to many cases, and they argue for careful modeling rather than simple generalizations.

This is where Carley's work (and others in the world of computational modeling) comes in. By simulating on a computer, she goes beyond the problem-solving focus of systems dynamics to build generalized theories of organizations. Moreover, she addresses the shortcomings in traditional theory development. Through the discipline of computational models, we are forced to explicate carefully the premises and microassumptions underlying our theory. We allow untold complexities to emerge and play out. We sacrifice simplicity (in that the resulting theoretical predictions are not intuitive and linear) for the benefit of logical accuracy (if not empirical accuracy) and generality. That is, computational theorizing is a step forward in completing the circle of theoretical development in the field of organizations.

Despite this obvious advantage, the field of organizations appears generally resistant to computational theorizing (e.g., Starbuck, 1976). For one thing, there seems to be a confusion in the field about the role the computer plays in this process. The computer does not test theory; it generates theory. It demonstrates the immutable logical consequences of a set of premises. From Dubin's (1978) perspective, there is no better theory than that.

But even in cases in which the computational models have successfully generated popular theory, the computer's role has been systematically ignored. For example, if we were to compile a "Top 10" list of theories of the past 30 years, the garbage can model of decision making would most likely make the list. Although it is a popular model of decision making that is included in many organizational theory textbooks (e.g., Daft, 1989), it is surprising how few scholars acknowledge that the theory itself was born from a computer program. A cursory reading of the original Cohen, March, and Olsen (1972) piece in *Administrative Science Quarterly* immediately reveals that the theory is based on a computer simulation of decision making. The authors even take up six pages (pp. 19–24) to include the FORTRAN source code of the computer program that produced their theoretical claims. This origin is well known among computational modelers, but textbook writers who summarize this work often leave out the fact that the model is computer-based (Daft, 1978, for example, has four pages of discussion of the model and no mention of a computer simulation as its origin). My informal observations are that most organizational scholars who are familiar with the garbage can model are not aware of the fact that it is a theory derived from computer simulations. By systematically ignoring the role the computer has played in the development of this theory, the field has unwittingly expunged the computer's rightful place in the history of this part of organizational theory.

Another barrier to acceptance of computational theorizing is the use of language. For example, Carley (as do others) uses the term *experiment* to describe the combination of premises and assumptions coded in the computer runs; *results* are observed as the computer spits out derivations. These terms also are used by noncomputational researchers, but the terms carry different meanings. The difference is not simply that one is performed with artificial data and the other with "real" data. Rather, the purposes of the two are different. An "experiment" to a social psychologist is an attempt to test a theoretical prediction, whereas an "experiment" in a computational model creates a theoretical prediction. The "results" of an experiment in social psychology allow a conclusion to be drawn about whether the theory was confirmed or disconfirmed. The "results" of an experiment in a computational model are the theory itself and its boundary conditions. A social psychologist (or other social scientist) is likely to dismiss computational modeling out of hand, arguing that one cannot do "experiments" and come up with "results" with any real meaning in the artificial world of the computer. And they would be right, if by "experiments" they meant the theory-testing variety. If computational theorists were to use different terms for these modeling components (Carley's occasional use of the term *virtual experiment* is a step in the right direction here), they might find less confusion and less resistance to their contributions.

Similarly, the way the experiments are talked about leads the reader to think of these as testing mechanisms rather than theory-generating mechanisms. For example, Carley states that density is expected to impact performance because the higher the density the higher the management work load but the greater the communication and so potential for noticing errors. A naive reader might interpret that as a hypothesis about to be tested in the computer runs. Also, when talking about the "results," Carley found that in a stable environment, despite being able to change, organizations get locked into competency traps not in what they do, but in how they do it. Again, this could easily be misinterpreted to mean that she found evidence that organizations actually do "get locked into competency traps," when, of course, what she has found is that under the conditions specified by the model, she now can make a reasonable theoretical prediction that organizations will find themselves so locked or incapable of adapting.

In closing, I would like to take the liberty of comparing computational theorizing with another popular brand of theorizing done by economists. Economic theorists are systems thinkers—witness their mantra "in equilibrium" or "an equilibrium solution." They understand the importance of feedback and dynamics. Yet the modal economic theorist in *Econometrica* insists on limiting herself to mathematically tractable statements. A set of assumptions is laid out, and mathematical theorems are derived. The problem with this approach to theorizing is that it is artificially limited in scope. It is not simply that the real world is more complex than that; the real world is more complex than any model or theory. The problem is that the theory itself is prevented from addressing interesting nonlinear dynamics, the kinds of dynamics that characterize and determine the behavior of virtually all systems. Thus, although economists are good theorizers (they clearly spell out premises and logically derive conclusions), they could be better theorists if they removed the shackles of pencil-and-paper mathematics and followed the lead of Carley and others into the realm of computational theory.

References

Cohen, M. D., March, J. G., & Olsen, J. P. (1972). A garbage can model of organizational choice. *Administrative Science Quarterly, 17,* 1–25.

Daft, R. L. (1989). *Organizational theory and design.* St. Paul, MN: West.

Dubin, R. (1978). *Theory development.* New York: Free Press.

Richardson, G. P. (Ed.). (1996). *Modeling for management.* Brookfield, VT: Dartmouth.

Senge, P. (1990). *The fifth discipline: The art and practice of learning in organizations.* New York: Doubleday/Currency.

Starbuck, W. H. (1976). Organizations and their environments. In M. D. Dunnette (Ed.), *Handbook of industrial psychology* (pp. 1069–1123). Chicago: Rand McNally.

Weick, K. (1979). *The social psychology of organizing.* Reading, MA: Addison-Wesley.

CHAPTER 12

Lessons Learned and Insights Gained

Daniel R. Ilgen
Charles L. Hulin

The scientific study of behavior in organizations must confront the interface between observations and theory. At the most fundamental level, theoretical propositions must be falsifiable, at least in principle, by a set of observations and those observations must be verifiable, either by replication or convergence among multiple sources of observation (see Seitz, Chapter 2, this volume). The interface between theory and observations is the subject of epistemology and part of any theory of the philosophy of science. Attempts to illuminate relations between theory and observations vary widely across disciplines; they change over time within disciplines. This book is an attempt to document the need for broad change as well as the benefits of a specific change for understanding behavior in organizations.

Cronbach's (1957, 1975) two disciplines of scientific psychology capture the views of the observation–theory interface that have dominated research in organizational psychology and behavior. Both disciplines describe the data–theory interface similarly; they agree on what constitutes legitimate observations for the science. Observations, typically termed *variables* and located in a multifaceted space defined by actors, behaviors, and contexts (Runkel & McGrath, 1972), are the data of science in both of Cronbach's disciplines. All organizational research is stamped from the same mold with respect to one crucial issue: observations of behavioral phenomena are the necessary data of an empirical science.

Theory may follow observations when it is constructed inductively in the positivist tradition; theoretical propositions emerge when observations are folded into internally consistent theoretical frameworks. Theory may precede observations when theoretical principles serve explicitly as guides for observations. Whatever the sequence, theories are evaluated in terms of the degree of fit between theory-based expectations, often termed *hypotheses,* and observations of phenomena in specific studies. Over time, the science of a domain should evolve as theory–observation episodes accumulate and theories are modified to maintain or create internally consistent relationships among theoretical propositions and accumulating observations. In the two-way relationship between theory and observation, our theories have a strong influence on the observations we obtain and how we interpret them.

There are disagreements within any science about what constitutes legitimate data. In organizational sciences, disagreements exist over whether qualitative or quantitative measures are legitimate (Van Maanen, Dabbs, & Faulkner, 1982), the nature and extent of control necessary for inferences about causation (James, Mulaik, & Brett, 1982), and other measurement and design issues (Hulin, Drasgow, & Parsons, 1983). These disagreements have been addressed in the past and will continue to be addressed. Their resolution, however, is orthogonal to the topics of this book.

Experimental and correlational methods have served the science of organizational behavior and psychology well. When cognitive and behavioral processes generate regular and relatively uninterrupted change, when constructs and their manifestations relate to each other linearly, when feedback or "feedacross" from outcomes onto antecedents of the next behavioral or cognitive episode are weak or inconsistent, and when the number of relevant constructs is limited, the two methods provide us with a way to link observations to theory in ways that advance understanding. Even with multiple variables and constructs under conditions of limited change and nonlinearity, the two methods may provide useful data that allow us to estimate processes or event histories in organizational and individual space. But the disciplines reach their limits when confronting data generated by stochastic, dynamic, nonlinear processes. The world of organizations fits the latter well.

Simplifying assumptions of linearity, smooth and differentiable functions, or the artificial creation of controlled environments (e.g., experimental studies in the laboratory) permit the use of our old and trusted methods, but they conceal much of the complexity of the dynamic, nonlinear world of organizations. As a result, the glimpses of the world of data they allow us may be locally accurate, but they may not be true. Understanding streams of behaviors in organizations often exceeds the capabilities of the two methods to provide observations that relate to issues important for developing theories of behavior in complex organizations. Such theories, if they are to be useful, must account for the interesting variance in dynamic and complex multivariate behavioral space.

In the face of similar constraints of traditional research disciplines, other fields have turned to computational modeling to fill gaps created by the limits of standard research methods. In physics, in addition to experimentation and pure theory, a third discipline exists, labeled *numerical analysis*. Numerical analysis represents the adoption by physicists of computational modeling. Studies using numerical analysis are referred to as studies "in silica." Some physicists argue that numerical analysis is the branch most likely to lead to the next major breakthrough in physics. The entire field of chaos theory owes much of its underpinning to modeling in the fields of meteorology, astrophysics, physics, and biology (Gleick, 1987). Organizational behavior and psychology need to be equally innovative and adaptive. We need to adopt methods that directly address our questions rather than frame our questions in ways that can be addressed comfortably by the two traditional disciplines.

Added Value of Computational Modeling

Systematizing Theory

Computational models of behavioral phenomena demand careful development of theoretical propositions underlying the behavioral constructs or other phenomena of interest. Ideally, theoretical propositions underlying all behavioral research would be carefully constructed before the research is undertaken. This is too seldom the case, in part because neither correlational nor experimental research designs force clear conceptual formulations before their execution. Data are often collected based on ill-conceived and internally inconsistent theories about key constructs and the relationships among them. Just as likely, existing theories and models may be interpreted in ways that test the usefulness of a model in situations or contexts whose existence the model denies.

Consider, for example, the classic job characteristics theory of Hackman and Oldham (1976). This model proposes that the impact of jobs on behavioral and attitudinal outcomes of job holders is mediated by the extent to which the job creates, in job incumbents, critical psychological states (experiences of doing meaningful work, a sense of responsibility, knowledge of results). Furthermore, both the link between jobs and critical psychological states and the link between these states and the behavioral and attitudinal outcomes are moderated by a stable individual difference, *growth need strength.* For those with high growth needs, job characteristics covary with psychological states, and psychological states covary with important behavioral and attitudinal outcomes. For those with low growth needs, the covariation is, at best, much lower. At the lowest levels of growth need strength, the theory predicts that changes in the nature of jobs have little or no impact on critical psychological states. Therefore, if growth need strength is low, the covariation between psychological states derived from the job and behavioral and attitudinal outcomes is far less than is the case when growth need strength is high.

When the model is formulated verbally as above or represented with boxes and arrows capturing the verbal description, the model makes good intuitive sense. But on closer scrutiny, the model breaks down for those with low growth need strength. If, indeed, critical psychological states for people with low growth needs are unaffected by the nature of the job, then there is little to moderate in the next link of the model, the link of psychological states to job outcomes for these persons. Technically, the model predicts that the link from the job to the outcomes is broken at the first stage of the model for people with low growth needs; the next link is meaningless for them. This fact, to our knowledge, is not acknowledged or recognized in typical presentations of the model. If a formal computational model of the job characteristics model had been attempted, the inconsistency would have been recognized because the modeler would not have been able to construct a formal model consistent with the theory as verbally stated.

With computational models, making presuppositions and assumptions explicit is absolutely necessary in order to translate models into symbolic representations that can be processed by a computer. A valuable part of this process involves systematically identifying any unstated assumptions that are necessary to make the model internally consistent or to keep its predictions from drifting off to infinity (where all or none of the behaviors are enacted by all or none of the individuals or agents in the simulation). An equally valuable part of modeling is the identification of limiting conditions in which the model does not apply, as is the case with the job characteristics theory described above. There is no guarantee that the theoretical bases for computational models are any more "correct" than any other theory. To develop and use computational modeling, however, the investigator must specify that model in something more than literary or metaphorical terms. Formalization of conditional probabilities—mathematical rules for behaviors—may require, for example, attitude–behavior theory, cognitive information-processing theories, or theories of emotions and aggression (Glomb & Miner, 1998).

The computational models reported in this book provide systematic treatment of their content domains. Systematizing the domains took several forms. In some cases, investigators started with a few simple but robust findings in the literature, used these as initial assumptions, and proceeded to model the consequences of these assumptions. Latané (Chapter 9) and McPherson (Chapter 10) each begin with observations about social interactions among people in order to construct models of the formation and distribution of subgroups and subgroup characteristics in populations over time.

Latané (Chapter 9) begins with a few basic assumptions from social impact theory about similarities and dissimilarities among people and the amount of their physical separation—whether they are adjacent to each other, one "unit" of distance away, and so forth. Temporal evolution and regional differentiation characterize the emergence of subcultures, described in terms of the consolidation of attributes within the subcultures, clustering of subcultures in the total population of interest, stable diversity within subcultures, and correlated individual differences within subcultures. These complex group-, cultural-, or organizational-level phenomena all are consequences of a few simple assumptions that have strict local origins and operations. Cultural, organizational, and group complexity arises from the applications of these simple local rules, much as work with fractals has generated extraordinary complexity of physical order from repetitions of simple rules at different scales (Gleick, 1987, pp. 81–118).

Latané's results become more compelling when his simulated results are applied to phenomena as diverse as work group norms or societal behavior patterns without reference to any overarching group or cultural processes. Other work that demonstrates complexity arising from simple local rules (often leading to chaotic regions and fractal geometry in biological and physical designs) has taken place at the Santa Fe Institute (Epstein & Axelrod, 1996; Holland, 1995).

In McPherson's model (Chapter 10), people are localized in subgroups nested within societies described by dimensions derived from the work of Peter Blau (1977) and named, in his honor, *Blau space*. The model is based on the assumption that people exist in localized groups that occupy niches and compete for members with other groups within a finite space. Agents (people) within groups have limited ability to scan their environments and locate other groups into which they may fit. McPherson then asks important questions about the underlying forces, such as homophily, that may drive stability or change in group membership. How are groups dispersed throughout a culture or organization as a result of competition with other organizations for members?

Zickar (Chapter 5) creates a model of faking on personality tests using a simple (but not simplistic) stochastic simulation program. Faced with weaknesses in the domain of theory on personality (see DeShon's comments on Zickar's chapter, pp. 109–114), Zickar anchors his model more in his own rationale for how faking would be manifested in test-taking situations than in what is known about personality constructs. However, his model is explicit. Readers can judge how well this model conforms to their own construction of the reality of item responding and faking.

As expected, Zickar found a serious negative effect of faking on the expected performance of those who were selected from the "top down" based on their personality assessments. The finding that the validity coefficient of the personality test was robust to faking was unexpected and important. Small decrements in the validity of the personality test, defined as its correlation with a performance criterion, were generated by Zickar's simulations even as the usefulness of the tests approached zero. Claims about the effects of faking on the usefulness of personality tests based on validity coefficients (e.g., Ones, Viswesvaran, & Reiss, 1996) need to be reevaluated in light of Zickar's findings.

DISCUSS, SPEAK, WORKER, and ORGAHEAD represent systematic developments of behavior domains that were constructed from more complex origins. To develop DISCUSS and SPEAK, Stasser (Chapter 7) began with empirical observations on consensus decision making in small groups and models of individual decision making. He argues that because group decisions are made by collectives of individuals mentally processing information, working models of the mind might be adapted to create a model of minds working together. In the development of DISCUSS, models of individual cognitive-processing heavily influenced analogically constructed models of group decision making. Constructs were added that are important in group decision making when group members hold preferences for alternatives at the time they join the group and when they share part, but not all, of their information during a group decision-making session. The model provided ways to test alternative explanations for phenomena that Stasser observed in his earlier empirical work (Stasser & Titus, 1987) with decision-making groups.

In the case of WORKER, the modeling software incorporated several existing theoretical models and was constructed to account for changes across time in the frequencies and covariances of withdrawal behaviors and related attitudes. The software was based on a literature that had not previously been integrated into a dynamic representation of the withdrawal process as it unfolds within environments characterized by combinations of incentives and disincentives for withdrawal behaviors. Other researchers had implicitly or explicitly assumed that key withdrawal behaviors and behavioral tendencies unfold and interact over time. Little consideration, however, has been given to dynamic changes in multivariate distributions of the variables over time. To develop WORKER, the investigators were forced to make all assumptions explicit.

In Chapter 3, Hanisch simulates the impact of organizational interventions targeting specific withdrawal behaviors; his findings are both expected and counterintuitive. When withdrawal behaviors were the targets of organizational incentives and disincentives, the behavior frequencies increased or decreased as expected. Following interventions, however, nontargeted withdrawal behaviors also changed in systematic ways that were not predictable from the specific models being simulated; several of these unexpected findings would be dysfunctional in organizations.

Munson and Hulin (Chapter 4) use WORKER to address a different set of issues. Data obtained from employees in one organization are input into WORKER to create a virtual representation of the organization from which the data were obtained. Comparing modeled data with observed data provides a way to interpret observed phenomena; the process created a partially illuminated theory–data interface that offered a look at underlying processes not available using traditional descriptions.

Carley's model, ORGAHEAD (Chapter 11), addresses a complex, multivariate domain: the structure and change of organizations in volatile environments. Her model relies on theory that is less well grounded in empirical observations than either WORKER or DISCUSS but incorporates findings from other research using computational modeling. In contrast to the existing literature on groups and on withdrawal behavior, an extensive, model-based literature is available for studying behaviors of whole organizations. Carley capitalized nicely on that literature to develop ORGAHEAD and guide its application.

The behavioral domains of interest to Coovert and Dorsey (Chapter 8) span several levels—individual, team, and organizational. The order that the authors impose on these levels evolved from a generalized mathematical model known as *Petri nets.*

The developmental process for Coovert and Dorsey progressed in a direction opposite to that of the other models in this book. Behavioral observations, theory, or logic provided the foundation on which the other models were constructed; implications of formalizing the theoretical descriptions of behavioral processes were explored using computational models. Coovert and Dorsey, in contrast, started with a formalized mathematical model and then looked for behavioral phenomena that could be represented by the model. Under such conditions, underlying assumptions are integral parts of the formalized models. These assumptions are assumed to operate in the behavioral domain that is to be modeled. In this version of the modeling process, if the focal behaviors do not fit the assumptions, the models are rarely redefined. More typically, if there is a poor fit, one looks for other behaviors to study that provide a better fit to the model. The model remains the focus of interest. Discovery of new behavioral domains that can be captured using the model represents knowledge and generalization.

Coovert and Dorsey's work, like that of Kleinman and Song (1990), is an exception to the usual modeling process. In Coovert and Dorsey's case, data derived from the model and observations of individual behaviors are compared, changes are made in the parameters of the model, and the comparison process is repeated in an iterative fashion until models and behaviors are aligned. The specter of overfitting a theoretical model to sample data is exorcised by replication of the iterated model on new behavioral samples taken from the same domain.

One final systematic method of organizing a domain using models is that of holding the model constant and "testing" a number of values for variables in that model. Schwab and Olson (Chapter 6) use this approach to test the effects of various merit pay conditions. They created models with systematically differing parameter values and compared the effects of several such configurations. Their modeled data led to unexpected findings, such as relatively small effects for reductions in the reliability of performance measures. They also found that higher levels of contingency between pay and performance did not lead to better performance in the long run under standard assumptions about the impact of contingent pay on performance.

Comparing Alternatives

At their basic level, computational models exist to address questions of the form "If conditions *X* exist, then what *Y* will result?" where both *X* and *Y* represent variables or samples of variables with prescribed distributions. A complete catalogue of permissible "if . . . then" statements in a model is known as the *propositional inventory* of the model. Useful models can be stated or described in propositional inventories. Models instantiated as propositional inventories provide excellent means of comparing alternatives and judging the efficacy of each one. In the simplest case, any alternative can be evaluated alone, in a sense, compared with the null model. Variables with assumed distributions are sampled. Models can be constructed or parameter values entered into existing models to observe the effects of the created conditions on appropriate dependent variables. The effects of these parameter values on performance, pay, and promotions over time can be simulated. The Schwab and Olson simulation is that kind of approach, known as a "What if . . . " study.

Another powerful procedure is to compare two or more models with each other, as Seitz does in Chapter 2. Hanisch (Chapter 3), Munson and Hulin (Chapter 4), and Stasser (Chapter 7) also apply this technique. Hanisch systematically created conditions consistent with one of three models of withdrawal behavior—independent, compensatory, and progressive forms of withdrawal—and compared the simulated behaviors generated by each model to determine the effects of an intervention on nontargeted behaviors. Stasser developed DISCUSS to explore questions generated by contrasting theories and data patterns, originating from the traditional experimental approach, that were difficult to interpret. The model provided a way to draw inferences about which theories seemed most reasonable under the conditions of the model.

Comparisons of the "What if . . . " form among models are valuable when the phenomena of interest function in dynamic environments or are themselves dynamic processes that have feedback and feedacross effects from enacted behaviors or other outputs influencing the status of variables and constructs in the process. In Chapter 4, Munson and Hulin compare the frequencies of eight withdrawal behaviors assessed in an organization to the structures among these behaviors simulated by five models represented in WORKER's library of theoretical models. WORKER created a virtual representation of the organization from which the data were collected. The 127 employees × 8 behaviors that form the observation matrix and the five theoretical models were underidentified with respect to each other, making it possible to test and falsify claims of some of the models. The competing claims of three of the five theoretical models were sufficiently different that all could not be supported. They all, however, could be rejected. The comparisons provided a basis for judging the ability of the computational models to study real-life situations in silica. These comparisons neither "validate" any model nor "prove" causation, but they do provide information that strengthens (or weakens) confidence in one or more alternative theoretical statements related to the model or to the data. They add information to our knowledge and reduce our uncertainty about the characteristic structures of data that should be observed if different specific models are useful accounts of the withdrawal process.

Conditions Not Possible

Every method of inquiry is flawed; computational models are no exception. Just as an investment portfolio can reduce risk through diversity of holdings, diversity of methods of inquiry helps protect our research against the effects of unrecognized flaws in our favorite method. Including computational modeling in a research portfolio that contains experimental and correlational research methods provides value; it contributes uniquely to discovery. The chapters in this book illustrate cases in which questions were addressed that are impossible to address by the two disciplines of empirical investigation. The method's unique contributions are most evident when addressing change over time. Human behavior in organizations does not occur in a vacuum. Events that have occurred in the past, as well as expectations of the future, affect how people behave in the present. Many theorists have described behaviors not as isolated events but as a stream of behaviors over time, whereby both time and other behaviors in the stream influence the signals that are extracted from the streams at any point in time when we integrate across windows of time (Atkinson & Birch, 1970; Naylor, Pritchard, & Ilgen, 1980).

No matter how dynamic our conceptualization, past behaviors influence current behaviors. Outcomes of current behaviors influence the trajectories of related behaviors. Current behavior streams dynamically link the influences of the past to the behaviors of the future and their outcomes. These propositions are nearly universally accepted in organizational sciences and are the basis for the recurrent cry for longitudinal research with multiple observations using any scientific method—correlational, experimental, or a combination of the two. In general, the cry for more longitudinal research is easier to enact than is the research; therefore, the cry goes unanswered. One-shot, cross-sectional studies involving one or two dependent variables dominate our empirical database. Part of the reason for this situation is that multivariate observations over time create data offering analytical challenges that have been difficult to address. Although great strides have been made addressing data analysis problems, SUDAAN, LISREL, and event history analysis, among others, offer only partial solutions to many problems caused by complex studies of dynamic behavioral processes. Modeling offers a way to inform researchers before they begin their empirical research about the expected structure of the multivariate behavior streams.

More serious limitations are conditions intrinsic to capturing change over time using traditional research disciplines:

- Changes occur slowly, making it difficult to study within researchers' own life spans.
- Changes occur quickly and generate data traces that may resemble nearly random configurations of events. A chaotic system (individuals) embedded within a nearly deterministic system (an organization), if viewed within normal time windows, may generate empirical data nearly uninterpretable within our normal research frameworks.
- Different cadences of change among events, with some things changing rapidly and others slowly, make it difficult to know when to assess variables at critical times in their temporal development.

- Often we have little or no understanding of what a meaningful unit of time is for the constructs of interest. The socialization of people into organizations occurs over time as people adapt to their work settings and they adapt the work settings to fit themselves. Yet to study this, should the time frame last hours, days, weeks, years, or a whole lifetime in the work setting?

Empirical data address some of these questions, but to observe and understand the nature of change over time requires that we (a) adequately sample events over time when often little is known about what time units should be used and (b) sample multivariate streams of behaviors when the resulting data sets may nearly defy analyses using standard techniques. Much of the field is still wrestling with the problems of selecting the variables to assess and the behaviors to sample in order to represent adequately the multivariate behavior streams; only now are we beginning to ask questions about time.

More subtle problems are revealed by questions about the expected duration of different forces operating on people. We might expect, for example, that basic work and cultural values will have a duration of influence extending from one's first job to retirement. These values may change slowly over the course of a working career, but their influence should continue. The values of one's peer group in high school might be expected to have an effective duration that is much shorter, lasting only a few weeks or months after the start of the first job. The influence of one's work group may be intermediate between these two; initially it may be strong, but after assimilation into the organization, individual values may continue far longer. One-shot empirical studies slice into the stream of time at an arbitrary point to study either an age or tenure cohort or a random cross-sectional sample of workers with various years of service in the organization. Such studies will almost certainly obtain data that provide substantially different answers to questions about what influences workers, the relative strengths of the different sources of values, and so forth, depending on the timing of the slice of data that provides the snapshot of the traces of the processes at work. These questions are nearly impossible to study using traditional research disciplines. They can be modeled, however, and we can be informed about the expected data that would result from different configurations and durations of forces that impinge on workers. These simulated results can provide the bases for interpreting empirical observations.

The very nature of time is the source of constraints that make it nearly impossible to study within the two disciplines of normal science. In other cases, different factors constrain our ability to observe organizational behaviors. Hanisch (Chapter 3) explores the simultaneous effects of organizational interventions on nontargeted withdrawal behaviors that would have been logistically impossible to study in any organizational setting. Some of Zickar's (Chapter 5) constraints involve ethics: Solid ethical reasons exist for not probing in the manner needed to observe unmanipulated faking behavior and for not creating conditions to entrap job applicants who fake on personality tests. The fuzziness of some "explanatory" constructs in the personality assessment area—social desirability—also make rigorous testing of many of the explanations impossible.

Limits on Adopting Computational Modeling

We noted earlier that computational modeling of behavioral processes in organizations is not a panacea for all the data- and theory-related ills of organizational science. It can, however, make important contributions because of its own strengths and because its strengths and limitations are often orthogonal to those of experimentation and correlational analyses of individual differences. It provides a necessary correction to overreliance on our two traditional disciplines of psychology—disciplines that often seem to be used because they are well known to us, not because they are well-suited to answering the research questions being posed.

This book was intended as a possible antidote to the apparent reluctance of organizational sciences to adopt the use of computational modeling as an alternative to normal science. We recognize that computational modeling is the newest of the research disciplines although elements of it have been in use since Gossett used Monte Carlo simulation methods in his work on the Student's *t* distribution. We had to await the confluence of developments in technology, theory, and epistemology to see the flowering of computational modeling in many research fields. It is reasonable that organizational researchers must be persuaded of its value because it is the newest tool in our bag of research methods. This book is an attempt at such persuasion. But proof of the value of computational modeling and awareness of its strengths can come only from researchers using it to answer questions about dynamic, nonlinear behavioral processes and systems in organizations. Confidence precedes use, but confidence also comes from use.

We still must overcome prejudices against computational modeling that involve the oft-repeated statements to the effect that "we get out of modeling only what we put into it; we can learn nothing not already contained in the theories and input parameter." Such statements reflect views of linear, deterministic models instantiated as a series of differential equations or simple stochastic unfolding across iterations. They are not accurate views of models incorporating dynamic, nonlinear processes. Yet the myths linger.

Computational modeling is quantitatively complex in ways not normally encountered by even the quantitatively sophisticated. Our understanding of multivariate statistics and ability to work easily with integrals in calculus may ill-prepare us for the linked partial differential equations, fuzzy set theory, and fuzzy calculus that undergird many of the more complex modeling programs. If much detail is provided about the programming and the quantitative basis of the models, many organizational researchers are likely to reject the approach as not being worth the intellectual effort. Reading articles or chapters on which the results and details of computational modeling are based is not a spectator sport.

We asked the contributors to omit the details and the quantitative bases of their programs. Our purpose is as much didactic as it is to present an integrated set of findings in organizational research obtained through computational modeling. However, the detail must be presented at some time to readers and potential users of the methods; if not now, then later. The question is one of how much detail is necessary and appropriate, rather than whether the details are needed. This question is illustrated in Fichman's commentary on Chapter 3 (Hanisch). He argues that the reader should be provided with the source code of the software that executes the modeling. Including source code, however, poses a dilemma both to investigators and to those interested in the investigators' work. Research with models involves substantial initial costs in time, money, and intellectual capital that can be recouped only once the program is used. For example, it took more than 7 years to develop WORKER to its current version. It is a tool the developers anticipate using for the next several years on a variety of problems. Some resistance on the part of the developers to releasing it into the public domain is understandable.

Consumers of modeling research face another problem with full disclosure: The level of abstraction and the sheer volume of information overwhelm understanding. Thus, the needs of peers to understand in order to meet the fundamental requirement of science—replication—bump up against some human limits of motivation and cognition. Again, the question is when, not if. With time, we will better understand where the limits lie and how to find a balance that meets the needs of those doing the research and those who need enough information to sufficiently evaluate and replicate results.

An intermediate solution between overwhelming the reader with programming detail and withholding detail is the one Latané (Chapter 9) adopts. Davis's comments on Chapter 9 highlight this solution in its title: "Simulation on the Cheap." Latané has developed a modeling program based on a standard spreadsheet that is easy to understand for anyone who is computer literate. Such programs can model sophisticated theories and processes. In the hands of someone who thoroughly understands the content of the theory and the capabilities of spreadsheets, there are few limits to their usefulness. Spreadsheet programs are easily explained, and they provide convenient answers to questions about disclosure of a program without overwhelming the reader. Unfortunately, programs built on such methods may not be able to answer the full range of questions that investigators in organizational science might ask.

A barrier to modeling in organizational research may inhere in the field itself and its researchers. For years we have had no tight or generally applied standards for theory; we have an abundance of sloppy "word" theory. Even theory that is relatively useful and accurate, given the standards of the field, is typically stated more as literary metaphor than as a scientific theory. Some of this theorizing has been used to provide answers to a wide range of questions, and many of those answers have become important parts of our empirical database. But metaphorical models qua theories have limited usefulness; we need to move beyond tolerating literary metaphors passing as scientific theory.

Another barrier to the adoption of computational modeling in organizational sciences is the general acceptance of the position that because we are a young science, we have the luxury of operating as a loosely connected federation of scientists who can simply gather data without limit while giving little thought to how the data fit together. Our field seems to share a blind faith that some day, a philosopher king will come along and fit all the pieces together. This creates a perceived freedom to partition our world of constructs into small pieces and collect data on those pieces at a single time in a specifically configured environment. Little concern exists about finding any global theory, only about developing local, ad hoc theory and achieving accuracy that may be no more than descriptions of specific findings. We continue doing research on individual behaviors, one at a time, without concern for how well one behavior might represent a behavior stream or how environmental characteristics influence multivariate distributions of behaviors, and even behavioral substitution, within a behavior stream.

It is comforting to believe that individual studies of isolated behaviors can be accumulated into an overall statement or model of organizational behavior. This view is reinforced by a misplaced faith in the meta-analysis fix. Schmidt (1992) even goes so far as to suggest that as scientists, we specialize into those who gather "real" data (make bricks) and those who conduct meta-analyses when the stack of bricks is big enough to build scientific edifices (theories).

Such rationalizing is comforting, but it denies reality. Many important questions need to be answered in studies of organizational behavior. The problem is not that the results of any local study of an isolated behavior are in error; they are likely to be accurate, but local accuracy does not imply truth or a more global usefulness. Specifically, they may be an accurate representation of the necessarily limited set of constructs observed for the sample, organization, place, and time. But if the constructs themselves unfold over time in complex interactions with multiple other constructs, relegating these unmeasured events to unreliability and sampling error can lead to only limited success in our discovery of fundamental and general processes in complex organizations.

Conclusion

Computational modeling is no universal elixir. That is not our point. Recall, however, that we have stressed that its strengths lie in the ability to handle complex sets of variables and to recreate dynamic interactions in ways that are orthogonal to the methods that dominate the conduct of science in organizational behavior and industrial–organizational psychology. Thus, the use of such models, in concert with methods subsumed under Cronbach's (1957, 1975) two disciplines, begins to sample more adequately the conceptually dynamic space of behavior in organizations. We ask no more and no less.

The potential scope and reach of computational modeling in organizational science is unknown at this time. The chapters in this book demonstrate that it can inform us about issues ranging from faking on personality tests to the behavior of organizations in volatile environments. Its contributions to other specific research areas and to the integration of local findings and theories, although unexplored, are likely to be as important as the contributions of modeling have been in other branches of science, specifically physics and biology as well as other soft sciences.

References

Atkinson, J. W., & Birch, D. (1970). *The dynamics of action* (2nd ed.). New York: Wiley.

Blau, P. M. (1977). *Inequality and heterogeneity.* New York: Free Press.

Cronbach, L. J. (1957). The two disciplines of scientific psychology. *American Psychologist, 12,* 671–684.

Cronbach, L. J. (1975). Beyond the two disciplines of scientific psychology. *American Psychologist, 30,* 116–127.

Epstein, J. M., & Axelrod, R. (1996). *Growing artificial societies: Social science from the bottom up.* Washington, DC: Brookings Institution Press.

Gleick, J. (1987). *Chaos: Making a new science.* New York: Penguin.

Glomb, T. M., & Miner, A. (1998, August). *Exploring patterns of aggressive behaviors in organizations: Assessing model/data fit.* Presented at the First Annual Conference on Emotions in Organizations, San Diego.

Hackman, J. R., & Oldham, G. R. (1976). Motivation through the design of work: The test of a theory. *Organizational Behavior and Human Performance, 16,* 250–279.

Holland, J. H. (1995). *Hidden order: How adaptation builds complexity.* Reading, MA: Addison-Wesley.

Hulin, C. L., Drasgow, F., & Parsons, C. K. (1983). *Item response theory: Applications to psychological measurements.* Homewood, IL: Dow-Jones.

James, L. R., Mulaik, S. A., & Brett, J. M. (1982). *Causal analysis: Assumptions, models, and data.* Beverly Hills, CA: Sage.

Kleinman, D. L., & Song, A. (1990). A research paradigm for studying team decision-making and coordination. *Proceedings of the 1990 Symposium on Command and Control Research.* Washington, DC: National Defense University.

Naylor, J. C., Pritchard, R. D., & Ilgen, D. R. (1980). *A theory of behavior in organizations.* New York: Academic Press.

Ones, D. S., Viswesvaran, C., & Reiss, A. D. (1996). Role of social desirability in personality testing for personnel selection: The red herring. *Journal of Applied Psychology, 81,* 660–679.

Runkel, P. J., & McGrath, J. E. (1972). *Research on human behavior: A systematic guide to method.* New York: Rinehart & Winston.

Schmidt, F. L. (1992). What do data really mean? Research findings, meta-analysis, and cumulative findings in psychology. *American Psychologist, 47,* 1173–1181.

Stasser, G., & Titus, W. (1987). Effects of information load and percentage of shared information on the dissemination of unshared information during group discussion. *Journal of Personality and Social Psychology, 53,* 81–93.

Van Maanen, J., Dabbs, J. M., Jr., & Faulkner, R. R. (1982). *Varieties of qualitative research.* Beverly Hills, CA: Sage.

Author Index

("n" indicates a note)

Subject Index

("i" indicates an illustration; "n" indicates a note; "t" indicates a table)

About the Editors

Daniel R. Ilgen, PhD, is the John A. Hannah distinguished professor of psychology and management at Michigan State University. He received his PhD in psychology at the University of Illinois in 1969, and was on the industrial and organizational psychology faculty at Purdue University prior to being appointed to his current position in 1983. He has also served as a visiting professor at the University of Washington and the University of Western Australia. He is a past president of the Society of Industrial and Organizational Psychology. He is the editor of *Organizational Behavior and Human Decision Processes,* and a member of the editorial boards of four other journals. His research addresses issues of work motivation and behavior in teams. Most recently he has been involved in research on the quality of decision making in teams. His works appear as books, book chapters, and articles in such journals as the *American Psychologist, Journal of Applied Psychology, Personnel Psychology,* and *Organizational Behavior and Human Decision Processes.*

Charles L. Hulin, PhD, is professor emeritus of psychology in the College of Liberal Arts, Institute of Labor and Industrial Relations, and the Institute of Aviation at the University of Illinois at Urbana-Champaign. He received his PhD in psychology from Cornell University in 1963. He has been a visiting professor at the University of California at Berkeley and the University of Washington at Seattle, and was a member of the Center for Advanced Study at the University of Illinois at Urbana-Champaign. He has served in a variety of committee and advisory positions for the U.S. government and for private industry. From 1975 to 1982, Dr. Hulin was the associate editor of *Journal of Applied Psychology,* and since 1972 he has been a member of the editorial board of *Organizational Behavior and Human Decision Processes.* He is a fellow of the American Psychological Association, American Psychological Society, and the Society of Industrial and Organizational Psychology. He has twice received the Ghiselli Award from the Society of Organizational Psychology and received the Career Scientific Contributions Award from the Society of Organizational Psychology in 1997. His research addresses issues of work motivation, job attitudes, job emotions, and organizational withdrawal, as well as the application of computational modeling to behaviors in organizations. He is a co-developer of WORKER, a computational modeling program that models how individuals withdraw from work organizations. He is a co-author of four books and has published in *Journal of Applied Psychology, Personnel Psychology, Psychological Bulletin, Human Factors, Journal of Cross Cultural Psychology, Journal of Vocational Behavior,* and *Organizational Behavior and Human Decision Processes.*

About the Editors